Hear, O Heavens and Listen, O Earth

Hear, O Heavens
and
Listen, O Earth

An Introduction to the Prophets

Joan E. Cook, s.c.

A Michael Glazier Book

LITURGICAL PRESS
Collegeville, Minnesota

www.litpress.org

A Michael Glazier Book published by Liturgical Press

Cover design by Joachim Rhoades, o.s.b.

Photo credits: pp. 43, 146, 280, istockphoto.com; p. 75, Hugh Witzmann, o.s.b.; pp. 95, 127, 187, 285, Corel Photos; p. 107, Kevin R. Locke; p. 201, Liturgical Press Archives; p. 244, Flat Earth Photos.

1   2   3   4   5   6   7   8

Library of Congress Cataloging-in-Publication Data

Cook, Joan E.
    Hear, O heavens, and listen, O Earth : an introduction to the Prophets / Joan E. Cook.
        p.   cm.
    Includes bibliographical references and index.
    ISBN-13: 978-0-8146-5181-0   (alk. paper)
    ISBN-10: 0-8146-5181-X   (alk. paper)
    1. Bible. O.T. Prophets—Textbooks.   I. Title.

BS1505.55.C66   2005
224'.061—dc22

                                                              2005034578

Contents

Abbreviations viii

Foreword ix

CHAPTER ONE
Introductory Topics 1

The Approach of this Book 1

Why Study the Prophets? 3

Which Books to Study, and Where to Find Them 3

Former and Latter Prophets 6

Major and Minor Prophets 8

Ancient Israel's Beliefs and Understandings 8

How to Study a Prophetic Book 13

Basic Forms of Prophetic Speech 17

Rhetorical Features 23

Prophecy Throughout the Ancient Near East 24

True and False Prophets 30

For Further Reading 31

CHAPTER TWO
The Early Prophets 33

Micaiah ben Imlah 33

Samuel 35

Nathan 38

Elijah 40

Moses the First Prophet and Model 41

For Further Reading 44

CHAPTER THREE

The Eighth-Century Prophets in the Northern Kingdom   45

Background Information   45

Amos   51

Hosea   68

CHAPTER FOUR

The Eighth-Century Prophets in the Southern Kingdom   87

Micah   87

First Isaiah   100

CHAPTER FIVE

The Seventh-Century Prophets
Zephaniah, Nahum, and Habakkuk   123

Background Information   123

Zephaniah   128

Nahum   135

Habakkuk   143

CHAPTER SIX

Jeremiah, Lamentations, and Baruch   155

Jeremiah   155

Lamentations   185

Baruch   186

CHAPTER SEVEN

Ezekiel and Obadiah   189

Ezekial   189

Obadiah   212

CHAPTER EIGHT

The Final Years of the Exile: Second Isaiah   219

Background Information   219

Second Isaiah   222

CHAPTER NINE

The Persian Period and the Second Temple:
Third Isaiah, Haggai, Zechariah 1–8   239

    Background Information   239

        Third Isaiah   245

        Haggai   253

        Zechariah 1–8 or First Zechariah   259

CHAPTER TEN

Fifth- and Fourth-Century Prophets:
Malachi, Joel, Zechariah 9–14   267

    Background Information   267

        Malachi   267

        Joel   275

        Zechariah 9–14 or Second Zechariah   284

CHAPTER ELEVEN

Jonah, the Unique Prophet   295

        Jonah   295

Conclusion   305

Index of Authors and Subjects   307

Index of Biblical References   311

LIST OF MAPS

Cities Identified with Israel's Prophets   7

The Kingdoms of Israel and Judah in the Eighth Century   47

Boundaries of the City of David and the City of Jerusalem
in Solomon's Time and in Nehemiah's Time   103

The Extent of the Persian Empire   241

Abbreviations

AB	Anchor Bible
ANE	Ancient Near East
FOTL	Forms of Old Testament Literature
ICC	International Critical Commentary
JBL	*Journal of Biblical Literature*
OBT	Overtures in Biblical Theology
OTG	Old Testament Guides
OTL	Old Testament Library
NCBC	The New Century Bible Commentary
LM	*Lectionary for Mass*
RCL	*Revised Common Lectionary*
MT	Masoretic Text
LXX	Septuagint
NAB	*New American Bible*
NRSV	*New Revised Standard Version*
RSV	*Revised Standard Version*
SBLDS	*Society of Biblical Literature Dissertation Series*
VT	*Vetus Testamentum*

Foreword

This textbook focuses on how to read the Old Testament books of the Prophets, addressing the concerns of graduate and advanced undergraduate students in theology and ministerial programs. The book is the product of years of teaching undergraduate and graduate students in theology and in preparation for ministry in the church. From a canonical point of view this study includes primarily those books designated as the Latter Prophets in the Jewish canon, with mention of several Former Prophets. In Christian terminology this involves a few prophets whose work is recorded in the historical books and all the prophetic books named for a prophet, with a brief mention of Lamentations and Baruch as part of the discussion of Jeremiah. It does not include a study of the apocalyptic book of Daniel, but it does include brief discussions of the apocalyptic sections of several of the later prophetic books.

The study proceeds chronologically, to the extent that it is possible to assign dates to the different prophetic books. This approach respects the importance of the specific historical contexts within which each of the prophetic books took shape, including the socioeconomic, political, and religious issues that impacted the lives of the people who heard the prophetic words or reinterpreted them in later circumstances.

Biblical quotations and references are based on the New Revised Standard Version, which is the best combination of literal translation and dynamic equivalence available to us today. When the versification differs from that of the Masoretic or Septuagint texts, or from the New American Bible translation, a note is made to that effect.

Specific ideological considerations include, first of all, the following current foci of scholarship on the prophets. First, the superscription names the historical setting of the earliest words of each book, with the understanding that later words and interpretations were added throughout the different books. Second, references to particular historical events included within the text, for instance in Isaiah 7, contribute to our knowledge of the historical setting. In the absence of such references I situate the words within the general contours of the book's setting. Third, many of the books include early efforts to interpret the prophets' words for a new audience in later circumstances. These early examples of resignification of the text offer models for us as we interpret the prophets' messages for our own day. Fourth, I stress the prophetic task of commenting on the present rather than foretelling the future.

A second ideological focus is three recent Roman Catholic documents on the study of the Bible in the church. The first is the Vatican II document, *Dei Verbum*, the Constitution on Divine Revelation. The other two were prepared by the Pontifical Biblical Commission: the 1994 text *On the Interpretation of the Bible in the Church*, which underscores the validity and importance of historical-critical methods and also discusses other approaches to biblical study, and the 2001 document *The Jewish People and their Sacred Scriptures in the Christian Bible*, which offers insights for how Christians should read the Old Testament. In particular it asserts that christological readings of Old Testament passages are retrospective interpretations on the part of the early Christians rather than text-based understandings of the biblical word.

The third ideological focus is an appreciation of ancient Israel's beliefs and understandings, which underpin their way of life and thus the prophetic words. The Introduction addresses these: the people understand themselves as chosen by the Lord; God is One, both transcendent and immanent, and ultimately a mystery; life is a grateful response to God; everyday life has value; the vulnerable members of the community are entitled to special care by the group; the spoken word has effective importance; the prophets spoke in the genres of their day. In addition ancient people tended to see suffering as punishment, a perspective prevalent throughout the prophetic books. This view is inadequate and highly problematic in today's world. The book offers alternative interpretations of the meaning of suffering.

Finally, I base this book on five pedagogical assumptions in my eagerness to encourage students to engage the biblical text. First, I assume a basic knowledge of Scripture and do not offer detailed explanations of such topics as the different historical-critical methods, the ancient project of story-telling as opposed to history-telling, or the question of authorship of biblical books. Second, I organize the chapters around a systematic approach to the task of exegesis. I explain this approach in the Introduction. Third, I focus on the rhetorical features of each book because the prophetic material has a strong persuasive dimension that is expressed in its rhetorical features. We do not use all the same features in today's persuasive speech; however, an examination of the ancient style underscores the means the prophets used in their efforts to persuade the people to turn to God in their need. Fourth, I invite interaction with the textbook, and ultimately with the biblical text, through questions imbedded throughout the book. Many of these questions direct the student to look for details in the biblical text. Others invite comparisons and contrasts with other biblical material. All these interactive questions are integral to this study as they call attention to significant details, motifs, and passages in the different books. Lastly, I encourage students to actualize the text: that is, to interpret it for our lives today. In order to achieve this end I include the use of each book in the *Lectionary for Mass* and the *Revised Common Lectionary* as well as the Jewish readings for Shabbat and holy days. I then suggest points for reflection and questions for thought and action based on each of the prophetic books.

I am grateful for the support and suggestions of colleagues who have contributed their insights, including Corrine Carvalho, Marilyn Chambliss, Walter Harrelson, Joseph Mindling, O.F.M.CAP., James Wallace, C.SS.R., and Joseph Wimmer, O.S.A. Students at St. Bonaventure University, Fordham University Graduate School of Religion and Religious Education, and Washington Theological Union engaged the biblical text with commitment and with critical eyes, and I am particularly grateful to Matt Allman, C.SS.R., Ericson de la Peña, O.F.M.CONV., Robert Hawkins, Christopher Ianizzotto, O.CARM., Andrea Kramer, Michael Meyer, Joseph Narog, O.S.A., Christopher Page, Carla Riga, Yvonne Stewart, Ericjohn Thomas, Marie Ulanowicz, and Andrew White for engaging the text of the book and the text of the Bible. Lorraine Delisle, S.C., and Patricia McQuinn, S.C., assisted with preparation of the indices.

Colleagues and friends at Tantur Ecumenical Institute and the Ratisbonne Institute in Jerusalem and at the Pontifical Biblical Institute in Rome offered hospitality and study space during the preparation of this manuscript. The editorial staff at the Liturgical Press, especially Linda Maloney and Colleen Stiller, gave ongoing assistance and encouragement.

Finally, I dedicate this book to my Religious Congregation, the Sisters of Charity of Cincinnati. Our mission statement proclaims, "As pilgrims we pray for the wisdom to know the needs of our sisters and brothers and we dare to risk a caring response."

Chapter One

Introductory Topics

Choose life! Moses challenged the people to live according to the framework established on Sinai in response to the Lord's faithful care for them. Throughout the years when ancient Israel developed an understanding of monotheism and its requirements and rewards, the prophets repeated that challenge to their audiences. They insisted that the one God who had led the people out of Egyptian oppression, throughout forty years in the wilderness and into the Promised Land continued to care for them with steadfast concern, and asked that in return the people worship God alone and treat one another with justice and compassion.

The purpose of this book is to guide students of religion, theology, and ministry in reading the prophetic books with academic and pastoral integrity. This study, linked with awareness of the values and needs of today's society, will enable students to re-signify the prophetic message for today's world with its own human longings, oppressive situations, and vexing tensions as well as its significant achievements and profound awareness of human dignity.

The Approach of this Book

This first chapter addresses introductory topics essential to a study of the prophets: Why study the prophets? Which books of the Bible does this study include, and where in the Bible are those books located? What is the meaning of the terms Former and Latter prophets, and Major and Minor prophets? Then we will explain the approach of this study and examine several topics implicit in our approach: a look at ancient Israel's beliefs and understandings, a discussion of how to study a prophetic book, a look at prophecy throughout the ancient Near East, and a brief survey of the question of true and false prophets. An examination of the genres of prophetic speech completes the chapter.

The following chapters focus on the different prophets, proceeding in chronological order to the extent possible. That is, in Chapter Two we will look at the Former Prophets, who lived and worked before the eighth century B.C.E., according to their genres, messages, and contributions to an understanding of prophecy. Then we will study the eighth-century prophets Amos, Hosea, Isaiah of Jerusalem or First Isaiah, and Micah; the seventh-century prophets Zephaniah, Nahum, and Habakkuk; the seventh- and sixth-century prophets Jeremiah and Baruch; the sixth-century prophets Ezekiel and Obadiah; the exilic prophet Isaiah of Babylon or Second Isaiah; and the prophets of the Persian period: Third Isaiah, Haggai, and Zechariah 1–8. Next will come the fifth- and fourth-century prophets: Malachi, Joel, and Zechariah 9–14. Last we will consider Jonah, the most problematic of the prophetic books as regards date of composition.

This schema divides two books, Isaiah and Zechariah, into several different parts. We will discuss Isaiah 1–39 in connection with the eighth century, Isaiah 40–55 in the context of the Babylonian exile in the sixth century, and Isaiah 56–66 in the Persian period. Zechariah 1–8 will also be discussed during the Persian period shortly after the Babylonian exile, and chapters 9–14 will be situated among the last prophets, probably as late as the third century B.C.E. The specific reasons for these divisions will be discussed in connection with the books themselves.

Situating the prophets in their historical settings makes it possible to consider their socioeconomic and religious contexts as well. This contextual information allows us to understand the immediacy of the prophets' words as well as their lasting significance. In other words, it gives us insight into how the prophets interpreted the fundamental values of ancient Israelite religion in light of their specific situations. That information can offer us examples of how the prophetic words can be interpreted for today's needs, holding fast to the basic values found in the Bible while addressing the particular circumstances of our own societies.

We will look at each prophetic book in its canonical or final form. This approach allows us to look at the prophetic messages as they were shaped by the scribes and editors, to note the overall meaning of each book as well as the themes of its individual passages. We will situate the books in the historical settings indicated in their superscriptions, that is, the list of kings given in the first verse. When possible we will also look at specific historical settings of individual passages. This is feasible, for example, when historical figures are named in the text, such as in Isa 7:1-20, which lists the rulers of Israel, Judah, Syria, and Assyria. We will also note sections of the books that appear to be later reworkings of the original prophetic words. These passages serve as examples of early interpretation and thus can be models for us as we strive to interpret the prophets' words for today. The chapters are organized according to the schema "How to Study a Prophetic Book," outlined in this chapter. Finally, the last chapter addresses the significance of the biblical prophets for today in light of the themes highlighted throughout our study.

Why Study the Prophets?

First of all, why study the prophets? For us the prophetic books both record the values of the ancient Israelites and speak to us in our own times. The better we understand the ancient context and meaning of the prophets' words, the more fully we can hear them speak to the concerns of our day. The ancient prophets called their audiences to be faithful to the values handed down to them throughout the generations. Within their different historical, socioeconomic, political, and religious contexts they exhorted and challenged the people around the issues and practices of their day. Identifying those societal issues and values yields valuable insights into ancient Israel's understanding of its foundational relationship with God, articulated in the Pentateuch and interpreted for later communities at specific times in Israel's history. We will note throughout all the prophetic books the concern for how these issues impacted and impinged upon the people in their relationships with God and with their communities. From this record of the interaction among the people, their concerns, and their God we can appreciate the underlying values on which the ancient Israelite communities based their lives. Then we can re-signify their ancient message for our own day.

Which Books to Study, and Where to Find Them

Next, which books of the Bible does this study include, and where in the Bible are they located? The specific books we will study are those named for prophets: Isaiah, Jeremiah, Ezekiel, Hosea, Joel, Amos, Obadiah, Jonah, Micah, Nahum, Habakkuk, Zephaniah, Haggai, Zechariah, and Malachi. In addition we will look at the stories about prophets in the

Pentateuch, Joshua, Judges, 1 and 2 Samuel, and 1 and 2 Kings. We will also examine briefly the books of Baruch and Lamentations as part of our study of Jeremiah, as we explain in the following paragraph.

The books that concern us are placed differently in Jewish and Christian Bibles. In the Jewish canon the books named for prophets follow directly after Joshua, Judges, Samuel, and Kings, which are known as the Former Prophets, as opposed to the Latter Prophets Isaiah through Malachi. The Jewish community refers to all the books from Joshua through Malachi as the Prophets, the second part of the Scriptures, after the Torah and before the Writings. In the Christian canon the books named for prophets are the final books of the Old Testament. Included among them are three books in addition to the fifteen named above: Lamentations and Baruch, which follow Jeremiah, and Daniel, which follows Ezekiel.

Lamentations is traditionally thought to have been composed by Jeremiah, which explains its position after Jeremiah in the Christian canon. It is a series of laments over the loss of the city of Jerusalem to the Babylonians. They are written in the style of Jeremiah's confessions or laments to God throughout the book of Jeremiah. Because of those similarities, tradition attributes the authorship of Lamentations to Jeremiah. Baruch is mentioned in the book of Jeremiah as the prophet's scribe, and for this reason the book named for him appears after Lamentations in the Roman Catholic canon. Other Christian Bibles include Baruch among the Apocrypha and Pseudepigrapha. This position reflects the view that Baruch is not one of the canonical prophets but is nevertheless considered a holy book.

The book of Daniel follows Ezekiel. The early Christians included Daniel among the prophets because they interpreted certain sections of the book as preparing the way for the coming of Christ. Daniel is not, however, a prophetic book but an apocalyptic work. For that reason we will not include the book in our study.

The Jewish arrangement of the books follows a somewhat chronological order, insofar as the Torah was the first to be canonized, the Prophets were edited next, and the Writings were the last to be composed. The Christian arrangement reflects the theological presupposition of the early church that the prophetic books predicted or foreshadowed the coming of Christ, whose life is recorded in the New Testament; therefore the books were placed immediately before the New Testament. This problematic theme of the relationship between the prophets and the coming of Christ will be discussed periodically throughout our study.

Jewish, Protestant, and Roman Catholic Canons

Jewish	Protestant	Roman Catholic
Genesis	Genesis	Genesis
Exodus	Exodus	Exodus
Leviticus	Leviticus	Leviticus
Numbers	Numbers	Numbers
Deuteronomy	Deuteronomy	Deuteronomy
Former Prophets	*Historical Books*	*Historical Books*
Joshua	Joshua	Joshua
Judges	Judges	Judges
1 and 2 Samuel	Ruth	Ruth
1 and 2 Kings	1 and 2 Samuel	1 and 2 Samuel
Latter Prophets	1 and 2 Kings	1 and 2 Kings
Isaiah	1 and 2 Chronicles	1 and 2 Chronicles
Jeremiah	Ezra	Ezra
Ezekiel	Nehemiah	Nehemiah
Hosea	Esther	Tobit
Joel	*Wisdom Books*	Judith
Amos	Job	Esther
Obadiah	Psalms	1 and 2 Maccabees
Jonah	Proverbs	*Wisdom Books*
Micah	Ecclesiastes	Job
Nahum	Song of Solomon	Psalms
Habakkuk	*Prophets*	Proverbs
Zephaniah	Isaiah	Ecclesiastes
Haggai	Jeremiah	Song of Songs (of Solomon)
Zechariah	Lamentations	Wisdom of Solomon
Malachi	Ezekiel	Ecclesiasticus (Sirach)
Writings	Daniel	*Prophets*
Psalms	Hosea	Isaiah
Job	Joel	Jeremiah
Proverbs	Amos	Lamentations
Ruth	Obadiah	Baruch
Song of Songs	Jonah	Ezekiel

Jewish	Protestant	Roman Catholic
Ecclesiastes	Micah	Daniel
Lamentations	Nahum	Hosea
Esther	Habakkuk	Joel
Daniel	Zephaniah	Amos
Ezra	Haggai	Obadiah
Nehemiah	Zechariah	Jonah
1 and 2 Chronicles	Malachi	Micah
		Nahum
		Habakkuk
		Zephaniah
		Haggai
		Zechariah
		Malachi

Former and Latter Prophets

The Jewish community refers to Joshua, Judges, Samuel, and Kings as the books of the Former or Preclassical Prophets and to Isaiah through Malachi as the Latter or Classical Prophets. This distinction acknowledges the different genres and contents of the two collections of books. The books of the Former Prophets include accounts and legends about the prophets, who acted on behalf of the vulnerable and attributed their success to the intervention of the one God. The Former Prophets include Moses, Balaam, Samuel, Nathan, Ahijah, Elijah, Micaiah, and Elisha.

The books of the Latter Prophets consist mainly of the words the prophets spoke to the people and to God. As did the Former Prophets, they emphasized the people's responsibility to the vulnerable members of the community, often referring explicitly to widows, orphans, and resident aliens. The prophets highlighted care for the vulnerable as the proper response to God's continuing care for them from their earliest beginnings. In addition these books highlight the necessity to worship the Lord. They underscore two aspects of worship: first, its importance as an expression of the relationship between YHWH and the people, and second, the need to complement worship with justice and righteousness in dealing with one another.

The Christian tradition refers to Joshua, Judges, 1 and 2 Samuel, and 1 and 2 Kings as the Deuteronomistic History, highlighting the books'

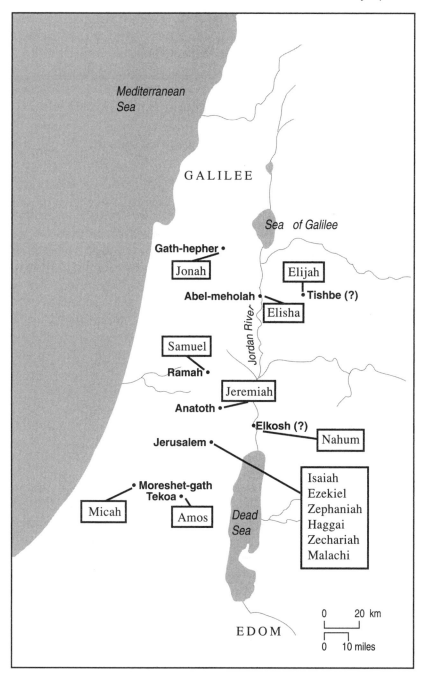

Cities Identified with Israel's Prophets

account of the history of Israel from the taking of the land under Joshua's leadership to its loss to the Babylonians in the early sixth century B.C.E. The designation calls attention to the Deuteronomistic perspective of the books; that is, their similarity to Deuteronomy in terms of themes and basic presuppositions. Within that frame of reference, the term "Former Prophets" refers not to the books but to the individuals listed above, and "Latter Prophets" refers to the fifteen named individuals from Isaiah through Malachi.

Major and Minor Prophets

Another set of terms by which to designate the prophets is "major" and "minor." The terms refer not to the relative importance of the books, but simply to their length. There are three major prophets (Isaiah, Jeremiah, and Ezekiel) and twelve minor prophets (Hosea through Malachi). The minor prophets are often referred to as the Twelve, a term that reflects the early custom of including all twelve on the same scroll, the total length of which is approximately the same as one scroll of the major prophets.

Ancient Israel's Beliefs and Understandings

In addition to the organizational features of the prophetic books, our study is based on an understanding of several ideological presuppositions of the ancient Israelite communities. The following ten points summarize the most salient of these features.

1. *This people is chosen by YHWH.* All ancient Near Eastern communities relied on the special protection of some particular god whom they looked upon as their own. The idea of chosenness *per se* was not the issue; that was implicit in the people's confidence in their gods. Rather, for each people it was a question of which particular deity had chosen them. Ancient Israel saw itself chosen by the God known as YHWH. This is a form of the name God gave to Moses when he requested it at the burning bush, "Thus you shall say to the Israelites: I AM has sent me to you" (Exod 3:14). The prophets frequently challenged the people to remember that they were chosen by YHWH. (See, for example, Jer 30:2-3; Hos 2:23; Amos 3:2.)

2. *God is One.* Implicit in the name "I AM" is the belief that Israel's God is One. Such a belief was almost unique in the ancient Near East. Briefly

in Egypt during the fourteenth century B.C.E. Pharaoh Akhenaton introduced belief in one god, the sun, but the belief did not endure after his death. Elsewhere throughout the ancient Near East it was customary for communities to believe in pantheons of deities, of whom each had dominion over one particular aspect of the community's life or over some natural or geological phenomenon. But Israel was called to believe in only one God whose love, power, and influence extended to every member of the community and to all the dimensions of life. Often the prophets reminded the people that their God is One. Second Isaiah articulated this belief in the most unequivocal terms of the entire Old Testament. (See, for example, Isa 42:8; 44:24; 45:4-6; see also Deut 4:35, 39.)

3. *God is both transcendent and immanent.* This belief is integral to the Hebrew Scriptures and appears both implicitly and explicitly in the prophetic messages. We know that the first two chapters of Genesis tell two stories of creation: Chapter 1 describes God in transcendent terms. God's word brings creatures into being, separates them from one another, and designates their place in the universe. We know that this creation story does not pretend to offer a scientific explanation of creation, but rather, from a theological point of view, to express the awesome point that divine creation of the universe is beyond human ability and comprehension. The Creator is described in transcendent terms.

But Genesis 1 is followed by Genesis 2, which describes God making creatures in a way we humans are able to understand. God takes some clay from the ground and shapes it into various creatures in an effort to find a suitable companion for the human being God has created. These creatures prove to be unsatisfactory insofar as none of them gives the human being the sort of companionship that would be ideal, until finally a creature is made out of a bone of the human being. The result is men and women, who are companions to one another. This we can understand! Shaping things out of dirt, desiring companionship, finding relationships that are satisfying as opposed to those that are disappointing—these are realities we know from our own experience, and they describe God in immanent terms. The juxtaposition of transcendent and immanent descriptions of God in Genesis 1 and 2 highlights the belief that God is both transcendent and immanent. The prophets' belief in these two aspects of God is apparent in all their words.

Throughout the Hebrew Scriptures the transcendent and immanent God is actively involved in the life of the people from the time of creation. This immersion in human affairs permeates the prophets' writings as well; in fact, it is at the heart of prophetic messages.

4. *Life is a grateful response to God.* Israel's life was understood as a grateful response to the one God who cares for them. The covenant at Sinai spelled out for the people how to live in recognition and gratitude for all God did for them. This included the specific terms of their relationship with God, which the people explicitly expressed in worship; and their relationship with one another, particularly the more vulnerable members of the community, which they expressed in their everyday dealings with one another. The people's lives gave witness to their understanding that the details of life have importance because they are a response to God for what God has done for us, not because they are written down or because they are required. This divine-human relationship was formally expressed in terms similar to the ancient suzerainty treaty, a solemn agreement between a superior or more powerful party (in this case, God) and a weaker or subordinate party (the people) who were given instructions on how to live in response to their protector.

5. *Everyday life has value.* Worship was the explicit expression of the people's relationship with God in the yearly, monthly, weekly, and daily cycle of feasts and worship times. But these "holy" times alternated with the larger blocks of "ordinary" time, which most of the people spent in daily chores and interaction with one another. Time spent on everyday activities, and the activities themselves, were understood by the prophets to be as important as worship because they were the arena in which people lived out their response to God's faithful care for them.

6. *The vulnerable must be cared for.* The ancient Israelite community, like other ancient Near Eastern communities, had an explicit mandate to care for its more vulnerable members. These people are frequently defined in the Pentateuch as widows, orphans, and resident aliens. (See, for example, Exod 22:21-22; Deut 10:18; 16:11-14; 24:17-21.) This injunction appears with particular emphasis in the eighth-century prophets (Isa 1:17, 23; Amos 2:6-7; 4:1). In many ancient Near Eastern societies one held a place in the community through family, in the husband's line. So if a woman lost her husband she lost her place in the community, and was therefore entitled to special protection from everyone in the community. The same was true of orphans. Because they were children of dependent age and no longer had a designated place in the community by reason of the loss of their parents, it became the responsibility of the entire community to care for them.

The situation of resident aliens was a bit different. The term refers to travelers, or people who were migrating but had not yet become permanent settlers. In the ancient world they were vulnerable because, as not-yet members of the community, they were outsiders. In a society that placed great emphasis on belonging, anyone without family ties to a particular group was looked upon as outside the natural boundaries of protection. It was therefore the obligation of the entire community to ensure that resident aliens were given proper protection. If we think of who would fit this category in our own society, we might think of those who come to the United States from various places in Central or Eastern Europe or Central and South America. Mainstream American society with its commitment to capitalism and individualism often runs counter to this biblical community-oriented injunction to offer special support to marginalized people.

7. *Suffering may signify punishment.* Frequently the Old Testament, including the prophetic books, identifies sin as the cause of people's suffering. Simply put, if a person or community experiences illness, untimely death, famine, military defeat, or any diminishment of its life, it is assumed that the actions or omissions of the person or group caused the suffering. Within that perspective the antidote for suffering is to repent of one's sins and live in faithfulness to the Lord. The warnings of Amos, Isaiah, and Jeremiah strongly express this connection. But Jeremiah struggles with it, as do some of the Wisdom books (Jer 12:1-4; Job 21) and these offer correctives to its overly simplistic cause-and-effect perspective.

The tendency to equate suffering with punishment exists in our own society, sometimes in insidious ways. For example, we hear people refer to AIDS as punishment for sin, or we meet people who assume that poverty is always the result of laziness. Finding meaning in the prophets' messages for today often entails challenging or refining this particular assumption.

8. *God is the ultimate mystery.* While it is true that the ancient Israelites believed that God is both transcendent and immanent, and they described the divine presence and actions from these two perspectives, they believed that, when all was said and done, God was beyond their understanding. The divine mystery transcended even the ancient Near Eastern belief that suffering is deserved and blessing is earned. For example, Moses declared to the people as they prepared to enter the Promised Land:

> . . . you are a people holy to the LORD your God; the LORD your
> God has chosen you to be a people for his own possession, out of

> all the peoples that are on the face of the earth. It was not because
> you were more in number than any other people that the LORD set
> his love upon you and chose you, for you were the fewest of all
> peoples; but it is because the LORD loves you, and is keeping the
> oath which he swore to your fathers, that the LORD has brought you
> out with a mighty hand, and redeemed you from the house of bond-
> age, from the hand of Pharaoh king of Egypt. (Deut 7:6-8)

The people stood in awe before this ultimate mystery.

9. *The spoken word has power.* We know that a significant part of the Old
Testament, including the prophets, was originally transmitted orally.
Several significant implications follow from this reality. First, many of
the words of the prophets are best understood when heard as persuasive
speeches. Second, ancient people ascribed to the spoken word the power
to accomplish what it signified. Genesis 1 recounts the power of the
Creator's spoken word to bring the universe into being. We read in
1 Sam 3:19, "As Samuel grew up, the LORD was with him and let none
of his words fall to the ground." Isaiah 55:10-11 asserts, "For as the rain
and the snow come down from heaven, and do not return there until
they have watered the earth, making it bring forth and sprout, giving
seed to the sower and bread to the eater, so shall my word be that goes
out from my mouth; it shall not return to me empty, but it shall accomplish that which I purpose, and succeed in the thing for which I sent it."
These passages illustrate the dynamism of the word, with its sacramental
ability to accomplish what it signifies.

The prophetic speakers profoundly hoped their listeners would repent
and reform their lives. Their disappointment at the people's lack of
response was often poignant. For example, Jeremiah reflects,

> Then they said, "Come, let us make plots against Jeremiah—for the
> law shall not perish from the priest, nor counsel from the wise, nor
> the word from the prophet. Come, let us smite him with the tongue,
> and let us not heed any of his words." Give heed to me, O LORD,
> and hearken to my plea. Is evil a recompense for good? Yet they
> have dug a pit for my life. Remember how I stood before you to
> speak good for them, to turn away your wrath from them." (Jer
> 18:18-20)

Once words were recorded they were understood to be "reduced to
writing." The written word preserved the message, but did not have the
dynamic power of speech. We today assess the relative authority of

spoken and written words quite differently. We rely on written documents, particularly those that are signed and witnessed. But an understanding of the ancient value enables us to hear the persuasive power of the prophets' words.

10. *Prophets spoke and wrote in familiar genres.* The prophets delivered their messages in the genres of their day, according to the standard conventions of communication in the ancient Near East. Form critics have identified these genres and the life-settings in which they were originally used. Some examples are accounts of symbolic acts, oracles of judgment and of salvation, prophetic lawsuits, and complaints. These will be discussed later in this chapter, and throughout our study of the individual prophetic books. Awareness of these genres adds to an understanding of the prophetic word and also highlights the importance of speaking in such a way as to maximize the listener's chances of understanding the message. We today would frequently use different genres from the ancient prophets, but what is crucial is to speak so that the message can be understood.

How to Study a Prophetic Book

The box provides an outline of the steps we will follow in looking at each prophetic book. The first is to learn the background information. This information is often referred to as the world behind the text. The prophets spoke to a specific group of people in particular circumstances, and we investigate their world to the extent possible. We ask: With what geographical location and period in history do we associate the book? In what socioeconomic conditions did the people find themselves? What political situation influenced the prophetic message? What was the social setting (family life, ways in which people communicated)? What were the religious issues of the day? When was the message delivered in spoken words, and when was it put into writing?

Then we turn to the world of the text, or the text itself. First we identify the book's structure by outlining it. The purpose of this step is to clarify what is often a complex collection of fragments of different speeches given by the prophets over a period of time. The resulting composite often seems choppy and even disconnected, unlike the Pentateuch and the historical books, which consist of continuous narratives. The process of outlining the book brings into relief its organizational pattern. Often that organizing principle seems to be a particular theme. For instance,

Amos begins by condemning the sins of seven neighboring peoples, then he denounces the sins of Israel itself. This organizational device becomes clear with a careful look at the repeated formulas in Amos 1–2.

Next we identify the genres in the book, along with possible life-settings in which that kind of message might have been delivered to the people. We will identify and discuss the most frequently used forms later in this chapter, in preparation for the analysis of genres used by each of the prophets.

How to Study a Prophetic Book

1. Learn background information:

    a. Identify historical and geographical settings.

    b. Learn socioeconomic, political, and religious background.

    c. Identify date(s) of composition, both oral and written.

2. Identify forms and structure:

    a. Outline the book.

    b. Identify significant genres (and life-settings).

    c. Look for rhetorical features.

3. Find the message of the prophet:

    a. Identify important themes the prophet conveys to the audience.

      (1) Note the specific nuances of the message.

      (2) Note the audience to whom the words are spoken.

    b. Relate these themes to other parts of the Bible, particularly the Pentateuch and historical books, observing similarities and differences. (Note that this is a way of reflecting on the traditions of Israel.)

    c. Identify the meanings the material can offer us today.

      (1) Note its liturgical use in the lectionary.

      (2) Note its significance for our dealings with people and events.

The next step is to look for the book's rhetorical features, that is, its persuasive patterns and devices and its use of key words. These different features, particularly the various forms of repetition, help to highlight the themes of the book. They also show us how each prophet delivered the message and offer models for how we can identify the significance of the prophetic word for today.

Our examination of the genres and rhetorical features brings into focus the message of the prophet. Identification of the structure, genres, and rhetorical devices allows the important themes of the prophet's message to emerge within its original historical setting. Then we relate those themes to other parts of the Bible, especially the Pentateuch and historical books, by looking for similarities and differences in the themes. This comparison highlights the roots of the prophetic word within the traditions of ancient Israel, reinforcing and developing beliefs that had been part of the community's memory since its beginnings in the wilderness.

Finally, we reflect on the world in front of the text, that is, our own world, and on how the message can speak to people today in a world that, although far removed from the communities to whom the prophet spoke, often bears substantial resemblances to it in terms of both basic values and pervasive problems. We do this in two ways: first, we note the appearance of the prophetic words in the lectionary and second, we reflect on the ways in which the message can influence everyday life in today's world. The task of re-signifying the biblical message in our context is both crucial and complex.

First we take a look at the use of the prophets in the lectionary, that is, which passages are included, on what days, and in relation to what other biblical passages. We will look at three of these: the Jewish Readings, the Roman Catholic *Lectionary for Mass,* and the *Revised Common Lectionary* used in many Protestant traditions.

The Jewish Readings is organized around the Torah or Pentateuch. In many Jewish congregations, during the course of the year the entire Torah is read at Sabbath services, and portions of the Former and Latter Prophets are paired with the Torah readings according to their themes and historical settings. Observing which prophetic passages appear and which Torah readings they interpret gives us insight into how the Jewish community understands both the prophetic messages and the traditions in which they are rooted.

The *Lectionary for Mass* is a major contribution of the Second Vatican Council. It marks a milestone in the use of the Old Testament in modern liturgy: the previous lectionary did not include any Old Testament readings on Sunday, and only a very few on weekdays of the year. This new lectionary was prepared by and for Roman Catholics, but initially some Protestant groups adopted it as well. The *Lectionary for Mass* has four volumes: Volume One for Sundays, Volume Two for the weekdays of Year I, Volume Three for the weekdays of Year II, and Volume Four for Special Occasions.

The Sunday lectionary is organized in a three-year sequence around the three synoptic gospels: Matthew in Year A, Mark in Year B, and Luke in Year C. Readings from John's gospel appear each year, particularly during the Christmas and Easter seasons. During the liturgical seasons of Advent, Christmas, Lent, and Easter the gospel readings are selected as they relate to the themes of the season. On the Sundays of Ordinary Time the second readings and gospel readings are semi-continuous. Readings from the Old Testament are paired with the gospels except during Easter Time, when the Acts of the Apostles is read. The Old Testament readings generally relate to the gospel passages in a typological way, resulting in a christocentric use of the readings. The weekday *Lectionary for Mass* in Ordinary Time includes semicontinuous readings. Selections from the Prophets are featured, especially in Year II. These readings generally represent the important themes sounded by the different prophets.

The third lectionary of interest to us here, the *Revised Common Lectionary*, grew out of a concern on the part of some Protestant groups that the typological use of the Old Testament in the *Lectionary for Mass* did not adequately convey the richness of the Old Testament. It made two changes in an effort to substitute a theocentric approach for the christocentric approach, and to give the Old Testament its own voice. First, it uses longer Old Testament readings. Second, it tells the story of Israel in a three-year arrangement throughout the Sundays of the year. In Year A the readings focus on the time from the flood to Israel's entry into the Promised Land. In Year B the story continues with the beginnings of the monarchy. It also includes Wisdom readings traditionally attributed to King Solomon. Year C concentrates on the prophets, beginning with Elijah and continuing chronologically, with particular focus on Isaiah and Jeremiah.

By observing which prophetic passages appear in each of the three lectionaries we get an idea how the different congregations understand the prophetic messages. This view of the readings also gives us an opportunity to move beyond typological understandings toward appreciation of the prophetic messages as they stand in their own right.

In addition to looking at how the words of the prophets appear in liturgical use we are also interested in how those words can influence life today. This, too, is a complex task. It consists, first of all, in recognizing the historical setting of the prophetic book whose words we wish to re-signify. Next we compare and contrast the socioeconomic, political, and religious concerns the book addresses with today's situation. Then we turn to the words themselves, bringing them to bear on comparable conditions today. For example, Amos' world was marked by deep economic divisions, inequalities, and injustices. The same is true in many sectors of life today. When we recognize the similarities between Amos' environment and our own we can turn with confidence to his words and bring them to bear on our own situation; for example, "But let justice roll down like waters, and righteousness like an everflowing stream" (Amos 5:24) is as urgent a message today as it was 2700 years ago.

Basic Forms of Prophetic Speech

The prophetic books consist almost entirely of the prophets' words to the people and to God. We would expect the prophets to speak according to the conventions of their day to increase the likelihood that their words would be effective in the ears of their audiences. Here we will look briefly at the major prophetic forms that are typical of ancient Near Eastern speech. In the following chapters we will examine these forms in greater detail as they appear in the different prophetic books.

1. *Messenger Speech.* The formula "Thus says the LORD" or "says the LORD" at the beginning or end of a speech indicates that the prophet's message comes from God. The formula was used in the ancient world by messengers who delivered messages from kings. In the prophetic literature the formula highlights the divine origin of the prophet's words. In Zech 1:3 the phrase appears three times: "Therefore say to them, Thus says the LORD of hosts: Return to me, says the LORD of hosts, and I will return to you, says the LORD of hosts." The messenger formula often appears as part of another form such as the judgment speech or salvation speech.

2. *Words of Judgment.* The prophets' words frequently condemn actions of individuals, groups within Israel, Israel as a whole, or foreign nations. These words appear in several forms.

a. ANNOUNCEMENT OF JUDGMENT TO ISRAEL. These speeches include an introductory summons, an accusation, and an announcement of judgment or divine intervention, usually introduced by the word "therefore." These speeches often include a messenger formula, either at the beginning or immediately before the announcement of judgment. For example, Mic 3:9-12 begins with a summons to the rulers of Israel. The speech accuses them of injustice, oppression, violence, bribery, and extortion. These evils are compounded by the complacency of the rulers who assume that all will be well because the Lord is with them. The announcement of judgment follows: therefore Jerusalem, including the Temple, will be destroyed. The announcement repeats this judgment three times, using different images each time: "Zion shall be plowed as a field; Jerusalem shall become a heap of ruins, and the mountain of the house a wooded height." The power of the divine word announced by the prophet was believed to set in motion the disaster the prophet named. At the same time the announcement of judgment implies the hope that the people will take the message to heart and amend their ways before it is too late and the judgment comes to pass.

b. Announcement of Judgment to the Nations. This form follows a pattern similar to the announcement of judgment to Israel, but its effect is not so much a warning to the nations as a reassurance to Israel: the destruction of the nations will make life safer for the Israelites. A further effect of these speeches is to highlight God's power over nations besides Israel. Yhwh is not only the God of Israel, but also of all nations. For example, Amos 1:2-5 is an oracle against Damascus, the capital of Syria. It relies on the previous verse for the summons that does not single out a particular audience but rather announces that the Lord is speaking in a loud voice that reverberates throughout the land. The divine voice in Jerusalem devastates the top of the Carmel range. The speech itself begins with the messenger formula, then enumerates the sins of the city. Using imagery associated with harvest, Amos condemns the terrible oppression of the Syrians. Then the announcement of judgment specifies the destruction that will come upon Damascus as punishment for its injustice. It will be destroyed by fire, its gates will be broken, its leaders will be cut off from help, and its inhabitants will go into exile. While this announcement spells terrible devastation for Damascus, its audience is the Israelites who take complacent comfort in the Lord's care for them. That complacency is shattered, however, when the words of judgment are directed at them in Amos 2:6-16 after first being directed at each of Israel's neighbors.

c. Woe Oracle. This form is addressed either to Israel or to another people and calls attention to the sins that will eventually cause their downfall. Its message implies that the oracle is given in response to a question from an individual or group, perhaps originally a priest. (See, for example, 1 Sam 28:6; 2 Sam 5:22-24.) It contains three elements: it begins with the word "woe" followed by a description of the sinners and a statement of the results that will follow the sinful action. Several modern translations substitute the words "ah" or "alas" for "woe." Jeremiah 22:13-19 is an example of a woe oracle. It begins "Woe to him . . ." and goes on to describe an evil action of King Jehoiakim: he had the people build a grand palace for him but did not pay them for their labor. The consequence of his unjust action is that he will not be given a respectful burial.

d. ADMONITION. The form is a warning or instruction, telling the people what they must do to avert divine judgment. Admonitions often begin with words such as "turn!" or "seek!" Amos 5 includes several admonitions to the people to seek God and live, to seek good and not evil, to hate evil and love good.

3. *Words of Salvation.* While words of judgment are spoken either to Israel or to a foreign nation, words of salvation are given only to Israel. They are proclaimed in times of distress and are usually spoken in the first person singular; that is, the speaker is identified as "I." In the Hebrew language a distinction is made between two kinds of salvation speech, according to the tense of the verb. Assurances of salvation are proclaimed in the perfect tense, which denotes completed action, and announcements of salvation are given in the imperfect tense, which denotes incomplete or future action. This distinction is not always evident in English versions of the Bible. We will point it out, though, because the difference carries meaning: speeches in the perfect tense express a stronger degree of certainty than those in the imperfect tense, conveying the message that the people's cries for help have already been heard. A third type of salvation-speech is a portrayal of salvation, which describes a situation that will exist in the future but transcends time and history. We will look at examples of each of these types.

a. The ASSURANCE OF SALVATION often recalls God's past dealings with Israel, proclaims, "Do not fear," and offers assurance of divine presence or a promise of divine intervention, a description of the results of God's acts, and an explanation of why God chooses to act. For example, Isa 41:8-13 begins with a divine reminder to Israel that God chose them, followed by the words "Do not fear" and the assurance "for I am with you, do not be afraid, for I am your God." The assurance continues with the divine promise to strengthen, help, and uphold the people. Then the result of God's acts is given: those who try to harm God's people will themselves be defeated. Finally, God's reason for acting is given: "For I, the LORD your God, hold your right hand; it is I who say to you, 'Do not fear, I will help you.'" In this speech the verbs "I have chosen," "I took," "I called," "I have chosen you and not cast you off," "I will strengthen you, I will help you, I will uphold you" are all in the Hebrew perfect tense that expresses completed action.

b. The ANNOUNCEMENT OF SALVATION frequently begins with a messenger formula, proclaims salvation, and includes a statement of divine purpose at work in the saving act. For example, Isa 43:16-21 begins, "Thus says the LORD, who makes a way in the sea, a path in the mighty waters, who brings out chariot and horse, army and warrior; they lie down, they cannot rise, they are extinguished, quenched like a wick." These words allude to some unspecified difficulty, recalling the crossing of the sea in Exodus, which was accomplished through God's intervention on behalf of the people in a former time of need. The announcement of salvation in vv. 18-21a continues the allusion to the Exodus in proclaiming a new era:

> Do not remember the former things, or consider the things of old. I am about to do a new thing; now it springs forth, do you not perceive it? I will make a way in the wilderness and rivers in the desert. The wild animals will honor me, the jackals and the ostriches; for I give water in the wilderness, rivers in the desert, to give drink to my chosen people, the people whom I formed for myself.

The announcement ends with a statement of divine purpose in v. 21b, "so that they might declare my praise." Here the people's memory of the past serves to encourage them and to introduce the announcement of the divine saving acts to come. These verbs are in the imperfect tense: "they lie down, they cannot rise," "do not remember . . . or consider," "it springs forth, do you not perceive it? I will make a way," "they will honor me," "so that they might declare." They denote actions either taking place in the present or soon to happen in the future, but without the certitude of verbs in the perfect tense.

c. The PORTRAYAL OF SALVATION is not related to time or to the historical setting of the prophet, but rather describes a future situation that will be in contrast to the present. For example, Isa 11:6-9 describes an ideal moment when creatures who are natural enemies will live together in peace. It begins, "The wolf shall live with the lamb, the leopard shall lie down with the kid," and ends, "for the earth will be full of the knowledge of the LORD as the waters cover the sea."

The prophets used several other types of speeches as well.

4. *Prophetic Lawsuit.* This form is adapted from legal proceedings. It includes three elements: the summons to the offender or to the witnesses; the trial itself, including speeches by one or both parties; and the sentence. For example, Isa 41:21-24 summons the foreign idols and challenges them to demonstrate their divine power by whatever means possible. The speech concludes from their lack of response, "You, indeed, are nothing and your work is nothing at all; whoever chooses you is an abomination."

5. *Disputation.* This form is a prophet's response to, or disputation of, charges made by the people against God or the prophet. Micah 2:6-11 is an example of this genre. It responds to false prophets and oppressors of the people with words of accusation against their manner of leading the people astray.

6. *Prophetic Instruction.* This prophetic genre offers guidance to a group or an individual. An example is Isa 1:10-17, which explicates the essence of genuine worship as opposed to superficial sacrifice. Mere offering of sacrificial oblations is not what the Lord asks; rather, goodness and justice, particularly care for the vulnerable in everyday life, are the requisites for genuine worship.

7. *Proverb.* This is a pithy saying that illustrates an everyday reality. It is frequently found in the book of Proverbs. Amos 3:3-5 contains several proverbs, such as "Do two walk together unless they have made an appointment?"

8. *Dirge.* This two-line form is associated with mourning. In Hebrew it can be recognized by the number of accented syllables, three in the first line and only two in the second, connoting an abrupt ending or stopping. Amos 5:2 is an example of this form.

In addition, the prophetic books contain words of the prophets to God. They are usually similar to psalm forms.

9. *Hymn and Thanksgiving.* The prophet prays to God in the psalm form of praise or thanksgiving, or sings about God's presence and action in the world. An example of this form is Jonah 2:2-9.

10. *Prayer of Lament.* The prophet prays to God in the psalm form of a lament or call for help. The prayer includes a cry to God such as "O God"

or "How long, O God?" This is followed by a complaint or elaboration on the difficulties the speaker experiences. The complaint leads to a request or petition to God, a statement of trust in God, sometimes a promise, then a statement of praise. For example, Hab 3:1-19 is a confident prayer for help.

Besides words spoken by the prophets, the books contain narrative reports about their activities or about events in their lives.

11. *Call Narrative.* This narrative describes the prophet's call and commission by God to serve as a messenger of God to the people. The elements of a call narrative are: God appears to the prophet in some way (theophany); God commissions the person to do a particular task; the person questions or objects to the call; God overrides the objection, reiterates the call, and gives the person a sign. The sign ratifies the call and gives assurance of divine presence and guidance to the recipient. The elements of the call foreshadow the nature of the prophet's work. For example, Jeremiah's call is recounted in Jer 1:4-10. It begins with a simple report in 1:4 that the word of the Lord came to Jeremiah. Then the words of the Lord announce to Jeremiah that he had been appointed from the womb to be a prophet to the nations (v. 5). In v. 6 Jeremiah puzzles over the appointment because of his youth. The Lord reiterates the commission more specifically in vv. 7-8, and touches Jeremiah's mouth as a sign of putting divine words in his mouth; the Lord then repeats the commission in vv. 9-10.

12. *(Auto)biographical Report, or account of prophetic activities.* For example, Jeremiah 36 describes Jeremiah's instructions from the Lord to write down all the Lord's words to him, his directive to Baruch to read the scroll publicly, King Jehoiakim's outrage when he heard the words and his subsequent burning of the scroll, and finally Jeremiah's dictation of a new copy to Baruch.

13. *Vision Report.* This form describes a vision received by the prophet. It is often given in the first person, beginning with "I saw" and giving details about what the prophet saw. This report usually includes an explanation of the meaning of the vision. Amos 7:7-9 is an example of a vision report followed by an explanation.

14. *Account of a Symbolic Act.* This form describes a prophet's action, requested by God, that symbolizes a deeper reality. It usually has three elements: God's instruction to the prophet to perform the act, often in a vision; the account of the act itself; and an explanation of the meaning

of the act. For example, Jer 32:1-15 recounts the Lord's instruction to Jeremiah to purchase a field. He reports that he did so; then the explanation is offered: "For thus says the Lord of hosts, the God of Israel: Houses and fields and vineyards shall again be bought in this land." In other words, the act symbolizes the divine assurance that, in spite of the exile in Babylon, the time will come when the people will again inhabit the land from which they were taken.

15. *Prophetic Legend.* This type of narrative recounts events in the life of the prophet that illustrate God's will being accomplished in the situation. The events may or may not be biographical; the intent in reporting them is to highlight the prophet's obedience and faithfulness to God as well as the divine power that makes possible the events described. This genre is found primarily in the narratives about Elijah and Elisha. For example, 2 Kings 4:1-7 narrates a miraculous expansion of the amount of oil in a widow's jar. Elisha instructs her to pour the oil into borrowed containers and sell it to pay off her debts. As she pours, the oil continues to flow until all the available containers have been filled. Elisha then instructs her, "Go sell the oil and pay your debts, and you and your children can live on the rest." The import of the narrative is not in the precise details but rather in its illustration of Elisha's reliance on God, and God's care for the widow in her indebtedness. We will look more closely at these forms in our study of each of the prophets.

Rhetorical Features

In addition to the forms or genres of their speeches, the prophets used specific rhetorical techniques to hold the attention of their listeners and to highlight the point they were making. Several examples are listed below; we will discuss these and others as they appear in the prophetic books.

1. *Repetition.* A frequent rhetorical feature is repetition of words or phrases such as in Jer 7:4: "Do not trust in these deceptive words: This is the temple of the Lord, the temple of the Lord, the temple of the Lord." The repetition highlights the people's pointless reliance on temple worship to save them from harm. Words or phrases might also be repeated at intervals throughout a passage or book, calling attention to the main point of the prophet's words.

2. *Rhetorical Questions.* These questions have an obvious answer that is not stated, and they are often followed by another, more probing question that expects the same response. Amos 3:3-8 begins with a series

of rhetorical questions: "Do two walk together unless they have made an appointment? Does a lion roar in the forest when it has no prey? Does a young lion cry out from its den if it has caught nothing?" Several more rhetorical questions follow, culminating with: "Does disaster befall a city, unless the LORD has done it?" This device catches the attention of the audience, who already know the answer to the first question, and prepares them to hear and ponder the final, more personal and penetrating question.

3. *Plays on Words.* Similar-sounding Hebrew words with unrelated meanings were sometimes used by the prophets to make a point. For example, Jer 1:11-12 refers to an almond tree (*šaqed* in Hebrew), followed by the words, "You have seen well, for I am watching (*šoqed* in Hebrew) over my word." We will take note of other examples of this feature in the prophets' words, and observe how they intensified the prophetic messages to their audiences.

Prophecy Throughout the Ancient Near East

Documents from ancient archaeological sites have shed light on prophecy throughout the ancient Near East (ANE). They reveal several similarities to biblical terms referring to the prophetic figure and also genres and motifs. We will look at some of these similarities, giving examples from the different locations where documents have been found.

The oldest and largest collection comes from Mari, a kingdom that thrived in the eighteenth century B.C.E. along the Euphrates River, controlling the trade routes between Babylonia and Syria. Thousands of tablets have been found in its royal palace. Of particular significance for a study of prophecy are letters from the time of two kings, Yasmaḫ-Addu, who ruled from 1792 to 1775, and Zimri-Lim, who ruled from 1774 to 1760, just before Mari was destroyed by the Babylonian King Hammurabi (Nissinen, *Prophets and Prophecy,* 13).

Messenger formulas indicate that the words come from the gods. For example, Malikdagan delivers a message from Dagan, "Now go, I send you, thus say. . . ." (Weinfeld in Gordon, ed., *The Place Is Too Small for Us,* 33).

- Compare and contrast this formula with the messenger formulas in Exod 3:10 and Isa 6:9.

Many of the Mari letters refer to divination, dreams, and prophetic oracles from diviners and high officials or royal ladies. For example,

Mari texts include the formula, "In my dream. . . ." and "he went into a trance, arose, thus said." A different Mari text reads, "I was left alone gazing at his great vision. . . . I became a sorry figure of a man, I retained no strength . . . I fell on the ground. . . . Suddenly a hand grasped me and pulled me up onto my hands and knees; he said to me: Daniel, attend to the words I am speaking to you and stand up where you are. . . . I stood up trembling . . . and he said: Do not be afraid . . ." (Weinfeld, "Ancient Near Eastern Patterns," 35, 36, 39).

- Compare and contrast these quotations with Gen 40:9, 16; 41:17, 22; Num 24:2; Judg 3:10; 11:29; 14:6, 19; 15:14; 1 Sam 10:6, 10; 11:6; 16:13; 2 Chr 20:14; 24:20; Ezek 2:2; 3:24.

The prophets served particular gods by divining the future in assistance to the king. Sometimes the messages came while a person was in a trance. They reported messages regarding, for example, political issues such as war and the king's welfare, and cultic concerns such as maintaining the temples and conducting the ceremonies and sacrifices (Weinfeld, "Ancient Near Eastern Patterns," 36–38).

For example, a woman named Timlû reports to the royal lady Adduduri, "I had a dream in your behalf." The message instructs her to entrust an important mission to six men from Mari. Another dream report reads, "In the temple of Annunitum, three days ago, Šelebum went into trance and said, 'thus says Annunitum: Zimri-Lim, you will be tested in a revolt! Protect yourself. . . . As regards the people who would test you: those people I deliver up into your hands.'" Another message, this one from the god Dagan through the prophet Lupahum to Zimri-Lim, reads, "Wherever you go, joy will always find you!" A further message delivered by Zimri-Lim's daughter to him states regarding Ešnunna, "I will gather him into the net that I knot. . . . Now protect yourself!. . . . Without consulting an oracle do not enter the city!" (Nissinen, *Prophets and Prophecy*, 28, 30, 47, 71).

The Mari documents include pronouncements similar to biblical words of salvation; for example, "There will be no armed conflict! For as soon as his [Zimri-Lim's] auxiliaries arrive they will be scattered. The head of Išme-Dagan will be cut off and placed under the feet of my lord, saying: 'the army of Išme-Dagan is large, but even if his army is large, his auxiliaries have scattered it. My auxiliaries are Dagan, Šamaš, Itur-Mer, Belet-ekallim, and Adad . . . the Lord of Decisions, who go before my lord'" (Nissinen, *Prophets and Prophecy*, 40).

- Compare these pronouncements with the divine assurances of
  protection in Exod 14:13; Num 10:35; Deut 7:17-24; 20:1-4; 31:1-8;
  1 Sam 23:4; 26:8; Pss 4:6; 68:2; 89:11; 144:6.

Cultic concerns are evident in several examples, such as "Concerning
the portion consecrated to Adad, about which I had written to you . . .
gather all the consecrated portion and let it be taken to the temple of
Adad in Aleppo." Another message declares to Zimri-Lim, "Dagan has
sent me to deliver a message concerning the execution of the . . . offerings: 'Send to your lord the following message: the new month has now
begun, and on the fourteenth day, the . . . offerings should be executed.
Not a single offering may be neglected.'" The offerings in question are
related to ceremonies commemorating the dead (Nissinen, *Prophets and
Prophecy*, 24, 55).

- Compare and contrast these words with the cultic instructions in Isa
  56:7; 66:20; Jer 17:26; Ezek 40:38-43; 43:18-27; Zeph 3:10; Mal 3:3-4.

The second-largest collection comes from the royal archive at Nineveh,
the capital of Assyria. These tablets were written over one thousand
years after the Mari tablets. Most of them come from the library of
Ashurbanipal, who was king in Assyria when the Neo-Babylonian
empire began its ascendancy (Nissinen, *Prophets and Prophecy*, 97).
    We know from these documents that many Assyrian prophets at the
time were women. They were affiliated with the temples of Ishtar, and
they reported her words to the king. These oracles are very helpful to
our study of prophecy because many of them include the four key elements of prophetic messages: they name the deity whose message is
being delivered, the message itself, the prophet who delivers the word,
and the one to whom the message is addressed. The addressees are
usually Esarhaddon (681–669) and Ashurbanipal (668–627), and the
messages address topics that were important in Esarhaddon's time
(Nissinen, *Prophets and Prophecy*, 99).
    The tablets express divine support for the king and for the stability of
his reign, often in the form of assurances of salvation with their characteristic words "Fear not." For example, the goddess Ishtar assures
Esarhaddon: "Esarhaddon, king of the lands, fear not! What is the wind
that has attacked you, whose wings I have not broken? Like ripe apples
your enemies will continually roll before your feet!" Another assurance
of salvation proclaims, "Do not trust in humans! Lift up your eyes and
focus on me! I am Ishtar of Arbela. I have reconciled Ashur to you.

I protected you when you were a baby. Fear not; praise me!" (Nissinen, *Prophets and Prophecy,* 102, 105).

A Babylonian text from around 133 B.C.E., the time of the Seleucids, records a message from the goddess Nanaya delivered by someone called Boatman. "[Boatman] responded to them, saying: 'I am a messenger of Nanaya; I will not deliver up the city to loot and plunder!'" The text continues, "The council of that temple responded to the people who were with that [Boatman]: 'Do not listen to the words of that fanatic!'" (Nissinen, *Prophets and Prophecy,* 198).

- Compare and contrast these expressions of divine support with those in Isa 30:12-16; Jer 9:4; 49:11; Mic 7:5.

Several oracles in the Nineveh archive are preserved in collections that were organized several years after they were originally delivered. This later compilation shows that the original oracles took on a larger significance beyond their original meaning, giving us early examples of ongoing interpretation of the prophetic message.

A small number of texts have been found in areas geographically and linguistically closer to Israel than Mari or Nineveh. Among them are several that are useful to our study of prophecy in the ANE. An eighth-century plaster inscription found at Tell Deir Alla, in a valley east of the Jordan River, mentions a person named Balaam. He has access to the divine council, who send out one of their members on a mission of destruction. Balaam is called a "seer" [*hozeh*], the same word used in biblical texts (for example, 2 Sam 24:11; Isa 29:10; Amos 7:12). This inscription calls to mind the account of Balaam in Numbers 22–24 (Nissinen, *Prophets and Prophecy,* 210–12).

Assurances of salvation appear among these letters. For example, an inscription in Aramaic from the vicinity of Aleppo celebrates the victory of Zakkur over Syrian enemies around 800 B.C.E. It records his pleas to the god Baalshamayn for help in defending his territory against them, then reports, "Baalshamayn spoke to me through seers and through visionaries and Baalshamayn said, 'Fear not, for I have made you king. . . . I will deliver you from all these kings who have forced a siege against you'" (Nissinen, *Prophets and Prophecy,* 206). Again we note the term "seer" as well as the formula "fear not" that introduces the assurance of salvation.

- Compare and contrast these words with Isa 7:4; 40:9; 44:2; Jer 30:10; Zeph 3:16; Hag 2:5; Zech 8:13.

Another area that has yielded inscriptions useful for our study is Lachish, a city about thirty miles southwest of Jerusalem. It was almost as important as Jerusalem at the time of the Babylonian invasion in the sixth century B.C.E. Among the ostraca, or pottery shards, found in Lachish are letters that illustrate prophetic activity in the face of Nebuchadnezzar's onslaught and give insight into the desperate situation of the Israelites at that time. One of the letters mentions "the prophet," perhaps referring to Jeremiah. Another, to Yaush, reads, "To my lord, Yaush. May YHWH cause my lord to see this period in peace. Who is your servant, a mere dog, that my lord has sent the letter of the king . . . saying, 'Read!'" (Nissinen, *Prophets and Prophecy*, 216, 218). We note the name YHWH not only here but in several other Lachish letters as well. The reference to a dog is reminiscent of Mephibosheth in 2 Sam 9:7-8.

- See also Jer 26:20-24; 28:1-17; 37:7-10 for descriptions of the desperate situation in Judah in the face of the Babylonian onslaught.

Several additional features are common to biblical and other ANE prophecy. We will look at examples that are particularly revealing for our study of biblical prophecy.

A formula for marriage and divorce found in texts from Old Babylonian through Persian times reads, "She is (not) my wife and I am (not) her husband." A similar formula for creating and breaking adoption reads, "You are (not) my son" (Weinfeld, "Ancient Near Eastern Patterns," 41–42). These formulas shed light on biblical passages such as Hos 1:6-8, which names Hosea's second son "Not My People," then explains, "You are not my people and I am not your God." The biblical name takes on added force when it is understood as the rendering of a legal formula for severing a relationship.

- Compare and contrast these formulas with Ps 2:7 and Mal 3:17.

An old Babylonian prayer of a diviner refers to purification of the mouth: "O Šamaš, I am placing in my mouth pure cedar (resin). . . . I wiped my mouth with . . . cedar (resin). . . . Being (now) clean, to the assembly of the gods I shall draw near." This ritual is similar to that in Isa 6:5-7, showing that Isaiah's experience was not unique; rather, it was a known ritual of purification (Weinfeld, "Ancient Near Eastern Patterns," 34).

The relative importance of morality and cult is found in Egyptian texts; for example, "Story of the Shipwrecked Sailor" and "Instruction to King

Merikare": "Make firm your place (= grave) with uprightness and just dealing for it is on that which their hearts rely; more acceptable is a loaf of the upright than the ox of the wrongdoer" (Weinfeld, "Ancient Near Eastern Patterns," 44–47).

• Compare these passages with Isa 1:11-17; Jer 6:20; 7:22; Mic 6:6-8.

The question of justice independent of cult also appears in ANE texts. A Sumerian hymn to Enlil asserts, "Hypocrisy, distortion, abuse, malice . . . enmity, oppression, envy, (brute) force, libellous [sic] speech, arrogance, violation of agreement, breach of contract, abuse of (a court) verdict, (all these) evils the city does not tolerate . . . the city endowed with truth where righteousness (and) justice are perpetuated" (Weinfeld, "Ancient Near Eastern Patterns," 48).

In an inscription from the time of Esharhaddon we find, "They (the Babylonians) were oppressing the weak/poor and putting them into the power of the mighty; there was oppression and acceptance of bribes within the city daily without ceasing; they were robbing each other's property; the son was cursing his father in the street . . . then the god (Enlil/Marduk) became angry, he planned to overwhelm the land and to destroy its people" (ibid.).

The king had special responsibility for upholding justice among his people. A Babylonian document, "Advice to a Prince," declares:

> If a king does not heed justice, his people will fall into anarchy and his land will be devastated . . . if he does not heed his nobles, his life will be cut short. If he does not heed his adviser, his land will rebel against him. . . . If citizens of Nippur are brought before him for judgment and he accepts bribes and treats them with injustice, Enlil, lord of the lands, will bring a foreign army against him. . . . If he takes the money of his citizens and puts it into his treasure . . . Marduk . . . will give his wealth and property to his enemy. If he mobilized the whole of Sippur, Nippur, and Babylon and imposed forced labor on the people . . . Marduk . . . will turn his land over to his enemy (Weinfeld, "Ancient Near Eastern Patterns," 48–49).

• Compare these words with the emphasis on justice in Deuteronomy 17; 1 Kings 12; Isa 1:21-23; Jer 22:13-17; Mic 7:1-7; Nah 3:18.

These few examples show us that the institution of prophecy was known throughout the ANE since before the era of Israel's classical prophets. It involved messages from a deity to a particular recipient who was often a ruler. The word was delivered by a messenger who frequently received it in a dream or vision. The messages often promise divine protection for the king and thus for all the people. In addition, several ANE parallels emphasize justice, particularly the king's responsibility to uphold justice in his kingdom. This theme is less prevalent among the parallels than in biblical prophecy, as we will see when we note the constant concern for the vulnerable members of the community in the biblical materials.

True and False Prophets

The question of the credibility of the prophets was often a vexing one, particularly among those listeners who chafed at the message the prophets delivered. The commission to serve as a prophet was solemn and serious. In fact the classical prophets, almost without exception, shied away from accepting the commission precisely because it was so serious and they saw themselves as unworthy of it. Nevertheless, there were people who usurped the prophetic office. Several biblical passages shed light on the topic:

Exodus 20:18-21

Deuteronomy 13:1-5; 18:15-22

1 Kings 18:7-46; 22:1-53

Jeremiah 6:13-15; 14:13-16; 23:9-17, 26-28; 28:1-17

Ezekiel 13:1-23; 14:1-11

True Prophets: The passages in Exodus and in Deuteronomy 18 specify that prophets serve as divinely appointed intermediaries between God and the people, even at the cost of death. They serve in order that the people can communicate indirectly with God rather than directly, because of their fear of getting too close to the Deity.

False Prophets: On the other hand, several characteristics of false prophets can be identified. They spoke in their own name, or in the name of a god other than YHWH, or relied on some source other than the divine word for their information. For example, if a prophet claimed to be a prophet of Baal or one of the other Egyptian or Mesopotamian gods, their word would not come to pass; if it did, the prophet would be punished because in Israel prophecy was understood as intermediation between the one God and the people.

In addition, false prophets spoke only encouraging words to the people (see, for example, Jer 5:12-15 and 6:13-15). This became a particularly troublesome issue during the exile in Babylon, when false prophets predicted a quick end to the exile (see, for example, Jer 28:1-17).

Finally, they spoke words that did not come to pass. This final characteristic is complicated. We know that many prophetic words did not come to pass (again, see Jeremiah 28). In fact, we are relieved that many predicted events never occurred. Some examples are Isaiah's warning, "Someone will even seize a relative, a member of the clan, saying, 'You have a cloak; you shall be our leader, and this heap of ruins shall be under your rule'" (3:6); the dire predictions of punishment in Amos 1–2; and Jonah's prediction, "Forty days more, and Nineveh shall be overthrown!" (3:4). Nevertheless, we take note that Deut 18:22 specifies, "If a prophet speaks in the name of the LORD but the thing does not take place or prove true, it is a word that the LORD has not spoken. The prophet has spoken it presumptuously; do not be frightened by it." Furthermore, in the Deuteronomistic view fulfillment was expected to occur within the memory of those who heard the words being spoken, that is, within a relatively short time. This puzzling characteristic must therefore remain unclear to us. We will refer to it again as we meet unfulfilled words in the prophetic books.

Now we turn to the prophets themselves and use the tools and insights we have reviewed in this chapter to break open their words and find their message.

For Further Reading

Blenkinsopp, Joseph. *A History of Prophecy in Israel.* Philadelphia: Westminster, 1983.

Bright, John. *A History of Israel.* 3d ed. Philadelphia: Westminster, 1981.

Heschel, Abraham Joshua. *The Prophets.* New York: Harper & Row, 1962.

Koch, Klaus. *The Prophets.* 2 vols. Philadelphia: Fortress, 1982 (insights on prophets as thinkers).

Mowinckel, Sigmund. *The Spirit and the Word: Prophecy and Tradition in Ancient Israel.* Edited by K. C. Hanson. Minneapolis: Fortress, 2002.

Nissinen, Martti. *Prophets and Prophecy in the Ancient Near East.* With contributions by C. L. Seow and Robert K. Ritner. Edited by Peter Machinist. Atlanta: Society of Biblical Literature, 2003.

Petersen, David. *The Prophetic Literature: An Introduction.* Louisville: Westminster John Knox, 2002.

Pontifical Biblical Commission. "The Interpretation of the Bible in the Church" in *Origins* 23:29 (Jan. 6, 1994) 497–524.

———. *The Jewish People and their Sacred Scriptures in the Christian Bible.* Città del Vaticano: Libreria Editrice Vaticana, 2002.

Pritchard, James B., ed. *Ancient Near Eastern Texts Relating to the Old Testament.* 3rd ed. Princeton: Princeton University Press, 1969.

Rad, Gerhard von. *The Message of the Prophets.* Translated by D. M. G. Stalker. New York: Harper & Row, 1962. (The same book can also be found under the title *Old Testament Theology.* Vol. 2. It offers a general historical and theological discussion.)

Stacey, David. *Prophetic Drama in the Old Testament.* London: Epworth Press, 1990.

Sweeney, Marvin A. *Isaiah 1–39 with an Introduction to Prophetic Literature.* FOTL. Grand Rapids: Eerdmans, 1996.

———. *The Twelve Prophets.* 2 vols. Berit Olam. Collegeville: Liturgical Press, 2000.

Weems, Renita. *Battered Love: Marriage, Sex, and Violence in the Hebrew Prophets.* Minneapolis: Fortress, 1995.

Weinfeld, Moshe. "Ancient Near Eastern Patterns in Prophetic Literature," *VT* 27 (1977) 178–95; repr. in Robert P. Gordon, ed., *The Place Is Too Small for Us: The Israelite Prophets in Recent Scholarship.* Winona Lake: Eisenbrauns, 1995, 32–49.

West, Fritz. *Scripture and Memory: The Ecumenical Hermeneutic of the Three-Year Lectionaries.* Collegeville: Liturgical Press, 1997.

Westermann, Claus. *Basic Forms of Prophetic Speech.* Translated by Hugh Clayton White. Philadelphia: Westminster, 1967.

———. *Prophetic Oracles of Salvation in the Old Testament.* Translated by Keith Crim. Louisville: Westminster John Knox, 1991.

Zucker, David J. *Israel's Prophets: An Introduction for Christians and Jews.* New York: Paulist, 1994.

Chapter Two

The Early Prophets

The prophets who get most of our attention are those for whom books are named, whom we call the "writing prophets," whose work began in the eighth century. But there were several who lived and taught before that time, and the biblical accounts of them help to shape our understanding of the institution of prophecy in ancient Israel. We will look first at Micaiah ben Imlah, about whom we read in 1 Kings 22:1-38. That account introduces the significant characteristics of the biblical prophets and their messages. Then we will examine the stories of other early prophets to become acquainted with the beginnings of the institution of Israelite prophecy.

Micaiah ben Imlah

The Micaiah ben Imlah episode appears within the Elijah stories found in 1 Kings 17–2 Kings 1. It involves Ahab, king of Israel (875–854) and Jehoshaphat, king of Judah (874–850), preparing for battle against the Syrians in order to take back the city of Ramoth-Gilead. As part of the preparation Jehoshaphat requests that Ahab ask the Lord whether or not to go to battle, so Ahab assembles about four hundred prophets and puts the question to them. They respond positively, assuring the king that the Lord will grant him victory. Jehoshaphat remains unconvinced and asks if there is no other prophet who might be consulted in this matter. Ahab names Micaiah ben Imlah, whom he did not consult with the others because of the prophet's record of predicting disaster rather than victory for Ahab.

At Jehoshaphat's request, Micaiah is summoned by a messenger who hints that all the other prophets have predicted victory and the king hopes Micaiah will do likewise. Micaiah, however, asserts that he will speak the word the Lord gives him. In fact, when the king puts the question to him, Micaiah gives him a positive response, prompting Ahab to insist on the truth. At that point Micaiah predicts defeat for the king of Israel. He explains his prediction by recounting a vision of the Lord in the heavenly court, asking who might entice Ahab to fight against the Syrians in order that he would be defeated. Finally a spirit volunteered, explaining, "'I will go out and be a lying spirit in the mouth of all his prophets.' Then the LORD said, 'You are to entice him, and you shall succeed; go out and do it.' So you see, the LORD has put a lying spirit in the mouth of all these your prophets; the LORD has decreed disaster for you" (22:22-23). Then Zedekiah, one of the four hundred prophets, slaps Micaiah, wondering how both could speak in the Lord's name and give different responses to the same question. The king orders Micaiah to be imprisoned and fed reduced rations until after the battle. Micaiah responds that if the king survives the battle, that will indicate that the Lord has not spoken to him. As Micaiah had predicted, Ahab suffers mortal wounds in the battle and dies that evening.

Several significant points in the account give us insight into early Israelite prophecy. First, the incident takes place in a specific historical context, the wars between Israel and Syria in the mid-ninth century. First Kings 20:1-43 introduces the conflict, describing the Syrian siege of Samaria and the Israelite attack on Damascus that followed the siege. In 799 B.C.E. the advisers of Ben-Hadad, king of Syria, advised him to wage battle on the plains because they thought the Israelite gods (they assumed Israel had many gods) would protect only the hills. In fact, the greatly outnumbered Israelite army defeated the Syrians on the plain, and as a result the Israelites made a treaty with the Syrians. Three years later the events described in 1 Kings 22 unfolded.

Second, the narrative sharply contrasts the prediction of the four hundred and that of Micaiah. We learn that this was not the first time Micaiah predicted negative results in contrast to the encouraging words of the four hundred; in fact, the king had come to expect such words from him. The account points out that Micaiah's first response to the request is a positive one, but the king presses him to tell the truth, knowing that Micaiah's words will not be encouraging. Then Micaiah gives the response that predicts the death of the king.

Third, Micaiah's words, as well as the commission to deliver them to the king, had a divine origin, as we see from the narrative. Micaiah had a vision that took him to the heavenly court, where the Lord was looking for a way to send Ahab into battle. Events unfolded as they did when a spirit volunteered, and the Lord promised him success through divine assistance. When the prophet Zedekiah questions Micaiah about the divine origin of his words, Micaiah responds that the results of the ensuing battle will make clear whether or not his words come from God. The outcome does, in fact, confirm the divine origin of Micaiah's words, showing at the same time that the words of the four hundred did not come from God and therefore the four hundred were not prophets of the Lord.

- Compare and contrast Micaiah's vision with that of Isaiah in Isaiah 6.

- Compare and contrast the theme of divine origin of prophetic words with Jeremiah 23.

Fourth, the vision makes clear that the Lord has power over Ahab. The Lord wants Ahab to fight the Syrians and suffer defeat at their hands, and arranges that the four hundred prophets will encourage him to go into battle. We are reminded here of the Lord's power over the Pharaoh, expressed in the Exodus narrative through divine power to make Pharaoh's heart harden. The outcome will demonstrate the Lord's power to control what happens to Ahab.

The entire incident is one of divine intervention in human affairs, making known to the people, through the prophet, something new from the divine realm that would not otherwise be knowable. This intervention depends on the vision, audition, and speech of the prophet in a particular set of circumstances, offering insight into the meaning of the events as they relate to God. In fact, these are the characteristics we find throughout the biblical prophets and their messages. We will now look at other early Israelite prophets in light of these characteristics.

Samuel

The next prophet we will consider is Samuel, whom we first meet when his mother Hannah names him at birth in 1 Sam 1:20. As is the case with Micaiah ben Imlah, Samuel lives and works in a specific historical context that gives meaning to his words and actions. He lived at the beginning of the transition period from tribal confederacy to centralized government and played a major part in initiating the monarchy in Israel. First Samuel records the circumstances of his birth. He was born to Hannah and Elkanah after Hannah promised the Lord that if she gave birth to a son she would lend him to the Lord. She fulfilled her promise by taking him to Shiloh, where the Ark of the Covenant was housed, to

serve as an apprentice to Eli the priest. The narrative makes clear that
the Elide priesthood was in a state of decline: Eli's sight (his insight) was
failing (1 Sam 1:12-17; 4:15) and his sons were violating both the sacrificial
laws and the women who came to the Shiloh shrine (2:12-17, 22). In larger
terms they were violating the sacred trust that had been placed in them
as priests at the Shiloh shrine. In contrast to the decline of the Elide
priesthood, Samuel's stature and divine favor increased (2:26; 3:19).

Samuel was commissioned to perform several tasks as an intermediary
between God and the people. First, the Lord called him to denounce the
Elide priesthood for its hypocrisy and abuse of office (3:11-17). Note the
elements of a call narrative in this account. Samuel is called by God three
times during his sleep. The first time he hears a voice Samuel runs to Eli,
thinking it was he who had called. The second time he does the same,
and Eli realizes it is God calling, so he instructs Samuel to respond to
God. The third time Samuel responds to God. He then hears the voice
of YHWH announce that Eli's house will suffer punishment for its sins.
Here the writer illustrates the point by juxtaposing two contrasting tra-
jectories. While the story reports Samuel's increasing favor with God, it
also describes the diminishment of Eli's sons' favor. This storytelling
technique of juxtaposing two contrasting realities recurs throughout the
Deuteronomistic History. Here Samuel's increase and the diminishment
of the Elide priesthood are woven together to illustrate that the two tra-
jectories develop simultaneously. While one institution disintegrates,
another begins to take its place. The Elide priesthood comes to an end
and a new priesthood begins with Samuel.

Not only the Elide priesthood but also the institution of judgeship was
disintegrating. Judges are identified in the Bible as commissioned by
God for a particular task. We see this in the theoretical introduction to
the cycle of judges in Judg 2:16. It is also stated in the accounts of particular judges; see, for example, Judg 3:9 regarding Othniel, 3:15 regarding Ehud, and 6:14 regarding Gideon. But 1 Sam 8:1 reports, "When
Samuel was old, he made his sons judges over Israel." This hereditary
succession ended the institution of judgeship.

The Deuteronomistic theme of prophecy and fulfillment is also evident
here. In the battle against the Philistines at Ebenezer, both of Eli's sons
die on the same day, bringing the Elide priesthood to a final, tragic end.
The narrative had predicted that end in the divine words to Samuel, and
then it came to pass (1 Sam 3:13-14; 4:11). The incident illustrates the Deuteronomistic understanding of prophecy and fulfillment: the fulfillment
occurs within the memory of those who heard the earlier announcement.

Samuel's second commission comes in response to the people's request for a king. Samuel is sent by God to appoint and anoint first Saul, then David, to rule over the people (1 Sam 9:1–10:27; 16:1-13). The establishment of the monarchy came about as a result of the interplay of several factors. According to the biblical text the people requested a king because they wanted to be like the nations (8:5). In addition, the request was made during a hinge point in human history. Historians and anthropologists have identified sociological, political, and military factors that contributed to a significant paradigm shift at the end of the second millennium B.C.E. (This historical period probably had much in common with our own day: the paradigms under which people had been living for centuries were breaking down but it was not clear what new paradigms would emerge to define the way people lived and worked and governed themselves.)

Agriculture had advanced with the use of iron tools, making it possible to grow surplus crops. This in turn led to barter as a means of exchange, and eventually to the growth of cities where young men from different families came together to bargain with one another, bartering one kind of food for another, or food for other necessities. This way of life necessitated a form of government based on a foundation other than family life, because the city dwellers were no longer living in family groups. A leader who was chosen or appointed needed some kind of validation of authority to take the place of family sanctions that had been vested in the head of the household.

Furthermore, the turn of the millennium saw the rise of powerful groups who were eager to amass territory and power. The Bible depicts the Philistines in this way, and describes the killing of Goliath the Philistine as David's first public act of heroism, in 1 Samuel 17. By the time of Samuel and Saul the increasing greed for land and power led to the development of standing armies among Israel's neighbors, whose training and weaponry were far superior to those of the Israelites.

In addition to these factors, 1 Samuel's account of the establishment of the monarchy lists religious infidelity as a significant reason for the shift in forms of government. The people's request for a king is interpreted as rejection of the Lord as leader of the people (8:6-9). Herein lies the reason for the Deuteronomistic portrayal of the classical prophets as intermediaries between God and the people, especially the king: to insure that the king as human leader would continue in the way of Moses as a divinely appointed leader who would honor the relationship between God and the people.

This background information clarifies the significance of Samuel's commission to find and anoint the one chosen by God to be king. The selection of the king is ultimately God's work, to be carried out by the divine representative. The prophet serves as a bridge between Deity and people by carrying out the divine command on behalf of the people, and by speaking to God as the people's representative. In addition, Samuel's role as bridge is specific to the need he was called to address; that is, to carry out the transition from tribal government to monarchy in such a way as to ensure that God would continue to rule in the person of the king.

A final aspect of Samuel's prophetic role is evident in 3:19, "As Samuel grew up, the LORD was with him and let none of his words fall to the ground." The account's assurance that the divine word spoken by Samuel would not "fall to the ground" is a way of saying that the word was protected by God and would therefore be effective. It would remain "in play" among the people, accomplishing its intended purpose.

With Samuel, then, the institution of prophecy becomes identified with the emerging monarchy. The prophet is chosen by God to serve in a particular historical context. He receives instructions from the Lord to speak and to perform certain actions in God's name, to incarnate the divine will among the people.

Nathan

Another early prophet we will consider is Nathan, whom the text situates in the generation after Samuel. The Bible does not give any biographical or other background about Nathan. One of David's sons was named Nathan (2 Sam 5:14), but he seems to be a different person because when Nathan first appears in 2 Samuel he is identified as a prophet *(nabi)*.

The books of 2 Samuel and 1 Kings recount three events in which Nathan participated, all of which concern David. The first is a conversation with David, who reveals to the prophet his desire to build a house for the ark of God (2 Sam 7:1-17). Nathan initially responds with encouragement, but that night he receives a message from the Lord regarding David's plan. The message has three points: first, the Lord is accustomed and content to move about among the people; second, the Lord has cared for David all along and will continue to do so in the future; and third, the Lord will continue to care for all the people by giving them a place where they will be free from enemies and by providing a house for

David. The message is built around a play on the word "house": David wishes to erect a house for God, but God promises David a different kind of house, a family.

Nathan appears in the narrative for a second time at the Lord's request after David violates Bathsheba. Nathan tells David a parable about a rich man who took the one lamb that belonged to a poor man because he wished to offer hospitality to a guest and did not want to slaughter one of his own flock. David does not understand this illustration of David's unjust and oppressive behavior until Nathan interprets the parable with his climactic accusation, "You are the man!" Then David takes the message to heart and repents of his sin, but his penance is not enough to save the child born to David and Bathsheba from death. When they eventually have another son, Solomon, God sends Nathan to David to announce that the child's name is to be Jedidiah, "Beloved of the Lord" (2 Sam 12:24-25), in keeping with the earlier promise of descendants to David.

The third incident involving Nathan takes place toward the end of David's life when one of David's sons, Adonijah, declares himself king (1 Kings 1:5-53). Nathan advises Bathsheba, Solomon's mother, to alert David to this development, referring to a promise that Solomon would succeed David. (This promise does not appear in the text.) Bathsheba does as instructed and the prophet Nathan reinforces her petition to her husband and king, David. When David hears that Adonijah has taken the throne he commands that his son Solomon be made king and be anointed by Zadok the priest and Nathan the prophet. This is done as commanded, after which Adonijah offers his allegiance to Solomon.

This particular incident is problematic in terms of Nathan's role as prophet. It is not said that Nathan is speaking on God's behalf, nor does the narrative report the promise on which Nathan bases his advice to Bathsheba, "Go in at once to King David, and say to him, 'Did you not, my lord the king, swear to your servant saying: Your son Solomon shall succeed me as king and he shall sit on my throne? Why then is Adonijah king?'" The silence of the text raises questions about Nathan's prophetic role in this instance. Is he serving in a strictly political capacity here?

The other incidents report Nathan speaking and acting at the Lord's instruction, making known to David the divine will in specific circumstances. His messages and actions make known the meaning of events from the divine point of view beyond their economic, political, and sociological significance. What is more, they offer assurance that God is present among the people in the events that are unfolding in their lives.

Elijah

The next prophet we will consider is Elijah. The Elijah material is found in 1 Kings 17–19; 21; 2 Kings 1:1–2:12. The text situates him a good hundred years after Nathan, during the reigns of Ahab (875–854) and his son Ahaziah (854–853) in Israel, the northern kingdom. Ahab inherited the throne from his father Omri, who had built the city of Samaria as the capital of the northern kingdom. Ahab strengthened the kingdom by his marriage to Jezebel of Sidon. During his reign Ahab encouraged the worship of the Phoenician deity Baal (1 Kings 16:32), but did not take care of the altar to YHWH (18:30).

The Elijah narratives include several different genres: for example, miracle stories in chapter 17, lament stories in chapter 19, conflict stories in 1 Kings 18 and 21 and 2 Kings 1. They also represent varying degrees of historical reliability. Those stories thought to be part of the original cycle of Elijah stories, connected to the historical context in which he is situated, are the drought and the Mount Carmel episodes in chapter 18, the incident at Horeb in chapter 19, the events surrounding Naboth's vineyard in chapter 21, and the account of Ahaziah's death in 2 Kings 1. Other hagiographic stories were added later; these magnify the miraculous dimension of Elijah and his work. Examples include the ravens feeding Elijah at the Wadi Cherith in 17:2-6, the widow feeding him at Zarephath in 17:8-16, and the angel providing food for him in the wilderness in 19:4-8. The stories gradually became a continuous narrative and were eventually included in the Deuteronomistic History.

> • What miraculous elements do you find in 17:2-6 and 17:8-16? How do these elements augment the depiction of Elijah as larger than life?

Elijah appears without warning and almost without introduction; we are told only that he is from Tishbe of Gilead. His work is described in a series of events that highlight the power of the Lord as opposed to the powerlessness of Baal. These incidents are organized around the theme of supplying food and drink for Elijah and all the people. In each instance the climactic moment is a miraculous intervention of the Lord. The powerlessness of Baal contrasts most dramatically with the power of YHWH in the incident when the four hundred fifty prophets of Baal are unable to call down fire from Baal to start a sacrificial fire, but Elijah prays to the Lord and immediately his sacrifice is consumed in the flames (1 Kings 18:20-40). The four hundred fifty men prepare a sacrifice and call on Baal to light the fire for it, but nothing happens. Then Elijah prepares his sacrifice and prays to the Lord. His sacrifice is consumed in flames, even after Elijah has his men pour twelve jars of water on the offering.

The legend is an example of addition of anecdotes to an already existing tradition. It describes the lengths to which Elijah went to be sure the power of YHWH would be unequivocally evident in the lighting of his sacrificial fire. Twelve jars of water was an extravagant amount to pour on the sacrificial offering and altar, especially during a drought. This detail is considered an anecdote added later to enhance Elijah's stature rather than a historically verifiable incident.

These early prophets, whom we know through the legends about them, set the stage for our study of the classical prophets in several ways. They introduce the phenomenon of intermediaries called by the Lord to fulfill a particular commission. They held before the people the values of faithfulness and obedience to the one God. They interacted in particular ways with the kings, calling them to faithful service as the Lord's appointed rulers of the people. The books of Kings include stories of other prophets as well: for example, Ahijah in 1 Kings 11:29-39; 14:1-18; Shemaiah in 1 Kings 12:21-24; two unnamed prophets in 1 Kings 13:1-32; Jehu in 1 Kings 16:1-4; and Elisha in 2 Kings 2:1–9:13. Now we turn to Moses, whom the book of Deuteronomy identifies as the first prophet, who serves as a model for all the others.

- What miraculous elements do you find in the Elisha stories in 2 Kings 2:1–9:13? How do these details enhance Elisha's reputation as a man of God?

Moses the First Prophet and Model

Within the Bible, Moses appears first among the prophets we are studying. But we save him for last in this introduction to the early prophets because the biblical identification of him as a prophet comes from a time at least as late as the Micaiah ben Imlah stories, when the Deuteronomistic History was beginning to take shape. The accounts of the Exodus and wandering in the wilderness do not identify him as a prophet, but Exodus 3 includes the elements of a prophetic call in the account of God's commissioning of Moses. This and other details provide the point of reference from which Deuteronomy identifies him as the model prophet, as we will see below.

- What elements of a prophetic call narrative do you find in Exodus 3? What characteristics of a prophet does this call highlight?

Deuteronomy 18:15-22 asserts that the Lord will appoint a prophet like Moses from among the people. The declaration is given twice, once from the mouth of Moses and once from God (18:15, 18). The first assertion explains that the appointment of a prophet is a response to the people's request for someone who would contact God directly, on behalf of the people who feared the divine presence. This request was recorded in Exod 20:18-20:

> When all the people witnessed the thunder and lightning, the sound of the trumpet, and the mountain smoking, they were afraid and trembled and stood at a distance, and said to Moses, "You speak to us, and we will listen; but do not let God speak to us, or we will die." Moses said to the people, "Do not be afraid; for God has come only to test you and to put the fear of him upon you so that you do not sin."

The second assertion in the Deuteronomy passage specifies what the prophet will be called to do: speak the word given by God.

Three ideas from the passage are important because they permeate the Prophets and also the whole Old Testament. First, Exod 20:18-20 describes the people's fearful response to the theophany that surrounds the giving of the Ten Commandments on Mount Sinai. Their reaction involves not only fright but also profound awe that God would speak directly to them. Such intimate communication with the Deity is too much for the people to bear; they request that Moses act as intermediary to receive and then speak the Lord's word to them. This combination of fright and awe is the meaning of the expression "fear of the Lord," and Deuteronomy identifies it as the cause of the divine commissioning of prophets. Thus for the Deuteronomist the institution of prophecy was a response to the people's request based on their fear of the Lord.

The second idea is the necessity for a divine voice among the people. The people remember Moses as the one who led their ancestors in the wilderness as God's representative. But for the Deuteronomist, contact with the Deity had become less direct and therefore less certain after the establishment of the monarchy. A human king surrounded by the trappings of office did not clearly signify God's presence among the people; furthermore, the people had no assurance that the king was acting as divine representative. The prophets made up for this lack by serving as intermediaries between God and king, or as the conscience of king and people in the face of injustice and oppression. (See, for example, Hos 12:13 and Sir 46:1.)

Mount Sinai

The third theme is that the prophets were chosen by God to serve in a specific situation or time. They did not inherit their position as did the dynastic leaders (see Amos 7:14-15). In fact, the lack of biographical information about most of the prophets makes it impossible to identify their family ties. Instead, they were chosen to serve as the need arose; hence their designation as charismatic leaders.

When the Deuteronomist quotes from Exodus 20 it is not an exact quotation but rather a quotation from the people's memory. What they remember is not the precise words but rather the profound sense of awe and unworthiness they experienced in the presence of God. This wonder accounts for their request for an intermediary to bridge the gap between God and the people. God validates the people's request by agreeing to send them a prophet, and to tell the prophet what to say: "I will put my words in the mouth of the prophet, who shall speak to them everything that I command" (Deut 15:18). Thus we see the role of the prophet defined in Deuteronomy in relation to Moses. This connection with Moses links prophets to the people's memory of divine guidance in the wilderness, during the period of their formation as a people.

The stories of the other early prophets also appear in the Deuteronomistic History, which includes its theological message within the narrative. Specifically, it highlights leaders chosen by God to care for the people as well as rewards that follow keeping the covenant and punishments that result from its violation.

For Further Reading

Blenkinsopp, Joseph. *A History of Prophecy in Israel.* Philadelphia: Westminster, 1983.

Bright, John. *A History of Israel.* 3rd ed. Philadelphia: Westminster, 1981.

Gray, John. *I & II Kings: A Commentary.* OTL. 2nd ed. Philadelphia: Westminster, 1970.

Jones, G. H. *1 and 2 Kings.* 2 vols. NCBC. Grand Rapids: Eerdmans, 1984.

Chapter Three

The Eighth-Century Prophets
in the Northern Kingdom

In the second half of the eighth century there appeared on the scene four prophets whose words were eventually recorded by their followers. The prophets in the eighth century and later did not completely differ from their predecessors but, in a departure from the prophetic legends of earlier times, the written record preserves their preaching to a much greater degree than it recounts their activities. Only two books record the words of prophets who worked in the northern kingdom. These two men, Amos and Hosea, both lived during the latter part of the eighth century. We turn now to these two, and in the next chapter we will look at the two southern prophets from the same period: Isaiah of Jerusalem, whose preaching is recorded in chapters 1–39 of the book of Isaiah, and Micah. This period marked the beginning of what is often called Classical Prophecy.

Background Information

Historical and Geographical Setting

The events from the beginning of the Assyrian expansion in 745 to the destruction of Jerusalem by the Babylonians in 587 followed one another quickly and formed a continuous pattern of political and military conquest. For this reason we look now at the sweep of history throughout that 150-year period to understand the context in which the eighth-, seventh-, and sixth-century prophets preached.

The second half of the eighth century was dominated by the expansion of the Assyrian empire, beginning with Tiglath-Pileser III in 745 and bringing to an end one hundred years of relative stability throughout the region. Tiglath-Pileser gradually took over the area, creating the first of the empires whose rise and fall would determine the life of the Fertile Crescent and surrounding areas throughout the ensuing millennia. The Assyrian Empire controlled the area for approximately 120 years, from Tiglath-Pileser's accession until the death of Ashurbanipal in 627, after which the Assyrian empire declined and the Babylonian empire began its ascent.

Tiglath-Pileser took over the surrounding nations systematically and relentlessly. He conquered Damascus, whose king was Rezin and whose ally was Israel under King Menachem (2 Kings 15:19-20). Four years later he conquered Gaza. A closer look at the different kingdoms and their relationships with Assyria will illustrate the Assyrian effect on Israel and Judah.

Under Jeroboam II of Israel (786–746) the northern kingdom reached the zenith of its political and economic power and stability. But Jeroboam's son and successor Zechariah, who came to the throne at the same time as Tiglath-Pileser, was assassinated after a brief reign of six months, ending the period of prosperity for the northern kingdom and marking the beginning of its rapid downfall. Over the next twenty-two years five kings ruled from Samaria; three of them were assassinated. One of the five was Shallum, whose coup in 745 probably led to Hosea's denunciations of the monarchy (see Hos 7:7) and Amos' predictions that the Jehu dynasty would suffer a violent end. (See Amos' visions in chs. 7, 8, and 9.)

Tiglath-Pileser was succeeded by Shalmaneser V. During his reign King Hoshea of Israel tried to unite with Egypt against Assyria, with the disastrous result of the siege and destruction of Samaria in 722. The fifth king was deported by the Assyrians when they defeated the city of Samaria, marking the Assyrian conquest of the northern kingdom (2 Kings 17:1-6). Hosea 13:9-11 very likely comes from the years just before 722 and refers to the deposing of Hosea and the end of the northern kingdom. Other prophetic passages that probably relate to this period are Isa 9:8-21; 28:1-4; Hos 6:11–7:7; 8:4.

The kingdom of Judah pursued its own interests in relative stability during the reigns of Uzziah (783–742) and his successor Jotham (742–735). But things changed dramatically during the reign of Jotham's son Ahaz (735–715). Syria and Israel (now under King Pekah) tried to convince Ahaz to join them in a new alliance, known as the Syro-Ephraimite Alliance, against Assyria. When they failed to convince Ahaz to join them they invaded Judah, at which time Ahaz turned to Assyria for protection

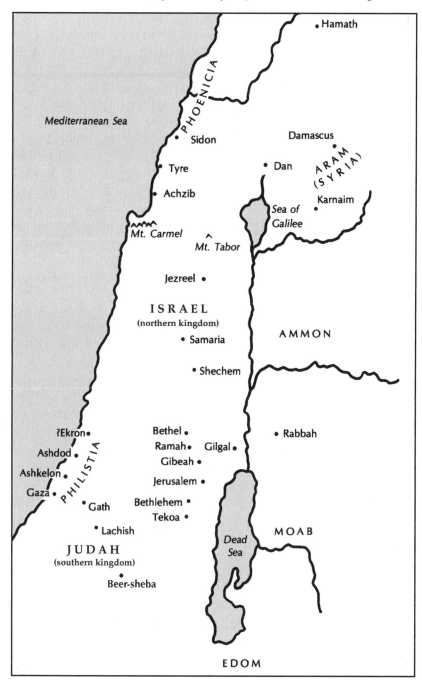

The Kingdoms of Israel and Judah in the Eighth Century

against the Alliance. Isaiah of Jerusalem tried to dissuade Ahaz from this move, but he did not succeed. As a result Judah became a vassal of Assyria, a situation that was never completely reversed. (See 2 Kings 16:5-10; Isa 7:1–8:15; 17:1-6; Hos 5:8–9:9.)

Shortly after the conquest of Samaria, Shalmaneser died and was succeeded by Sargon II (722–705). (Sargon's annals can be found in *ANET*, 3rd ed., 287.) During his reign the Assyrian expansion continued with the conquest of Gaza and, a few years later, of Ashdod. According to Assyrian records King Hezekiah of Judah (715–689) participated in Ashdod's efforts to withstand the Assyrian onslaught. He also welcomed Babylonian envoys into the palace when they visited him during his illness (2 Kings 20:12-19). The prophet Isaiah chastised the king for allowing his Babylonian visitors to see the palace treasures, warning the king that Babylon would eventually use that knowledge against Judah. But while Hezekiah acted imprudently toward his Babylonian guests, he took precautionary defensive measures as well. He fortified the capital city, Jerusalem, strengthening the city wall, part of which is still visible in the Jewish Quarter. In an amazing feat of engineering he brought the water supply into the city by having a tunnel carved through the rock from the Gihon Spring to the Pool of Siloam (2 Kings 20:20; 2 Chr 32:30). These measures assured Jerusalemites that they would have access to water in the eventuality of an Assyrian siege or attack, which occurred under Sargon's successor.

During the reign of the Assyrian emperor Sennacherib (705–681) the Assyrian army reached Jerusalem. The city was saved from destruction, but the burden of its tribute was increased. The biblical account gives two descriptions of the event: 2 Kings 18:13-16 coincides with Assyrian records that assert that Jerusalem was "shut up like a bird in a cage," while 19:35-37, immortalized in Lord Byron's poem, "The Destruction of Sennacherib," recounts the miraculous destruction of the Assyrians and the salvation of the inhabitants of Jerusalem.

Assyria's domination of the Fertile Crescent stemmed in large part from its military strength and strategies. It supported a standing army, troops who trained together full time and thus worked well as units without the need to go home for seasonal agricultural duties. Assyria's military strategies included siege warfare and atrocities committed against civilians, large numbers of whom were deported. Administratively, the emperor set up provinces throughout the conquered territories and appointed Assyrian rulers in each. Neighboring states dependent on Assyrian protection signed treaties and became vassal states. These tactics contributed to the conquest of Israel, as a result of which thousands of people were deported and foreign groups were gradually moved into the territory to take their place. The area became an Assyrian province (Isa 7:8b), and the ten tribes that had inhabited the Northern Kingdom dissolved.

In the years that followed, Assyria's expansionist activities continued, but at a slower pace. Twenty years after the siege of Jerusalem, Sennacherib was killed in a palace uprising (2 Kings 19:37). His successor Esarhaddon (680–669) conquered Egypt in 671. He was succeeded by Ashurbanipal (668–627), whose reign was marked by internal restlessness and external pressures, including Egypt's regaining its independence from Assyria. At Ashurbanipal's death the Assyrian empire fell into rapid decline, while Babylon began its ascendancy under Nabopolassar, who became king in 625. His relentless expansion led to the conquest of the Assyrian capital of Ashur in 614, Nineveh in 612, and Egypt in 605, solidifying Babylonian domination of the Fertile Crescent.

In Judah, Hezekiah was succeeded by Manasseh (687–642), Amon (642–640), and Josiah (640–609). After Josiah died his son Jehoahaz reigned for three months, during which time Judah became a vassal of Egypt. Pharaoh Neco then replaced Jehoahaz with his brother Jehoiakim, who reigned eleven years (609–598), continuing to pay tribute to the Egyptian ruler. His tenure saw the initial conquest of Jerusalem by the Babylonians. His son Jehoiachin followed him and reigned for only three months; Nebuchadnezzar of Babylon laid siege to Jerusalem and eventually broke through its walls, took the valuables from the Temple, forced the city's influential people into exile in Babylon, and appointed Jehoiachin's uncle, Zedekiah, king (597–587). Zedekiah eventually rebelled against Babylon, causing the new empire to besiege the city a second time, this time for eighteen months, until Jerusalem was destroyed.

The Socio-economic Situation

During the eighth century the socio-economic effects of urbanization and surplus farming had become acute, first in the northern kingdom, then eventually in Judah as well (Bright, *History of Israel*, 272–73). We recall that in Samuel and Nathan's time, at the beginning of the monarchy, urbanization brought about a change in family life and also in government because of the shift in the economic structure. In earlier times people had possessed relatively equal amounts of goods, and they lived at a subsistence level. But once farmers began to grow surplus crops, the more industrious and the more fortunate produced larger yields while others produced less. The result was that those who had larger crops, which they bartered for other goods, became wealthier and more powerful while those who had smaller yields had access to fewer other goods, and they became less wealthy and powerful than those who had more. That inequality, and the oppression it implied and fostered, was a constantly recurring theme among the eighth-century prophets, who condemned it as a grave societal evil.

Religious Issues

Throughout the Assyrian period both Israel and Judah felt the religious effects of Assyria's imperial expansion. The empire does not seem to have dealt with the local cults in its conquered territories in any consistent way. But worship and financial support of the principal Assyrian deity Ashur, "lord of all lands," and other Assyrian deities was sometimes imposed on conquered peoples.

In Samaria, when Assyria defeated the city, the people who were brought there from other conquered lands did not worship YHWH. The emperor, in an effort to placate the god of the land, ordered that a priest be brought back from exile to teach the people how to worship YHWH. But the settlers also continued to worship their own deities, and syncretistic religious practices became typical (see 2 Kings 17:24-41). After all, from the perspective of the defeated peoples it seemed that Ashur had prevailed over YHWH and the gods of the other conquered nations. In particular some feared that they had caused the disaster by their abandonment of their own vegetation gods (see Jer 44:15-19).

According to the Deuteronomistic historian, the religious lessons Judah could learn from Samaria were taken seriously by some of the kings and ignored by others. Jotham (742–735) tolerated worship in places other than the Temple (see 2 Kings 15:35). Ahaz paid tribute to Assyria, against Isaiah's counsel, in an effort to protect Judah from invasion by Israel and Syria. What is more, he had a copy of the Damascus altar built and placed in the Jerusalem Temple to replace the altar to YHWH, and he removed other furnishings at the insistence of Tiglath-Pileser (see 2 Kings 16:1-18). Hezekiah (715–689), on the other hand, took measures to purify the cult in the Temple and throughout Judah (2 Kings 18:4).

Following Hezekiah's death Manasseh reigned in Judah from 689 to 642. He in turn undid the reforms his father had initiated, setting up statues of Baal and Asherah and violating the prohibitions against consulting mediums and wizards. Because of his infidelity he was blamed for the destruction of Jerusalem, the first wave of which occurred less than fifty years after his death at the hands of the Babylonians. Manasseh's son Amon ruled for only two years (642–640; see 2 Kings 21:19-26), after which his son Josiah reigned until 609. Like Hezekiah, Josiah initiated reforms including repairing and purifying the Temple, removing altars from the high places throughout Judea and even Samaria, and commanding the celebration of Passover (see 2 Kings 22:1–23:30).

One additional point to note when we consider the religious issues of the later eighth century is that the people looked upon the good things of life, including health, a large family, a long life, and the wealth brought by surplus crops, as divine rewards for their faithfulness. Conversely, lack of those goods was understood as punishment for unfaithfulness. We will see this perspective expressed throughout the prophetic books. We in the twenty-first century take a more complex view of the reasons for suffering. We realize that much suffering exists for which we cannot offer a satisfactory explanation. But we recognize the zealous efforts of the prophets to convince the people of the importance of faithfulness to God, a value that is as essential today as it was in the eighth century B.C.E.

AMOS
"But let justice roll down like waters,
and righteousness like an everflowing stream." (Amos 5:24)

Background Information

We have considered this book's eighth-century historical, geographical, socio-economic, and religious settings above, in the historical section. The specific setting of the book of Amos is identified in its superscription and in Amos 7:14-15. The prophet Amos was from Tekoa, in the kingdom of Judah. He was working as a shepherd and dresser of sycamore trees when he was called by God to preach in Israel during the reigns of Jeroboam II in Israel (786–746) and Uzziah in Judah (783–742). A more precise indication of the date is the note that he preached two years before the earthquake (1:1), but the date of that event is not known. It is likely that he spoke at the shrine in Bethel (see, e.g., 4:4 and 7:13). The words recorded in the book were probably spoken over a short span of time, perhaps only a year. The outline below suggests that the words were collected and arranged according to genre. The redaction process might well have continued for several centuries following Amos' death.

Organization of the Book

Outline

The book is organized primarily according to the principal genres Amos used in delivering his message to the people.

1:1-2	Superscription and introduction
1:3–2:16	Announcements of judgment
3:1–6:14	Specific condemnations
7:1–9:10	Vision reports
9:11-15	Conclusion

Genres

The outline lists several genres Amos used in expressing his message to the people. He actually spoke in a large number of genres, of which we will look at ten. We will examine them in detail because Amos' words are clear examples of the forms, and also because they demonstrate how each form expresses the prophet's message. Amos' use of this wide variety of genres illustrates his knowledge of the rhetorical conventions of his day as well as his ability to appeal to the people from different perspectives: coaxing, condemning, grieving, encouraging, assuring. The elements of each genre are discussed in Chapter One and can serve as a reference for the examples below.

MESSENGER SPEECH. Amos 1:3–2:16 contains eight messenger speeches delivered to different nations. All eight begin with the phrase, "Thus says the LORD," and several end with the phrase "says the LORD." These formulaic expressions highlight the divine origin of the message, reminding the reader that Amos is not speaking his own words, but rather the words the Lord sent him to deliver.

(AUTO)BIOGRAPHICAL REPORT, OR ACCOUNT OF PROPHETIC ACTIVITIES OR FATE. Chapter 7:10-15, Amos' description of his call, is an autobiographical report. After Amaziah the priest tried to send Amos away for stirring up the people and condemning the injustices of the day, he replied, "I am no prophet, nor a prophet's son; but I am a herdsman, and a dresser of sycamore trees, and the LORD took me from following the flock, and the LORD said to me, 'Go, prophesy to my people Israel'" (7:14-15). Sycamores are trees that require their buds to be pinched off at a precise point in their growth process to enable their fruit to grow. It was highly specialized work, and the yield of the trees depended on its being accomplished skillfully. Amos' talent was thus of great value in his home town, but God called him from this work and sent him to preach to the people of the Northern Kingdom. When Amaziah tried to send him away Amos said, in effect, "I can't stop preaching because I am not talking on my own authority; I say the words God gave me to say, and they must be said."

This is all the biographical information about Amos that we are given. It is enough, though, to illustrate the kind of response Amos' message received from the priest at Bethel in Israel. He objected to it, fearing it would undermine those in authority, and accused Amos of conspiracy against the king—in fact, of saying words the book does not record. Perhaps they were spoken but not written down, or perhaps they were not spoken but illustrate the interpretation Amaziah placed on Amos' message. They also speak to Amos' determination and perseverance in speaking the word of the Lord in spite of opposition.

VISION REPORT. Amos 7:1-3, 4-6, 7-9; 8:1-3; 9:1-4 relate five visions that involve everyday things and events. For example, 7:1-3 gives Amos' report of his vision of a plague of locusts. The swarm came at the end of the growing season, after the king had taken the first cutting, which was used to feed the army, and just before the beginning of the dry season when crops could not grow. What is more, a plague of locusts recalls the eighth plague in Egypt before the people escaped. Like Moses in Egypt, Amos pleads to God on behalf of the people—"Lord, forgive!"—using the verb *slḥ*, which describes only divine actions (see also, e.g., Exod 34:9 and Num 14:18-20). The meaning of the vision is evident in Amos' request: the plague represents punishment for the people's sins. Amos offers God a reason to forgive the people: "How can Jacob stand? He is so small!" (7:2). Amos does not pretend that the people are deserving of forgiveness; instead he appeals to divine compassion for the people in their vulnerability, even though they have not shown compassion for the poor and needy among them. Smallness in size or number can be understood as a metaphor for small-mindedness and smallness of virtue as well. The divine response is to desist from the announced punishment. The word "repent" gives an anthropomorphic description of the divine decision not to carry out the threatened punishment in response to Amos' plea.

• In 7:4-6, how does the vision symbolize destruction?

ANNOUNCEMENT OF JUDGMENT. Amos includes several of these, for example the series of indictments of Israel's neighbors, and finally of Israel itself, in 1:3-5, 6-8, 9-10, 11-12, 13-15; 2:1-3, 4-5, 6-16. The indictments are arranged geographically in a spiral that tightens with the name of each area until it reaches its intended audience, Israel. Each indictment is introduced by the messenger formula. The three elements that comprise the announcement of judgment can be illustrated by 1:3-5: the introductory call to attention in v. 3a begins with the messenger formula, followed by the formula that introduces each announcement of judgment in chapters 1 and 2: "For three transgressions of Damascus, and for four, I will not revoke the punishment." The description of the sinful situation follows in v. 3b, "because they have threshed Gilead with threshing sledges of iron." The harvest imagery is tinged with violence: not crops but a people has been threshed, that is, tossed up in the air, allowing the wind to carry it off. Furthermore, the implement is made of iron, a metaphor of strength and harshness. The metaphor expresses not only harvest but also control and conquest by division.

The announcement of judgment follows in vv. 4-5: "So I will send a fire on the house of Hazael, and it shall devour the strongholds of Ben-hadad. I will break the gate bars of Damascus, and cut off the inhabitants from the Valley of Aven, and the one who holds the scepter from Beth-eden; and the people of Aram shall go into exile to Kir, says the LORD." The violent oppression the inhabitants of Damascus have inflicted on others will be visited on them. Just as Gilead, the Israelite land immediately south of Aram, was tossed into the air to land where the wind carried it, likewise the inhabitants of Aram will be taken into exile to Kir in Mesopotamia.

The announcement of judgment against Israel (the Northern Kingdom) in 2:6-16 is a more complex example of the form. Verse 6a repeats the messenger formula that introduced the previous seven announcements, bringing to a climax the catalogue of condemned nations by speaking directly to and about his audience in Israel with the formula that introduces each of the eight announcements: "For three transgressions of Israel, and for four, I will not revoke the punishment." (We will look at this rhetorical feature, known as the graded numerical saying, in the next section, "Rhetorical Features.")

Then vv. 6b-8 describe Israel's sin:

> They sell the righteous for silver, and the needy for a pair of sandals
> —they who trample the head of the poor into the dust of the earth,
> and push the afflicted out of the way; father and son go in to the same
> girl, so that my holy name is profaned; they lay themselves down
> beside every altar on garments taken in pledge; and in the house of
> their God they drink wine bought with fines they imposed.

The list of Israel's sins is much longer than the preceding seven lists, but it does have a characteristic in common with the one preceding, against Judah. That is, these two condemn sins against the covenant. The earlier announcements listed war crimes committed by one nation against another. But here the sins are committed by members of the community against one another. The more powerful are accused of exploiting the vulnerable, specifically debtors, the powerless, and young women.

Several items involve customs and laws that need explanation. "Sell the righteous for silver and the needy for a pair of sandals" (v. 6) refers to selling people into servitude for minor offenses, a violation of the law permitting debt servitude as a means of paying off heavy debts (see Lev 25:39-46; 2 Kings 4:1-7). "Father and son go in to the same girl" (v. 7) refers to sexual violation of a young woman by an older man. It is sinful in two ways: first, a father is most likely a married man and thus commits adultery; in addition he interferes with the girls' eligibility for marriage. The son is required to marry her as a result of the affair, but the father complicates the situation by compromising her eligibility (see Lev 18:15; 20:12). "Lay themselves down . . . on garments taken in pledge" (v. 8) violates the command not to take as collateral something that is necessary to life. Sleeping beside the altar violates the shrine, which belonged to God as did the poor whose garments had been taken and not returned by nightfall (see Exod 22:26-27; Deut 24:12-13, 17). It is difficult for us who have large wardrobes to imagine having only one garment. This was the case, though, for those to whom Amos spoke; their outer garment served as a coat during the day and as a blanket at night. The reference to the altar also serves as a reminder that the sins of oppression listed here offend not only other people but also God, whose care for all the people is compromised by the people's injustice.

The list of sins is interrupted at this point (vv. 9-11) by a recital of ways God has acted on behalf of the people, giving them land after leading them out of Egypt and through the wilderness, making possible the defeat of the much larger, stronger nation of the Amorites and giving the people leaders to guide them. Then v. 12 returns to the list of Israel's sins with the accusation that they refused to accept their divinely appointed leaders, and did not allow them to serve (v. 12), thus compounding their own sin.

Verses 13-16 are the final element; they announce the coming judgment. God will press down the people, or in the words of the NAB, will crush them. The implications of the punishment follow in vv. 14-16: those who have power of any kind, whether physical strength or prowess, intellectual influence or courage, will lose it. The punishment is thus in keeping with the people's sin: just as they have oppressed the weak, God will crush the influential among them. The punishment is described in terms of battle, recalling the war crimes of which the other nations are accused in 1:3–2:5. Furthermore, the punishment will overturn the people's expectation of the "Day of the Lord," to which they looked forward as a time of joy and triumph. Here the announcement is of "that day" as a time of punishment (see also 5:18-20).

The effective power of the word would set in motion the punishment it named. The people who exploited the weak members of the community would suffer the same fate they had inflicted on the vulnerable.

- Note the elements of the announcement of judgment in 1:6-8, 9-10, 11-12, 13-15; 2:1-3, 4-5. In what ways is the announcement of judgment against Israel more harsh than the indictments against Israel's neighbors? How do you explain this harshness?

WOE ORACLE. This form appears in Amos 5:18-20; 6:1-3, 4-7. We will take a close look at 6:4-7. It begins with "Woe!" or "Alas!" as the first of the three elements (6:4a). The description of the sinners follows in 6:4b-6:

> Alas for those who lie on beds of ivory, and lounge on their couches, and eat lambs from the flock, and calves from the stall; who sing idle songs to the sound of the harp, and like David improvise on instruments of music; who drink wine from bowls, and anoint themselves with the finest oils, but are not grieved over the ruin of Joseph!

These verses describe those who enjoy life's luxuries of food and drink, music and physical comfort, but do not concern themselves with the plight of others. The third element, the result, is stated in v. 7: "Therefore they shall now be the first to go into exile, and the revelry of the loungers shall pass away." The verdict specifies that the tables will be turned on those who enjoy their leisure without regard for other people: they will be sent into exile. It is important to note here that the condemnation is not handed out simply to those who have the means to enjoy life. Rather it is given to those who enjoy life in complete disregard for those who do not have the same niceties.

ADMONITION. Amos 5:4-5, 6-7, 14-15 are examples of Amos' efforts to convince the people to do good and avoid evil. Specifically, 5:4-5 asserts, "For thus says the LORD to the house of Israel: Seek me and live; but do not seek Bethel, and do not enter into Gilgal or cross over to Beer-sheba; for Gilgal shall surely go into exile, and Bethel shall come to nothing." Here Amos instructs the people to seek God and not to visit the shrines in either the Northern Kingdom (Bethel and Gilgal) or the Southern (Beer-sheba). The admonition might refer to empty rituals taking place at those shrines (see 5:21-24), or it might refer to places that, even though holy, are still not substitutes for God. In the final analysis only God is the source of life.

Amos 5:14-15 instructs, "Seek good and not evil, that you may live; and so the LORD, the God of hosts, will be with you, just as you have said. Hate evil and love good, and establish justice in the gate; it may be that the LORD, the God of hosts, will be gracious to the remnant of Joseph." The straightforward lesson is given twice: "Seek good and not evil" and "Hate evil and love good." A specific way to love good is added to the second command, "establish justice in the gate." The instruction refers to the custom of assembling at the city gate for legal trials at which the plaintiff, defendant, and witnesses presented their cases to the elder who served as judge. In fact, the motif repeats the admonition of vv. 6-7.

These two admonitions summarize Amos' instructions throughout the book: seek God and seek good. These are not new commands, but rather summary statements of how to live in relationship to their God, YHWH. In fact, all of chapter 5 is pivotal: it summarizes in capsule form the lessons in Amos' teaching.

- Whom does Amos admonish in 5:6-7? What does he advise them to do?

HYMN. The hymns in Amos celebrate God's actions in the world. We find them in Amos 4:13; 5:8-9; 9:5-6. For example, 4:13 acclaims: "For lo, the one who forms the mountains, creates the wind, reveals his thoughts to mortals, makes the morning darkness, and treads on the heights of the earth—the LORD, the God of hosts, is his name!" Here Amos praises God the Creator, specifically naming three creatures: mountains, wind, and morning darkness. He goes on to praise God's interaction with creation, both human and natural: sharing divine thoughts with people and walking upon the earth. The position of this hymn at the end of chapter 4 reinforces the message of vv. 6-12: the people have still not returned to God. Amos repeats that refrain five times: "Yet you did not return to me, says the Lord" (vv. 6, 8, 9, 10, 11). Then the hymn in v. 13 celebrates God who not only causes all the calamities listed in vv. 6-12 but, even before that, created the entire universe.

• What divine actions do 5:8-9 and 9:5-6 celebrate?

DIRGE. Amos 5:2 is a dirge, or word of mourning. While it is easily recognized in Hebrew by its rhythm of a three-accent line followed by a two-accent line, that rhythm is not evident in English: "Fallen, no more to rise, is maiden Israel; forsaken on her land, with no one to raise her up." A rhythmic translation is: "She fell, no more to rise, maiden Israel; forsaken on her land, none saves." Both the words and the 3-2 rhythm connote grief over the destroyed and abandoned Israel.

PROVERB. Amos 3:3-6 includes six proverbs, concise sayings based on observation of natural phenomena. Here all six are rhetorical questions to which the response is "no." The series leads up to the crucial point in vv. 6b-8: the people's sins have prompted the Lord's response. It is all the more fearsome in light of the intimate bond between the Lord and the people expressed in vv. 1-2 in an effort to persuade them to act in ways befitting people who have been chosen.

ANNOUNCEMENT OF SALVATION. Amos 9:11-12 is an announcement of salvation. It reads,

> On that day I will raise up the booth of David that is fallen, and repair its breaches, and raise up its ruins, and rebuild it as in the days of old; in order that they may possess the remnant of Edom and all the nations who are called by my name, says the LORD who does this.

The saying implies that the people have cried to God in their distress at the destruction they have suffered through the fall of the royal house. This event actually occurred when the Babylonian army took the city of

Jerusalem in the sixth century. The placing of these words at the end of Amos shows the eagerness of later scribes to relate Amos' words to their own specific situation, perhaps 150 years later than Amos' message was first delivered to the people. In terms of the elements of the form, the actual announcement of salvation is explicit in the same words that allude to a previous lament. God promised to raise up, repair, and rebuild the city. The divine purpose in these actions is to restore the lands of David's kingdom. The placement of this announcement of salvation close to the end of the book of Amos enables the entire book to look with hope toward the future. The announcement assures the people that, while punishment must follow their misdeeds, it will come to an end, and will be followed by a time of restoration. Throughout all these seasons God is with the people, putting into effect the divine purpose.

ASSURANCE OF SALVATION. This assurance is found in Amos 9:13-15, the final passage of the book. It alludes to Israel's past in its promise to rebuild their cities. Divine actions will assure the return of agricultural prosperity as well as urban renewal. To assure the people of God's presence and active concern for them, the passage makes clear that the promised new life will come from God.

• How does this final assurance of salvation affect the meaning of the entire book of Amos?

These examples illustrate Amos' rich and wide use of ancient Near Eastern genres to express the divine message he had received. In addition, he spoke with a rhetorical flair that contributes to the eloquence and urgency of his message. We will look at several of his specific rhetorical devices.

Rhetorical Features

INTENSE LANGUAGE. Amos uses intense language, for example: "The LORD roars from Zion, and utters his voice from Jerusalem; the pastures of the shepherds wither, and the top of Carmel dries up" (1:2); "They have ripped open pregnant women in Gilead in order to enlarge their territory. So I will kindle a fire against the wall of Rabbah, fire that shall devour its strongholds" (1:13-14); "As the shepherd rescues from the mouth of the lion two legs, or a piece of an ear, so shall the people of Israel who live in Samaria be rescued, with the corner of a couch and part of a bed" (3:12); "As if someone fled from a lion, and was met by a bear; or went into the house and rested a hand against the wall, and was bitten by a snake" (5:19). The vividness and horror of the words grab our attention, just as they surely seized the minds and hearts of Amos' audience, shocking both listener and reader to soul-searching and repentance.

• Find another example of intense language in Amos. What emotion does the language add to the thought of the passage?

ANTITHESES. Amos spoke in antitheses or opposites, naming what was acceptable versus what was unacceptable, or what the people expected versus what was unexpected. For example, in 5:14-15 he counseled the people, "Seek good and not evil. . . . Hate evil and love good." By naming both of the opposite poles Amos underscored how different the extremes were from each other, and at the same time related the two extremes like flip sides of the same coin. And most of all, he underscored the vital importance of doing what is good. The admonition continues with reasons for doing good: "that you may live" and "that the LORD, the God of hosts, will be with you." The importance of doing good is to enhance life in relationship to God.

• What additional antitheses do you find in Amos?

SIMILES AND METAPHORS. These appear frequently in Amos. Examples of similes are: "he will break out against the house of Joseph like fire" (5:6); "but let justice roll down like waters" (5:24); "I will make it like the mourning for an only son, and the end of it like a bitter day" (8:10); "all of it rises like the Nile, and sinks again, like the Nile of Egypt" (9:5). Metaphors include "Hear this word, you cows of Bashan" (4:1); "Fallen, no more to rise, is maiden Israel" (5:2); "Is not the day of the LORD darkness, not light, and gloom with no brightness in it?" (5:20). These vivid comparisons create word pictures for both listener and reader, drawing on both human relationships and natural phenomena to concretize Amos' message.

• Identify a simile or metaphor in Amos, and explain how it enhances Amos' message.

QUOTATIONS. Several times Amos quotes his audience, for example in 6:13 and 9:10. The latter reads: "All the sinners of my people shall die by the sword, who say, 'Evil shall not overtake or meet us.'" This device shows that Amos knew his audience and makes them present to the reader. It underscores his message that the people brought about their condemnation by their own actions. In this case it was their complacent arrogance in assuming that nothing would happen to them that brought about their downfall.

• How does the quotation in 6:13 intensify Amos' message?

GRADED NUMERICAL SAYINGS. Amos uses these to introduce each of the eight announcements of judgment in 1:3–2:16. The formula, which names a number followed by that number plus one, is often found in wisdom literature. It calls attention to the final element in the list, the "plus one." Amos charged, "For three transgressions of . . . and for four, I will not revoke the punishment," implying that the sins of all the nations, especially Israel, could be included in an ever-increasing list.

• In the lists introduced by graded numerical sayings in 1:3, 6, 9, 11, 13; 2:1, 4, what sins does Amos condemn? Which ones will be punished by military means?

PUNS. Amos uses puns, which would catch the listeners' ear and cause them to look for meaningful connections between the similar-sounding words. Puns are evident in the Hebrew text and are often explained in the notes of translated versions. For example, 8:1-2, which reports Amos' vision of a basket of summer fruit, involves a play on words. "Summer fruit" is the translation of the Hebrew *qayiṣ*. That word is pronounced similarly to "end," or *qeṣ*. At first reading a basket of summer fruit is interpreted, "The end has come upon my people Israel." Summer fruit does not keep well; once it is ripe, it will soon be overripe and therefore at its end. This interpretation is reinforced by the similar sounds of the two words.

These rhetorical features illustrate Amos' rhetorical creativity and also convey his passion. He used his familiarity with the land and the wild animals that inhabited it as a device to persuade the people to turn away from their sins of empty worship and social injustice and to urge faithfulness to the terms of the covenant on which the people's life was based.

Amos' Message

The vivid rhetorical devices we have analyzed express a rich and profound message. It can be understood in two dimensions: God's intimate involvement with the people and the people's unfaithful response to God's care. Amos speaks for a God who is passionately involved with the people, who creates, chooses Israel, asks for justice and righteousness in return, condemns injustice, shows compassion, and extends divine concern to all nations by condemning their sins and using them as divine instruments. But the people do not respond in kind; they worship with empty gestures and engage in unjust, oppressive dealings with one another. The contrast between God's loving care and the people's response is the heart of Amos' message. We will look at several specific aspects of that message.

Themes

GOD CREATES BOTH THE NATURAL AND THE HUMAN WORLDS, as we saw in the discussion of the hymn form in 4:13. The hymn in 5:8-9, with its reference to earth, sky, and sea, gives the same message:

> The one who made the Pleiades and Orion, and turns deep darkness into the morning, and darkens the day into night, who calls for the waters of the sea, and pours them out on the surface of the earth, the Lord is his name, who makes destruction flash out against the strong, so that destruction comes upon the fortress.

God's creation is not limited to the beginning of the universe, but is ongoing and continuous.

GOD CHOOSES ISRAEL: Amos reminds the people of the Exodus and wandering in the wilderness, when God went with them and provided for their needs, creating them as the people of God. Amos asserts, "I brought you up out of the land of Egypt, and led you forty years in the wilderness, to possess the land of the Amorite" (2:10); "Hear this word that the LORD has spoken against you, O people of Israel, against the whole family that I brought up out of the land of Egypt: You only have I known of all the families of the earth; therefore I will punish you for all your iniquities" (3:1-2); and "Did I not bring Israel up from the land of Egypt?" (9:7). All these words address the unique relationship between God and the people, formed and deepened throughout the forty years of wandering in the wilderness. Throughout that time God cared for the people, providing food, drink, and a home for them. The importance God attaches to that bond is evident in God's sadness at the people's unfaithfulness, which is tragic in light of God's special care for them.

The final words of the book reiterate God's passionate involvement in the lives of the chosen people with a promise of restoration and protection. "I will restore the fortunes of my people Israel . . . I will plant them upon their land, and they shall never again be plucked up out of the land that I have given them, says the LORD your God" (9:14).

The people's lives, however, do not reflect the faithfulness God asked of them. Rather, they seem to be just the opposite. We find specific indictments in Amos' harsh critiques of their empty worship and their lack of care for one another. For instance, he cries:

> Come to Bethel—and transgress; to Gilgal—and multiply transgression; bring your sacrifices every morning, your tithes every three days; bring a thank offering of leavened bread, and proclaim freewill offerings, publish them; for so you love to do, O people of Israel! says the LORD God. (4:4-5)

Again he announces: "For thus says the LORD to the house of Israel: Seek me and live; but do not seek Bethel, and do not enter into Gilgal or cross over to Beer-sheba; for Gilgal shall surely go into exile, and Bethel shall come to nothing" (5:4-5). In another instance he proclaims:

> I hate, I despise your festivals, and I take no delight in your solemn assemblies. Even though you offer me your burnt offerings and grain offerings, I will not accept them; and the offerings of well-being of your fatted animals I will not look upon. Take away from me the noise of your songs; I will not listen to the melody of your harps. But let justice roll down like waters, and righteousness like an ever-flowing stream. (5:21-24)

The sin is not in the act of worship itself, but in its emptiness; their worship does not affect their everyday life.

Amos bitterly condemns the people's lack of care for one another. He decries their failure to live in justice and righteousness in his words: "Ah, you that turn justice into wormwood, and bring righteousness to the ground!" (5:7). He refers explicitly to their lack of these virtues, particularly in their dealings with the vulnerable, who have been identified for special consideration since the foundation of the people. See, for example, Exod 22:21-22; 23:9, where instructions are given to care specially for widows, orphans, and resident aliens.

Amos' first words of judgment against the people of Israel specify the sins the wealthy and powerful are perpetrating against the poor and against those who lack power: ". . . they sell the righteous for silver, and the needy for a pair of sandals—they who trample the head of the poor into the dust of the earth, and push the afflicted out of the way . . . [the verse continues with the passage about father and son having intercourse with the same young girl and defiling altars with garments taken in pledge; see the analysis above under "Announcement of Judgment"] "and in the house of their God they drink wine bought with fines they imposed" (2:6-8).

He names specific sins of injustice such as bribery (5:12), cultic excesses and hypocrisy (4:4-5). He issues a particularly strong condemnation of the excesses in the lifestyle of the wealthy (3:15; 4:1; 5:11; 6:4-6, 8, 11), whom he condemns not for their wealth *per se,* but rather for their complacent inattention to the needy (6:6). These sins result from the socio-economic gap between rich and poor that emerged as a result of economic prosperity and came to a head in the eighth century.

The bottom line for Amos is that the people do not know how to do right (3:9-10); that is, their sins have destroyed their ability to make just decisions and do compassionate deeds. This tragic result of their sins is all the more poignant in light of the divine words, "You only have I known of all the families of the earth" (3:2). The people's sins violate the special relationship that has been established between God and the people.

GOD PUNISHES UNFAITHFULNESS: The people's unfaithfulness to God, shown in their lack of knowledge, empty worship, and oppressive treatment of the vulnerable, evokes God's punishing destruction. We see this in the initial condemnation of Israel, after the judgments against the neighboring peoples:

> So I will press you down in your place, just as a cart presses down when it is full of sheaves. Flight shall perish from the swift, and the strong shall not retain their strength, nor shall the mighty save their lives; those who handle the bow shall not stand, and those who are swift of foot shall not save themselves, nor shall those who ride horses save their lives; and those who are stout of heart among the mighty shall flee away naked in that day, says the LORD. (2:13-16)

Specific calamities will be an earthquake (1:1; 9:1), war (3:11; 6:14), defeat (5:3), captivity (7:17), destruction (8:2). In another instance we find: "Therefore thus says the LORD God: An adversary shall surround the land, and strip you of your defense; and your strongholds shall be plundered" (3:11), and again "The eyes of the LORD God are upon the sinful kingdom, and I will destroy it from the face of the earth—except that I will not utterly destroy the house of Jacob, says the LORD" (9:8). These judgments followed repeated efforts to convince the people to turn away from their sinfulness and toward God. But the future holds hope as well, as we see in 9:11-15.

GOD SHOWS COMPASSION: The Israelites' specially beloved status is evident not only in divine condemnation of their sons, but also in God's eagerness for them to change their ways and God's readiness to forgive and restore them. Amos issues the divine invitation: "Seek me and live!" (5:4). He reminds the people: "You only have I known of all the families of the earth" (3:2). We see that compassion in God's sadness at the people's unfaithfulness: "I brought you up out of the land of Egypt, and led you forty years in the wilderness, to possess the land of the Amorite. And I raised up some of your children to be prophets and some of your youths to be nazirites. Is it not indeed so, O people of Israel? says the LORD" (2:9-11).

In another instance Amos points to God's turning back from the punishment intended for the people. We see this in the visions in 7:1-3, 4-6. In both instances Amos pleads, "O LORD God, forgive, I beg you! How can Jacob stand? He is so small!" It was not because of Israel's righteousness that Amos asked God for mercy, but because the people were unable to desist on their own strength. Amos goes on to report, "The LORD relented concerning this; this shall not be." Even though the people did not themselves protect the fragile ones in their own midst, Amos pleaded with God to desist because the people were "so small." His pleas caused God to relent.

Finally we note in 9:8 that, although severe punishment is coming, it will not consist in complete destruction: "I will destroy [the sinful kingdom] from the face of the earth—except that I will not utterly destroy the house of Jacob."

GOD'S ACTIONS AFFECT THE NATIONS: God intervenes not only among the people of Israel, as we have seen, but among all the nations. We see this in the oracles against Damascus, Gaza, Tyre, Edom, Ammon, Moab, and Judah in 1:3–2:5. They, too, are punished for their political and military offenses. At the same time God uses them as instruments of divine judgment against Israel. This is particularly evident in 6:14: "Indeed, I am raising up against you a nation, O house of Israel, says the LORD, the God of hosts, and they shall oppress you from Lebohamath to the Wadi Arabah" (that is, from the northern edge of the Northern Kingdom of Israel to the southern end). As divine instruments they will carry out the divine punishments the people deserve because of their sins. Thus they, too, come under the divine influence and power, just as the Israelites do.

• How many different kinds of divine involvement with humans does Amos include? How does this variety of divine actions strengthen Amos' message to the people?

Amos' Meaning for Us Today

Amos in the Lectionary

Amos appears in the Sunday *Lectionary for Mass (LM)* three times and in the *Revised Common Lectionary (RCL)* five times. In Year B 7:12-15 is paired with Mark 6:7-13 in *LM* and 7:7-15 in *RCL* is paired with Mark 6:14-29 on the Fifteenth Sunday of the Year. On the Twenty-Eighth Sunday in Ordinary Time 5:6-7, 10-15 is an option in *RCL*, paired with Mark 10:17-31.

In Year C, on the Fifteenth Sunday in Ordinary Time, 7:7-17 is an option with Luke 10:25-37 in *RCL*. On the Sixteenth Sunday in Ordinary Time, *RCL* offers Amos 8:1-12 as an option with Luke 10:38-42. On the Twenty-Fifth Sunday in Ordinary Time, 8:4-7 is paired with Luke 16:1-13. This pair of readings highlights the final words of the gospel reading, "You cannot serve both God and wealth." On the following Sunday, the Twenty-Sixth of the year, Amos 6:1, 4-7 is paired with Luke 16:19-31 in *LM*, and is an option in *RCL*. Again the two readings highlight a common theme, the injustice of disregard for the poor.

In the weekday *Lectionary for Mass*, Amos is read in Year II for the six days of the Thirteenth Week in Ordinary Time. The six readings are a representative sample of Amos' message, including 2:6-10, 13-16, the announcement of judgment against Israel; 3:1-8; 4:11-12, rhetorical questions that highlight the impending destruction because of the people's sins; 5:14-15, 21-24, Amos' plea for justice and righteousness as opposed to empty worship; 7:10-17, the account of Amos' call; 8:4-6, 9-12, further words of condemnation of injustice; and 9:11-15, the final hymn.

• Look at Amos 7:12-15, the *LM* first reading for Year B, the Fifteenth Sunday in Ordinary Time, in relation to the gospel for that day, Mark

6:7-13. What thematic connections do you see between the two readings? What difference does it make to an understanding of Amos to include *RCL*'s longer passage?

It is also instructive to see the passages from Amos that are read in the synagogue, as a window into how the Jewish communities understand Amos. Amos 2:6–3:8 is paired with Gen 37:1–40:23. Both the Genesis passage, about Joseph and his brothers, and the Amos passage talk about the terms of the relationship between God and the people. Amos 9:7-15 is one option to be paired with Lev 19:1–20:27. The Leviticus reading is part of the Holiness Code, and the Amos passage highlights the relationship between God and the people.

Amos' significance for our daily life

Amos can speak to people and situations in our own day because the socio-economic situations are very similar: the gap between the "haves" and the "have-nots" is wide and deep, with significant implications for everyday life: access to housing, food, education, medical care, and leisure varies greatly according to people's level of income. While these conditions can be related to one's industry and determination, they are also affected by circumstances beyond one's control, such as language barriers or family history. The problems are exacerbated by the individualism that pervades American life today. Amos' condemning words to those who enjoy what money can provide without regard for the vulnerable, and his constant reminders of God's loving concern speak eloquently and urgently to these concerns.

- Select a particular passage in Amos that speaks to a situation of injustice or oppression of which you are aware. Explain how that passage addresses the situation you have in mind.

- Illustrate an aspect of the book of Amos with a photo or drawing.

- Compose an announcement of judgment in which you condemn a contemporary evil.

Passages for study:

6:1-7

9:1-6

For Further Reading

Andersen, Francis I., and David Noel Freedman. *Amos*. AB 24A. New York: Doubleday, 1989.

Doorly, William J. *Prophet of Justice: Understanding the Book of Amos*. New York: Paulist, 1989.

Jeremias, Jörg. *The Book of Amos: A Commentary*. Trans. Douglas W. Stott. Louisville: Westminster John Knox, 1998.

Mays, James Luther. *Amos: A Commentary*. OTL. Philadelphia: Westminster, 1969.

Paul, Shalom. *Amos: A Commentary on the Book of Amos*. Hermeneia. Minneapolis: Fortress, 1991.

Sweeney, Marvin A. *The Twelve Prophets*, vol. 1. Berit Olam. Collegeville: Liturgical Press, 2000.

Wolff, Hans Walter. *Joel and Amos: A Commentary on the Books of the Prophets Joel and Amos*. Trans. Waldemar Janzen, S. Dean McBride, Jr., and Charles A. Muenchow. Hermeneia. Philadelphia: Fortress, 1977 (forms and literary features, pp. 91–100; message, pp. 100–106; redaction, pp. 106–13).

HOSEA

And I will take you for my wife forever;
I will take you for my wife in righteousness and in justice,
in steadfast love, and in mercy.
I will take you for my wife in faithfulness;
and you shall know the LORD. (Hos 2:19-20)

Background Information

The book of Hosea is a love story about God's constant concern for the people, in the midst of and in spite of their pervasive lack of faithfulness to God and to what God asks of them. The book was probably compiled by scribes in Judah, working shortly after the fall of Samaria. Like Amos, the book of Hosea gives little biographical information about the prophet. His father's name was Beeri, and he was probably a person of some means, according to the amount he paid for the woman in 3:2— fifteen shekels of silver, a homer of barley and a measure of wine. The superscription sets the dates of his work in the reigns of Uzziah (783–742) through Hezekiah (715–689) in Judah, and Jeroboam II in Israel (786–746). But the book does not mention the reigns of Jeroboam's successors in Israel or the successors of Uzziah in Judah until the fall of Samaria, nor does it allude to the latter event. Hosea was thus a contemporary of Amos, but his work extended over a longer period of time than did Amos' and most likely ended before 722.

From the text we learn that he worked in the Northern Kingdom. For example, Hosea's first child is named Jezreel to acknowledge the coming destruction of the house of Jehu, and Hosea announces that the Lord "will break the bow of Israel in the valley of Jezreel" (Hos 1:4-5). He criticizes the northern cities of Bethel, Mizpah, Samaria, and Tabor, but not Shechem, except to accuse the priests of murder on the road to Shechem. These factors suggest the possibility that Shechem was his home. Hosea's geographical, socio-economic, and religious concerns are similar to those of Amos.

Organization of the Book

Outline

The book is organized according to its contents, which fall into four groups:

1–3	Hosea's marriage
4:1–9:9	Words of condemnation
9:10–13:16	Israel's sinful past
14	Words of hope

Genres

Hosea's message was expressed not in clearly defined genres as was Amos', but rather in adaptations and combinations of genres and in juxtapositions of words of judgment and salvation. In this section we will look at the genres and adaptations that appear in the book, examining several of them carefully to note how they convey the message of the book.

MESSENGER SPEECHES appear only rarely in Hosea: see 1:2; 2:13; 2:16; 2:21; 11:11. For the most part the prophet speaks in the first person as the divine spokesperson. Some examples are 5:8-15 and 10:9-15. The lack of messenger formulas in the book contributes to the difficulty in finding the beginnings and endings of the different oracles. It also expresses the very close relationship between Hosea and God; Hosea's words are God's own.

(AUTO)BIOGRAPHICAL REPORT: Hosea 1 is a biographical report, and Hosea 3 is an autobiographical report. Both chapters have to do with God commanding Hosea to marry a prostitute. In 1:2 the Lord instructs Hosea, "Go, take for yourself a wife of whoredom and have children of whoredom, for the land commits great whoredom by forsaking the LORD." This is a biographical report giving information about Hosea, the woman Gomer, and the three children they had, but, in fact, it is much more: it is also a report of a symbolic act. We will look at the symbolic dimension of the passage below.

- In the autobiographical report in chapter 3, what information does Hosea give about himself? Compare and contrast it with the report in chapter 1.

SYMBOLIC ACT: Hosea 1:2-3; 3:1-5 describe several symbolic acts that create the metaphor for the entire book: Hosea's marriage to Gomer and the births of their children. We will look closely at the first of these. All three elements are straightforward: the Lord gives instructions to Hosea and immediately explains the meaning of the requested action in 1:2, then Hosea carries out the instructions in 1:3. The requested act is that he marry a prostitute and have children by her. The Lord explains this shocking request: the marriage mirrors the land's unfaithfulness to the Lord. Hosea does as the Lord asks, marrying Gomer and having three children: a son, Jezreel; a daughter, Lo-ruhamah, and another son, Lo-ammi.

The symbolic meanings of the three names express the serious rupture of the divine-human relationship. Each name is explained, detailing the horror of the unfaithful situation. The word Jezreel means "God sows." Several violent acts were committed in Jezreel: It was the location of Naboth's vineyard, for which Jezebel arranged his murder (1 Kings 21:1-16), and where the murdered bodies of Joram and Jezebel were left (2 Kings 9:14-37). These violent acts were blamed on the corrupt Israelite kingship, and the very ground cried out in horror at the atrocities, because of which it would be destroyed. Lo-ruhamah's name, which means "not-cared-for," signifies a different aspect of the impending tragedy: Hosea's daughter will not receive the care a child would usually experience from her parents. The name reverses the divine promises to have compassion on the people (see, e.g., Deut 13:17; 30:3). Thus the foundation of the covenant relationship between God and the people is called into question. The name of the third child is even more chilling: Lo-ammi means "not my people." This name negates the very words of the covenant: "I will be your God, and you will be my people" (see, e.g., Exod 6:7; Lev 26:12; 2 Sam 7:24; Jer 7:23). It depicts the depths to which the people's unfaithfulness has sunk.

The symbol of marriage here is an apt one because it highlights three characteristics of ideal marriage: it is mutual, permanent, and exclusive. That is, it is based on a serious commitment by both husband and wife to spend a lifetime loving and caring for one another and their children, and setting aside the possibility of such a relationship with another person. Hosea uses the symbol of marriage to highlight the qualities of the relationship between God and the people. It is mutual and permanent insofar as both parties agree to a lasting relationship. Finally, it is exclusive insofar as commitment to the Lord precludes faith in any other deity.

This report of symbolic acts has given rise to much speculation regarding the actual biographical reality described here. I will mention three possible interpretations of the command. One is that Hosea was commanded to marry a woman who had adulterous tendencies. Another is that she was not a prostitute in the physical sense, but rather that she was a typical Israelite of the time, unfaithful to God and therefore described as adulterous. A third possibility is that she had participated in a fertility rite commonly practiced in Israel in Hosea's time. The account does not give us enough information to clarify this dilemma. However, it does invite us to pose a different, more fruitful question: What is God trying to tell the people through this symbolic act? The response to that query is embedded in the explanation given to Hosea with the initial instruction to marry the "wife of whoredom": "For the land commits great whoredom by forsaking the Lord" (1:2). What is crucial for Hosea is that the people have turned away from the one God, and this renunciation strikes at the heart of the relationship between God and the people.

In 2:16-23 this message is reversed, and the bonds of a faithful relationship between God and the people are reestablished. We will look at that passage below in our discussion of the salvation oracles in the book.

  • In 3:1-5, whom does Hosea purchase? What does he pay for this purchase? What is the meaning of this purchase?

ANNOUNCEMENT OF JUDGMENT: Hosea makes adaptations to the genre in 5:1-2 and 13:4-8. For example, in 13:4-8 he begins not with a call to attention, but with a reminder of the divine care in the wilderness: "Yet I have been the LORD your God ever since the land of Egypt; you know no God but me, and besides me there is no savior. It was I who fed you in the wilderness, in the land of drought." Then he names their sin: "When I fed them, they were satisfied; they were satisfied, and their heart was proud; therefore they forgot me." The sin is the same as the one Hosea announced in the initial report of a symbolic act: The people have become unfaithful to God. Hosea names the sin in its relational dimension: remembering is fundamental to the divine-human relationship, but the people have forgotten. (See the commands not to forget in Deut 4:9-31; 6:12; 8:11-19.) The actual announcement of judgment follows: "So I will become like a lion to them, like a leopard I will lurk beside the way. I will fall upon them like a bear robbed of her cubs, and will tear open the covering of their heart; there I will devour them like a lion, as a wild animal would mangle them." The judgment is expressed in a series of similes that describe the divine punishment in terms of wild animals that destroy their prey. One simile in particular, "like a bear robbed of her cubs," captures the relational focus of Hosea's speech by referring to the frantically protective actions of a mother animal whose offspring are in danger. The Lord, whose people have gone astray, will attack the source of the trouble: in this case, the very people who have gone astray. We will look more closely at the similes in Hosea in the next section.

- In 5:1-2, to whom does Hosea address the words of judgment? For what sin?

WORDS OF SALVATION: Hosea adapts these as well, in 1:10-11; 2:16-23; 14:4-8. In 1:10-11 he juxtaposes the past, present, and future, the names of two of Hosea's children and the elements of the salvation oracle in a message of deliverance. The reference to the past in v. 10b is given from the perspective of a later time. Its promise of divine intervention plays off the name of Hosea's youngest child, "Not my people," looking forward to the time when the people will be too numerous to count and God will reclaim them, reversing their name to "children of the living God." The description of the results plays off the first child's name: "The people of Judah and the people of Israel shall be gathered together, and they shall appoint for themselves one head; and they shall take possession of the land, for great shall be the day of Jezreel." The promised salvation includes unification of the two kingdoms as one people.

In the words of salvation in 2:16-23 Hosea again alludes to past, present, and future as well as the names of his children, his wife, and past unfaithfulness, and promises a future filled with faithfulness, righteousness, justice, steadfast love, and mercy forever.

> On that day, says the LORD, you will call me, "My husband," and
> no longer will you call me "My Baal." . . . On that day I will answer,
> says the LORD, I will answer the heavens and they shall answer the
> earth; and the earth shall answer the grain, the wine, and the oil,
> and they shall answer Jezreel; and I will sow him for myself in the
> land. And I will have pity on Lo-ruhamah, and I will say to Lo-ammi,
> "You are my people," and he shall say, "You are my God."

With these words Hosea overturns the unfaithful marriage between God
and the people. In its place will be harmony among God, the people,
animals, lands, and crops. The explicit use of the children's names highlights the healing of the infidelity that will be accomplished by the Lord's
intervention. The characteristics of the new relationship are those associated with the covenant and used frequently by the prophets: righteousness, justice, steadfast love, and mercy (v. 19).

• In 14:4-8, what saving word is given?

LAWSUIT: Hosea includes several lawsuits, for example 2:2-9; 4:1-3;
4:4-10. In 2:2-9 the divine plaintiff speaks to the children in the hope of
convincing their mother to set aside her adulterous ways. The elements
are not neatly separated in this lawsuit, but are intertwined within the
verses. Verse 2a is the summons, which acknowledges the complex
relationship between father, mother, and offspring. The naming of the
offenses and the punishment are found in alternating pairs: offenses are
listed in vv. 2b, 5, and 8 and the punishments are given in vv. 3-4, 6-7,
and 9. The offenses are all related to the unfaithful marriage, and the
children's mother is described in an extended metaphor that alludes to
fertility religion in its depiction of the land as provider. In this complex
juxtaposition of elements and motifs, unfaithfulness consists in looking
to the land to supply what, in fact, only God can give. The fertility that
yields plentiful crops is the gift not of the "lovers," but of God. In the
end she will return to the Lord, her first husband, not realizing that it
was the Lord who provided for her all along.

Metaphors use the language and concepts of Baal religion to name the
emptiness and futility of fertility religion as opposed to the Lord's exclusive ability to provide for the people. For example, "she said, 'I will
go after my lovers; they give me my bread and my water, my wool and
my flax, my oil and my drink.' . . . She did not know that it was I who
gave her the grain, the wine, and the oil, and who lavished upon her
silver and gold that they used for Baal" (2:5, 8). Her punishment will be

the loss of these gifts, which really came from God. Implicit in this punishment is the hope that, once she is deprived of divine gifts, she will come to her senses and realize that they come not from the fertility gods, but from YHWH.

Another lawsuit is found in 4:4-10. Verse 4 is the summons: "Yet let no one contend, and let none accuse, for with you is my contention, O priest." Just as in the first example, the suit and punishment alternate in the remaining verses. Verses 5, 9-10 contain the punishment and vv. 6-8 include both lawsuit and punishment; the two parts are not easily separated because sin and punishment are inextricably linked. In this lawsuit the Lord indicts the religious leaders for rejecting knowledge and forgetting the law of God. They have turned their office of service to the Lord into an opportunity to feed their own greed. In punishment the Lord will negate the positive results of their work; they will not see its expected results because it represents their rejection of the God who gave them their office. The Lord accuses the leaders of not knowing and of forgetting and forsaking the Lord. The sinful acts point to the underlying sin: violation of the divine-human relationship. Hosea links this indictment to the original metaphor of the unfaithful marriage when he accuses the leaders of devoting "themselves to whoredom."

- In the lawsuit in 4:1-3, identify the summons, the suit itself, and the sentence. Which of the Ten Commandments have the people violated? What is the underlying sin that these sins illustrate? Why does the land mourn?

Rhetorical Features

SIMILES AND METAPHORS: We noticed in the discussion of Hosea's genres that similes and metaphors appear frequently and add vividness to the prophet's message. The metaphors often rely on personification to express the message of judgment and salvation. The similes are often based on the land, particularly agricultural and pastoral life. They compare some aspect of God or the people to some natural phenomenon in order to illustrate Hosea's point. We have seen several of these in our discussion of Hosea's forms. Many other examples can be found:

"The number of the people of Israel shall be like the sand of the sea, which can be neither measured nor numbered" (1:10). Grains of sand would be nearly impossible to count, which underscores how large their numbers would grow.

"I will make [your mother] like a wilderness, and turn her into a parched land" (2:3). The one the people ought to be able to depend on will not be able to care for them, as her resources for nurturing the people will be depleted.

"[The LORD] will come to us like the showers, like the spring rains that water the earth" (6:3). In contrast to the previous simile, here the Lord's nourishing touch is compared to the rain that provides water for the ground.

Hosea uses many other similes; see, for example, 9:10, 13; 10:4; 13:3; 14:7, 8.

• How do these similes enhance Hosea's message?

Metaphors likewise rely on agricultural and pastoral life, particularly the necessity of water if crops are to grow:

"Ephraim is stricken, their root is dried up, they shall bear no fruit" (9:16).

"Israel is a luxuriant vine that yields its fruit" (10:1).

"Although he may flourish among rushes, the east wind shall come, a blast from the LORD, rising from the wilderness, and his fountain shall dry up, his spring shall be parched" (13:15). For other agricultural metaphors see 10:11-13.

Hosea's similes and metaphors often refer to animals; for example:

"I will be like a lion to Ephraim, and like a young lion to the house of Judah" (5:14).

"Ephraim has become like a dove, silly and without sense" (7:11).

"For they have gone up to Assyria, a wild ass wandering alone" (8:9).

"Ephraim's glory shall fly away like a bird" (9:11). See also the comparison of the LORD to a lion, leopard, and bear in 11:10; 13:7-8, referred to above. Each of these examples draws on the characteristics of different animals to describe some aspect of the people's life or of the divine-human relationship.

Occasionally the figures allude to urban life. For example: "My judgment goes forth as the light" (6:5), and "I will send a fire upon his cities, and it shall devour his strongholds" (8:14). Others use the imagery of cooking: "For [mockers] are kindled like an oven, their heart burns within them, all night their anger smolders; in the morning it blazes like a flaming fire. All of them are hot as an oven" (7:6-7), and "Ephraim is a cake not turned" (7:8).

Wild Asses Foraging in the Herodian Hills (see Hos 8:9)

Several similes and metaphors refer to childbirth and childcare. For example: "When Israel was a child I loved him, and out of Egypt I called my son" (11:1); "Yet it was I who taught Ephraim to walk, I took them up in my arms" (11:3); "I bent down to them and fed them" (11:4); "The pangs of childbirth come for him, but he is an unwise son, for at the proper time he does not present himself at the mouth of the womb" (13:13). These highlight the tenderness of God's care for the people at their most vulnerable, when they are most in need of nurturing.

Several of Hosea's metaphors are personifications, particularly of the land; for example, "the land commits great whoredom by forsaking the Lord" (1:2). Chapter 2 is an extended personification of the land as mother. In later chapters we find "the land mourns" (4:3), and "the new moon shall devour them along with their fields" (5:7). These metaphors have several layers of meaning. The land represents the people and also suffers the consequences of the people's sins.

The reliance of these figures of speech on motifs of land, fertility, and growth alludes to the imagery of fertility worship, on which the people depended for successful farming. For Hosea the comparisons are a graphic way to condemn the people's trust in the gods of fertility rather than the one God who loves and cares for them.

- Read chapter 14 and list the figures is uses. Explain these in light of Hosea's message. What are the two points of comparison? How is each of these appropriate?

Hosea's Message

Themes

Hosea's pervasive concern was the relationship between the Lord and Israel. In fact, this theme, which relies on the metaphor of marriage, sets the tone for all twelve Minor Prophets because Hosea is the first of the Twelve. Hosea conveys this message in words of love, sadness, judgment, and hope. He describes the relationship through references to history, a focus on faithfulness and unfaithfulness, and references to fertility and infertility. We will look at how each of these themes contributes to Hosea's focus on the divine-human relationship.

HISTORY: First, Hosea refers frequently to the history of Israel, describing it as the family history of God and the people. He reminds the people that God has cared for them from the time of creation, but "Israel has forgotten his Maker" (8:14). Hosea often refers to Israel as Jacob, recalling the ancestor's struggles with his brother Esau, with God, and with Laban in 12:2-6, 12-14. The people themselves are frequently referred to by the name of Ephraim, Jacob's favored grandson. For example, in 11:8 the Lord wonders, "How can I give you up, O Ephraim? How can I hand you over, O Israel?" These familial references underscore the personal, intimate focus of the Lord's relationship with the people since their earliest beginnings.

- Notice the number of times the word Ephraim appears in chapters 5 and 9. How does the use of this word personalize Hosea's message?

Hosea's reflections on Israel's history continue with the Exodus and wandering in the wilderness. The Lord reminisces with tenderness about Israel's childhood. In chapter 11 the Lord's care for the people is described in terms of a parent nursing and nurturing a toddler; sadly, the people rejected the Lord's concern.

- Compare and contrast Hos 11:1-4 with Exodus 32 and Numbers 11. What differing memories of the time in the wilderness do you find in these passages?

FAITHFULNESS AND UNFAITHFULNESS: Throughout Israel's history God remained faithful to the people, but they were not faithful in return. Several key words speak to this theme; these words recur throughout the prophetic books: *ḥesed* (steadfast love), *mišpat* (justice), *ṣedeq and ṣedaqah* (righteousness), and *raḥamim* (mercy). Hosea clusters these words in 2:19-20; 4:1; 6:4-6; 10:12; 12:6. In addition, *mišpat* (judgment) appears in 5:1, 11; 10:4. All these terms describe the qualities of faithfulness the Lord looks for in the people. For instance, in 2:19-20 the Lord offers assurance: "I will take you for my wife forever; I will take you for my wife in righteousness (*ṣedeq*) and in justice *(mišpat)*, in steadfast love *(ḥesed)*, and in mercy *(raḥamim)*. I will take you for my wife in faithfulness *(ʾemunah)*; and you shall know the Lord."

Again in 4:1 we find: "There is no faithfulness or loyalty, and no knowledge of God in the land," followed by a list of specific sins that violate the Ten Commandments. In 12:6 Hosea pleads, "Hold fast to love and justice, and wait continually for your God." In both these instances the key words name the qualities the Lord looks for in the people.

- Note the key words in 6:4-6. These qualities are contrasted with what others? Note the key words in 10:12. Contrast the thought with 10:13.

Note the agricultural metaphor here. How does that metaphor enhance Hosea's message?

The first three chapters focus on faithfulness and unfaithfulness in Hosea's marriage. The biographical information uses Hosea and Gomer's unfaithful marriage as the symbol of the people's unfaithfulness to God, who nevertheless continues to care for the people, pleading with them to give up their unfaithful ways. Elsewhere throughout the book Hosea directly condemns the religious leaders who, instead of leading the people to God, lead them astray. Priests and prophets receive scathing criticism: "Yet let no one contend, and let none accuse, for with you is my contention, O priest. You shall stumble by day; the prophet also shall stumble with you by night" (4:4-5). Civil leaders, too, experience Hosea's condemnation. Officials, princes of Judah, and the king are all targets of his criticism.

- Whom does Hosea condemn in 5:1-2, 10; 9:7-8? For what sins of unfaithfulness does he indict them?

Not only the leaders, but all the people are guilty of unfaithfulness. They reject the king, claiming they have no need of him. But their actions have deeper significance: to reject the king is to reject God who appointed him. The people further reject God by turning to foreign rulers for protection in time of trouble. What is more, even their most basic deeds violate the Ten Commandments, the foundation on which faithfulness is based.

- Whom does Hosea condemn in chapter 7? What sins of unfaithfulness have they committed?

Not only empty worship of the Lord, but also idol worship illustrate the people's unfaithfulness. Hosea offers a biting critique in 13:1-3: "People are kissing calves!" he scoffs. Here the prophet condemns Baal worship and the casting and worship of silver calves. The people's rejection of God and their reliance on Canaanite religion will come to a disastrous end when the Canaanite objects of worship are taken to Assyria in the conquest of Samaria (10:3-8; 11:5-7).

- In 8:4-6, what condemnation of idolatry do you find?

Throughout the indictments and condemnations, the Lord remains faithful to the people and eager to win them over to faithfulness. For example:

> How can I give you up, O Ephraim? How can I hand you over,
> O Israel? How can I make you like Admah? How can I treat you like
> Zeboiim? My heart recoils within me; my compassion grows warm
> and tender. I will not execute my fierce anger; I will not again destroy
> Ephraim; for I am God and no mortal, the Holy One in your midst,
> and I will not come in wrath. . . . (11:8-11)

Here condemnation is mixed with sadness and with the hope that the
people will turn aside from their unfaithfulness and turn back to God.

• What does 14:1-7 say about faithfulness and unfaithfulness?

Hosea 6:4-6 focuses on the divine desire for the people in spite of their
fickleness. The Lord wonders how to shake the people out of their unfaithfulness. Similes that depict nature in the early morning ("Your love
is like a morning cloud, like the dew that goes away early," 6:4b) evoke
the people's short-lived dedication, like morning mist that lasts only
until the heat of the day burns it off. "For I desire steadfast love and not
sacrifice, the knowledge of God rather than burnt offerings" (6:6). Empty
religious practices are no substitute for determined, persevering knowledge and love for God.

These examples show that for Hosea the issue of faithfulness and unfaithfulness is deeply personal and fundamental to the intimate relationship between the Lord and Israel. This relationship expresses itself in
law and covenant and depends on knowing both the Lord and the Lord's
expectations. We will consider each of these three ideas: knowing,
covenant, and law.

Hosea uses the words "know" and "knowledge" seventeen times.
Eight times the Lord laments that Israel did not know (e.g., 2:8; 5:4; 7:9).
In contrast, God knows; for example: "I know Ephraim, and Israel is not
hidden from me" (5:3). Hosea includes lack of knowledge among the
sins for which Israel is condemned. The three connotations of the word
"knowing" fit well with the intimacy of Hosea's message. The first is
having information; for example: "She did not know that it was I who
gave her the grain, the wine, and the oil . . ." (2:8). The lack of knowledge
that Hosea condemns is itself understood as the consequence of sin.
When Hosea points out that the people do not know, he is implicitly
condemning the sins that took away the people's knowledge.

The second connotation of "knowing" is being acquainted with someone; for example, "There is no faithfulness or loyalty, and no knowledge
of God in the land" (4:1). The third connotation is experiencing sexual

intimacy, as in "I will take you for my wife in faithfulness; and you shall know the LORD" (2:20). The first two connotations are basic to any relationship. The third indicates the depth and intensity of the tie between the Lord and Israel.

When Hosea speaks about faithfulness and unfaithfulness his words include all three of these connotations of knowing. The people's actions attest that they forgot it was God who cared for them, and they mistakenly thought it was their own efforts that made possible life's benefits. This was a misunderstanding of the basic reality of Israel's existence: that God's care for them was the source of their very being. Hosea's condemnations of their lack of knowledge highlight the gravity of their unfaithfulness. Their punishment would be the loss of God's gifts: as long as they counted on their own efforts or on the favors of nonexistent gods they would not see the results for which they hoped. For example, Hosea warns in 2:9-13 that the land will stop producing and become desolate because Israel forgot the Lord. They do not know that neither their own efforts nor the Baals can make the land bear fruit. What is more, they forgot the Lord; in other words, they lost sight of their intimate acquaintance with the Lord.

But for Hosea condemnation is not the end. He alternates his words of accusation with assurances that, just as the people will suffer the consequences of their unfaithful history, likewise the Lord will bring them back in the future. For example, the condemnation in 2:9-13 is followed in 2:14-23 by the divine promise of intimacy, food, safety, renewal of the relationship between God and the people, return of their knowledge, and reestablishment of the covenant.

- In 11:5-11, what does the Lord condemn? What assurance follows the condemnation?

Hosea's covenant message was solidly based in the traditions of Israel. The specific terms of the covenant, articulated in Israel's law, appear throughout the book. Working with the commandments as they appear in Exodus 20, we find that Hosea alludes to the first commandment, identifying the Lord as the God of the people, in 7:13. The second commandment, against making idols, is implicit in "My people consult a piece of wood, and their divining rod gives them oracles" (4:12). The third commandment, prohibiting wrongful use of the name of the Lord, is evident in 10:4, "They utter mere words; with empty oaths they make covenants." Hosea refers to the fourth commandment, to honor the Sabbath, in condemning its violation in 2:11. The fifth commandment, to honor one's parents, is implicit in Hos 11:1-3, while violations of the sixth through ninth commandments, against murder, adultery, stealing, and false witness, are evident in 4:2: "Swearing, lying, and murder, and stealing and adultery break out; bloodshed follows bloodshed." Finally, the tenth commandment, against coveting, is implicit in Hosea's unfaithful marriage as well as in the words, "She shall pursue her lovers, but not overtake them; and she shall seek them, but shall not find them" (2:7).

Further similarities between Hosea's covenant stipulations and those in the Pentateuch can be found by comparing it with both Priestly and Deuteronomistic passages. Leviticus 26 is reflected in several passages in Hosea, as this chart indicates:

Leviticus	Hosea
26:16	4:10
26:18	10:10
26:22	5:14
26:30	8:6
26:37	4:5; 5:5

• What similarities do you find in these parallel passages? What differences do you identify?

Likewise, comparisons can be made between Hosea and Deuteronomy:

Deuteronomy	Hosea
4:9; 6:6-13; 8:11-20	4:1-3
9:15-21	8:5-7
17:14-15	8:4
28:1-68	8:3
31:9-11; 33:10	8:12

• What similarities do you find in these parallel passages? What differences do you observe?

FERTILITY AND INFERTILITY: Hosea uses the theme of fertility and infertility with particular richness. The unfaithful people believed that the Baals of Canaan were responsible for the land's fertility, but Hosea insists that the produce of the land and the children of the people are gifts of the Lord, not of the Baals (e.g., 2:8, 13, 16, 17; 11:2; 13:1).

Using the language of the fertility religions gives Hosea a vast array of images with which to condemn the people's unfaithfulness. The fertility theme appears throughout the biographical section in chapters 1–3, always highlighting the Lord, not the Canaanite gods, as the author of fertility. This theme, like the theme of faithfulness and unfaithfulness, is expressed in alternating words of judgment and salvation. Hosea's wife bore three children at God's command, and God gave them names signifying the people's violations of the divine-human relationship (1:2-9). The symbolic meanings of these names were discussed above. Those harsh words of indictment are followed immediately by assurances that the realities signified by the children's names will be reversed, and the people will become as numerous as the sand of the sea (1:10-11; 2:2-3).

Hosea warns that both land and people will become infertile in punishment for their unfaithfulness (9:16-17; 10:1). Elsewhere he threatens that fertility will serve a harmful purpose: noxious plants will proliferate (10:8). At times Hosea uses the language of fertility to symbolize the concrete realities of the people's life: for example, in 10:11-13 the metaphor of working the land and reaping its fruits teaches the people that they must cultivate the characteristics of faithfulness.

Hosea uses the language of fertility to promise salvation in 14:4-8. Here, using language that connotes prosperity, he assures the people that they will become numerous and their crops will flourish, multiplying good fortune. At the same time the imagery implicitly condemns the fertility religions by reminding the people that fertility in plant life as well as in human growth comes from God.

- Note the language of cultivation and fertility in the following passages: 2:8-9, 13, 23; 9:16-17; 10:1-2, 11-12. How does this language contribute to Hosea's message?

Hosea's Meaning for Us Today

Hosea in the Lectionary

In the Sunday *LM*, Hosea is read twice: once in Year A and once in Year B. In *RCL* it is read four times. In Year A, on the Tenth Sunday of Ordinary Time, *LM* pairs Hos 6:3-6 with Matt 9:9-13. On that day the *RCL* offers Hos 5:15–6:6 as an option with Matt 9:9-13, 18-26. In Year B on the Eighth Sunday in Ordinary Time Hos 2:16b, 17b, 21-22 is paired with Mark 2:18-22 in *LM*, and Hos 2:14-20 is paired with Mark 2:13-22 in *RCL*. In Year C *RCL* includes two semi-continuous readings from

Hosea as options during Ordinary Time: the reading for the Seventeenth Sunday is Hos 1:2-10 with Luke 11:1-13, and for the Eighteenth Sunday Hos 11:1-11 with Luke 12:13-21.

- How would you relate the two *LM* readings for the Tenth Sunday of Ordinary Time in Year A?

- In Year B, Eighth Sunday of Ordinary Time, which readings do you prefer, *LM* or *RCL*? Explain.

In the weekday *Lectionary for Mass* Hosea is read on five consecutive days in the fourteenth week of Ordinary Time in Year II, immediately following the consecutive reading of Amos. The five readings: 2:16-17, 21-22; 8:4-7, 11-13; 10:1-3, 7-8, 12; 11:1, 3-4, 8-9; and 14:2-10 are representative of Hosea, as they include the themes of judgment and salvation and focus on God's tender love for the people. In addition, on Friday and Saturday of the third week of Lent we read passages from Hosea that focus on God's healing love, an apt theme for the season: Hos 14:2-10 and 6:1-6.

In the Jewish community Hos 12:13–14:10 is one of the options paired with Gen 28:10–32:3, Jacob's journey to find a wife, his dream of the ladder, his marriages, and his escape from Laban. The Hosea passage reflects on the Israelites' journey out of Egypt, characterized by God's constant care and the people's infidelity. The alternative passage is 11:7–12:12, about Jacob. Then on the following Sabbath this same passage is paired with Gen 32:4–36:43, Jacob's reconciliation with his brother Esau, Shechem's violation of Dinah, and Jacob's continuing travels beyond Shechem, followed by a genealogy. If the alternate reading is used on the previous Sabbath, a reading from Obadiah is paired with the Genesis passage. Hosea 2:1-22, pleading with unfaithful Israel, is paired with Num 1:1–4:20, the census of the tribes. And on the Sabbath between Rosh Hashanah and Yom Kippur, Hos 14:2-10, about divine healing of the people, is one of the options to be paired with the weekly portion of the Pentateuch.

Hosea's significance for our daily life

The marriage metaphors give us insight into the depth and intimacy of God's love for us. The comparisons with an ideal marriage highlight the commitment, permanence, and depth of God's ongoing care. These metaphors offer support and reassurance to people who struggle with issues of acceptance and self-image. They serve as reminders that God's love for us is a bond as strong as the ideal marriage. God loves people regardless of our own degree of faithfulness. In fact, the depth of God's love serves as a call to repentance and healing.

- What precautions would you take in applying Hosea's message to victims of another person's unfaithfulness?

Passages for study:

>   2:2-15

>   11:1-11

For Further Reading

Dempsey, Carol J. *Hope Amid the Ruins: The Ethics of Israel's Prophets.* St. Louis: Chalice Press, 2000.

Habel, Norman C., ed. *The Earth Story in the Psalms and the Prophets.* Earth Bible 4. Cleveland: The Pilgrim Press, 2001.

Mays, James Luther. *Hosea.* OTL. Philadelphia: Westminster, 1969. General Introduction.

Sweeney, Marvin A. *The Twelve Prophets,* vol. 1. Berit Olam. Collegeville: Liturgical Press, 2000.

Wolff, Hans Walter. *Hosea.* Hermeneia. Philadelphia: Fortress, 1974. Pp. xxiii–xxv for literary features; xxix–xxxii for redaction.

Chapter Four

The Eighth-Century Prophets in the Southern Kingdom

The historical setting of the eighth century was described at the beginning of Chapter Three. While the political and military situation in Judah in the second half of the eighth century was more stable and the Southern Kingdom of Judah was less immediately threatened by the Assyrian onslaught than was the Northern Kingdom of Israel, the messages preached by two prophets, Micah and Isaiah, to the people of Judah were similar to those of Amos and Hosea in Israel.

MICAH

"He has told you, O mortal, what is good;
and what does the LORD require of you but to do justice,
and to love kindness, and to walk humbly with your God?" (Mic 6:8)

Background Information

Micah was a contemporary of Hosea and Isaiah, and most likely of Amos as well. His name is a shortened form of Micaiah, or "Who is like YHWH?"—an apt name for one whose words praise the many actions of God. He lived in Moresheth, a village about twenty-five miles southwest of Jerusalem. The village was very likely part of the Jerusalem perimeter that was fortified for the protection of the city. Micah's words reveal his understanding of rural life and the tensions faced by the villagers under military presence.

According to the superscription, Micah preached during the reigns of the southern kings Jotham, Ahaz, and Hezekiah in the second half of the eighth century. His message was concerned with both the northern and southern kingdoms in face of the Assyrian threat. His words were inter-preted over the next few centuries, especially during the Babylonian ascendancy, and edited into their present arrangement after the exile.

Organization of the Book

The book looks forward to the rule of God by announcing both judg-ment and salvation. Three times the prophet cries, "Hear!" in 1:2; 3:1; and 6:1, dividing the book into three parts. Each of the three divisions contains words of judgment followed by words of salvation. Catchwords and motifs, sometimes similar, sometimes contrasting, link the different units into a coherent whole.

The versification in Micah differs among the versions of the Bible, according to the chart below.

RSV, NRSV	*MT, LXX, NAB*
5:1	4:14
5:2-15	5:1-14

Outline (according to NRSV versification)

1:1	Superscription
1:2–2:11	Judgment for the people's sins
2:12-13	Words of salvation
3:1-12	Judgment for sins against justice
4:1–5:15	Words of salvation
6:1–7:7	Judgment because of the people's shortcomings
7:8-20	Words of salvation

Genres

We can see from the outline that the oracles are grouped around judg-ment and salvation. Several oracles are straightforward expressions of specific forms, but often they adapt the prophetic genres to fit the specific situation. The following genres appear:

ANNOUNCEMENT OF JUDGMENT: These announcements figure promi-nently throughout the book; for example, three announcements of judg-ment against the leaders are found in chapter 3, vv. 1-4, 5-8, 9-12. The first and third are quite similar: both are addressed to the rulers, who are responsible for the administration of justice among the people (vv. 1 and 9). The first announcement describes the sinful situation in vv. 2-3, focusing on the leaders' injustices toward their people. Micah elaborates on this evil with an extended metaphor suggesting cannibalism. The impending disaster declared in the first announcement is that God will turn away from them just as they have turned away from God (v. 4).

The second announcement (3:5-8) condemns a different group of leaders, the prophets, summoning them in v. 5a, describing their sin of misuse of their prophetic office in v. 5b, and announcing the disaster that will come upon them in vv. 6-7. Their guilt lies in misguiding the people with words and actions that are deceitful and self-interested rather than divinely given. As a result they themselves will suffer the confusion of divine silence in the face of their cries. In v. 8 Micah contrasts the false prophets' situation with his own. They cry "Peace" in times of prosperity and "War" in times of hunger, but Micah's words come from the power and spirit of God, preaching condemnation of the people's sins. This assertion is as close as Micah comes to describing his call from God to be a prophet.

The third announcement (3:9-12), like the first, is addressed to the rulers. It also repeats the accusation of the first, focusing explicitly on the violence and bloodshed, bribery and extortion rampant in the city. It indicts chiefs, priests, and prophets and condemns their avarice, lawlessness, and immorality. This announcement makes a more sweeping condemnation than the first, predicting the total destruction of the city in v. 12. This announcement was most likely made at the time of the Assyrian threat to Jerusalem which, as we know, did not materialize. The words struck home 150 years later when the Babylonians succeeded in taking the city and sending many of its leading citizens into exile in Babylon. Jeremiah 28:16 quotes this announcement, putting the words into the mouths of the elders, who apply them to the Babylonian threat.

- In 1:2-7, to whom are the words addressed? How will the land suffer for the sins of the people?

- In 6:9-16, identify the elements of the announcement of judgment. Compare and contrast this announcement with the three in chapter 3.

WORDS OF SALVATION: Chapter 4 includes words of salvation in vv. 6-7, 8, 9-10. In vv. 6-7 the oracle promises divine intervention on behalf of the lame, the banished, and the wounded (v. 6); the promised result proclaimed in v. 7 is that those God gathers will become a remnant and a powerful nation, with the Lord as their leader forever.

Verse 8 addresses Jerusalem with titles that emphasize its elevation. "Former dominion" alludes to an earlier time of sovereignty and offers assurance that the city will again be free from external control.

Verses 9-10a allude to the people's complaint of abandonment. The description uses the vivid image of a woman in labor to suggest that the people's pain is necessary in order to give birth to the future. That image continues in the announcement of salvation proper in v. 10b, which asserts that Babylon, the place of exile, will in fact be the locus of delivery from their enemies to the new life of redemption by the Lord.

- What similarities do you find among 4:6-7, 8, and 9-10?

- In 2:12-13, how does the image of shepherd and sheep offer hope to the people?

PROPHETIC LAWSUIT: Micah 6:1-5 exemplifies this form. It begins with a summons to three parties: a general audience designated by the plural "Hear" in v. 1, an individual addressed in "Rise, plead" in v. 1, and the mountains in v. 2. The summons suggests that the Lord is the plaintiff, but in the trial itself the divine defendant asks the puzzled question, "What have I done to you?" and then reviews details of rescuing the people from slavery (vv. 3-4). The trial does not contain a sentence as such, but instead the prophetic *torah* that follows in vv. 6-8 serves thematically as the outcome of the trial. We will look closely at these verses below.

- Which historical details are included in vv. 3-4? How do these details respond to the question, "What have I done to you?"

PROPHETIC INSTRUCTION: Micah 6:6-8 raises and responds to questions about sacrificial offerings. Because of its association with the cult it is often referred to as a Priestly *torah*. Here the lesson is given in response to the request in v. 6a: "With what shall I come before the LORD, and bow myself before God on high?" The questioner continues in vv. 6b-7 with specific inquiries about the acceptability of several sacrificial offerings. The response in v. 8 does not directly answer those questions, but instead implies that a different question must be posed. The required sacrifice is not the offering of another creature's life, but of one's own daily living. This *torah* follows the lawsuit in 6:1-5, and in that context it is the outcome of the trial. This concise summary of life in relation to God and others, given in response to the question about appropriate sacrifice, completes the legal proceeding introduced by the Lord's summons to trial in 6:1.

- What covenant responsibilities does the instruction include?

DISPUTATION: Micah 2:6-11 is a disputation. In v. 6 the prophet addresses listeners who are identified in vv. 8-10 as leaders whose preaching misleads those who trust in them. These preachers deny the possibility that disaster might come upon Jerusalem, contrary to Micah, whose words warn of impending disaster. The false optimism of the preachers will victimize women and children. When the preachers object to Micah's warnings, his rhetorical questions accuse them of oppressive actions, specifically of stealing the clothing and homes of women and children (vv. 8-9). As a result the land itself has become unclean and is no longer fit for habitation. In v. 11 Micah utters a final word of scorn for one who is spiritually bankrupt and yet would preach to the people.

- In this disputation, contrast the words of Micah's accusers with their actions. How do their actions invalidate their own words?
- How are these words similar to the words of 3:12?

INDIVIDUAL LAMENT: Micah 7:1-7 is similar to a type of psalm called "individual lament." The prophet grieves over the disappearance of faithfulness from the land and the prevalence of unrighteousness that has displaced concern for one another. He cautions his audience not to put their trust in other humans. Then he utters his own words of trust in God. A significant element of the lament, the petition to God, is not explicit in this prayer but is implied in its final line: "My God will hear me." The prayer expresses confidence in divine help in the present difficulty.

- In this lament, which leaders does Micah condemn, and for what sins? Compare and contrast this condemnation with that in 3:5-8.
- In 1:8-16, what is the source of the prophet's grief?

Rhetorical Features

The rhetorical features in Micah link the various passages to one another and highlight the prophet's message. We will look first at those features that serve as links among the passages, then at others that appear throughout the book.

CATCHWORDS: These repeated words or phrases appear throughout the book, connecting different passages and highlighting the meaning that runs through them. For example, the word "mountain" or "mountains" occurs three times in 4:1-2, in the expressions "mountain of the LORD's house" and "highest of the mountains" in v. 1, and "mountain of the LORD . . . house of the God of Jacob" in v. 2. These words emphasize the importance of Jerusalem and the Temple, which will be the center of pilgrimage and the source of instruction for many people. Then the expression "Mount Zion" appears in v. 7, repeating the meaning associated with "mountain" and connecting it with the phrase "daughter Zion" that appears in 4:8, 10, 13. In each case the speaker uses the title in addressing the city of Jerusalem. The first time the phrase is in the context of a divine promise; the second time it announces the coming exile that will be followed by redemption; the third promises that Jerusalem will participate in demonstrating God's power. These catchwords focus our attention on Jerusalem as the topic of the chapter.

- How many catchwords do you see in chapter 3? How do these repetitions unify the chapter? Which words in chapter 3 are repeated in chapter 4? How do these catchwords connect the words of judgment of chapter 3 with the words of salvation of chapters 4–5?

SIMILES: Micah uses similes, often in vivid pairs and as synonymous parallels. For example, he describes the Lord coming in judgment: "Then the mountains will melt under him and the valleys will burst open, like wax near the fire, like waters poured down a steep place" (1:4), and "I will make lamentation like the jackals, and mourning like the ostriches" (1:8). In the first example Micah compares the mountains to wax that melts and runs down like water, to underscore the fearful response to the Lord's coming in judgment: even nature itself will cower. In the second example the mourner's lament is compared to the cries of jackals and ostriches, animals of the wilderness.

Paired similes offer comfort as well as judgment; for example, "I will set [the survivors of Israel] like sheep in a fold, like a flock in its pasture" (2:12). Here he compares the survivors to sheep who know the care of their shepherd.

- How does each of the paired similes in 1:8; 3:3; 4:9-10; 5:7-8; 7:17 enrich Micah's message?

QUOTATIONS: Micah quotes his hearers, turning their words back on them, e.g.: "[Jerusalem's] rulers give judgment for a bribe, its priests teach for a price, its prophets give oracles for money; yet they lean upon the LORD and say, 'Surely the LORD is with us! No harm shall come upon us!'" (3:11). The insertion of the audience's words into Micah's speech intensifies the words and underscores the complacency of the leaders' declaration. Rulers, priests, and prophets mistakenly believe that nothing can happen to them because they are the Lord's people, even though their hypocritical, oppressive actions violate the basic covenant responsibility to care for the people, especially the vulnerable.

• How do the quotations in 6:6-7 and 7:10 intensify Micah's teaching?

PUNS: In 1:10-15 Micah names eleven cities located southwest of Jerusalem, making wordplays on many of their names. For example, in v. 10, "in Beth-leaphrah roll yourselves in the dust" plays on the word *'aphar*, "dust," to describe grieving people. Rolling or lying in dust, or putting it on one's head, were acts of mourning in ancient Israel. In v. 13 Lachish, an important fortified city, is warned to prepare to flee because of its sins. Its fortifications will not hold up in face of the people's unfaithfulness. These two examples illustrate how Micah uses the name of the city to highlight the punishment that will come upon it in consequence of the people's sins.

IRONY: In 3:5-8 Micah warns the false prophets that they will lose the ability to see because they lead the people astray. This punishment is particularly ironic because prophecy depends on seeing the situation in light of the relationship between God and the people.

• In 3:11-12, what irony do you find?

KEY WORDS: Micah uses three words that occur frequently among the prophets: steadfast love *(ḥesed)*, judgment *(mišpat)*, and righteousness *(ṣedaqah)*. We recognize these three terms from our study of Hosea. They are not so easily identified in Micah because they are given several different translations. The *NRSV* translates *ḥesed* as "kindness" in 6:8, "clemency" in 7:18, and "unswerving loyalty" in 7:20. Likewise, *ṣedaqah* appears in Micah in 6:5 and 7:9, translated "saving acts" and "vindication," describing divine action on behalf of the people. Micah uses *mišpat*, "justice" or "judgment," in 3:1, 8, 9; 6:8; 7:9. The term emphasizes the covenant responsibility of the people, particularly their leaders, to deal fairly with one another. Two of the three terms, *ḥesed* and *mišpat*, appear in the well-known verse 6:8, clarifying the kind of sacrifice the Lord asks of the people: not taking the lives of animals, but living the lives of covenant partners with the Lord. Two of the terms are paired in 7:9 as well, focusing on the Lord's actions on behalf of the people.

- Micah 5:5-9 is particularly rich in rhetorical features. How many do you find? How does each contribute to the meaning of the passage?

Micah's Message

Themes

Many of the themes in Micah appear also in Isaiah 1–39. Historically the two prophets, who were contemporaries, might well have been familiar with common traditions. Canonically, the effect of the similarity is that the two books offer a commentary on each other, enriching the message of both books. Here we take a close look at the themes we find in Micah.

THE SWEEP OF HISTORY. Micah portrays all of history as the arena of God's actions on behalf of all people. God punishes sins and offers salvation throughout all time. This overarching theme is explicit in the organization of the book, with its two main divisions into words to a universal audience followed by words to Israel, and the two parallel subdivisions of words of judgment and words of salvation. The message applies with particular urgency to Israel and Judah, specified in the superscription that announces Micah's message concerning the two capital cities of Samaria and Jerusalem. Micah's words then indict the two cities, threatening destruction for their sins of idolatry and injustice in chapters 1–3. Words of reassurance relieve the flow of condemnatory accusations, promising divine salvation to a righteous remnant in 2:12-13, peace to be centered in Jerusalem and a new ruler to come from Bethlehem after a period of exile (chs. 4–5). Then Micah turns his words directly to the people of all Israel, condemning their empty worship and their acts of injustice and again warning of impending destruction and exile in 6:1–7:7. The final section of the book promises defeat of Israel's enemies. More importantly, it assures the people of God's forgiveness and the people's return to faithfulness. The organization of Micah's words places all these realities within the realm of divine action on behalf of the people.

Several specific themes emerge within this overall schema. The Lord comes in judgment, which takes the form of the destruction of Jerusalem; the people's sins are the cause of this catastrophic event; and guilt rests

Manger Square in Bethlehem (see Mic 5:2)

predominantly on the leaders who are misusing their authority. The Lord will bring about a new beginning, restoring the destroyed city and protecting the righteous remnant who remain faithful throughout the time of hardship and destruction. We will now look more closely at these themes.

GOD OF ALL NATIONS. Micah's opening words announce to all people, not only the people of Israel and Judah, that the Lord is coming in judgment because of their sins of unfaithfulness and injustice. He later proclaims that many will come to Jerusalem, the central place where God resides. Among all peoples, the leaders are singled out for intense condemnation because they are not only corrupt but also complacent in assuming that no harm can come to God's people. At the end of the book, the promise of restoration includes the assurance: "In that day they will come to you from Assyria to Egypt, and from Egypt to the River, from sea to sea and from mountain to mountain" (7:12). This pledge highlights the far-reaching influence of divine sway, centered in Jerusalem.

JERUSALEM WILL SUFFER DESTRUCTION. Micah announces the end of the city and exile in Babylon that would come about because of the corruption of its leaders. His warnings are given in vivid similes, relating Jerusalem to a woman in labor and the destruction to a plowed field. Responsibility for the impending destruction will rest primarily with Jerusalem's leaders, whom Micah accuses of avarice and oppression (2:1-9). Those who administer justice, as well as priests and prophets, are accused of unjust decisions, violence, bribery, and extortion (3:1-7, 9-12). He indicts all the people in sweeping condemnations of their behavior throughout chapters 2 and 3, and also in 1:2-6; 6:1-5.

YHWH WILL BRING ABOUT A NEW BEGINNING. The rebirth would begin in Bethlehem, the town of King David and his ancestors. Hence Bethlehem was a city of divine favor and its rebirth would coincide with return from exile in Babylon (5:2-4), which the Lord will bring about with compassion (7:18-20). The reference to the ruler who is to come from Bethlehem has been used retrospectively by the Christian community to refer to Christ the messiah. Here we see that its original meaning is related to the people's hope for a human king in the spirit and line of David, who also came from Bethlehem. (This expectation differs from Isaiah's announcements of a messiah to come in Jerusalem.) The new beginning would include restoration of the kingdom to the vulnerable, and to the city of Jerusalem (4:6-8), where the remnant would be gathered in and become numerous (5:7).

FAITHFUL ENDURANCE. The time of waiting for the restoration is to be one of patient expectation. Micah counsels the people to acknowledge their sinfulness and wait patiently and hopefully for the redeeming action of God (7:8-10). Even the accustomed cultic practices are secondary to the practice of the three virtues of *mišpat* (justice/judgment), *ḥesed* (steadfast love), and "walking humbly with your God," or living always with God's will and promises in mind (6:8). This instruction highlights the awesome privilege inherent in being God's people. They have the assurance of divine care for them and the certainty of knowing what God asks of them in grateful response to God's actions on their behalf.

Micah's message is solidly rooted in the traditions of Israel from its earliest beginnings. He refers to the Exodus and wilderness wandering in the Lord's question:

> O my people, what have I done to you? In what have I wearied you? Answer me! For I brought you up from the land of Egypt, and redeemed you from the house of slavery; and I sent before you Moses, Aaron, and Miriam. O my people, remember now what King Balak of Moab devised, what Balaam son of Beor answered him, and what happened from Shittim to Gilgal, that you may know the saving acts of the LORD. (6:3-5)

In addition, as we saw above, he refers to David's birthplace when promising a new king to come from Bethlehem in 5:2. These references give added solemnity to Micah's words by connecting the people's lives with their treasured memory of divine care for them.

• Compare and contrast the divine reference to Balak and Balaam to the account in Numbers 22–24.

Micah's Meaning for Us Today

Micah in the Lectionary

Micah appears in the Sunday *LM* and *RCL* on the fourth Sunday of Advent in Year C, when 5:2-5a (vv. 1-4a in *NAB*) is read. This passage celebrates Bethlehem as the city from which the "one who is to rule in Israel" will come when "she who is in labor has brought forth." This messianic passage assures the people that after their exile a new ruler will come from Bethlehem, the city of kings. It is paired with Luke 1:39-45. This placement in the lectionary with the passage from Luke on the Sunday before Christmas adds a christological layer to its messianic meaning. It is useful to recall that this kind of reading is a retrospective one, added to the original assurance of God's concern for the people in their immediate circumstances. Within the context of the Old Testament this passage celebrates God's promise to David that his descendants would sit on the throne of Israel (see 2 Sam 7:16).

In addition, the *RCL* uses Mic 6:1-8 on the Fourth Sunday after Epiphany in Year A, pairing it with Matt 5:1-12. The two readings summarize how we are to live as covenant people. On the Thirty-First Sunday in Ordinary Time or 26A, *RCL* reads Mic 3:5-12 as an option with Matt 23:1-12.

In the weekday *LM* Micah is read three times in the cycle of continuous readings, during the fifteenth and sixteenth weeks in Ordinary Time, Year II. The readings are 2:1-5; 6:1-4, 6-8; 7:14-15, 18-20. The first of these condemns socio-economic injustice, the second is the well-known trial speech and prophetic instruction, and the third is Micah's prayer of confidence in God's care for the people. Micah also appears twice during Lent: 7:7-9 is read on the optional Lent 4 weekday; that is, any day in the Fourth Week, especially in Years B or C when the gospel is not John 9:1-41, the healing of the man born blind; and 7:14-15, 18-20 is read on the Saturday of the Second Week of Lent.

In the Jewish community Mic 5:6–6:8 is paired with Num 22:2–25:9 in a weekly Sabbath portion. On Shabbat Shuvah (the Sabbath during the week between Rosh Hashanah and Yom Kippur) Mic 7:18-20 is paired with the weekly Pentateuch portion, and on Yom Kippur afternoon the same passage is read with the book of Jonah and Lev 18:1-30.

Micah's significance for our daily life

Micah, like the other eighth-century prophets, insists that justice is essential in our dealings with other people. This charge applies with particular intensity to religious and civil leaders, but no one is excused from the responsibility to treat other people fairly and respectfully. Those who merit special consideration are the vulnerable, who often suffer oppressive treatment by the powerful and influential members of the community.

Micah's words call attention to the environmental dimension of human actions, acknowledging that all of nature suffers the consequences of our actions (e.g., 1:4). The summary statement in 6:8 calls all of us to join with the ancient Israelites to do justice, love kindness, and walk humbly with our God.

- Which twenty-first century social, economic, and political institutions might Micah criticize for complacency, injustice, and oppression?

- Which ecclesial institutions might be called upon to help put Micah's words into practice?

- What specific actions might individuals take in order to live in justice, steadfast love, and humble awareness of God's presence?

- How can knowledge of our history as God's people inspire us?

- Compose a lament in the spirit of Mic 7:1-7.

Passages for study:

> 2:1-5
> 4:1-5
> 7:8-20

For Further Reading

Anderson, Francis I., and Freedman, David Noel. *Micah.* AB 24E. New York: Doubleday, 2000.

Dempsey, Carol J. *Hope Amid the Ruins: The Ethics of Israel's Prophets.* St. Louis: Chalice Press, 2000.

Hillers, Delbert. *Micah.* Hermeneia. Philadelphia: Fortress, 1984.

Mays, James Luther. *Micah.* OTL. Philadelphia: Westminster, 1976.

Sweeney, Marvin A. *The Twelve Prophets,* vol. 2. Bertit Olam. Collegeville: Liturgical Press, 2000.

Wolff, Hans Walter. *Micah: A Commentary.* Trans. Gary Stansell. Minneapolis: Augsburg, 1990.

FIRST ISAIAH

"And one called to another and said:
'Holy, holy, holy is the LORD of hosts;
the whole earth is full of his glory.'" (Isa 6:3)

Background Information

Isaiah is the first of the three major prophets. We recall that the designation "major" relates to the length of the book. The book of Isaiah is actually a compilation of words spoken over a long span of time, with most of the activity centering around three periods: the second half of the eighth century, the end of the exile in Babylon, and the time of return and reconstruction after the exile. For the most part chapters 1–39 come from the first of the three periods, chapters 40–55 from the second, and chapters 55–66 from the third. Accordingly, the person associated with the first part is called First Isaiah or Isaiah of Jerusalem because his words indicate that he lived and worked in that city. The person connected with the second part is called Second Isaiah or Isaiah of Babylon because his words are associated with Babylon at the end of the exile. Finally, the person linked with the last part is called simply Third Isaiah, reflecting the small amount that can be known about the author from the words recorded in chapters 56–66.

In this chapter we will concentrate on the writings associated with Isaiah of Jerusalem, chapters 1–39.

Organization of the Book

Outlines

The content of the book is evident in the following outline, which also shows the groupings of particular genres.

1–12	Judgment on Israel
13–23	Sayings against foreign nations
24–27	Isaian apocalypse celebrating the downfall of an unnamed city
28–31	Judgment on Israel (Judah)
32–35	Poems and prayers dealing with the coming age of judgment and redemption

36–39	Biographical "legends"
36–37	Events of 701
38	Hezekiah's illness
39	Predictions of exile from the visit of Merodach-baladan

A detailed outline of chapters 1–12, on which we will focus most of our consideration, shows the complexity of the material. The outline combines themes and genres.

1	Introduction
2:1–4:6	Early oracles
5	Warnings
6	Isaiah's call
7:1–9:6	Syro-Ephraimite oracles
9:7–10:4	Warnings
10:5-34	Assyria
11–12	New Age

Genres

As we might expect, a book of thirty-nine chapters includes a wide variety of genres. Many of them have been introduced earlier, but several are new to our study of the prophetic forms.

CALL NARRATIVE: Isaiah's call is reported in 6:1-13. It took place in the year of King Uzziah's death, 742. The opening theophany is a vision of the heavenly court, with the Lord sitting on a throne, the hem of his robe filling the temple. He is surrounded by six-winged seraphs celebrating the holiness of the Lord. The transcendent atmosphere of the scene is heightened by the description of the quaking building supports and the smoke-filled room. Isaiah's description is similar to the plan of the temple, whose inner sanctuary contained two cherubim (1 Kings 6:23-28). Isaiah's declaration of unworthiness is unusual in that he utters it in reaction to the vision, before he hears the call, rather than as a response to the call itself. The prophet acknowledges his own ritual impurity, which would disqualify him from entering the temple; yet there he is in the Holy of Holies. This terrifying realization is acknowledged and rectified by one of the seraphs, who touches Isaiah's mouth with a burning coal.

That gesture purifies him, provides the sign typical in a call narrative, and foreshadows divine presence and guidance in carrying out his commission.

Then Isaiah hears a question: "Whom shall I send?" in response to which he expresses his availability. His commission follows, with the Lord's instruction to deliver a message to the people. That message appears to be defeatist, suggesting that even though the people are to look and listen, they will not understand. In fact, Isaiah is commissioned to stop them from comprehending and thus from being healed. Isaiah then asks a question for clarification: "How long, O LORD?" This question, which often appears in psalms of lament, expresses Isaiah's heavy-hearted response to the commission he has just been given. The response confirms the near finality of the commission, emphasizing the desolation and emptiness that will eventually befall the cities when their inhabitants are gone. Then the commission picks up a different metaphor, comparing the situation to a tree stump that is burned in an effort to remove it. But this metaphor concludes on a hopeful note: a holy seed will remain. In other words, new life is assured.

Thus Isaiah is called to witness to divine holiness among the intransigent, hardhearted people. The harsh word he is given to announce recalls the situation of the Egyptian Pharaoh in his interaction with Moses during the plagues. God assures Moses, "I will harden his heart" (Exod 4:21); then throughout the account of the plagues and the escape through the Sea the narrative reports the Lord's hardening of the Pharaoh's heart eight more times (7:3; 9:12; 10:1, 20, 27; 11:10; 14:4, 8). In addition it tells us that Pharaoh hardened his own heart three times (8:15, 32; 9:34), and six times that Pharaoh's heart was hardened (7:13, 14, 22; 8:19; 9:7, 35). We know that the Exodus account demonstrates the Lord's power over Pharaoh's ability to rule his people, and also Pharaoh's loss of the ability to make wise decisions because of his own failure to do so. With that background in mind, we can understand that the words Isaiah is given to deliver to the people are an expression of the people's own hardheartedness, which prevents them from understanding the meaning in the events surrounding the Assyrian onslaught. In that sense the people are experiencing the consequences of their own actions. At the same time we see here an example of equating suffering with punishment for sin, an equation that is problematic if it is used as a blanket explanation for suffering.

• Compare and contrast this call narrative with 1 Kings 22:19-23.

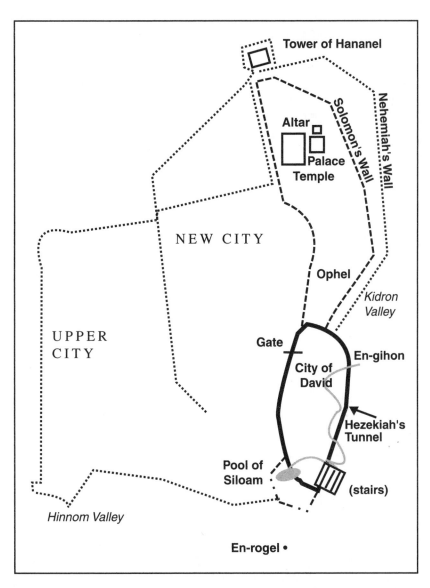

Boundaries of the City of David and the City of Jerusalem in Solomon's Time and in Nehemiah's Time

ANNOUNCEMENT OF JUDGMENT: In 1:21-25 the sinful situation is described with imagery, first of prostitution, then of precious metal. In each case the image describes the evil that Isaiah addresses. Prostitution destroys marital relationships, and contamination of silver results in a worthless product. Likewise, faithlessness is at the heart of other sins: murder, theft, bribery, lack of concern for the vulnerable. The actual announcement of judgment continues the second image: "I will turn my hand against you; I will smelt away your dross as with lye and remove all your alloy" (1:25). This announcement is followed immediately by a proclamation of salvation, joined so seamlessly to what precedes that we almost miss its change of tone. The Lord promises to restore the original leaders, who in turn will restore righteousness and faithfulness to their city.

The oracle in 8:5-8 opens with a description of the sinful situation, expressed through the metaphor of water: the people have refused the gentle water of the Siloam stream from the Gihon spring; in other words, the protection of the Lord, and instead are cowering in fear before the human rulers Rezin of Syria and Pekah, son of Remaliah. The actual announcement of judgment continues the water metaphor: the torrential flood of Assyrian conquest will inundate the land of Judah.

- The announcement of judgment in 3:16-26 ridicules the empty lives of the women of Jerusalem by mocking their manners and their finery. How would you rewrite this announcement to address an inclusive audience?

- In 9:8-12 and 13-21 what sins are named, and what judgment is announced against them?

- What images do you find in the announcement of judgment in 30:8-14?

The announcement of judgment against Assyria in 10:12-19 begins with the naming of the evil in v. 12: the pride of the Assyrian king leads to arrogant self-sufficiency. The judgment is then elaborated in both literal and figurative descriptions: literally, sickness will afflict the troops. Figuratively, fire will consume a forest until only a remnant is left. This comparison of the remnant to the aftermath of a fire connects this announcement with Isaiah's call (6:13).

- Chapter 13–23 contain words of judgment against what other foreign nations? Locate these places on a map. Note the specific condemnations of the different nations, and the sins that cause these condemnations.

WOE ORACLE: After the Song of the Vineyard in 5:1-7 the woe oracle in vv. 8-10 begins with the characteristic word "Woe" (the *NRSV* uses "Ah"). It then describes the greedy landowners who accumulate so much land and so many houses that they end up alone on their vast holdings. The result will be desolation: uninhabited houses and unproductive land.

- What evils do the woe oracles in 5:11-13, 18-24 condemn? What will be the consequences of those evils?

- In 10:1-4, 5-11 what evils do the woe oracles condemn?

CONVERSATION BETWEEN ISAIAH AND AHAZ: In 7:10-25 Isaiah and Ahaz converse. This section can be set historically during the Syro-Ephraimite crisis because the names of several kings are given: Rezin of Damascus and Pekah of Israel, as well as Ahaz and Isaiah (see the discussion of the Syro-Ephraimite crisis in the historical section of Chapter 3 above). Ahaz feared that the allies Syria and Israel would succeed in attacking Jerusalem, so he turned for protection to Assyria. This background information is given in 7:1-3, immediately before the words of salvation in vv. 4-9, which we will discuss below. The Lord sends Isaiah to talk to Ahaz and discourage him from counting on Assyria, assuring him that human alliances cannot substitute for trust in God.

Isaiah instructs Ahaz to ask God for a sign that will reassure him of divine protection, but Ahaz refuses to ask. He uses the excuse that such a request would be tempting God. To appreciate the lack of faith Ahaz's words express we can recall the numerous signs given throughout the Old Testament as reassurance to people God commissions. Moses is given signs in Exod 3:12, 20 and 4:2-5, 6-8, 9. Isaiah is given a sign of cleansing in 6:6-7. We will see that Jeremiah, too, is given a sign. Ahaz is invited to request any sign he chooses, but he refuses. Then Isaiah responds that the Lord will give the sign of a pregnant woman who will bear a son to be named "God With Us." He goes on to explain to Ahaz that by the time the child is able to make decisions Israel and Syria will be defeated by Assyria.

Then, in vv. 18-25, Isaiah elaborates on the consequences of the sign of Immanuel. Four are given, each beginning with the formula "On that day," in vv. 18, 20, 21, and 23. The first two use symbols to illustrate the

Lord's actions on behalf of the people of Judah. In vv. 18-19 the fly and the bee refer to the rulers of Egypt and Assyria, elaborating on v. 17. Verse 20 uses the image of a razor to indicate that the Lord will use the Assyrian king as a divine instrument of destruction. The shaving of hair was a way of humiliating captives. Verses 21-22 refer to the shortage of food that will result from the Assyrian occupation, and vv. 23-25 describe the desolation the land will experience.

Various suggestions have been made as to the identity of the pregnant woman: for example, Isaiah's wife, Ahaz's wife, or a woman who happened to be passing by as Ahaz and Isaiah were speaking. We do not know if any of these is the correct identification. What we do know is that the child to be born represents hope for the future. Life will continue under the Lord's protection throughout all the suffering the people will soon endure.

WORDS OF SALVATION: Isaiah of Jerusalem adapts this form, often implying rather than expressly articulating the divine purpose. For example, in 7:4-9 the announcement begins with the messenger formula, "Then the Lord said to Isaiah, 'Go out to meet Ahaz, you and your son Shear-jashub, at the end of the conduit of the upper pool on the highway to the Fuller's Field, and say to him. . . .'" It then alludes in vv. 4-6 to the people's fear of King Rezin of Syria and King Pekah of Israel, who threaten to destroy Jerusalem. The Lord offers assurance that the two rulers are mere humans and therefore will not endure. The conclusion of the announcement is not so much a statement of divine purpose as a divine reminder to hold fast to faith in God. The names of the rulers make it possible to associate these words with the Syro-Ephraimite crisis.

- What saving assurance is offered in 4:2-6?

- In 10:20-27 what promise of salvation is made to those who survive?

- What is promised in 11:1-5? How does the tree imagery relate back to Isaiah's call in chapter 6? What actions will the "shoot" perform on behalf of the people?

In 11:6-9 the prophet paints an idyllic picture of an ideal time when improbable relationships will thrive. All of this will be possible because "the earth will be full of the knowledge of the Lord as the waters cover the sea." These words are a portrayal of salvation, that is, a depiction of

"Guns into Plowshares" Monument, Washington, D.C.
Esther K. Augsburger and Michael D. Augsburger, Sculptors

a future that will be dramatically different from the present but that is not related to a particular moment in history.

- What specific improbable relationships are named in 11:6-9? What one human image does the portrayal include?

PROPHETIC INSTRUCTION: Isaiah 8:19–9:6 instructs the people not to consult various mediums or engage in other superstitious actions. This kind of action will only bring dissatisfaction and confusion.

- In 8:19–9:6 what specific superstitious acts are forbidden? How does the passage make fun of those who engage in superstitious acts? What will be the result of the superstitious acts? In contrast, what will be the situation of those who "were in anguish"?

ACCOUNT OF SYMBOLIC ACT: In 8:1-4 the Lord instructs Isaiah to write "Belonging to Maher-shalal-hash-baz" on a large tablet, in the presence of witnesses. Then Isaiah and his wife have a child whom the Lord instructs them to name Maher-shalal-hash-baz, interpreted as "The spoil speeds, the prey hastens." The symbolic meaning of the name is a warning of the impending Assyrian destruction of Syria and Israel (the Northern Kingdom). This warning is one of several signs offered to assure the people of divine protection for Jerusalem and Judah in the face of the imminent Assyrian onslaught. They, and particularly their king, Ahaz, can count on divine help; there is no need to rely on treaties with neighboring peoples.

HYMN OF THANKSGIVING: Isaiah 12:1-6 is a hymn of thanksgiving for the Lord's comfort and salvation. It is divided into two parts, each beginning with a word of instruction. In v. 1 the instruction is given to one person: "You will say in that day," followed by praise of God for turning away the divine anger and offering comfort, then an expression of trust in the God of strength and salvation. Then in v. 3 an instruction is given to many, using the same expression, "You will say in that day," but in the plural. This part offers thanks and praise for divine deeds and divine greatness. This hymn, because of its position in chapter 12, summarizes the first eleven chapters of the book and glorifies God whose words and actions those chapters report. It ends with the title "Holy One of Israel," recalling the words of the seraphs, "Holy, holy, holy" in chapter 6. We will look again at the motif of God's holiness below.

- In 9:1-7, for what does the hymn give thanks? How might vv. 6-7 relate to 7:14?

Rhetorical Features

RHETORICAL QUESTIONS: Isaiah uses this technique to challenge his listeners to look at themselves and their unfaithful, self-destructive ways. For example, in 1:5 the prophet asks the sinful nation (v. 4), "Why do you seek further beatings? Why do you continue to rebel?" Later in the same chapter he poses another question: "What to me is the multitude of your sacrifices? . . . When you come to appear before me, who asked this from your hand?" (1:11-12). The first question highlights the counter-productivity of the people's sins of unfaithfulness. The second and third questions condemn the emptiness of the people's worship, which is negated by their evil dealings with one another. In contrast, Isaiah admonishes in 1:16-17, "Wash yourselves; make yourselves clean; remove the evil of your doings from before my eyes; cease to do evil, learn to do good; seek justice, rescue the oppressed, defend the orphan, plead for the widow."

- In chapter 10, how do the rhetorical questions in vv. 3-4, 8-9, 15 enhance Isaiah's message?

- What other rhetorical questions do you find in Isaiah 1–39? How do they enhance the prophet's teaching?

QUOTATION OF THE LISTENERS: Isaiah puts words into the mouths of his audience, sometimes describing the present situation and at other times anticipating the future. For instance, in 5:19 the prophet attributes words to those who mock God and divine actions: "Let him make haste, let him speed his work that we may see it; let the plan of the Holy One of Israel hasten to fulfillment, that we may know it!" This taunt by sinners suggests that if God is truly able, God will act immediately on behalf of the people. Since divine actions come, in reality, in God's time, the taunters blame the wait on God's ineffectiveness and inability to care for the people.

In 9:10 Isaiah quotes the proud and arrogant: "The bricks have fallen, but we will build with dressed stones; the sycamores have been cut down, but we will put cedars in their place." The quotation expresses the denial that prevails among the proud. They glibly claim that even though houses built of bricks and sycamores have been destroyed, the people will build palaces with even better materials: dressed stones and cedars.

- In chapter 21, how do the quotations of the audience in vv. 8-9, 12 enhance Isaiah's message?

• What other quotations do you find, and how do they enhance Isaiah's teaching?

PERSONIFICATION OF NATURE: In 14:8 Isaiah creates human speech for the cypresses, who say to the cedars of Lebanon: "Since you were laid low, no one comes to cut us down." A few verses later, in vv. 13-14, Isaiah creates speech for the Day Star: "I will ascend to heaven; I will raise my throne above the stars of God; I will sit on the mount of assembly on the heights of Zaphon; I will ascend to the tops of the clouds; I will make myself like the Most High." Just as trees and the Day Star are not really able to speak, likewise human beings are limited to human actions, contrary to their arrogant talk. These verses are part of a taunt song, originally directed against a king and here addressed to the king either of Assyria or of Babylon. Whichever king is meant, and hence whichever date can be assigned to these words (eighth or sixth century), the quotations offer a graphic example of arrogance overstepping its boundaries.

• What is personified in 23:4? How does this personification enhance Isaiah's message? What other examples of personification of nature do you find in Isaiah 1–39?

PUN: In 5:7 the meaning of the verse depends on the similar sounds in two pairs of words. If we insert the relevant words in Hebrew we have "he expected justice *(mišpat),* but saw bloodshed *(mišpaḥ);* righteousness *(ṣedaqah),* but heard a cry *(ṣeʾaqah)*!" Then the meaning becomes clear: he expected one thing and received something that, on the surface, seemed quite similar, while in reality it was completely different. Instead of the two virtues extolled throughout the Old Testament (justice and righteousness) he found harm in the form of bloodshed and a cry.

KEY WORDS: Several key words that occur throughout the prophetic books are used frequently in Isaiah 1–39. The words *mišpat* (justice or judgment) and *ṣedeq* and *ṣedaqah* (both of which mean "righteousness") occur frequently, often together. For example, 1:27 assures, "Zion shall be redeemed by justice, and those in her who repent, by righteousness." In 5:7 the pun juxtaposes the words "justice" and "righteousness." Both these instances emphasize the importance of justice and righteousness in the people's dealings with one another. In 9:7 the two words appear together again, "He will establish and uphold it with justice and righteousness from this time onward and forevermore." In this example "he" is the child born to be king (see v. 6). The two key virtues characterize his rule, which will be peaceful because he will govern with justice and righteousness.

- In 3:14, whom does Isaiah condemn for lack of justice to the vulnerable? Compare and contrast the meaning here with 5:7.

- Note the juxtaposition of the two words in 1:21. What contrast between past and present do they express?

- According to 5:16, what is the outcome of the practice of justice and righteousness?

- In 10:1-2, who is accused of injustice? Of what injustice?

- According to 11:4-5, who will practice righteousness?

- Note the juxtaposition of these two key words in 16:5. What assurance do these words offer to their listeners?

- What insight into judgment and righteousness do we get from 26:7-9? from 32:1–33:5?

Another key word in Isaiah is *'emunah* (faithfulness). This word is related to the word "Amen!" which means "I believe!" At several points in Isaiah it appears in conjunction with the two words discussed above. For example, it is listed in 11:5 along with righteousness as a characteristic of the shoot to come from the stump of Jesse.

- In 26:2, who is characterized by righteousness and faith?

- In 33:6 the *NRSV* uses the word "stability" for *emunah*. What insight into all three words—stability, justice, and righteousness—do you find in 33:5-6?

Isaiah's Message

Themes

We mentioned in our discussion of Micah that many themes appear in both books. In fact, we noticed that one passage appears almost verbatim in Isa 2:2-4 and Mic 4:1-3. In *NRSV* the Isaiah version reads:

> In days to come the mountain of the LORD's house shall be established as the highest of the mountains, and shall be raised above the hills; all the nations shall stream to it. Many peoples shall come and say, "Come, let us go up to the mountain of the LORD, to the house

of the God of Jacob; that he may teach us his ways and that we may walk in his paths." For out of Zion shall go forth instruction, and the word of the Lord from Jerusalem. He shall judge between the nations, and shall arbitrate for many peoples; they shall beat their swords into plowshares, and their spears into pruning hooks; nation shall not lift up sword against nation, neither shall they learn war any more.

We will look first at those themes common to both books, then at those particular to Isaiah.

THE SWEEP OF HISTORY: Like Micah, Isaiah portrays history as the arena of divine action on behalf of all. This understanding is evident in the quotation above, which portrays all nations streaming to the Lord's mountain in order to learn to walk in the ways of the Lord. It permeates the conversation between Isaiah and Ahaz in which Isaiah, the divine messenger, assures Ahaz in 7:17 and 8:7 that the Assyrian king is the Lord's instrument to accomplish the divine purpose. The theme underlies the portrayal of salvation in 11:6-9 as well, offering assurance that all of creation will live in harmony because all will know the Lord.

GOD OF ALL NATIONS: This theme is closely related to the previous one. The Lord is God not only of all time, but also of all people, as the quotation about people streaming to the Lord's mountain suggests. There is a slight difference between the two themes, though. Throughout the sweep of history God uses even those who know and worship other deities to bring about the divine purpose. But in contrast, both Micah and Isaiah promise that all will know the Lord. We see this sense in such examples as 11:10, as well as in the quotation above. We will see this theme developed further in Second Isaiah (chs. 40–55).

- In 11:10-16, what evidence do you find of the divine sway over all of creation and all of history?

Isaiah also includes some themes that are not in Micah. These include:

HOLY ONE OF ISRAEL: This title for God appears frequently throughout Isaiah: twelve times in First Isaiah, eleven in Second Isaiah, and twice in Third Isaiah. It is very rarely used elsewhere in the Old Testament (but see Hos 11:9, 12). Ezekiel also emphasizes God's holiness, as we will see in our discussion of that book.

For Israel the essence of divine holiness is closely related to divine Otherness; that is, God is like no other being. It also connotes divine supremacy over all creatures and total divine freedom from ritual contamination, which might result from contact with anything unclean or sinful. For instance, in chapter 6 Isaiah hears the seraphs calling "Holy, holy, holy is the Lord of hosts." The threefold repetition of "holy" calls attention to that divine attribute. The very building trembles and fills with smoke at the words, creating an out-of-the-ordinary atmosphere that conveys the otherness of God. A sense of unworthiness overcomes Isaiah because he is in the presence of God, but he experiences himself as unclean and therefore unworthy to be in the divine presence. The seraph touches Isaiah's lips with a burning coal, removing his uncleanness and making him worthy to be in the presence of the divine Other. This incident shows the close relationship between the motifs of divine otherness and ritual purity in Isaiah.

We will see that throughout the prophetic books elements of the prophetic call often foreshadow aspects of the prophet's life and work and highlight themes that recur throughout the book. Here the repetition of the word "holy" and the interplay of the motifs of otherness and ritual purity accent those dimensions of Isaiah.

For Isaiah true worship and humble living involve acknowledging one's complete dependence on God, who is holy and wholly other and yet at the same time is actively present among us. When Judah is faced with the threat of invasion from Israel and Syria, Isaiah cautions Ahaz against entering into an agreement with Assyria because human alliances are ultimately insufficient. Isaiah pleads with Ahaz: "If you do not stand firm in faith, you shall not stand at all" (7:9).

- How does 1:18-20 express the need for complete dependence on God?

In contrast, not to recognize these divine qualities is a sin of pride, of not acknowledging one's relationship of complete dependence on God. We see this contrast in 10:20: "On that day the remnant of Israel and the survivors of the house of Jacob will no more lean on the one who struck them, but will lean on the LORD, the Holy One of Israel, in truth."

- In 8:11-15 and 17:7-8 what contrast do you find that involves the Holy One of Israel?

- In 30:8-11, 12-14, 15-17 how does the topic of a rebellious people develop around the title Holy One of Israel? What contrasts does the entire passage, 30:8-17, contain?

Israel: For Isaiah the terms "Israel" and "house of Jacob" seem to be religious terms for "people of Yhwh" rather than designations for the Northern Kingdom or even for both the northern and southern kingdoms. Isaiah uses the terms when admonishing and pleading with the people to return to faithfulness to the Lord. They highlight the relational quality of Isaiah's message: he counsels faithfulness not to a set of rules, but to the Lord who provides for the people. In 2:5-6 Isaiah accuses the people of abandoning the ways of their ancestors and pleads: "Come, let us walk in the light of the Lord!" In 8:17 Isaiah again calls attention to the relational character of religion, observing that the Lord "is hiding his face from the house of Jacob."

- How does 29:22-24 highlight the relationship between the Lord and the people?

This relationship is founded on the covenant between God and the people, but Isaiah never uses that term in the book. He does, however, call the people to live in grateful response to all that God has done for them. For instance, in the Song of the Vineyard in 5:1-7 he underscores the tender care the Lord has given the people, comparing it to the work of tending a vineyard. In spite of all the careful nurturing of the vineyard, it yielded wild grapes. Then the Lord asks the people: "What more might I have done for my vineyard?" before announcing the destroying punishment. At the end of the parable Isaiah identifies the Lord's vineyard as the house of Israel and the people of Judah who respond to divine care, not with justice but with violence.

- How does 1:2 focus on the relationship between the Lord and the people?

Zion: Another term Isaiah frequently uses is Zion, which appears twenty-eight times in chapters 1–39, eleven times in 40–55, and six times in 56–66. The word stands for Jerusalem as the religious center; for example, "For out of Zion shall go forth instruction, and the word of the Lord from Jerusalem" (2:3). Zion is seen as the dwelling place of the Lord, as in "See, I and the children whom the Lord has given me are signs and portents in Israel from the Lord of hosts, who dwells on Mount Zion" (8:18). The term is often paired with the word Jerusalem in parallel phrases; for example, "Then the moon will be abashed, and the sun ashamed; for the Lord of hosts will reign on Mount Zion and in Jerusalem, and before his elders he will manifest his glory" (24:23). The use of this special religious name for Jerusalem accentuates the holiness and otherness of the Lord who lives there: Jerusalem is not merely the political capital; it is the dwelling place of the Lord.

Several times in the book the term "daughter Zion" is used. It calls attention to the special relationship between the Lord and the inhabitants of Jerusalem. We see this, for instance, in 1:8: "And daughter Zion is left like a booth in a vineyard, like a shelter in a cucumber field, like a besieged city."

The city that is the dwelling place of the Lord and the religious capital of the people serves as a model of righteousness and justice, especially for the vulnerable members of the community. We find this idea in 14:32: "What will one answer the messengers of the nation? 'The LORD has founded Zion, and the needy among his people will find refuge in her.'"

- What connotations of the term Zion do you find in 4:3-5; 10:12; 12:6; 16:1; 18:7; 28:16?

MONARCHY AS DIVINE INSTRUMENT OF SALVATION: In his call, Isaiah reports, "I have seen the King, the Lord of hosts!" His use of the title "king" highlights the importance of kings, and of the monarchy, for the well-being of Israel. We have observed that God sent Isaiah to speak with King Ahaz during the Syro-Ephraimite crisis. Isaiah's instruction to the king at that time was to trust in the Lord rather than in human political alliances, as we saw in chapter 7. Had the king trusted in God, his trust would have mediated salvation for all the Israelite people. Isaiah conversed with King Hezekiah as well, offering him divine words of encouragement and guidance. For example,

> When the servants of King Hezekiah came to Isaiah, Isaiah said to them, "Say to your master, 'Thus says the LORD: Do not be afraid because of the words that you have heard, with which the servants of the king of Assyria have reviled me. I myself will put a spirit in him, so that he shall hear a rumor, and return to his own land; I will cause him to fall by the sword in his own land'" (37:5-7).

Through this message Isaiah assures Hezekiah that the Lord is with him, using him as the instrument by which the Lord cares for the people.

- What insights do the following verses offer into the monarchy as divine instrument of salvation: 32:1-4; 37:21-25?

HOPE FOR A MESSIAH: This theme recurs throughout many of the prophetic books. In Isaiah it is closely related to the theme of monarchy, which Isaiah sees as the divine instrument of salvation. The term "messiah" is the English translation of the Hebrew word *mešiaḥ*, or anointed one. In ancient Israel anointing was the rite by which priests were ordained, holy places were consecrated (Exod 40:10-15; Lev 8:10-12), and kings were installed (1 Sam 15:1; 2 Sam 2:4; 1 Kings 5:1). In David's time the monarch was referred to as "the Lord's anointed" (1 Sam 24:6-10; 26:9-16; 2 Sam 1:14-16).

Isaiah records the Lord's unsuccessful efforts to guide King Ahaz along a path of faithfulness to the Lord through the intervention of the prophet. When it became clear that Ahaz would not heed Isaiah's advice he used various means to direct the people's attention to a future king, very likely Ahaz's successor Hezekiah, with the promise that he would rule in a spirit of justice and concern for the vulnerable. We see this, for example, in 7:10-17; 9:1-7; 11:1-5; 33:17-22.

This theme continued to develop throughout the prophetic books. We will trace this development in our study of later books, particularly those composed after King Jehoiachin was imprisoned in Babylon and the Davidic line seemed to have been broken. Hope for a good king gradually looked farther and farther into the future, even outside history through miraculous divine intervention. But these passages in Isaiah have assumed special importance in Christian communities, who began to associate them with Jesus of Nazareth. While we recognize the applicability of the words to Christ (from the Greek translation of *mešiaḥ*), we also understand that the words were originally spoken to encourage the people of Jerusalem in the late eighth century as they struggled with the question of how to be faithful to God in the face of the Assyrian expansion. There is some thought that 9:2-7 was composed during the Exile and expressed the hope that focused on Zerubbabel.

The Pontifical Biblical Commission has assisted us in understanding how to differentiate between original meanings and later Christian interpretations in its 2001 document, "The Jewish People and Their Sacred Scriptures in the Christian Bible." (See bibliographic information, p. 32.) The Commission members explain:

> Although the Christian reader is aware that the internal dynamism of the Old Testament finds its goal in Jesus, this is a retrospective perception whose point of departure is not in the text as such, but in the events of the New Testament proclaimed by the apostolic

> preaching. It cannot be said, therefore, that Jews do not see what has been proclaimed in the text, but that the Christian, in the light of Christ and in the Spirit, discovers in the text an additional meaning that was hidden there.

This explanation highlights the importance of reading the text with its ancient audience in order to understand the message the prophets delivered to their listeners. Christian interpretations are an additional layer of meaning that fits the early Christian efforts to describe Jesus by referring Old Testament passages to him. It was common in the Greco-Roman world to look to earlier writings as "foretellings" of the coming of famous people, and the early Christian use of Isaian passages to describe Jesus was no exception.

Isaiah's Meaning for Us Today

Isaiah in the Lectionary

Of all the prophets, Isaiah appears most frequently in the lectionary. Chapters 1–39 appear in the Sunday readings seven times in Year A, twice in Year B, and twice in Year C. In the weekday lectionary many of the readings are used in both Years I and II, and in addition during Year II six readings appear in the cycle of continuous readings. Unfortunately, these readings do not, for the most past, express the heart of Isaiah's message. Rather, many of them are messianic passages that Christian communities have retrospectively applied to Christ. We will look at these readings and at how we might interpret them in a way that respects both their original meanings and their place in the Christian lectionary.

First, a look at the Sunday readings from Isaiah. In Year A the readings for all four Sundays of Advent are from First Isaiah. On the First Sunday of Advent Isa 2:1-5 promises that Jerusalem will become the center of divine activity on behalf of the people. It is paired with Matt 24:37-44 in *LM* (vv. 36-44 in *RCL*). This gospel reading underscores the importance of watchfulness, because it is not known when the Son of Man will come. Both of these readings set the Advent tone of watchful expectation. On the Second Sunday of Advent Isa 11:1-10 is paired with Mark 3:1-12 in both the *LM* and the *RCL*. The Isaian passage announces to the eighth-century Jerusalemites the coming of a new king who would care for the people in a spirit of justice and compassion. The early Christian community understood it retrospectively as a prediction of the coming of Christ, hence its place in the lectionary in early Advent. The Matthean reading describes Jesus' cure of the man with a withered hand and the subsequent eagerness of the crowd to call him Son of God. In this context we recognize the Christian application of the Isaian words to Christ, whose miraculous cures encouraged the crowd to identify Him as the hoped-for Messiah, but we keep in mind that this interpretation is retrospective on the part of the Christian community; the words were a source of comfort and encouragement to the eighth-century community who hoped that a new king in their own time would rule with justice and compassion. Both readings describe the characteristics of good leaders.

On the Third Sunday of Advent the First Reading is 35:1-6a, 10 in *LM* and 35:1-10 in *RCL*. It describes an ideal time outside of history when the world will be at peace. It is paired with Matt 11:2-11, the account of John the Baptist's question from his prison cell about whether Jesus, who is identified in the passage as the Messiah, is the awaited one. Both readings highlight the result of divine presence among us.

On the Fourth Sunday of Advent the First Reading is 7:10-14 in *LM* and 7:10-16 in *RCL*, Ahaz's opportunity to ask for a sign, his refusal, and Isaiah's announcement of the coming birth of a child as the sign of divine protection. Just as we see in the reading for the Second Sunday, here again we have a pericope that the early Christian community understood retrospectively as a prediction of Christ's coming. Again it is important to keep in mind that Isaiah's words were spoken to the people of Jerusalem, offering them hope in the form of a child to be born, signaling that a new generation would soon begin and Jerusalem would be spared from the onslaught of its eighth-century enemies. This reading is paired with Matt 1:18-24 in *LM* and 1:18-25 in *RCL*, Matthew's account of the birth of Jesus. Both readings focus on the hope for the future that the birth of a child represents.

In all three years the First Reading for Midnight Mass is 9:1-6 in *LM* and 9:2-7 in *RCL*. This, too, is a messianic reading the early Christians applied to Christ. Before this retrospective interpretation was attached to it, the reading offered hope for a new king who would rule in the spirit of justice and compassion the people expected from their rulers. The gospel reading is Luke 2:1-14 in *LM*, with the option of continuing to v. 20 in *RCL*. This is Luke's account of the birth of Christ. Again both readings address the hope we place in good leaders.

In Ordinary Time of Year A, 9:1-4 (8:23–9:3 in *NAB*) is read on the Third Sunday. This reading, a shortened form of the reading for Midnight Mass, is paired with Matt 4:12-17 (optional vv. 18-23) in *LM* and 4:12-23 in *RCL*.

This reading from the beginning of Jesus' ministry in Galilee quotes Isa 9:1-2. The pairing offers the homilist an opportunity to explain the early Christian tendency to use scriptural language to describe Jesus. (The Scriptures of the early Christians were what we today call the Old Testament.) That explanation would provide the occasion to talk about the original as well as the early Christian understandings of the Isaiah passage, and also about our ongoing efforts to interpret Scripture in light of current issues.

On the Twenty-first Sunday in Ordinary Time 22:19-23 is read in the *LM*, but a different reading is assigned in the *RCL*. This Isaian passage promises that a descendant of David will be appointed by God as ruler and will be given the key of the house of David. The reading is another passage with a messianic message, understood by early Christians as applying to Christ but originally understood by the people of Jerusalem as an assurance of divine protection in their own time. It is paired with Matt 16:13-20, Peter's declaration that Jesus is the Messiah followed by Jesus promising him the keys of the kingdom of heaven. Both readings refer to the giving of keys as a symbol of office. This similarity offers an opportunity to highlight the responsibilities of leaders and the need for all of us to pray for them in the exercise of their responsibilities.

The First Reading for the Twenty-seventh Sunday in Ordinary Time is 5:1-7, the Song of the Vineyard, in *LM*. The same reading is one of the options for the day in *RCL*. It is paired with Matt 21:33-43 in *LM*, 21:33-46 in *RCL*, Matthew's parable of the vineyard. This set of readings offers the kind of opportunity we have suggested above, of focusing on the similarities in the two readings.

On the following Sunday, the Twenty-eighth of Ordinary Time, 25:6-10a in *LM* and 25:1-9 as an option in *RCL* promises that the Lord will care for all from Mount Zion. The gospel reading is Matt 22:1-10 with optional vv. 11-14 in *LM*, and in *RCL* 22:1-14, the parable of the wedding banquet to which the invited guests did not come, so the king's slaves invited all the people they could find in the streets. Both of these passages address a leader's concern for the followers who depend on wise and just leadership.

In both Years B and C there is only one Sunday reading from Isaiah. In Year B, on the Twenty-third Sunday of the Year, 35:4-7a is paired with Mark 7:31-37 in *LM*. In *RCL* the Isaiah passage is one option, and is paired with Mark 7:24-37. The Isaiah passage promises that those who are blind, deaf, and mute will be cured. The gospel describes Jesus' cure of a person who is deaf and mute. The pairing of the two passages illustrates the

Christian tendency to look at the Old Testament as promise and the New as fulfillment, a relationship that sees the meaning of the Old Testament in relationship to the New rather than in its own right. When working with this pair of readings one might call attention to the common theme of the healing power of God.

In Year C, 6:1-2a, 3-8, the call of Isaiah, is read on the Fifth Sunday of the Year. The *RCL* includes the entire passage, 6:1-8, adding the option of vv. 9-13. The gospel in both lectionaries is Luke 5:1-11, the call of Peter, James, and John. This pair of readings is easy to discuss from the point of view of divine calls to all people, inviting us to follow God in faithfulness.

In the *Weekday Lectionary* Isaiah is read during the First Week of Advent in both Years I and II. On Monday, 2:1-5 describes the time of peace that will originate on Mount Zion, and Matt 8:5-11 recounts the cure of the centurion's servant. (Alternatively, in Year A in the Sunday *LM*, 4:2-6 describes the restoration of Jerusalem after its cleansing punishment.) On Tuesday, 11:1-10 announces the coming of a new king in the same reading as for the following Sunday, and Luke 10:21-24 describes the relationship between Father and Son. On Wednesday, 25:6-10a, the same reading as on the Twenty-eighth Sunday of the Year in Year A, promises the Lord's care for all from Mount Zion. That day's gospel, Matt 15:29-37, recounts the feeding of the crowd. The readings for the next several days carry similar messages, celebrating the victory of those who trust in the Lord. These are: on Thursday, 26:1-6 with Matt 7:21, 24-27; Friday, 29:17-24 with Matt 9:27-31; and Saturday, 30:19-21, 23-26 with Matt 9:35–10:1, 5a, 6-8. On the Second Monday, 35:1-10 is a slightly longer form of the reading for the following Sunday, promising a world at peace. That day's gospel is Luke 5:17-26, the healing of the paralytic man.

During the weekdays of Lent in both Years I and II, 1:10, 16-20 is read on Tuesday of the Second Week. This reading gets to the heart of Isaiah's plea to the people to live up to the obligations of their relationship with God. It is paired with Matt 23:1-12, about the hypocrisy of the scribes and Pharisees.

On the weekdays of Year II a series of readings appears, beginning on the Fourteenth Saturday with 6:1-8, the account of Isaiah's call, which appears in slightly abbreviated form on the Fifth Sunday of Ordinary Time in Year C. Then during the Fifteenth Week the readings become semi-continuous: on Monday is 1:10-17, a condemnation of empty worship; on Tuesday, 7:1-9, a promise of divine protection during the Syro-Ephraimite war; on Wednesday, 10:5-7, 13b-16 against Assyria; on

Thursday, 26:7-9, 12, 16-19, words of confidence in God; and on Friday, 38:1-6, 21-22, 7-8 recounts Hezekiah's illness, his prayer for help, and the divine promise of delivery given to Hezekiah through Isaiah.

In the Jewish community First Isaiah appears in three weekly Sabbath portions: 27:6–28:13; 29:22-23 is paired with Exod 1:1–6:1; Isa 6:1–7:6; 9:5 (6:1-13 in the Sephardi ritual) with Exod 18:1–20:23; and Isa 1:1-27 with Deut 1:1–3:22. Additionally, on the Eighth Day of Passover Isa 10:32–12:6 is read with Deut 15:19–16:17 and Num 28:19-25.

First Isaiah's significance for our daily life:

- Express "they shall beat their swords into plowshares" (2:4) in contemporary terminology.

- Discuss a contemporary situation to which the words in 10:1-2 might apply. Then select another passage in Isaiah that can apply to a contemporary situation; explain.

- Prepare a lesson for a high school class, a Bible Study group, an adult faith formation group, or some other group, in which you explain the importance for Christians to understand the original meanings as well as the Christian interpretation of Old Testament passages such as Isaiah 7, 9, and 11. Include in your explanation specific information about Isaiah 7, 9, and 11.

- Prepare a schema for homilies during Advent of Year A in which you focus on the season of Advent, the original meanings of the Isaiah passages, and also their meanings in relation to the gospel readings.

Passages for study:

    1:10-20

    9:8-21

    10:1-11

For Further Reading

Barstad, Hans M. *A Way in the Wilderness.* Manchester: University of Manchster Press, 1989.

Barton, John. *Isaiah 1–39.* OTG. Sheffield: Sheffield Academic Press, 1995.

Berrigan, Daniel. *Isaiah: Spirit of Courage, Gift of Tears.* Minneapolis: Fortress, 1996.

Blank, Sheldon H. *Prophetic Faith in Isaiah.* Detroit: Wayne State University Press, 1958.

Clements, Ronald E. *Isaiah 1–39.* NCBC. Grand Rapids: Eerdmans, 1980.

———. *Isaiah and the Deliverance of Jerusalem: A Study of the Interpretation of Prophecy in the Old Testament.* Sheffield: Department of Biblical Studies, University of Sheffield, 1980.

Conrad, Edgar W. *Reading Isaiah.* OBT. Minneapolis: Fortress, 1991.

Davies, Eryl. *Prophecy and Ethics: Isaiah and the Ethical Traditions of Israel.* Sheffield: JSOT Press, 1981.

Evans, Craig A. *To See and Not Perceive: Isaiah 6.9-10 in Early Jewish and Christian Interpretation.* Sheffield: Sheffield Academic Press, 1989.

Sawyer, John F. *The Fifth Gospel: Isaiah in the History of Christianity.* Cambridge and New York: Cambridge University Press, 1996.

Schmitt, John. *Isaiah and His Interpreters.* New York: Paulist, 1986.

Thompson, Michael E. W. *Situation and Theology: Old Testament Interpretations of the Syro-Ephraimite War.* Sheffield: Almond Press, 1982.

Wildberger, Hans. *Isaiah 1–12: A Continental Commentary.* Trans. Thomas H. Trapp. Minneapolis: Fortress, 1991.

Chapter Five

The Seventh-Century Prophets
Zephaniah, Nahum, and Habakkuk

The seventh century saw the Assyrian empire reach the height of its power throughout the ancient Near East. Then, in the 620s, a new power, the Neo-Babylonian empire, began to threaten the Assyrian hegemony. Four prophetic books are set during this period: Jeremiah, Zephaniah, Nahum, and Habakkuk. Jeremiah and Zephaniah are associated historically with the seventh century in their superscriptions, and Nahum's superscription sets it geographically in Nineveh. Habakkuk does not identify its historical or geographical setting, but its message fits the tension and instability of the time and so is generally thought to have originated in the seventh century. In this chapter we will look at the three seventh-century minor prophets, then in the next chapter we will study Jeremiah.

Background Information

Historical and Geographical Setting

The seventh century proved to be a very unstable and uncertain time in the Ancient Near East. Assyria's expansionist activities, begun in the previous century, continued at a slower pace. The Assyrian King Sennacherib was killed in a palace uprising in 681 (2 Kings 19:37). His successor Esarhaddon (680–669) conquered Egypt in 671. He was succeeded by Ashurbanipal (668–627), whose long reign was marked by internal and external pressures; for example, Egypt regained its independence from Assyria. The small entities of Judah, Moab, Ammon, Edom, and the Philistine kingdoms remained vassals of the Assyrian empire in spite of a show of independence against Assyria by Judah around 629. At Ashurbanipal's death the Assyrian empire fell into rapid decline.

Babylonia began its ascendancy under Nabopolassar, who became king in 625 and ruled until 605. Relentless in his expansion of the empire, he conquered the Assyrian capital of Ashur in 614, the Assyrian city of Nineveh in 612, and the Egyptian city of Carchemish in 605, destroying the Assyrian empire and solidifying Babylonian domination of the Fertile Crescent. The smaller provinces, including Judah, were caught in the middle of the ongoing conflict. Judah became a victim of Babylonian ascendancy under Nabopolassar's successor Nebuchadnezzar, who ruled from 605 to 562.

In Judah, Hezekiah was succeeded by Manasseh (687–642), who sided with Babylon against the Assyrian Ashurbanipal. His reign is recorded in 2 Kings 20:21–21:18 and 2 Chr 32:33–33:20. Manasseh's son Amon (642–640) was assassinated, most likely in connection to the struggle between Egypt and Babylon (2 Kings 21:18-25; 2 Chr 33:20-25). Amon's son Josiah (640–609) became king at the age of eight. Throughout his reign he saw the disintegration of Assyria's power and the rise of Babylonia. The Bible is silent on the political effects of this turmoil. It does, however, discuss the ambitious religious reform over which Josiah presided. We will describe this below in the section on Religious Issues.

In 609, in the battle between Babylonia and Egypt at Megiddo, Josiah sided with Babylonia rather than with Egypt and Assyria. He was killed in the battle; his son Jehoahaz II (also called Shallum) ruled for three months in the year 609 until he was deposed by Egypt (2 Kings 23:30-34; 2 Chr 36:1-4). Another of Josiah's sons, Jehoiakim, (609–598) was appointed and controlled by Egypt (2 Kings 23:35–24:7; 2 Chr 36:4-8). Then in 605 Egypt was defeated at Carchemish, a city on the Euphrates, in an effort to assist Assyria against Babylonia; Jehoiakim now had a new master, Babylonia (2 Kings 24:7). In 600 Babylonia made its first attempt to take Jerusalem. Although this effort failed, the Babylonian push for land and power continued. During this time Jeremiah was particularly vehement in his condemnation of Jehoiakim's policies and positions, and the king in turn tried to silence the prophet (2 Kings 22:13-20; Jer 36:20-26).

Jehoiakim's son Jehoiachin reigned for three months in the year 597, until the Babylonians deported him along with members of his family, his court, and many of the kingdom's professional people (2 Kings 24:6-17; 25:27-30; 2 Chr 36:8-10). His loss of the throne of Judah marked the end of the Davidic succession (Jer 22:26-30). Then Josiah's third son Zedekiah (597–587) was appointed by Babylon (2 Kings 24:17–25:21; 2 Chr 36:11-21). Throughout his reign struggles continued between the pro- and anti-Babylonian inhabitants of Jerusalem.

By 587 Jerusalem could not hold out any longer. The Babylonians breached the walls of the city and took it over, deporting more Jerusalemites to Babylon. Zedekiah tried to flee but was taken into custody, forced to witness the execution of his sons, then blinded and taken into exile (2 Kings 25:6-7; Jer 52:9-11). The Babylonians appointed Gedaliah to govern those who remained in Judah (2 Kings 25:22-26). A faction in Jerusalem, suspecting Gedaliah of collaboration with the enemy, assassinated him. Many then fled to Egypt for safety. It is likely that Jeremiah was among those who fled.

The Socio-economic Situation

During the seventh century the socio-economic inequities of the eighth century continued to intensify, complicated by the international strife we discussed above. The prophets witnessed socio-economic excesses and injustices and spoke out vehemently against them. The Assyrian king Esarhaddon required vassal kings to supply building materials for his construction projects. In Judah, Jehoiakim built a new royal palace, squandering funds and using forced labor in his effort to aggrandize his home and therefore his standing (Jer 22:13-19). In addition, Egypt levied heavy tax burdens on the people.

Religious Issues

The religious issues the Bible describes are related to monotheism and idolatry. King Manasseh restored the shrines to local deities that had been suppressed under Hezekiah. Foreign cults, with their practices opposed to Yahwistic religion, flourished. Altars to foreign gods were even erected in the Temple. Because of his support of foreign cults 2 Kings calls Manasseh the worst king the people had ever known. In addition, Manasseh perpetrated violent injustice and practiced divination and magic, all of which were denounced by Jeremiah and Zephaniah (2 Kings 21:3-16; Jer 15:1-4; Zeph 1:4-9; 3:1-7).

Josiah undertook significant rebuilding and reform measures during his reign. According to 2 Kings 22:3–23:25 he was a religious reformer like Moses, who worked to eliminate syncretistic practices. An important event early in the reform was the finding of the Book of the Law, a scroll unearthed by one of the workers in the Temple. It is thought that the scroll contained part of what is today the book of Deuteronomy, perhaps Deuteronomy 12–26. Second Chronicles 34:1–35:19 considers Josiah a

priest-king, more like Samuel than Moses. It focuses on Josiah's rebuilding of the Temple rather than on the discovery of the scroll that is described in Jeremiah (2 Kings 21:26–23:30; 2 Chr 33:25–36:23). When
Assyria conquered territories it did not impose its religion on its victims;
however, it is reasonable to assume that some local elites adopted the
practices of their victors. It was those practices that Josiah worked to
bring to an end.

Examples of the desire for independence from Assyria under Josiah,
perhaps also under Hezekiah, include rules governing warfare in Deut
20:1-20, treaty formulations including curses in Deut 27:15-26; 28:15-68,
xenophobia and the insistence that a prophet must be a native Israelite
in Deut 18:15, 18.

Josiah's repudiation of the Assyrian cult was surely helped by the
dramatic political weakening of the Assyrian empire. Josiah's reform
involved purging foreign cults and practices as well as symbols of native
practices such as divination and magic from the Jerusalem Temple. Perhaps the repairs to the Temple were part of the purification after the removal of those objects (Deut 12:13-18; 18:6-8.) Josiah extended his reform
into the north, particularly the city of Bethel, and he succeeded in cen-
tralizing the cult in the Jerusalem Temple. The finding of the scroll would
not in itself offer a sufficient explanation of the need for or the specific
details of Josiah's reform. The political situation was a major factor,
though. Reform was possible because of the resurgent nationalism that
accompanied the weakening of Assyrian domination and anxiety over
the shifting locus of power throughout the Ancient Near East. A return
to their ancient traditions was a safety net for the people at this precarious
time.

The success of the reform was certainly significant. Those people who
lived in the north opposed the centralization Josiah tried to enforce
(2 Kings 23:9), and the Jerusalem clergy were not eager to welcome those
from elsewhere into the Temple. The result was a priestly monopoly in
Jerusalem. Meanwhile, lack of access to cultic life in the outlying areas
limited the practice of religion in those parts of the kingdom. In addition,
it concentrated on externals, creating a false sense of security against
which Jeremiah railed in 5:20-31 and 6:16-21. Compliance superseded
the more important inner transformation. When Josiah died in battle
many interpreted his tragic end as a negative evaluation of his reform.
All the biblical writers idealized Josiah and his reform; nothing is said,
though, of his foreign policies.

Dome of the Rock, on the Site of the Ancient Temple in Jerusalem

Josiah was not the first king to mandate reform. Asa and Jehoshaphat encouraged reform in the late tenth and early ninth centuries (1 Kings 15:11-15; 22:43-46). Hezekiah, too, took steps to disestablish the high places (2 Kings 18:4, 22) in an effort to avoid the fate the north had suffered.

Deuteronomy regulates cultic practice as well. Support for the priests is spelled out in 18:1-8. In addition, support of the cult at pilgrimage festival times was to be proportionate to the individual's means (16:16-17).

Deuteronomy also addresses social concerns; for example, it legislates in favor of the marginalized, disadvantaged, orphans, widows, and unemployed clergy. It specifies the triennial tithe for these groups (14:28-29; 24:17-22; 26:12-15), remission of debts every seventh year (15:1-3) with special concern for those in need (15:7-11), prohibition of usury (23:19-20) and abusive debt collection (24:6, 10-13, 17), insistence on proper administration of justice (16:18-20), provision for protection and even emancipation of slaves (15:12-18; 23:15-16; 24:7), and fair treatment in case of involuntary homicide (19:1-13). It insists on respect for animals and property as well; for example, mother birds (Deut 22:6-7) and boundary markers (Deut 19:14; see also Mic 2:2). It also specifies conditions for release from military service in Deut 20:5-9; 24:5. In fact, the monarchy itself is to be subject to the law (17:14-20).

ZEPHANIAH, NAHUM, HABAKKUK

Three Minor Prophets are set in the seventh century: Zephaniah, Nahum, and Habakkuk. Each is a very short, straightforward book, which makes it possible to look carefully at each one as a whole. We will do this in chronological order, to the extent that can be determined, looking first at Zephaniah, then at Nahum, and finally at Habakkuk. Nahum and Zephaniah proclaimed the downfall of Nineveh.

ZEPHANIAH

"For I will leave in the midst of you a people humble and lowly.
They shall seek refuge in the name of the LORD." (Zeph 3:12)

Zephaniah is a short, tightly unified book, the most frequently encountered of the three Minor Prophets of the seventh century.

Background Information

The superscription sets the book of Zephaniah in Judah in the days of Josiah. A four-generation genealogy names Zephaniah's great-great-grandfather as Hezekiah, most likely someone other than the king unless Zephaniah was the descendant of one of the king's younger sons. The listing of four generations of ancestors is unique among all the prophetic books. The name of the father is given for each of the major prophets as well as a few minor prophets, but only here do we find such a lengthy genealogy. It identifies him as a native of Judah, thus a credible prophet according to the Deuteronomistic criterion (see Deut 18:15). The book might well have been composed in several stages until it reached its final form after the Exile.

As we learned from reading the historical background, Josiah's reign was a time of strength for Judah. Assyria was no longer a threat; Babylonia had begun its rise to dominance, but it would not subjugate Judah until a few years after Josiah's death. Josiah's reign marked a Golden Age when reform in Judah was possible while both Assyria and Babylonia were caught up in the international upheaval that would soon alter the face of the Ancient Near East.

Organization of the Book

Outline

The book consists almost entirely of oracles of judgment against Judah and Jerusalem and against the nations; it concludes with an oracle of salvation addressed to Jerusalem. The outline illustrates how these genres alternate in the book.

1:1	Superscription
1:2–2:3	Judgment against Judah and Jerusalem
2:4-15	Oracles against the foreign nations
3:1-20	Judgment, then deliverance, of Jerusalem

Genres

The outline illustrates that Zephaniah consists primarily of words of judgment and oracles of salvation. We will look at the genres that convey these messages.

ANNOUNCEMENT OF JUDGMENT: Zephaniah 1:14-18 is an abbreviated announcement of judgment. There is no introductory call to attention;

rather, judgment is proclaimed in the first words and continues throughout most of the passage. That judgment is linked to the Day of the Lord,
which Zephaniah describes in vivid, urgent, battle-ridden, violent language. We are told immediately that this day is imminent: "The great
day of the Lord is near, near and hastening fast." References to war and
warriors include "the warrior cries aloud," "a day of trumpet blast and
battle cry against the lofty city and against the lofty battlements."
Weather-related images add intensity to the scene: "a day of darkness
and gloom, a day of clouds and thick darkness." The effect on the people
will be devastating: "they shall walk like the blind . . . their blood shall
be poured out like dust, and their flesh like dung." In fact, the destruction will be total: "the whole earth shall be consumed; for a full, a terrible
end he will make of all the inhabitants of the earth." In the middle of the
passage the sins of the people are summarized in a sweeping condemnation: "they have sinned against the Lord."

- Which sins associated with Manasseh's reign are denounced in 1:4-6,
  8-9, 12; 3:11?

- Against which peoples are the words of judgment in 2:4-15 directed?
  For what sins are these groups condemned?

WOE ORACLE: Zephaniah 3:1-5 begins with "Ah!" *(hoy)* and continues
with a description of the sinners of the city. The city itself, that is, all its
inhabitants are guilty of four sins: "It has listened to no voice; it has ac-
cepted no correction. It has not trusted in the Lord; it has not drawn near
to its God." Four groups: officials, judges, prophets, and priests misuse
their power. The first two are compared to wild animals: roaring lions and
evening wolves. The abuses on the part of the prophets and priests are
named in straightforward terms. "Its prophets are reckless, faithless per-
sons; its priests have profaned what is sacred, they have done violence to
the law." Then, instead of naming the results of these sins, the oracle implies them in a contrasting statement of the Lord's righteous, faithful acts.
These divine actions bring about the judgment of the unfaithful ones.

- Compare and contrast this description of the Day of the Lord with
  1:7-13.

WORDS OF SALVATION: In 3:9-13 Zephaniah reassures the people of the
positive dimension of the Day of the Lord: it will be one of transformation and peace for those who trust in the Lord. The opening words of
v. 9, "At that time," link the passage with the discussion of the Day of
the Lord that precedes in v. 8. The words allude to a former time when

the people's words were unclean, then shift to words of universal salvation. The Lord promises to change the speech of the people, making it possible for all to trust and serve the Lord together. The verse has several layers of meaning. Pure speech is the opposite of impure or idolatrous speech and also the opposite of unintelligible speech as, for example, in Gen 11:1-9; Isa 33:19; Ezek 3:5-6. In fact, the end of the sentence reads literally "and serve him with one shoulder," suggesting the common effort of a yoke of oxen who pull together to accomplish their work. The reference to Ethiopia reinforces the promise of universal transformation the Lord will bring about. Even from that remote location people will worship the Lord, bringing offerings. (The point is similar to Isa 18:7.)

The divine purpose is expressed in 3:9: the Lord will change the speech of the people so that all will worship and serve the Lord. Then vv. 11-13 offer another image of the transformation the Lord will bring. After the opening "On that day" that links the words with what has come before, Zephaniah turns to another aspect of the promised transformation. God speaks to Jerusalem, evident in Hebrew because "you" is feminine singular, the grammatical genre of cities. In consoling words the Lord promises to remove the cause of shame, the people's pride. The lowly will be spared because they remain faithful, as they were promised in 2:3. The phrase "proudly exultant" vividly underscores the contrast between the pride to be abolished and the humility of the faithful ones. The term "Israel" here is not a geographical designation but an ideological one. The word links the people of Jerusalem and Judah with the descendants of Jacob, the people in the earliest days of the covenant, and with the one God. They have emerged from the coming Day of the Lord purified and transformed. They will "do no wrong" (3:13), a phrase that links this passage with 3:5, and their speech will be cleansed as v. 9 promises. Then the passage ends with the image of sheep, safe and secure in their pasture under the care of the divine shepherd. Their enemies are gone and they have nothing to fear in a future full of hope.

- How does this description of the positive aspect of the Day of the Lord balance out the words of 1:14-18?

- Compare and contrast the description of humility here with its descriptions in Pss 10; 25; 34; 37; 147 and Prov 15:33; 18:12; 22:4.

Rhetorical features

First- and second-person speech: Zephaniah consists entirely of divine words, introduced by the formula "The word of the Lord" that opens the book. Much of the discourse is first-person, for example, "I will utterly sweep away everything from the face of the earth" in 1:2. The first-person words alternate with second-person speech as in 2:3: "Seek the Lord, all you humble of the land, who do his commands; seek righteousness, seek humility; perhaps you may be hidden on the day of the Lord's wrath." This non-stop speech creates unrelenting intensity, adding a sense of urgency to the message.

- Note the same feature in the words of comfort in 3:8-20. What urgency do you find in these words, including the instruction to "wait"?

PERSONIFICATION/APOSTROPHE: Zephaniah speaks not only to the inhabitants of the lands but also to the lands themselves. For example, after addressing the inhabitants of the seacoast in 2:5 he turns to the seacoast itself and proclaims, "And you, O seacoast, shall be pastures, meadows for shepherds and folds for flocks" (2:6). These words remind the listeners that their actions affect not only themselves but also other people, and even nature itself.

- In 2:13-14, what effect will the people's sins have on nature?

- The words of 3:14 are addressed to Jerusalem. How do they refer to the city? What invitation do they extend to the city?

MOTIF: THE WORD OF THE LORD. These opening words of the book are the same as those that introduce the eighth-century minor prophets. They focus attention not on the one who delivers the message, but on the message itself and on the God whose words the prophet speaks. A variation of them appears in 2:9, the only other interruption of the words of the prophet throughout the book

Zephaniah's Message

Themes

FAITHFULNESS TO THE LORD. All Zephaniah's words of judgment condemn the people's lack of faith in the Lord, expressed either in turning to other gods or in unjust, oppressive treatment of other people. This holds for all people, those in Judah as well as in other nations. In fact, the destruction of the unfaithful will be a reversal of creation.

- Compare and contrast Zeph 1:3 and Gen 6:7 with regard to faithfulness to the Lord.

But Zephaniah does not stop with condemnation; he preaches hope for transformation in his words of assurance: "At that time I will change the speech of the peoples to a pure speech . . ." (3:9). Zephaniah proclaims that all the foreign gods and all the people will worship the Lord (2:11 and 3:9-10.) While Deut 4:35, 39 mentions this belief, it is not elaborated until Second Isaiah asserts repeatedly "I am the Lord, and there is no other." (See especially Isaiah 45.) In fact, the ideal community will trust completely in God rather than in political leaders.

Day of the Lord. Zephaniah uses this theme found in several other prophets, especially Amos. In chapter 1 the day is portrayed as a tremendous sacrifice of punishment for all whose lives are unjust and oppressive: officials, kings' sons, those who mimic foreign customs, the violent and fraudulent, traders, those who fail to acknowledge divine action on behalf of the people. It will be a time of utter destruction: a day of wrath, of distress and anguish, of ruin and devastation, of darkness and gloom, of clouds and darkness, of trumpet blast and battle cry. Zephaniah pleads with the people in 2:3 and 3:8 to seek the Lord in order to avoid the coming destruction.

But the Day of the Lord is not ultimately one of unmitigated destruction; it is a time of refinement and transformation. At the end of the book Zephaniah offers assurance that those who trust in the Lord need not fear because the Lord is with them. The Lord's comforting presence is integral to the Day of the Lord. Isaiah, too, sounded this message of the restorative effect of divine judgment.

Remnant of Judah in 1:4; 2:7, 9. Zephaniah uses several themes that appear in Isaiah, including the Remnant. In Zeph 1:4 the term refers not to the faithful Judahites but to those in Judah and Jerusalem who continue to worship Baal. Their unfaithfulness to the Lord will be punished. In 2:7 and 2:9 the term designates those who remain faithful to the Lord. As a result the Lord will give them the lands taken from the Ammonites and Moabites.

- What people are described as the remnant in 3:12-13? What specific faithful actions will they perform?

Several themes in Zephaniah are similar to Micah. Both condemn an unnamed city (Mic 6:9; Zeph 3:1); both denounce the evils of idolatry, especially the Baal cult; both condemn corrupt officials (Mic 3:9-12; Zeph 3:3-5). Micah's program spelled out in 6:8 could have provided the underlying principles that guided the "humble of the land" in Zeph 2:3 and 3:11-13.

Zephaniah's Meaning for Us Today

Zephaniah in the Lectionary

In *LM* Zephaniah is read twice on Sundays. In Year A on the Fourth Sunday of Ordinary Time 2:3; 3:12-13 is paired with Matt 5:1-12a; both describe faithful communities. In addition, *RCL* includes Zeph 3:14-20 as an option for the Easter Vigil in Years ABC, and Zeph 1:7, 12-18 as an option for the Thirty-third Sunday in Ordinary Time, with Matt 25:14-30. Both these readings exhort the people toward faithfulness to their covenant responsibilities in preparation for the end time.

In Year C, on the Third Sunday of Advent, 3:14-18a is paired with Luke 3:10-18, inviting the people to celebrate the Lord's consoling presence by honoring covenant obligations. The *RCL* expands these readings to Zeph 3:14-20 and Luke 3:7-18.

In the Weekday *LM*, 3:1-2, 9-13 is read on Tuesday of the Third Week of Advent, paired with Matt 21:28-32, the parable of the two sons in the vineyard. These readings condemn the people's lack of trust in the Lord before offering assurances of transformation. Zephaniah 3:14-18 is an option for December 21, assuring the people of God's presence among them. It is paired with Luke 1:39-45, the story of the Visitation. These readings focus, for the most part, on the comforting aspect of Zephaniah's words.

The Jewish community does not include any readings from the book of Zephaniah.

• How does the reading for the Third Sunday of Advent express the Gaudete theme of the day?

Zephaniah's significance for our daily life

While the language of destruction in Zephaniah might be offensive to us today, it serves as a reminder of several points. First, God cares for the entire universe and all of us who inhabit it. Second, we are responsible for our actions. Everything we do has consequences not only for ourselves but for other people and for the earth as well. Finally, God is eager for us to trust in divine love and care in all the events of our lives.

• Compose a song of joy about a contemporary concern, in the spirit of Zeph 3:14-20.

Passages for study:

> 1:7-13
>
> 3:9-13
>
> 3:14-20

For Further Reading

Berlin, Adele. *Zephaniah: A New Translation with Introduction and Commentary.* AB 25A. New York: Doubleday, 1994.

Roberts, J. J. M. *Nahum, Habakkuk, and Zephaniah: A Commentary.* OTL. Louisville: Westminster John Knox, 1991.

Robertson, O. Palmer. *The Books of Nahum, Habakkuk, and Zephaniah.* Grand Rapids: William B. Eerdmans Publishing Company, 1990.

Sweeney, Marvin A. *The Twelve Prophets,* vol. 2. Berit Olam. Collegeville: Liturgical Press, 2000.

NAHUM

"Look! On the mountains the feet of one who brings good tidings,
who proclaims peace!" (Nah 1:15)

Background information

The superscription identifies Nahum with Elkosh, a place that is not mentioned anywhere else in the Bible and is unknown to archaeologists and historians. It does not offer any specific clues as to the date of the book; however, it describes the destruction of Nineveh, which took place in 612. This suggests that the book is set in the late Assyrian period, the latter part of the seventh century. (Tobit 14:4-9 notes that Nahum predicts the fall of Nineveh.) Nahum probably preached shortly after Zephaniah and shortly before Habakkuk. Manasseh, during whose reign Nahum proclaimed his message, is not mentioned in the text. The rabbis claim that the omission was because of his wickedness. Another unique feature of the superscription is the reference to "the book." This is the only prophetic superscription that uses the word "book."

On a larger scale, while the book is directly concerned with predicting Nineveh's doom, its final form appears to be the effort of a redactor to urge his own community to faithfulness by putting before them the experience of Nineveh at the hands of the Babylonians.

Organization of the Book

Outline

The book is an almost unrelenting chorus of words against Assyria and its capital, Nineveh. Twice the judgment is mitigated by words of encouragement to Judah, reminding the people that Assyria's destruction will bring relief to the people of Judah.

1:1	Superscription
1:2-8	Hymn to the avenging God
1:9-14	Oracle against Nineveh
1:15	Reassurance to Judah
2:1	Oracle against Nineveh
2:2	Reassurance to Judah
2:3–3:19	Oracle against Nineveh

Genres

The book does not include any sort of call narrative; in fact, there is no narrative at all. It consists almost entirely of oracles against the nation of Assyria, with two reminders that these are messenger speeches (1:12, 14) and two brief words of consolation to Judah in 1:15 and 2:2, reminding the people that Nineveh's downfall will bring relief to Judah. Like the book of Jonah, Nahum does not mention the sins of Judah or call the people to repentance.

SUPERSCRIPTION. The first verse identifies the prophet's words as an oracle concerning Nineveh, and identifies these words as a book.

HYMN.The opening hymn shapes the theological agenda of the entire book by announcing that punishment for sin comes from God. It is an acrostic; that is, it uses the first eleven letters of the Hebrew alphabet to begin the lines of the hymn. The hymn acknowledges the power of the Lord to forgive sin.

WOE ORACLE. Nahum 3:1-17 is a woe oracle directed to the city of Nineveh. Oracles against nations appear frequently in the prophetic books. While they explicitly address a foreign nation or city with words of condemnation, they indirectly offer reassurance to Israel: the enemy's downfall is the salvation of Israel.

In the *NRSV* translation the oracle begins with "Ah!" (In Hebrew, *hoy*). The description of the sinners follows in vv. 1 and 4. Verse 1 highlights the violence and looting rampant in the city, while v. 4 underscores the prostitution that seduces whole nations. The largest part of the oracle describes the results to follow the sinful acts of the city. Verses 2-3 focus on the violence of battle; vv. 5-6 turn the tables on Nineveh, threatening that the rapist will become the victim of rape. Verses 8-11 pose a rhetorical question to Nineveh, comparing the city to Thebes. Just as that once-proud and beautiful city was destroyed by the Assyrians in 663 B.C.E., likewise Nineveh will struggle unsuccessfully to defend itself. The city's vulnerability is compared to trees fragile with ripe fruit that is ready to fall, troops that are fearful and weak, and city gates that have been burned away. Given the situation of imminent destruction, the oracle urges Nineveh to prepare for a siege, which will in the long run prove ineffective. Even large numbers of leaders will fail in defending the city: they will disappear at the moment of conflict.

ANNOUNCEMENT OF JUDGMENT: Nahum 3:18-19 is an announcement directly addressed to the Assyrian king. His kingdom is compared to shepherds who fall asleep on their watch while the sheep wander off. These verses continue the thought of vv. 16-17, which name specific groups of Ninevite leaders and influential people: merchants, guards, and scribes who neglect their duties. Then the oracle pronounces judgment on the king: he receives the death blow on behalf of all the people. Even his own, who have endured his oppressive rule, celebrate his defeat. We are reminded here of the cosmic battle between the Lord and Pharaoh in the first few chapters of Exodus. Ultimately the Lord triumphs over evil and oppression. But the passage also expresses divine grief over the tragedy that has befallen all the people of Nineveh. Just as we read in 3:7, "Nineveh is devastated; who will bemoan her? Where shall I seek comforters for you?" likewise in 3:19, "There is no assuaging your hurt, your wound is mortal" refers to the utter aloneness of the royal victim who has not only suffered defeat but also endured the complete aloneness of the leader who failed to protect his people in time of need. The passage offers further food for thought on the complex need to bring justice to bear on evil and at the same time to have compassion of the people who suffer, either as victims or as perpetrators of that evil. The book ends on this note of total devastation of Assyria. Just as we mentioned with regard to 3:1-17, this announcement also offers indirect assurance to Israel that its enemies will be defeated.

• In 1:2-14, another oracle against Nineveh, what sin does the prophet condemn? What punishment will result?

WORDS OF SALVATION. Two brief breaks in the words of judgment offer encouragement and hope to the people: 1:15 and 2:2. Both of these allude to the difficulties the people experience. In 1:15 this is apparent in the words "never again shall the wicked invade you; they are utterly cut off," and 2:2 refers to those who have ravaged the land. Both announce the coming of one who brings restoration. In addition, 1:15 encourages the people to carry out their religious celebrations in gratitude for the Lord's removal of their enemies from their midst.

Rhetorical features

ACROSTIC. The first eight verses of the book are an acrostic based on the first eleven letters of the Hebrew alphabet. The first letter, *aleph*, begins 1:2 and creates a group of six lines; then the second letter, *beth*, opens the third line of v. 3. From then through v. 8a the pattern continues with two lines per letter, two letters per verse. (This pattern depends on revising the first letter of v. 7b to *waw* instead of *yod*.) The pattern is created by combining previously composed texts, resulting in a composite recital of divine actions and attributes, all of which depict God's power.

VIVID IMAGERY. This book contains some of the most graphic descriptive passages in the entire Bible, especially in the battle scenes. Graphic descriptions catch us up in the intensity and horror of war and destruction. Vivid verbal snapshots depict the attack on Nineveh in all its cacophany and confusion. Officers' sharply barked commands set the fighting in motion: "Guard the ramparts; watch the road; gird your loins; collect all your strength" (2:1) and "Draw water for the siege, strengthen your forts; trample the clay, tread the mortar, take hold of the brick mold!" (3:14). Action-packed images bombard us with the overpowering sights and sounds of battle: "The crack of whip, and rumble of wheel, galloping horse and bounding chariot!" (3:2). "The shields of his warriors are red; his soldiers are clothed in crimson. The metal on the chariots flashes on the day when he musters them; the chargers prance. The chariots race madly through the streets, they rush to and fro through the squares; their appearance is like torches, they dart like lightning. [The officers] stumble as they come forward; they hasten to the wall, and the mantelet is set up. The river gates are opened, the palace trembles" (2:3-6). "Horsemen charging, flashing sword and glittering spear, piles of dead, heaps of corpses, dead bodies without end—they stumble over the bodies!" (3:3).

The images linger over the human dimension of the fighting. "It is decreed that the city be exiled, its slave women led away, moaning like doves and beating their breasts" (2:7). "Devastation, desolation, and destruction! Hearts faint and knees tremble, all loins quake, all faces grow pale!" (2:10). The aftermath is reported from the perspective of the victor: "Plunder the silver, plunder the gold! There is no end of treasure! An abundance of every precious thing!" (2:9) and of the victim: "She became an exile, she went into captivity; even her infants were dashed in pieces at the head of every street; lots were cast for her nobles, all her dignitaries were bound in fetters" (3:10).

This chaotic picture contrasts dramatically with the image of comforting leadership for Judah: "Look! On the mountains the feet of one who brings good tidings, who proclaims peace!" (1:15).

- Nahum creates vivid images around the four elements of earth, air, fire, and water. Locate these throughout the book, and describe how these verbal snapshots enhance the message of the book.

SIMILES. In 3:15-17 the consuming fire is compared to grasshoppers and locusts that multiply and devour everything in their reach. Then the same insects are compared to two groups of people, guards and scribes, who multiply but then disappear. The simile emphasizes the futility of depending on human leaders who cannot be counted on. Then after the simile the text names two more groups in the list of unreliable ones: shepherds sleep and nobles slumber. As a result the leaderless people scatter and lose their sense of common identity.

- Fire is the point of comparison in the similes in 2:4. What characteristics of fire does this verse highlight?

- What other similes do you find in the book?

PERSONIFICATION. The horribly graphic depiction of the divine violation of Nineveh is an example of Nahum's use of personification. Throughout the prophets, cities are often referred to as feminine. Recall, for instance, the references to "Daughter Zion" in Isaiah and Zephaniah. Here Nahum carries the image further, describing the violation of Nineveh as the rape of a woman. "I will lift up your skirts over your face; and I will let nations look on your nakedness and kingdoms on your shame" (3:5). In a literal sense the city will suffer the intrusion of the conqueror. But describing the city's fate in terms of rape focuses explicitly on its women, who must endure humiliating violation from the advancing army. The human outrage is thus highlighted, and Nahum's implicit suggestion that she asked for it (3:4) does not mitigate the shame suffered by each victimized woman.

- What inanimate objects are personified in 2:4? How does the personification add to the graphic description of battle?

RHETORICAL QUESTIONS draw the reader into the complexity and ambiguity of the scene. "Who can stand before his indignation? Who can endure the heat of his anger?" (1:6) underscores the futility of hoping for survival against the divine punishment. "Who will bemoan her? Where shall I seek comforters for you?" (3:7) captures the utter humiliation and aloneness of the rape victim. Even though that victim has been identified as the dreaded enemy Nineveh, we are horrified at the violation and shame it suffers. At the same time the second question hints at the conqueror's realization that the victim might wish for comfort: no one can be found to offer consolation. It is not likely that anyone will offer consolation, but nevertheless the need is acknowledged.

- The final words of the book are a rhetorical question. To whom is the question addressed? What effect does this final question have on the reader of the book?

AMBIGUOUS ANTECEDENTS. Frequently throughout the book the hearer of God's word is not immediately clear, nor is the one spoken about. For example, all of chapter 1 announces God's powerful support of the faithful and destruction of their adversaries. Not until 1:15 does it become clear that the words are addressed to Judah. But along the way clues are given in the Hebrew text because the gender and number of "you" and "your" is identifiable. "You" in 1:12-13 is feminine singular, the usual form for cities in Hebrew. But in v. 14 all the "yous" except the first are masculine singular. Then in v. 15 (2:1 in Hebrew) "you" returns to feminine singular. This gender distinction clarifies the antecedent of "you" as a city, and the reference to Judah in v. 15 suggests that the city is Jerusalem. Then, in 2:1; 2:13–3:17 (2:2; 2:14–3:17 in Hebrew) "you" is always feminine singular, referring to Nineveh, specified in 3:7. And in 3:18-19 "you" is masculine singular, referring to the king of Assyria who is identified in 3:18.

Nahum's Message

Themes

GOD IS ALL-POWERFUL. God is depicted in a variety of ways in the book: jealous, avenging, wrathful, raging, slow to anger, great in power over nature and over people, good, a stronghold, a protector. Sometimes these characteristics seem to contradict one another, as in "His wrath is poured out like fire, and by him the rocks are broken in pieces. The LORD is good, a stronghold in a day of trouble; he protects those who take refuge in him, even in a rushing flood. He will make a full end of his adversaries, and will pursue his enemies into darkness" (1:6-8). The alternation of attributes and actions that punish the evil and reward the good expresses the complexity and confusion rampant in the Babylonian takeover of the Assyrian empire. Identifying and classifying those who are good and those who are evil becomes extremely difficult in the midst of the violence and tension. In addition, the alternation reminds us of God's infinite power and goodness. The thought is similar to that expressed in Exod 20:5; 34:6, 14; Num 14:18; Deut 32:21.

DIVINE VENGEANCE. Of all the divine attributes related to power this book contains, the most-frequently named is vengeance. In 1:2-3 vengeance is depicted in detail: "A jealous and avenging God is the LORD, the LORD is avenging and wrathful; the LORD takes vengeance on his adversaries and rages against his enemies. The LORD is slow to anger but great in power, and the LORD will by no means clear the guilty. His way is in whirlwind and storm, and the clouds are the dust of his feet."

• Compare and contrast this passage with Exod 34:5-7.

The Old Testament looks upon divine vengeance positively, as a dimension of God's goodness (see Jer 11:20), which overcomes evil by divine power. Nahum 1:6-8 underscores the divine power that overcomes evil with good: "Who can stand before his indignation? Who can endure the heat of his anger? . . . The LORD is good, a stronghold in a day of trouble; he protects those who take refuge in him, even in a rushing flood." The words assure Judah that the Lord sees the suffering of the people and will avenge the oppression of the Assyrians.

• In the following passages, note the depiction of divine vengeance as a means of protecting the faithful people: Deut 32:43; Pss 17; 37; 58.

• Can the book of Nahum be understood as advocating passive resistance while trusting in divine power to protect the faithful?

FEMININE DIMENSIONS OF POWER. In 3:3-4 Nahum compares Assyria to a seductress whose sexual wiles enslave those drawn in by her charms. Then the following verses promise that the perpetrator will suffer in kind, enduring rape by its conquerors. Then in v. 13 Nahum seems to imply that women are weak and cowardly. But these verses can also suggest that power takes unexpected forms and can reside in those whom society looks on as weak or insignificant.

Nahum's Meaning for Us Today

Nahum in the Lectionary

Nahum does not appear in the Sunday *LM* or *RCL,* nor does it appear in the Jewish readings. It appears only once in the Weekday Lectionary, on Friday of the Eighteenth Week in Ordinary Time in Year II, following the weekday readings from Jeremiah. The reading consists of Nah 1:15; 2:2; 3:1-3, 6-7 (2:1, 3; 3:1-3, 6-7 in *NAB*), fragments of several units within the book. The thought of this chain of verses is difficult to summarize because the verses belong to different passages within the book. A common thread running through the verses might be identified as divine power to punish and to save. Such a message might offer an opportunity to reflect on how we define power in our own surroundings, and how we respond to violence.

Nahum's significance for our daily life

Nahum describes divine power throughout the book. In fact, much of the book depicts power in terms of violence. This raises difficult questions for our world today, especially for peacemakers. On the other hand, it encourages us not to respond to violence with active resistance. It notes the importance as well as the difficulty of empathizing with those who have sinned.

- What is your own image of divine power?

- Do you think the book glorifies war and violence? Explain your opinion.

- The book raises questions about empathizing with another person's pain in 3:7 and 3:19. What insights do these verses offer regarding empathy? With whom ought one to empathize? Who, if anyone, is beyond empathy in today's world? Must someone else suffer in order that one's own suffering can be relieved?

• How can we come to terms with the divine rape of Nineveh in 3:5-7? Is it sufficient to say that Nineveh is the enemy oppressor? And what female/feminine power is acknowledged in 3:4? Does this mitigate or offer an alternative understanding of the unmitigated violation described in the rape in 3:5? See also Ezek 16:37-43 and Hos 2:5-7. Compare and contrast the rape of Jerusalem in Lam 1:7-10.

Passages for study

> 1:2-8
>
> 3:1-7

For Further Reading

O'Brien, Julia Myers. *Nahum*. New York: Sheffield Academic Press, 2002.

Roberts, J. J. M. *Nahum, Habakkuk, and Zephaniah: A Commentary*. OTL. Louisville: Westminster John Knox, 1991.

Robertson, O. Palmer. *The Books of Nahum, Habakkuk, and Zephaniah*. Grand Rapids: William B. Eerdmans Publishing Company, 1990.

Sweeney, Marvin A. *The Twelve Prophets*, vol. 2. Berit Olam. Collegeville: Liturgical Press, 2000.

HABAKKUK

"For there is still a vision for the appointed time;
it speaks of the end, and does not lie.
If it seems to tarry, wait for it;
it will surely come, it will not delay." (Hab 2:3)

Background Information

The third of the seventh-century Minor Prophets is Habakkuk. Habakkuk follows Nahum and in two ways seems to complement Nahum's message. First, the book addresses the question of justice and injustice internally among Habakkuk's own people. This approach differs from that of Nahum, who reassures the Judahites by condemning the violence and oppression of the Assyrians. Second, the prophet's sense of compassion toward all humanity is more explicit than is Nahum's.

The book does not offer precise clues as to its geographical setting or time of writing. It does mention the Chaldeans, who helped defeat the Assyrians and eventually became identified with the Babylonians (see, for example, Jer 25:12). Several details in the book support a setting in Judah in the final years before the Babylonian takeover of Jerusalem and Judah. For example, the passages that condemn greed can be understood as a critique of King Jehoiakim's lifestyle. He lived beyond his own and all the people's means, and at their expense. Another possibility is that the oracles were collected after the devastating events of 597, when the Babylonian threat was no longer a possibility but a reality and the people of Judah turned to the terms of Torah, especially words of concern for justice and the cult, in the hope of forestalling further Babylonian incursions into Judah.

The superscription does not identify a historical setting either. Habakkuk is one of three books whose superscription calls it an oracle. The other two are Nahum and Malachi. The superscription identifies Habakkuk only as "the prophet," *nabi,* the same identification we find in Haggai and Zechariah. This designation, and the liturgical prayer in chapter 3, lead some people to speculate that Habakkuk was a professional or cultic prophet. The book itself does not clarify the point, which in any case is not necessary for understanding its message. The rabbis attribute the lack of a king's name in the superscription in both Nahum and Habakkuk to the fact that Manasseh, who was king at the time, was too wicked to have his name inscribed in the book. In spite of these uncertainties we can understand the message of the book within the context of the unstable and uncertain years around 597.

Organization of the Book

Outline

Habakkuk is unusual in not including any words of the prophet to the people. Instead, the book consists almost entirely of dialogue between him and God. His words to God are in the form of complaint and praise, and the divine words are announcements of judgment and woe oracles. Superscriptions in 1:1; 3:1; 3:19 define the following basic structure.

1:1–2:20	Interchange between Habakkuk and God
3:1-19	Prayer-Hymn of Habakkuk

We observed that the book of Nahum begins with a hymn, and we see from this outline that the book of Habakkuk ends with a hymn. Just as the opening hymn sets the theological tone of Nahum's message, the final hymn in Habakkuk shapes this book's meaning as well.

The book can be easily outlined according to genres as well.

1:1	Superscription
1:2-4	Habakkuk's first lament
1:5-11	God's response, an oracle of judgment
1:12–2:1	Habakkuk's second lament and soliloquy
2:2-5	God's response, the commissioning of Habakkuk
2:6-20	Woe oracles
3:1-15	Habakkuk's psalm of praise
3:16-19	Habakkuk's response to his commission

Both outlines point to a progression of thought throughout the book, from complaint to resolution.

Genres

LAMENT. This form appears in 1:2-4; 1:12–2:1; 3:2-15. The lament in 1:12–2:1 is Habakkuk's second, in which he decries the treatment of the people at the hands of the enemy. The passage begins with words of praise in vv. 12-13a, acknowledging God's holiness and immortality. (Early texts that read "you shall not die" were amended by the Masoretes to read "we shall not die" in order that people would not think God might be mortal.) The praise continues with words of confidence that the Chaldeans will be defeated. Then in v. 13b the prophet's complaint begins with the puzzled question, "Why?" He wonders why God, who "cannot look on wrongdoing," seems not to notice when evil people prevail over the righteous ones. He then compares the righteous to fish who are trapped by the enemy on a hook or in a net. That enemy regards his fishing implements as deities because they provide food for him. Then in 2:1 the prophet returns to words of confidence, positioning himself at his watchpost and waiting for the divine response to his prayer.

- In Habakkuk's first lament in 1:2-4, what complaint does he bring before God?

Habakkuk's lament in 3:2-15 begins with the invocation "O LORD," and continues with alternating words of praise, confidence, complaint, and petition. Habakkuk asks of God, "In our own time revive [your renown and your work]; in our own time make it known; in wrath may you remember mercy" (v. 2). Habakkuk describes his vision of the power of God manifest in creation, in geological phenomena such as earthquakes and floods, and in divine victory in battle against enemies. Toward the end of the lament, in v. 13, Habakkuk praises the divine purpose "to save your people, to save your anointed."

- Compare and contrast this prayer with Deuteronomy 33 and Ps 77:17-20.

Cuneiform on a Clay Tablet—the earliest form of writing known

ANNOUNCEMENT OF JUDGMENT. The announcement in 1:5-11 follows Habakkuk's first words to God, in which the prophet laments the lack of divine intervention in the face of injustice on the part of the people. Here the Lord addresses the people, urging them to look around them at the nations (v. 5), specifically the Chaldeans (v. 6). The imminent divine action will shock the inhabitants of Judah: the very Chaldeans who are known for their arrogant, self-sufficient power and military might will sweep through at the Lord's instigation. But in the end their arrogant self-sufficiency will be their undoing: "They transgress and become guilty; their own might is their god!" (v. 11).

The announcement speaks of God's power over all nations, even those whose violent strength can destroy the people of Judah. Though the Chaldeans do not realize it, their actions will accomplish the Lord's purpose. This becomes explicit in the woe oracles in chapter 2, discussed below.

Soliloquy. After the divine response in 1:5-11 Habakkuk addresses God again in 1:12-17. Then the text records his brief soliloquy in 2:1, followed by instructions from the Lord to the prophet. In the soliloquy Habakkuk mentally steps back from the words he has just spoken to the Lord and wonders aloud how those words will be received by the divine hearer, and what sort of response he might expect. He plans to position himself in a prominent spot so as not to miss the divine message when it comes. (Compare this with Jonah 4:5, where Jonah positions himself in a spot removed from the city to watch what happens from a more distant, remote location and perspective.)

Prophetic instruction and call. In 2:2-5 we see the divine response to Habakkuk's soliloquy in the form of instructions to the prophet followed by an explanation. Habakkuk is instructed to write the vision clearly on tablets in large characters so it can be easily read. This instruction is the prophet's call: God commissions him to make public the divine word to the people by writing the vision plainly for all to see. Then the Lord intimates that the vision might not be immediately evident but will come at its proper time and will be a message concerning the end. Habakkuk is instructed to wait, as the vision will definitely come. Then the Lord points out the proud, contrasting them to the righteous, who live by their faith. This sentence sums up the message to Habakkuk: it is the Lord who nurtures the people; this understanding sustains those who live by it. Then the Lord elaborates on the plight of the proud, the wealthy, and the arrogant: they will destroy themselves by their own greed and self-sufficiency. The Lord compares them to Sheol itself, which swallows up everyone but will not endure.

Woe oracles. Chapter 2 contains five woe oracles that begin in 2:6, 9, 12, 15, and 19. Each of the five condemns one of the evils denounced by Habakkuk in chapter 1.

The first oracle, in 2:6-8, addresses the plunderers mentioned in 1:6. It describes the sin, then announces its consequences: the plunderers will in turn be plundered. The second, in 2:9-11, decries the greed first mentioned in 1:4. In consequence the very houses built or acquired by the greedy will cry out in condemnation. The third, in 2:12-14, condemns violence. This sin is first named in 1:17, which accuses the enemy of "destroying nations without mercy." The woe oracle accuses those who "build a town by bloodshed, and found a city on iniquity." In consequence the situation will be reversed, and knowledge of the Lord's glory will cover the earth.

The fourth oracle, in 2:15-17, condemns drunkenness. In the Hebrew, and in some English translations, 2:5 reads: "Wine is treacherous." From that translation we see the parallel between 2:5 and the woe oracle that begins in 2:15. In consequence, those who force drink on other people will themselves be overwhelmed with contempt and violence. The final phrase of this oracle, "to cities and all who live in them," is repeated from 2:8. In both instances these words emphasize the vast extent of the injustice that is being condemned and of the consequent punishment of the perpetrators.

The fifth oracle, in 2:18-20, denounces idolatry, which was first condemned in 1:16. The making of idols is ridiculed because their makers then worship what they themselves have made. This final woe oracle concludes not by naming a specific consequence but by making a contrast with the divinity of the Lord. The people who make idols will call out to their wooden product in an effort to awaken it, but the whole earth will be silent in the presence of the Lord.

• Compare and contrast the fifth woe oracle with Isa 44:9-20.

AUTOBIOGRAPHICAL REPORT. After the lament in 3:2-15 Habakkuk describes his reaction to the vision of divine intervention. He is awestruck: fearful, aware of his own unworthiness, and also joyfully calm in his knowledge of the Lord's sustaining care. He lives in faithful expectation despite the uncertainty of the times, comparing it to agricultural and pastoral anomalies: "Though the fig tree does not blossom, and no fruit is on the vines; though the produce of the olive fails and the fields yield no food; though the flock is cut off from the fold and there is no herd in the stalls" (3:17). Then he continues his prayer of faith with a metaphor from animal life. He expresses his hope that God will make him as sure-footed as a deer that can maneuver in high places: "Yet I will rejoice in the LORD; I will exult in the God of my salvation. God, the Lord, is my strength; he makes my feet like the feet of a deer, and makes me tread upon the heights" (3:18). The prayer ends with instructions similar to those found in the Psalms.

• Compare and contrast these words with Phil 4:11-13.

Rhetorical features

The book is unusual in that Habakkuk never directly addresses the people. We know, though, from the commission he receives in 2:2-3, that he accepts the Lord's instruction to make the vision plain (2:2), so people can understand God's sending of the Chaldeans to punish them. Habakkuk speaks to God forthrightly, in a way typical of laments. God's first response (1:5-11) makes it clear to Habakkuk that the situation is extremely serious. The prophet's soliloquy in 2:1 implies that he is confident of receiving a response from God, which comes in 2:2-6a with the commission to write down the vision and the assurance of the vital importance of faith for righteous living. The actual pronouncement begins in 2:6b with the first of the five woe oracles in God's second reply to Habakkuk. Again the divine message is an extremely sobering one for Habakkuk.

CONVERSATION BETWEEN THE PROPHET AND GOD. Chapters 1 and 2 are an interchange between Habakkuk and God in which Habakkuk presents his initial complaint to God (1:2-4); then God speaks to the prophet, announcing the awesome and terrifying coming of the Chaldeans as divine instruments of destruction (1:5-11). Habakkuk speaks again to God, this time expressing his faith in divine goodness and the contrasting futility of idolatry. In chapter 2 Habakkuk states his plan to station himself in a prominent place, high up, where he will be able to learn the Lord's response. It comes in the form of a commission to Habakkuk to record the vision plainly for all to see. Habakkuk responds with a prayer of faith in God. Then God speaks to Habakkuk, not with direct responses to the prophet's concerns but with words of assurance that what really matters is faith in God. It is clear from Habakkuk's prayer in chapter 3 that the divine words bring him peace of mind.

This book, especially chapters 1–2, is similar to the interchange between Job and God in Job 38–42. Job pleads with God to speak to him and explain why Job suffers. Eventually God does speak to Job, not with the information Job has requested, but with a message that transforms Job's relationship with God.

Descriptive language. Particularly in the portrayal of the coming of the Chaldeans, the vivid descriptions bring the battle scene to life. We can visualize the enemy: fierce and impetuous, dread and fearsome. Their speed is like that of leopards and eagles, and their violence touches everything in their path: they march throughout the earth, seize other people's homes, charge on fierce horses, take captives, scoff at kings, laugh at fortresses. Finally they cause their own downfall when "they transgress and become guilty; their own might is their god!"

• The excessive cruelty of the Chaldeans is evident in the comparison of the number of their captives to sand in 1:9. Compare and contrast this image with Gen 22:17; 32:12; 41:49.

Key words: The word "violence" appears six times in chapters 1 and 2, beginning at 1:2 in the prophet's initial plea to God for help. It refers once to the Chaldeans in 1:9, and the other times to the human situation. It appears in parallel with the words "human bloodshed" and "destruction," describing the situation from which Habakkuk cries out for relief. In fact, the phrase "because of human bloodshed and violence to the earth, to cities and all who live in them" appears twice, in 2:8 and 2:17. This repetition underscores the widespread consequences of violence not only to individual people but also to communities, not only to humans but to all creation.

The word "earth" appears ten times in the book of Habakkuk, in 1:6, 10; 2:8, 14, 17, 20; 3:3, 6, 9, 12. Nine times the Hebrew word *ʾereṣ* is used. This is the same word as in Gen 1:1, "In the beginning God created the heavens and the earth." The tenth time, in Habakkuk 1:10, the word is *ʿapar*, which is usually translated "dust," as in "The Lord God formed the human from the dust of the ground" (Gen 2:7). The word *ʾereṣ* has several different connotations in Habakkuk. Several times it refers to physical space and is paired with another word or phrase that includes the people who live on earth. We see this in 1:6: "[the Chaldeans] march through the breadth of the earth to seize dwellings not their own." Other examples include 2:8 and 2:17: "violence to the earth, to cities and all who live in them," 3:6: "[God] shook the earth . . . and made the nations tremble," and 3:12: "you trod the earth . . . you trampled nations."

At other times the word "earth" is used alone to include both physical space and those who live in it. We see this meaning in Hab 2:14: "The earth will be filled with the knowledge of the glory of the Lord," 2:20: "let all the earth keep silence before him!" 3:3: "The earth was full of his praise." Only 3:9, "You split the earth with rivers," does not include at least an implicit reference to people. It alludes to the act of creation, when God separated the waters from the land, and also to the Lord's victory mentioned in Hab 1:8. These references to earth as a place inhabited by creatures, especially people, remind us of the integral bond between the earth and its inhabitants. When the earth is harmed, we who live on it are harmed as well. Likewise, when we sin, all creation, including the very earth on which we live, feels the consequences of our sin.

- In 3:8, what is the expected response to the questions? How do these questions express the relationship between people and the earth?

Habakkuk's Message

Theme

FAITHFULNESS: The book is a testimonial to the prophet's faithfulness, particularly in the face of injustice. As the book opens Habakkuk cries out to God for help against the unfaithfulness of his own people and the violent onslaught of the Chaldeans. In the middle of the book he announces his determination to remain present and wait for the divine response (2:1). At the end he professes his trust that God will keep him steadfast. Throughout the body of the book the graphic depictions of unfaithfulness and violence underscore the contrasting depth of the faith that sustains the prophet in the midst of these troubles. The book offers the same insight to the reader: "The righteous live by their faith" (2:4). This affirmation begins to call into question the traditional view of suffering as punishment for sin.

Here difficulty is presented as an opportunity to live in the calm conviction that God is with us and will intervene in God's time. Habakkuk remains quietly faithful, standing at his watchpost and waiting patiently for the Lord (2:2). Even if nature itself fails, he remains steadfast, knowing that the Lord is with him (3:17).

CHALDEANS AS DIVINE INSTRUMENTS: A related theme is the role of the Chaldeans as the divine instrument to call the people back to faithfulness. This becomes clear in 1:6, "I am rousing the Chaldeans." We discussed this theme with regard to the Assyrians in Isaiah; we will see it again in Second Isaiah with regard to Cyrus.

- Compare and contrast the theme of faithfulness in time of trouble in Ps 7:1 and Isa 8:8-10.

Habakkuk's Meaning for Us Today

Habakkuk in the Lectionary

Habakkuk appears once in the Sunday readings in *LM*. On the Twenty-seventh Sunday in Ordinary Time, Year C, 1:2-3; 2:2-4 includes Habakkuk's first lament and God's response to his second lament. (*RCL* assigns 1:1-4; 2:1-4 to this Sunday.) The reading is paired with Luke 17:5-10 in both *LM* and *RCL*, and pertains to the importance of faith.

The fragmentary nature of the Habakkuk reading can present difficulties for preaching. The homilist might explain that the first reading is part of a larger reading, or might simply discuss the larger reading without calling attention to the fragmentary nature of the lectionary reading. With a long-term Bible study group it can be helpful to discuss the larger reading in detail, to help readers understand the nuances of the message.

Habakkuk appears in the Weekday *LM* in Year II, on Saturday of the Eighteenth Week in Ordinary Time, on the day after the reading from Nahum. The reading is 1:12–2:4, a coherent presentation of the second part of the dialogue between Habakkuk and God. Habakkuk speaks in 1:12–2:1 and God replies in 2:2-5, of which only the last verse is omitted from the reading. It is paired with Matt 17:14-20, on the importance of faith.

- Imagine that you have been asked to recommend revisions for the Lectionary. What changes might you make in the Habakkuk readings?

Habakkuk does not appear in the Jewish readings.

Habakkuk's significance for our daily life

The book's focus on faithfulness in the face of trouble has much to offer us today. Injustice, oppression, illness, misunderstandings, financial strains, and other difficulties are sources of great stress that touch everyone in one way or another. Habakkuk serves as a reminder that we cannot escape these difficulties that are often beyond our control. What we can do, however, is remain confident that God is present with us.

When encouraging others to remain faithful in the face of difficulties that strain their resources, we might suggest that they sit with Habakkuk's words, particularly in 2:1 and 3:16-19.

• Compose a lament in the spirit of Habakkuk 1, in which you bring a troublesome problem to God.

Passages for Study

     1:12–2:1

     2:2-5

     3:17-19

For Further Reading

Roberts, J. J. M. *Nahum, Habakkuk, and Zephaniah: A Commentary.* OTL. Louisville: Westminster John Knox, 1991.

Robertson, O. Palmer. *The Books of Nahum, Habakkuk, and Zephaniah.* Grand Rapids: William B. Eerdmans Publishing Company, 1990.

Sweeney, Marvin A. *The Twelve Prophets,* vol. 2. Berit Olam. Collegeville: Liturgical Press, 2000.

Chapter Six

Jeremiah, Lamentations, and Baruch

JEREMIAH

"But this is the covenant that I will make with the house of Israel after
those days, says the LORD: I will put my law within them, and I will write
it on their hearts; and I will be their God, and they shall be my people."
(Jer 31:33)

Background Information

Historical and Geographical Setting

The superscription situates the book of Jeremiah from the thirteenth
year of the reign of Josiah (627) through the reign of Jehoiakim until the
eleventh year of Zedekiah's reign and the fifth month of Jerusalem's
captivity (587). As we saw in the historical summary in Chapter Three,
these dates represent a long and tumultuous span of forty years during
which the Assyrian empire rapidly declined and the Babylonian empire
just as quickly rose to dominate the Ancient Near East. Babylonian
ascendancy resulted in exile in Babylon for those people from all the
conquered cities who were skilled in building trades and community
organizing, who might foment insurrection against the Babylonian-
appointed governor. Some exiles assimilated into the local culture in
Babylon; others remained as separate from that culture as possible; still
others (perhaps the largest group) found a middle ground between those
two extremes, enjoying the cosmopolitan world of Babylon and adapting
their way of life to their new surroundings. Jeremiah's genealogical
information and also the list of kings given in the superscription situate
him in Judah from shortly before the Babylonian takeover of Jerusalem
until the fall of Jerusalem. While he did not go to Babylon, he may have

gone to Egypt with others who fled there in order to escape either the threat of exile in Babylon or the possibility of living under the sway of a Babylonian governor in Jerusalem. Documents found in Elephantine, Egypt corroborate the presence of a Jewish community there during the time of the exile.

Social and Religious Issues

While the communities of Judah were well aware of the sorry end that had come to the Northern Kingdom at the hands of the Assyrians, and of the interpretation that had been placed on it (punishment for sin), they did not see any possible connection between that reality and the impending Babylonian threat to themselves. The covenant community in Jerusalem understood itself within the context of the monarchy and temple-centered practice of religion. This understanding was at least partly the result of their own overconfident interpretation of the divine promise of successors to David (2 Sam 7:12-16), which the people saw as an unconditional assurance of divine support for their life in Jerusalem without any corresponding responsibility on their own part. The resulting tension between the terms of the divine-human covenant and the assumptions of the royal and Temple authorities is a constantly recurring theme for Jeremiah. He highlights the fundamental significance of the covenant that transcends both temple and monarchy and is concretized in a program of living in which the community, with or without monarchy or temple, remains faithful to God, who is eternally faithful to the community. His message offers a vision based on social values rather than a concrete set of proposals.

Organization of the Book

The contents and arrangement of the book suggest that Jeremiah proclaimed eloquent and powerful oracles based solidly in the traditions of Israel during the period immediately preceding the Babylonian destruction of Jerusalem, and into the early stages of the exile as well. Jeremiah's oracles were then interpreted for later communities, probably over the course of several generations. The later interpretations were inserted into the text according to genre and theme rather than in chronological order. Prose sections were inserted into the text sometime after 585, and the text gradually took on the canonical form we know today. This arrangement according to genre and theme creates difficulties for those who seek to sort out Jeremiah's original words and their precise historical and social contexts. It does, however, enable us to focus our attention on the book's message and significance for the pre-exilic Jerusalem community and for the exilic community in Babylon, on the example the book provides for interpreting an original message for a later time, and on how the book might be interpreted for our time, which has its own uncertainties and instabilities.

Outlines

Jeremiah is the longest book of the Old Testament. This factor, along with several others, presents us with three special challenges when we attempt to outline the book. The first is that the first part of the book, 1:1–25:14, includes various interwoven forms and themes. Then from 25:15 to the end of the book the arrangement is straightforward according to form and theme, making the second part easier to delineate in an outline. The presence of these two contrasting means of organization suggests two stages of editing before the book reached its final canonical form. The second challenge is our lack of certainty as to which parts are actually the "original core" of Jeremiah's words and which parts represent interpretations of that core for later generations. We will comment on this topic throughout our discussion of the book.

The third challenge is the most complex of the three: the presence of significant differences between the ancient Hebrew and Greek versions of the book. There are several kinds of differences, many of which involve material found in the Hebrew text, called the Masoretic text or MT, but not in the Greek text, called the Septuagint or LXX, with the result that the Greek version is about seven-eighths as long as the Hebrew. For example, MT 33:14-26, with its focus on David and the covenant, is not included in LXX. Another kind of difference is in the placement of material. For instance, the oracles against the nations that are found in MT chapters 46–51 are located in LXX after 25:13, and are thus found in 25:14–31:44 in LXX. In addition, complex passages in MT are found in a simpler form in LXX. For example, MT 28:8-9 includes the words "war, famine, and pestilence" in v. 8 and "of that prophet" in v. 9. These words (that is, their Greek equivalents) are omitted in LXX.

There is no simple explanation for these differences. Ancient manuscripts found at Qumran suggest that different Hebrew versions circulated even before the book was translated into Greek, with the Greek translation representing one of the Hebrew versions. Some of the variations suggest that the version that became the LXX is the earlier text. For example, it is more likely that the extra words in MT 28:8-9 were added to an earlier text than that they were omitted in a later version. Likewise, the position of the oracles against the nations in LXX is thought to be the earlier position, following the words "I will bring upon that land all the words that I have uttered against it, everything written in this book, which Jeremiah prophesied against all the nations." The possibility of Jerusalem's fall and restoration follows in LXX in chapters 33–52. The oracles against the nations may have been moved to the end at a later time, perhaps during the Maccabean period when people looked back on the Babylonian empire as a decisive moment in history. Another puzzling feature about these oracles is that they are not in the same order in the two versions. The order in MT is more likely the earlier one. English translations today follow the MT, and our discussion of the book will do the same for the most part. We will, however, consider the differences in the versions as they offer clues to the historical settings of different passages and stages of composition of the text.

What is clear in the midst of these complexities is that the message of the book alternates between words of destruction and promises of new life, an alternation introduced in the six verbs of Jeremiah's call: "to pluck up and to pull down, to destroy and to overthrow, to build and to plant" (1:10). Divine judgment brings an end to Jerusalem, and divine deliverance offers hope to the exiled community. The book ends, in fact, with the report of Jehoiachin's release from a Babylonian prison, a sign of hope that new life can emerge from the people's suffering. This ending parallels 2 Kings 25:27-30, the final verses of that book. Because of these complexities we present several outlines, each of which contributes to our knowledge of the shape of the book.

First, following the twofold division suggested above, we can divide the book in the following way:

1:1–25:14   Original core of Jeremiah's words, with interpretive
             additions throughout.

25:15–52:34 Appendices to the original collection.

The first of these two divisions is difficult to outline because it includes various interwoven themes and forms. The second is a straightforward arrangement according to forms and themes.

An outline according to the book's genres, broadly defined, suggests the following division.

1–25	Poetry and preaching
26–45	Prose and biography
46–51	Prophecies against foreign nations (25:14–31:44 in LXX)
52	Historical appendix

A more detailed outline that combines genres and time periods is the following.

1–25	Anti-Judah oracles	
	1–6	from the time of Josiah or shortly later
	7–20; 25:1-14	from the time of Jehoiakim
	21–24	from later periods
	25:15-38	against the nations during the Babylonian empire
26–45	Biographies and salvation oracles	
	26–35	salvation oracles, including the Book of Consolation (chs. 30–31) and the Little Book of Comfort (chs. 32–33)
	36–45	Biographical details of the fall of Jerusalem and about Jeremiah, much of which was probably written by Baruch
46–51	Oracles against the nations (25:14–31:44 in LXX)	
52	Historical appendix = 2 Kings 24:18–25:30, about the fall of Jerusalem and the early exile	

This third outline according to genres might well illustrate the organizing principle around which the book was arranged into its final form.

Genres

We begin our discussion of the genres of the book with a look at its narrative sections. These are the call narrative, biographical and autobiographical narratives, and historical summaries.

CALL NARRATIVE. We find the account of Jeremiah's call in 1:4-10. The elements of this call are discussed in the list of genres in Chapter One. This particular call focuses on God's selection of Jeremiah from before he was born. The six verbs by which the Lord explains his commission to Jeremiah begin with words of destruction and end with words of reconstruction. They describe several spheres of activity: agricultural, military, and urban. There are different interpretations of this call. It might be an actual account of a personal experience, or perhaps of a liturgical experience. It may also be an editorial construction that gives an overview of the entire book, with alternating words of condemnation and comfort. In that case the report of the call attests to the divine authority of Jeremiah's words. Or it may indicate the community within which Jeremiah's words were edited, one whose concerns ranged from overconfidence to hopelessness.

One element of Jeremiah's call strongly resembles an incident in Isaiah's. That is, in both instances the mouth of the prophet was touched, preparing him to speak the words given him by the Lord. The report of this action reassures the listener and the reader that the words spoken by the prophet are in reality the word of God.

• How do the words of 1:14-19 continue the message of Jeremiah's call?

BIOGRAPHICAL REPORT. Chapters 36–45 contain much biographical material, and Jeremiah 36 served (in Chapter One above) to illustrate the biographical report. In that incident Jeremiah was commanded to write down the words the Lord had spoken to him, in the hope that the written word would convince the people of the seriousness of the situation. Jeremiah dictated the words to Baruch, who copied them and then carried the scroll to the Temple to read aloud to the people. He did so in the hearing of all the people, but then was summoned to appear before a royal assembly. When the royal officials heard the words Baruch read, they urged him to take Jeremiah and go into hiding. Then the scroll was read to the king, who burned it piece by piece. After the scroll was destroyed, the Lord dictated it again, adding words of condemnation for Jehoiakim. This information gives us insight into the difficulties Jeremiah faced in carrying out his prophetic duties. He suffered persecution from the king himself because of his preaching. Jeremiah's words of condemnation offended the king, who destroyed the scroll but could not destroy the word of God. Baruch is thought to be the writer of much of the biographical information in the book, especially in chapters 36–45.

Chapter 37 describes Jeremiah's imprisonment, and chapter 38 his experience of being thrown into a cistern. Archaeologists have identified an ancient cistern in the City of David that may have been the site of this episode; whether or not it is the actual site, that cistern helps us to imagine the dank darkness of Jeremiah's underground confinement.

- In chapters 37–38, what details of Jeremiah's punishments does the narrative report?

- Why do his persecutors inflict these sufferings on him?

- Compare Jeremiah's situation in chapter 36 with that of Amos in Amos 7:10-17.

AUTOBIOGRAPHICAL REPORT. In 16:1-13 Jeremiah recounts the instruction he received not to marry or have children. A horrible death will come to children in the land, and to their mothers. For the community who believed that their name would live on in their descendants, this is a harsh command from God. Jeremiah is not to participate in the grieving of the community, not even in the people's celebrations. The reason for this strange and isolating demand is the people's unfaithfulness. They will either perish in their own land or be removed from it and taken to a place where the people worship other gods, because that is what they are actually doing: the very future itself becomes questionable. The instruction calls attention to the loneliness of Jeremiah's life as a prophet. He will not share the sorrows or the joys of the people, as a sign that the entire community will lose the life they currently know. The very future of the people is called into question.

- What autobiographical information are we given about Jeremiah in 32:6-15?

- How does this information offer hope for the future?

HISTORICAL SUMMARY. Chapters 36–45 provide biographical and historical information, especially about the Babylonian takeover of Jerusalem and its aftermath. These reports are straightforward accounts that provide us with details of the siege and actual destruction of the city as well as particulars about how the Babylonians dealt with their hostages, especially the royal family.

At points these summaries closely resemble the reports in 2 Kings. Jeremiah 39:1-10, which reports the fall of Jerusalem, is very similar to Jer 52:4-16 and 2 Kings 25:1-12. Likewise, Jer 40:5–41:18 gives a more detailed summary of the incidents recorded in 2 Kings 25:22-25. In addition, Jer 52:31-34 (the final verses of the book) is very similar to 2 Kings 25:27-30, the final verses of that book.

- Compare and contrast the accounts in Jer 39:1-10 and 2 Kings 25:1-12. Note especially the details that appear in only one of the two accounts.

Next we look at the various kinds of words attributed to Jeremiah.

DISPUTATION: The words of 2:4-13 take the disputation genre as their starting point and adapt the genre as Jeremiah's expression of the Lord's concern for this unfaithful people. Here Jeremiah challenges the people to explain their unfaithfulness in the face of the Lord's continuing care for them from the time they were in Egypt throughout all the years of wandering in the wilderness. He addresses his words to "all the families of the house of Israel" and refers to their "ancestors," setting an intimate tone in his accusation. He then intensifies the indictment against three groups of leaders of the people: priests, rulers, and prophets. His words call attention to the contrast between the difficult life the people led in Egypt and the life of plenty the Lord provided for them in their new land. He couches the speech in legal language, beginning with "What wrong did your ancestors find in me?" and ending with "I accuse you." The legal language adds a solemn note to the speech. Jeremiah juxtaposes this legal formality with the familial language we noted at the beginning of the passage, ending with a reference to "your children's children."

The indictment continues in vv. 10-13 with Jeremiah's challenge to find another people who have abandoned their gods, even nonexistent ones. How much more tragic and incomprehensible that God's own people have abandoned their God and switched their allegiance to other, nonexistent gods. Jeremiah calls on heaven to witness this unthinkable turn of events. He then uses the metaphor of a cistern as a further illustration of the tragic situation: the people have given up relying on a water source in favor of depending on a mere water container. What is more, that container cannot hold water because it is not watertight. By means of this metaphor Jeremiah reiterates his critique of the people's unfaithfulness, which is even more incomprehensible in light of the Lord's special care for them.

Throughout the entire disputation the theme is the violated relationship between God and the people. And yet, in spite of the people's violations of Torah, YHWH remains open in mercy to the people.

- Compare and contrast this theme with Ps 143:1-2.

• How does 2:14-37 continue the disputation form, familial language, and historical references to condemn the people's unfaithfulness? What will be the final outcome of their unfaithfulness?

LAMENT: Six prayers of Jeremiah are recorded in 11:18–12:6; 15:10-21; 17:14-18; 18:19-23; 20:7-13; 20:14-18. These are called his Confessions because of their honest expression of Jeremiah's suffering brought on by his prophetic commission. The Confessions are actually complaints to God in the form of laments, found frequently among the Psalms. A lament begins with a cry to God such as "O God" or "How long, O God?" This is followed by a complaint or elaboration on the difficulties the speaker experiences. The complaint leads to a request or petition to God, a statement of trust in God, sometimes a promise, then a statement of praise.

The first Confession does not begin with the traditional cry to God, but rather with Jeremiah's statement of his difficulty. He compares himself to a lamb who is led to the slaughter without understanding why this end comes to him. Then he requests God to bring retribution on those who seek to harm him. A brief prose response follows in vv. 21-23, a warning of punishment to the people of Anathoth, which is identified in 29:27 as Jeremiah's home. These verses respond to Jeremiah's request for vindication by indicting the people who tried to stop Jeremiah from prophesying in the Lord's name. The verses also give a clue as to one kind of suffering Jeremiah endured as a prophet. Then Jeremiah returns to his prayer, agonizing over the prosperity of the wicked. He compares evildoers to crops that thrive. Then Jeremiah expresses his confidence in God, who knows the faithfulness of Jeremiah's heart. He repeats his request that the wicked be destroyed, then returns to his description of the evil situation. This time he points out the suffering of the land itself because of the evil of those who live on it. God responds in vv. 5-6 by challenging Jeremiah not to take seriously the words of his family and townspeople.

In the final confession in 20:14-18 Jeremiah expresses the wish that he had never been born. He contrasts the joy of his birth announcement with the misery of his present condition. This unrelenting cry of anguish is not tempered by any word of confidence in God or praise of God. It speaks only of the desperation Jeremiah experiences in trying to fulfill his prophetic commission in the face of complete misunderstanding and lack of contrition or reform on the part of the people.

The speaker pours out his heart to the God who commissioned him, even in his most painful moment. Jeremiah's straightforward conversation with God has many parallels in the Psalms. It is also similar to the portrayal of Tevye in "Fiddler on the Roof," who talks to God as to a friend. In fact, it is not certain that the prophet Jeremiah actually spoke these words. They might have been composed by another member of the community and inserted into the text as an expression of the community's suffering and their trust that God would see them through. Even though we cannot be certain about the one who originally spoke the words, we can recognize the honesty that attests to an intimate relationship with God.

The Confessions can offer a model of prayer for Christians who tend to be very uncomfortable with prayers of complaint. Giving one's suffering to God is an act of confidence that God will transform those difficulties into reconciliation, sometimes with those who cause the hurt, always with ourselves and with God. The well-known Christian writer C. S. Lewis reminds us how important it is to give voice to whatever experience we have and feel, in order to give it to God and be healed of it. In this way our complaints become mini-liturgies in which we bring our concerns to God, who then releases us from our burdens and transforms us.

- With which of the Confessions do you identify? In your opinion, which of the divine responses, if any, would offer comfort to someone who is suffering today?

Jeremiah's Confessions can be compared with those of Augustine. Both responded to the theological and political crises they faced, each in his own day, according to how they perceived their relationship with their God. Jeremiah faced Nebuchadnezzar and the Egyptians, plots against his life, and temple religiosity. Augustine faced Pelagius and the Donatists. He wrote: "Is there no middle ground where the life of man is not on trial? Woe to the prosperity of this world, once and again, both from fear of adversity and from corruption of joy. Woe to the adversities of this world, once and again, and a third time, from desire for prosperity, and because adversity itself is hard, and because it can make wreck of endurance. Is not the life of man upon earth a trial, without any relief whatsoever?" (*Confessions* 10, 28).

SERMON: Jeremiah 7:1–8:3 is a lengthy prose sermon that we can identify by its introduction in the first two verses. We can picture Jeremiah stationed at the Temple gate, challenging the worshipers with the admonition, "Amend your ways and your doings, and let me dwell with you in this place." He specifies how to amend their ways: by not oppressing the alien, orphan, and widow, the three traditionally vulnerable groups in Israelite society; by not shedding innocent blood; by not turning to other gods. He goes on to catalogue the sins by which the people have violated the Ten Commandments, which is all the more offensive because they blithely assume that temple worship is all that is necessary. In fact, Jeremiah warns, this complacent approach to worship makes a mockery of the holy place. It will suffer the same destructive end as did the earlier shrine at Shiloh, and the people will be cast out as were the early worshipers at Shiloh.

Jeremiah reiterates the now-familiar theme of the people's unfaithfulness, describing the offerings they make to the queen of heaven, perhaps a reference to the Babylonian goddess Ishtar or some other deity. Later he condemns their sacrifice of their own children to pagan deities instead of giving them to God as commanded in Exod 13:2. Ultimately their sacrifices to pagan gods will hurt the people and also the land and its animals and plants.

Then in a tone dripping with irony he reminds the people that when God first brought them out of Egypt they were commanded not to offer sacrifices but rather, "Obey my voice, and I will be your God, and you shall be my people; and walk only in the way that I command you." In fact, the word "obey" is a translation of the Hebrew word *šemaʿ*, the first word of the injunction in Deut 6:5: "Hear, O Israel, the Lord is our God, the Lord alone." Throughout this sermon Jeremiah holds before the people the essence of faithful living: adherence to the commandments and especially to the injunction to care for the vulnerable. Without this kind of faithfulness, temple worship is meaningless. The coming judgment is described in 8:1-3 with graphic images of disinterment of the bones of the dead. Such a scene of horror captures the unthinkable magnitude of the people's unfaithfulness to God.

- Compare and contrast this temple sermon with the sermon and its aftermath in chapter 26. Why did Jeremiah's listeners want to put him to death?

- How do these two sermons contradict the prevailing ideology that Jerusalem was safe because of the presence of the Temple?

LETTER: Jeremiah 29:1-23 records a letter Jeremiah wrote at the Lord's request to the exiles in Babylon, according to the introductory information at the beginning of the chapter. The letter includes two themes: first, the Exile will last a long time; second, it will come to an end. In the first part Jeremiah instructs the exiles on how to conduct themselves in Babylon. His advice is to build, plant, marry and have children, work for the good of the city where they are currently living, and pray to the Lord for Babylon. He goes on to assure them that the Exile will continue for as long as the Lord has determined, long enough for the exiles to turn to God. After that God will gather them up and return them to their home. His words make clear that the Exile will continue for a long time, and during that time the people are to continue with their normal lives. He repeats two verbs from his initial call: to build and to plant (see 1:10). Here Jeremiah's commission extends to all the exiles: they are all called to participate in Jeremiah's work of bringing new life to the people. Exile will not be a time of passive waiting or escapism, but rather an opportunity to make a positive contribution to life in their city of exile. Jeremiah's letter offers long-term hope for return and restoration but assures the people that their own return to God is a necessary first step.

Second, the letter makes clear that both exile and return are part of God's plan for the people. The Lord assures the exiles that their welfare is God's ultimate concern. There is reason to hope: the Lord is waiting for the people to trust wholeheartedly in God. The promise is given: "if you seek me with all your heart, I will let you find me, says the LORD, and I will restore your fortunes and gather you from all the nations and all the places where I have driven you, says the LORD, and I will bring you back to the place from which I sent you into exile" (29:13-14).

WORDS OF SALVATION: Chapters 30–33 are a cluster of words of salvation known as the Book of Comfort or Consolation because their dominant theme is comfort. The book motif introduces the chapters: "Write in a book all the words that I have spoken to you." The words were very likely originally spoken at various times and in various circumstances, then collated over a period of time into their present shape. The individual segments are not always clearly delineated, nor do they follow precisely the elements of the various genres. For these reasons we will look at these chapters as a whole. Rather than try to pinpoint the original settings of individual sayings, we will focus on the context of the Exile, following Jeremiah's letter to the exiles in chapter 29, because the period of Exile in Babylon was the backdrop for much soul-searching on the part of the exiles. It raised fundamental questions for them regarding their relationship with the God whose promises had sustained them ever since the Exodus. In addition, it caused them to examine their own God in relation to the gods of the Babylonians and of the other exiled peoples among whom they found themselves in Babylon. Jeremiah's words in the midst of this agonizing search for meaning offer reassurance that the Exile, while it will last an unknown length of time, will indeed come to an end and the people will return to their land and their former lives.

From a pastoral point of view this encouragement gave the people hope to endure their situation of alienation from their land, king, and Temple. But the words go much deeper: this pastoral encouragement is solidly based not in the pragmatic reality of the people's present circumstances, but rather in the nature of God. Two divine attributes in particular are at the heart of the assurance that is offered. These are God's faithfulness and God's power: faithfulness insofar as God remains the God of the people throughout their history and in spite of all their unfaithfulness, and power insofar as God is able to break into the tragic situation in Babylon with new life and a new beginning. We will look at these two characteristics of God as they appear in the various segments of the Book of Consolation.

In 30:4-11 the Lord acknowledges the people's fear in vv. 4-7, then reassures them in vv. 8-9 that the Lord will break the bonds of their exile. The bonds to be broken are both geographical, holding them in Babylon, and spiritual, holding them in thrall to a strange god and a foreign king. Then the words of salvation follow in vv. 10-11, with encouragement not to fear because the Lord is present and will intervene on their behalf. The oracle specifies that the people are being punished for their unfaithfulness, but they will not be destroyed; the Lord will save them by defeating their captors.

Perhaps the best-known passage in the entire book is 31:31-34. These words of God do not simply promise a return to the former political reality. This assurance is far more radical: God will give them a new covenant. Before offering specific information about this new covenant, the Lord reminds them that after the Exodus their ancestors broke the former covenant. Then the new covenant is explained: it will not be written on stones, as were the Ten Commandments, but in the hearts of the people. Its terms will be the same as before: "I will be their God, and they shall be my people." Its new location in the hearts of the people assures that they will know the covenant and the God who gave it to them without having to be taught. Then, as a further reassurance, the Lord continues: "I will forgive their iniquity, and remember their sin no more."

This amazing promise lifts the people out of the pragmatic reality of their current exile and offers a whole new way of knowing. This covenant is not simply about knowing what is asked of them, but of knowing the

Lord, the giver of the covenant and, in fact, of their very lives. The assurance ends with an even more awesome promise: the Lord promises to forgive their sins. In giving this promise the Lord creates a clean break with the sins that have caused the exile, so that a new beginning can truly happen. Once again the Lord initiates a new way of interacting with the people, to break the bond of their unfaithfulness as the Lord has done so many times ever since the Exodus.

Members of the Christian community tend to see these words as a promise of a new covenant the terms of which will be different from the old. A careful reading of the text itself clarifies that the new element is not the actual terms of the covenant but rather the location of the covenant within the hearts of the people. This new arrangement is a gift of God to the people in exile, offering them immediate access to the bond between them and God. While Christians see Jesus as the embodiment of a new covenant, and point to this passage from Jeremiah to support that belief, the Christian interpretation is a retrospective one that comes not from the text itself, but rather from the experience of the early Christians in light of the biblical text. In actuality, what is new with Jesus Christ is that his life of faithfulness to the very covenant that defined the lives of the ancient Israelites provides us a model to follow in our own efforts to be faithful.

The words that follow in vv. 35-36 ignore the historical reality of defeat and discouragement, focusing instead on continuity. The words recall the memory of the creation of the sea and the heavenly bodies and the experience of God's ongoing sustaining power evident in the eternal cycle of day and night. This cycle remains fixed in the universe; likewise the people can count on the Lord's ongoing care for them.

- In 30:18-22; 31:1-6; 31:7-9, what assurances does the Lord make to the exiles? How do these promises illustrate divine faithfulness and power?

In 31:35-37 Jeremiah's words rise above the historical reality of defeat and the discouragement that accompanies it, focusing instead on the continuity of the cosmos. God's ongoing care for the universe assures that it will thrive; likewise, God's people will prosper under divine care. Just as it would be impossible for God's oversight of the universe to cease and for humans to comprehend completely the heavens and the earth, likewise, it would be impossible for God to reject the people, even after all their unfaithfulness.

Chapter 32:1-15 recounts Jeremiah's purchase of a piece of land at the Lord's instruction. The book situates this event during the Babylonian siege of Jerusalem, toward the end of the reign of Zedekiah, who had confined Jeremiah within the palace courtyard. The reason for Jeremiah's confinement was that he had announced the fall of Jerusalem. Here the text reports that Jeremiah received word from the Lord that he was entitled to purchase a piece of land in Anathoth. Jeremiah made the necessary arrangements through Baruch, who purchased the land and placed the deeds in a clay jar for safekeeping. An explanation of the meaning of the event follows in v. 15: "Houses and fields and vineyards shall again be bought in this land." The explanation assures the people that they can look forward to a future time when they will again enjoy life in the land. The exchange between Jeremiah and the Lord that follows in vv. 16-44 offers a historical overview of the Lord's care and the people's unfaithfulness, culminating in the punishment of exile but offering assurance that the punishment will end and the people will return to the land. This section repeats the theme of 31:31-34, promising as well that the Lord will renew the covenant.

Chapter 33 contains seven promissory oracles, each of which includes two common points: God's expression of resolve, and the relating of that resolve to the future of the community. The seven highlight God's on-going commitment to Israel, not only in the present but also in the future. The seven oracles are vv. 1-9, 10-11, 12-13, 14-16, 17-18, 19-22, and 23-26.

- What promise does each of the seven oracles make?

- In the New Testament, Heb 8:8-13; 9:15-22; 10:16-17 alludes to these chapters of Jeremiah, but casts their message in a different light that might be seen as supersessionist. What difference do you see between Jeremiah 30–33 and Hebrews, especially in the references listed above?

ORACLES AGAINST THE NATIONS: Chapters 46–51 are a series of oracles against the nations: against Egypt in 46:1-26, against the Philistines in 47:1-7, against Moab in 48:1-47, against the Ammonites in 49:1-6, against Edom in 49:7-22, against Damascus in 49:23-27, against Kedar and Hazor in 49:28-33, against Elam in 49:34-39, and against Babylon in 50:1–51:58. The list begins and ends with the two archenemies of Israel, Egypt, and Babylon. The oracles begin with a messenger formula, followed by the announcement of judgment that will come upon the people because of their sins.

The oracle against Egypt includes three sections, each beginning with a messenger formula. Verses 1-12 announce a day of shame to come upon Egypt, vv. 13-24 specify that Egypt's shame will come at the hands of the Babylonians, and vv. 25-26 reiterate the announcement of Egypt's destruction by the Babylonians, to be followed by restoration to its former glory.

The oracle against Babylon is the most dramatic and graphic of all, applying historically to the sixth-century empire and also symbolically to all dominant and oppressive powers. It includes four messenger formulas, in 50:1, 4, 33, and 51:1. The first introduces the announcement of defeat that is about to overcome Babylon. It specifies the shame about to be visited on Babylon's deities by a nation from the north. In v. 8 the threat mushrooms to include not just one foe but a company of nations from the north who will attack Babylon and put its once-proud people to shame. Verses 17-20 specify that Babylon's downfall will avenge its violation of Israel. The rest of the words against Babylon describe in vivid detail the destruction that will come to it as a result of its defeat and destruction of Israel. The final verse sums up the totality of the destruction: "Thus says the Lord of hosts: The broad wall of Babylon shall be leveled to the ground, and her high gates shall be burned with fire. The peoples exhaust themselves for nothing, and the nations weary themselves only for fire" (51:58).

These words are not merely condemnations of Israel's enemies; they are a promise to Israel that the enemies will be defeated and the Lord will restore Israel to peace. The promises have sacramental power to unleash the events they describe. This quality of the oracles offers insight into the violent depictions of battles, destruction, and revenge. The words express the desperation of the community suffering under its enemies, offering assurance that the Lord—and not the exilic community—fights against the enemy to reestablish justice for the people, offering them hope in the midst of the oppression they suffer without their having to join the battle.

- What sins do the oracles against Moab in chapter 48 and against the Ammonites in chapter 49 condemn?

- In the oracle against the Ammonites in chapter 49, what assurance is given that Israel is not guilty?

Rhetorical features

REPETITION. Throughout the book repeated words and phrases call attention to the themes. For example, in the Temple Sermon in 7:1-15

Jeremiah repeats "This is the temple of the LORD, the temple of the LORD, the temple of the LORD" (7:4). The words accuse the audience (and the reader) of the foolishness of presuming that God will protect the people from impending destruction simply because they worship in the Temple.

- How many times do you find the word "turn" or "return" in 2:35–4:8? How does this repetition enhance Jeremiah's message?

A further example of repetition involves the verbs in the call narrative. We noted that there are six, of which the last two express a new beginning, "to build and to plant" (1:10). These two verbs reappear in Jeremiah's letter to the exiles: "Build houses and live in them; plant gardens and eat their produce" (29:5). By repeating the two verbs, both of which promise a hopeful future, Jeremiah encourages the exiles to make a home for themselves in Babylonia, and to look forward to their eventual return to Jerusalem.

- Note the repetition of the "call" verbs in 18:7-10; 24:6; 31:28; 42:10; 45:4. How does the repeated use of these verbs enhance the message of the book?

PUN. In 1:11-12 Jeremiah uses two words that seem unrelated, but are connected by their similar sounds. The word "almond tree" is *šaqed* in Hebrew, and the word "watching" is *šoqed*. The juxtaposition of the two similar-sounding words creates an auditory reminder that God watches over the events of history. In 5:6 the same word describes the leopard's action: "A leopard is watching against their cities." The word appears twice in 31:28: "And just as I have watched over them to pluck up and break down, to overthrow, destroy, and bring evil, so I will watch over them to build and to plant, says the LORD," referring to the same two stages we found in Jeremiah's call: destruction and rebuilding. The verse also repeats the six verbs used in his call: pluck up, break down, overthrow, destroy, build, plant. The pun, and the further repetition of the word "watch," serve as a reminder that all human governance is provisional: ultimately it is God who watches over the events of history.

MARRIAGE LANGUAGE. Jeremiah, like Hosea, uses the metaphor of marriage to highlight the bond between God and the people. In 2:2 the prophet refers to the years in the wilderness as the time of Israel's youth, when the people were the faithful bride of the Lord. While this memory differs from the descriptions of the people's unfaithfulness throughout the Pentateuch, the marriage metaphor appeals to the intimacy, permanence, and exclusivity of the relationship between God and the people

and calls poignant attention to the current tragedy of the people's unfaithfulness.

- Compare and contrast the description of faithfulness and unfaithfulness in the wilderness in Jeremiah with Exod 16:1–17:7; Num 11:1-15;
  Hos 2:14-15.

IMAGES. These appear frequently throughout Jeremiah, particularly in
his description of the people's unfaithfulness to God. For example, 1:11-
16 gives two vision reports, each of which involves images. We discussed
the vision of the almond tree above in our consideration of puns. The
second vision (1:13-16) involves "a boiling pot, tilted away from the
north," an image of something spewing out and rolling over the land,
destroying everything in its path. The pot in the vision is most likely an
allusion to Babylon. Beyond that we can only speculate on the identity
of the "tribes of the kingdoms of the north," but we can recognize in the
symbols the divine judgment that will come against God's unfaithful
people. This vision, which comes shortly after the report of Jeremiah's
call, specifies quite explicitly that Jeremiah will have to suffer (1:17-19)
in carrying out his commission. God promises to be present with Jeremiah but at the same time alerts him that his life and mission as a prophet
will not be easy.

- In 47:2 we find a symbol similar to that in 1:13-16. Compare and
  contrast the two symbols.

- What is the symbolism of the figs in 24:1-10 and of the yoke in
  27:1–28:17?

- In the oracle against Babylon in chapters 50–51, what images convey
  the destruction Babylon will suffer at the hands of the divine
  warrior?

METAPHORS. Jeremiah's frequent metaphors add to his graphic descriptions of the situation in which the people find themselves. Several of the
metaphors involve the land. For instance, 3:1 uses the metaphor of land
pollution to describe marital infidelity. Then 3:2-5 elaborates on that
metaphor to call attention to the people's shameless unfaithfulness. The
land becomes a barren, dry wilderness, a metaphor for the emptiness of
the people's turning to other gods in spite of calling God their father.
The reference to defilement of the land anticipates the imminent exile in
Babylon, when both YHWH and the people will depart from the land.

- Compare and contrast 3:1-5 with Lev 26:19 and Ezek 8:6.

In 2:21 Jeremiah describes the people as a grape vine from a pure, carefully selected vintage. The vine degenerated into a wild one. The passage recalls Isa 5:1-7, the Song of the Vineyard, which describes the details of the vinedresser's careful cultivation of the vineyard. The prevalence of vineyards in ancient Israel, and also today, assured that the people could picture the literal meaning of Jeremiah's words. His interpretation made clear that the real issue is the people's unfaithfulness, which is all the more tragic in light of the amount of care that goes into cultivating grapes.

- Compare and contrast the vineyard metaphor in Jer 2:21 with 12:10-11; 31:5; 32:15. How do the metaphors depict the people's faithfulness or unfaithfulness?

- In 23:1-4 discuss the metaphor of the sheep and shepherd in light of the exile.

Circumcision in Jeremiah is a metaphor for conversion of heart. In 4:4 he instructs: "Circumcise yourselves to the LORD, remove the foreskin of your hearts, O people of Judah and inhabitants of Jerusalem, or else my wrath will go forth like fire, and burn with no one to quench it, because of the evil of your doings." In 9:25 he reports: "The days are surely coming, says the LORD, when I will attend to all those who are circumcised only in the foreskin." Both quotations highlight the need for a change of heart for the covenant people; physical circumcision alone does not suffice.

- Compare and contrast these Jeremiah passages with Deut 10:16 and 30:6.

Jeremiah's Message

The message in Jeremiah developed over a long span of years during which Israel's people as well as its institutions of monarchy and temple endured destruction and transformation. We will notice these profound changes in our discussion of the specific themes of the book as we observe the portrayals of God and God's transforming actions in the life of the people. Then when we consider Jeremiah's significance for our daily life we will see that the development of the themes throughout the book of Jeremiah begins the process of resignifying them for later communities, including our own.

Themes

The book of Jeremiah holds in tension divine judgment for the people's sins, divine love for the people, and divine promise of salvation. In addition it highlights Israel's traditional institutions: covenant, temple, monarchy, priesthood, prophecy. We will look at how judgment, divine love, and salvation intersect in Jeremiah's treatment of each of Israel's institutions.

COVENANT. Jeremiah recalls the covenant elaborated in Deuteronomy, with its delineations of God's actions on behalf of the people and of the faithful response that is expected in the people's lives. Their unfaithfulness to their covenant obligations will result in disaster, a theme prominent in chapter 11. Jeremiah rehearses the people's experience of Exodus and wandering in the wilderness, when God spelled out the terms of the covenant. He goes on to accuse the people of violating its terms just as their ancestors did, particularly in turning against their God and honoring other gods. The consequence will be disaster from which the people cannot escape, and from which the gods to whom they cry cannot protect them.

- What particular covenant responsibilities does Jeremiah name in 22:1-9? What will be the consequence of neglecting these responsibilities?

When the people cry out to God for help they base their prayer on their chosen status expressed in the covenant. In 14:19-22 they acknowledge their own unfaithfulness to God and see their sufferings as the consequence of their evil. Then they pray to God not to act as they have done in not living up to what they have promised. They plead, "Do not spurn us, for your name's sake; do not dishonor your glorious throne; remember and do not break your covenant with us" (14:21).

Jeremiah assures the people that they will no longer need the ark of the covenant, where the tablets of the commandments were housed. Instead, the Lord will send shepherds to teach the people what they need to know and understand (3:15-16). The promises of transformation become more explicit in chapters 30–33. The Lord promises a new covenant that will have the same familiar terms as the former one: "I will be their God, and they shall be my people" (31:33). The promise that the covenant will be within the people appears again in 32:36-41. The revolutionary dimension is that the covenant will be written on the hearts of the people where they will not have to search for it or learn about it, because it will always be within them.

• What assurance of transformation do you find in 33:14-26?

While Jeremiah highlights the centrality of the covenant in the life of the people, God is not bound to reward or punish people's actions. Rather, the Lord breaks into human affairs in new ways that change the course of history, transcend the ability of humans to control events, and open up a deeper understanding of God. This message helped Israel to survive the tragedy of exile, with all the uncertainty and alienation it meant for them. In our own day it challenges us to discern our own situation in terms of our relationship with the God who constantly intervenes in our lives in surprising and unsettling ways, inviting us, like the exiles in Babylon, to a deeper understanding of God..

IMPORTANCE OF THE TEMPLE. The Temple is a pervasive theme in Jeremiah, and he approaches it from several different points of view. Repeatedly throughout the book Jeremiah speaks from the entrance or a court of the Temple. For instance, he stands in the Temple court to warn the people of impending destruction because they have refused to pay attention to the Lord's word (19:14-15). In another instance King Zedekiah meets Jeremiah at the entrance to the Temple to seek reassurance from him. Jeremiah tells him bluntly that he will be spared from the Babylonian onslaught only if he obeys the Lord. Jeremiah stands at the gate of the Temple, at the Lord's instruction, to deliver the sermon recorded in chapter 7. The location of the sermon reinforces the futility of depending on the Temple, and the chosenness it represents, for salvation unless the people's actions on behalf of one another fulfill the terms of the covenant.

The Temple is significant in other ways in addition to being the location of Jeremiah's words. In his sermon in chapter 7, Jeremiah uses the Temple as an example of the people's complacency. Worship, even at the central religious place, is worthless unless it honors the one God. And that is not enough: adherence to the terms of the covenant stipulations to treat one another, particularly the vulnerable, with justice and compassion is the measure of genuine worship. Jeremiah recalls the destroyed shrine at Shiloh as an example of what will happen to the Jerusalem Temple unless the people take his words to heart (7:12-14).

But the importance of the Temple in Jeremiah goes beyond its representation of what is wrong in the life of the community. It is also described as a center of renewed life. When the time for return comes, the sound of returning exiles reclaiming the Temple will be heard round about (50:28; 51:11). The Lord promises the people that if they honor the Sabbath, then once again people will come to the Temple from far and near to offer sacrifices in it (17:24-26). These various perspectives on the Temple illustrate its importance in the life of the people as the religious center and place of sacrifice. When genuine worship complements faithfulness to the covenant, the Temple will thrive as a place of *shalom*. On the other hand, when the people are unfaithful in worship and in their dealings with one another the Temple will languish, as will the people themselves.

- Compare and contrast the points of view and the themes in chapters 7 and 26.

IMPORTANCE OF THE MONARCHY. Temple and monarchy are closely related in Jeremiah. Just as there are several different perspectives on the Temple, we find different points of view about the institution of monarchy and about the kings themselves throughout the book. Jeremiah's call foreshadows the significance of his ministry in relation to kingdoms with the words, "See, today I appoint you over nations and over kingdoms . . ." in 1:10. That role is evident in the large number of references to different kings throughout the book. It names specific kings of Judah: Hezekiah, Manasseh, Josiah, Jehoiakim, Jehoiachin, Zedekiah; it also mentions kings of neighboring lands including Uz, Ashkelon, Gaza, Ekron, Ashdod, Zimri, Elam, Media, Arabia, and Egypt. Often the references express the Lord's power over the kings; for example, the Lord will make Zedekiah and his officials "a horror, an evil thing, to all the kingdoms of the earth—a disgrace, a byword, a taunt, and a curse" (24:9).

The book refers frequently to Nebuchadnezzar and his conquering power as the Lord's instrument in the region; for example,

> It is I who by my great power and my outstretched arm have made the earth, with the people and animals that are on the earth, and I give it to whomever I please. Now I have given all these lands into the hand of King Nebuchadnezzar of Babylon, my servant, and I have given him even the wild animals of the field to serve him. All the nations shall serve him and his son and his grandson, until the time of his own land comes; then many nations and great kings shall make him their slave. But if any nation or kingdom will not serve

this king, Nebuchadnezzar of Babylon, and put its neck under the yoke of the king of Babylon, then I will punish that nation with the sword, with famine, and with pestilence, says the LORD, until I have completed its destruction by his hand. (27:5-8)

Jeremiah makes clear as well that when the time comes, "after seventy years are completed, I will punish the king of Babylon and that nation, the land of the Chaldeans, for their iniquity, says the LORD, making the land an everlasting waste" (25:12).

In other words, the Lord is king over all the earthly kings, those who rule in Israel and Judah and also those who reign in other lands, even those who do not know the Lord. The Lord uses the earthly kings to accomplish the divine purpose, an idea we met in our study of Isaiah. All the actions of all the kings are guided by the hand of the Lord, whether or not they are aware of their role as divine instruments. This theme calls attention to the importance of kings as rulers and also as servants of the divine king. The kings are not all evil, though, and their role is not exclusively as instruments of destruction. The Lord promises, "The days are surely coming . . . when I will raise up for David a righteous Branch, and he shall reign as king and deal wisely, and shall execute justice and righteousness in the land" (23:5). Just as we have noted in relation to the other themes in Jeremiah, here, too, we see the divine love and concern for the people breaking through their cycles of evil and unfaithfulness, offering the people a new opportunity for transformation by promising them a good king.

The responsibilities and privileges of the king are summarized in 22:15-16, addressed to Josiah's son Shallum and focusing not on the king's wealth, but on his faithfulness to the covenant that entails living justly and righteously and caring for the vulnerable members of the kingdom: "Are you a king because you compete in cedar? Did not your father eat and drink and do justice and righteousness? Then it was well with him. He judged the cause of the poor and needy; then it was well. Is not this to know me? says the LORD."

PRIESTS AND PROPHETS. Jeremiah himself was a priest and prophet, but at the Lord's command he indicts the priests and prophets who, instead of living exemplary lives as models of justice and concern for others, act only on their own behalf. For example, he accuses them in 6:13: "For from the least to the greatest of them, everyone is greedy for unjust gain; and from prophet to priest, everyone deals falsely," and in 23:11: "Both prophet and priest are ungodly; even in my house I have found their wickedness, says the LORD." When Jeremiah warned the people of impending disaster in consequence of their sins, the priests and prophets tried to have him put to death (see 26:7-19).

The prophets are the object of particularly sharp condemnation because they speak comforting words instead of the truth. In 14:13-16 Jeremiah complains to the Lord because the prophets are misleading the people with words of reassurance. The Lord declares that the prophets who speak falsely will, in fact, experience precisely what they deny will happen: war and hunger. Jeremiah accuses them of being empty wind (5:13), of speaking false words (5:31), and of having no knowledge (14:18). He condemns the prophets of Israel for prophesying by Baal, but criticizes the prophets of Judah even more sharply for adultery, lying, and encouraging evil (23:13-14). They receive particularly harsh condemnation because of their position in the community: they are leaders whom the people ought to be able to respect but they misuse their position by their evil actions and their untruthful words, leading all the people astray by their bad example and their false teaching.

But not only the prophets are evil. Some of the condemnation is reserved for those who refuse to take to heart the words of prophets who speak the Lord's word, for example in 35:15.

- In the following passages, whom does the Lord condemn, what is their sin, and what will be its consequences: 23:9-40; 25:1-14; 28:1-17; 29:15-23; 35:12-17?

But just as we have seen in the case of other institutions Jeremiah condemns at the Lord's request, the Lord does not completely give up on either the priests or the prophets. With regard to the priests, the Lord promises: "I will give the priests their fill of fatness" (31:14). He gives assurance that there will always be priests to offer the prescribed sacrifices (33:18). And the Lord continues to speak to the people through the prophets Jeremiah and Baruch, promising a new form of divine presence among them and a new ability to understand the Lord's word (31:31-34).

The poignancy of the Lord's condemnation of priests and prophets reflects the value of both offices for the community. They serve as intermediaries between the people and the Lord: priests by their intercession and prophets by their teaching. Jeremiah does not preach destruction of the institutions themselves, but rather of those people who misuse the institutions in order to serve their own interests. After the time of punishment, the Lord promises, priests will again offer sacrifices. No explicit promise of future prophets is made, but the Lord continues to speak through the prophet Jeremiah, showing by that example that the institution of prophecy will continue.

DIVINE PATHOS. We have seen throughout our discussion of the different institutions Jeremiah addresses, often in condemnation but also in consolation, that the Lord's ongoing love for the people expresses itself in a variety of ways: harsh condemnation of sin, pleas for repentance, threats of punishment, sadness over the people's unfaithfulness, and also eagerness to find new ways of breaking into the life of the community to maintain and strengthen the divine-human bond. The Lord's anguished concern is expressed in some of the most poignant language of the entire Bible. We will look now at some examples.

In 4:19-28 the Lord's heartbeat quickens at the sights and sounds of impending battle. The juxtaposition of verses does not offer a rationale for the coming disaster, but rather suggests that the people's lack of knowledge is breaking the Lord's heart. Then the metaphor shifts to a scene of desolation caused by an earthquake. Jeremiah describes the scene in the same language we find in Genesis 1:1, "earth was a formless void," translated here as "it was waste and void," harking back to the chaos that existed before creation began. Again what follows is not a rationale but rather an allusion to the divine purpose at work in the desolation. The destruction will not be total. The Lord offers the assurance, "I will not make a full end," thus promising, in the spirit of Isaiah, that a remnant will survive the calamity. The scenes of horror depict the tragic reality of the people's unfaithfulness and its heartbreaking effect on the Lord.

Another example of the Lord's anguished concern is 8:22–9:6, in which the Lord laments the sickness of the people and the lack of care that might offer a cure. No amount of tears would suffice to express the divine grief at the extent of disease. At the same time the Lord expresses the desire to flee from the people's unfaithfulness, adultery, deception, and oppression. The juxtaposition of conflicting emotions addresses the complexity of the situation and the cacophony of responses it calls forth in the Lord.

Through all the displays of unfaithfulness on the part of the people, the Lord's willingness to forgive the people remains steadfast. In 5:1-6 people are urged to search quickly and thoroughly throughout the city in the hope of finding one truthful and just person. One will suffice to give the Lord reason to pardon the entire city of Jerusalem. We are reminded here of Abraham's efforts to find righteous people in the city of Sodom. The Lord agreed to save that city for the sake of ten people; now even one would be enough to save the city of Jerusalem (see Gen 18:22-33). Then the Lord excuses those who have had fewer opportunities to know and looks among those who have more knowledge and wealth, but does not find a faithful person among them. The consequence is expressed in terms of wild animals: a lion, a wolf, and a leopard will destroy the people who have turned their backs on their saving God. (Psalms 14 and 53 express this same theme. See also Lev 26:21-22 and Hos 5:14-15.)

Divine eagerness to forgive leads to new ways of caring for the people, even when they are in exile. The Lord promises personally to bring them home from Babylon and provide new leaders to care for them. This promise is expressed within the metaphor of the sheep and shepherd, adding a tender note to this word of assurance in 23:3-4. Then 23:7-8 promises that the homecoming from exile will be even more dramatic than the Exodus from Egypt, and will become the new model of divine power and concern.

- Which of the concerns mentioned above are found in 31:15-22?

- In chapter 2, what particular infidelities of the people does Jeremiah lament?

Jeremiah and Other Old Testament Books

RELATIONSHIP BETWEEN JEREMIAH AND DEUTERONOMY. We noted above some similarities in language and themes between Jeremiah and Genesis. There are many connections between Jeremiah and another book of the Pentateuch, Deuteronomy. This is not surprising when we think of Jeremiah's emphasis on the covenant, a form and theme central to the book of Deuteronomy. In addition, both Jeremiah and Deuteronomy were very likely in the process of composition during and immediately after the exile, when questions about faithfulness were pressing concerns for the people. For example, Jer 3:1, a passage that raises questions about the consequences of unfaithful marriage, is similar to Deut 24:1-4. Both address the topic of divorce and remarriage, both use the metaphor of polluting the land, and both connect the marriage with the relationship with the Lord.

- Compare and contrast Jer 22:1-5 and Deuteronomy 11.

RELATIONSHIP BETWEEN JEREMIAH AND 2 KINGS. Several sections of Jeremiah that describe the final siege of Jerusalem, its capture and the exile of many of its citizens, are very similar to 2 Kings. Jeremiah 52, the final chapter of the book, is almost exactly the same as 2 Kings 24:18–25:30. In fact, Jer 52:4-16 is the same as Jer 39:1-10 and 2 Kings 25:1-12. The differences among the three accounts are slight: Jer 52:28-30, which reports the number of people taken into exile, is not included in Kings. In another divergence among the texts, 2 Kings 25:22-26, the appointment of Gedaliah as governor of Judah, is not reported in Jeremiah 52 but rather in Jer 40:5–41:18. The account would have originated in 2 Kings, with the few additional details added to the account in Jeremiah, because there would have been no reason for the Deuteronomistic historian to omit those details if they were already present in the text.

The presence of the account in two places in Jeremiah attests to its pivotal importance in the life of the community. Indeed, the Exile became the hinge point in the history of the community, when the institutions of the life they had known in Jerusalem came to an end and the seeds of the new life they would adopt on their return were just beginning to germinate in the words of Jeremiah, and also Ezekiel, as we will see in the next chapter.

Jeremiah's Meaning for Us Today

Jeremiah in the Lectionary

Jeremiah appears much more frequently in *RCL* than in *LM* because *RCL* offers options for a semi-continuous reading of the prophets on the Sundays of Ordinary Time. In *LM* Jeremiah appears a total of nine times on Sundays against twenty-two times in *RCL*: in Year A, twice in *LM* and three times in *RCL*; in Year B, twice in *LM* and four times in *RCL*; and in Year C, five times in *LM* and fifteen times in *RCL*.

In Years ABC when Epiphany is celebrated on January 6 during the week, *RCL* offers Jer 31:7-14 as an option for the Second Sunday of Christmas, paired with John 1:(1-9) 10-18. Both readings celebrate the presence of God among us.

In Year A, *RCL* offers Jer 31:1-6, a promise of restoration after the exile, as an option on Easter. It is paired with Matt 28:1-10, an exhortation not to fear. In *LM,* both readings for Year A are in Ordinary Time. On the Twelfth Sunday 20:10-13, the end of Jeremiah's Fifth Confession, is read in *LM* and Jer 20:7-13 is an option in *RCL,* paired with Matt 10:26-33 in *LM* and Matt 10:24-39 in *RCL*. On the Thirteenth Sunday *RCL* offers the option of Jer 28:5-9, paired with Matt 10:40-42, an exhortation to hospitality. On the Twenty-second Sunday in Ordinary Time 20:7-9, the beginning of Jeremiah's Fifth Confession, is paired in *LM* with Matt 16:21-27, an instruction on the inevitability of suffering in following God. In *RCL,* Jer 15:15-21 from the Second Confession is an option paired with Matt 16:21-28.

In Year B one reading appears during Lent: on the Fifth Sunday 31:31-34 in both *LM* and *RCL* promises a new covenant written on our hearts. It is paired with John 12:20-33, in which Jesus teaches about death as a path to life. The other two readings in *LM* are in Ordinary Time. On the Sixteenth Sunday of Ordinary Time 23:1-6 gives a warning to unreliable shepherds in *LM* and as an option in *RCL.* The reading is paired with Mark's account of the feeding of the five thousand, Mark 6:30-34 in *LM* and Mark 6:30-34, 53-56 in *RCL.* On the Twenty-fifth Sunday *RCL* offers Jer 11:18-20, the threat on Jeremiah's life, as an option, paired with Mark 9:30-37, Jesus' teaching on his coming death and resurrection. On the Thirtieth Sunday in Ordinary Time, in 31:7-9 God promises to bring the people home after their dispersion both in *LM* and as an option in *RCL,* paired in both Lectionaries with Mark 10:46-52, the giving of sight to Bartimaeus. Both readings highlight God's care for the vulnerable.

In Year C, Jer 33:14-16, a messianic promise, is read on the First Sunday of Advent in both *LM* and *RCL.* It is paired with Luke 21:25-28, 34-36 in *LM* and 21:25-36 in *RCL,* urging watchfulness because the Kingdom of God is near. We recognize the interpretive stance of this passage from Jeremiah, which is read retrospectively with regard to Christ. Then on the Sundays in Ordinary Time, on the Fourth Sunday Jer 1:4-5, 17-19, from the call of Jeremiah, is read in *LM* and Jer 1:4-10 in *RCL,* paired with Luke 4:21-30, Jesus' experience in the synagogue in Nazareth. The two passages describe the beginnings of the ministries of Jeremiah and Jesus. On the Sixth Sunday 17:5-8 in *LM* and 17:5-10 in *RCL* contrasts those who trust in humans with those who trust in the Lord. It is paired with Luke 6:17, 20-26 in *LM* and 6:17-26 in *RCL,* Luke's version of the Beatitudes. On the Twentieth Sunday, Jer 38:4-6, 8-10 recounts Jeremiah's imprisonment in *LM* and Jer 23:23-29, a critique of false prophets, is an option in *RCL.* The Gospel reading for the day is Luke 12:49-53 in *LM* and Luke 12:49-56 in *RCL,* a warning of the misunderstandings that often accompany belief in God.

In Year C, beginning on the Twenty-first Sunday in Ordinary Time, *RCL* offers the option of a semi-continuous reading of Jeremiah, starting with 1:4-10, the prophet's call. On the Twenty-second Sunday the option is Jer 2:4-13, accusations against the people. On the Twenty-third Sunday *RCL*'s option is Jer 18:1-11, the metaphor of potter and clay. *RCL*'s option on the Twenty-fourth Sunday is Jer 4:11-12, 22-28, descriptions of the coming destruction. On the Twenty-fifth Sunday the option is Jer 8:18–9:1, the prophet's grief over the people. On the Twenty-sixth Sunday the option is Jer 32:1-3a, 6-15, the account of Jeremiah's purchase of the field. The option for the Twenty-eighth Sunday is Jer 29:1, 4-7 from Jeremiah's letter to the exiles. On the Twenty-ninth Sunday the option is Jer 31:27-34, the words of comfort to the exiles. On the Thirtieth Sunday the option is Jer 14:7-10, 19-22, the people's plea to the Lord for help. And on the Last Sunday in Ordinary Time, on the feast of the Reign of Christ, *RCL* assigns Jer 23:1-6, the promise of return and a new king in the Davidic line after the exile.

In the Weekday Lectionary in Years 1 and 2 on December 18, Jer 23:5-8 promises a messianic ruler (see my comment above regarding the christological interpretation of this reading by reason of its place during Advent). It is paired with Matt 1:18-25, Matthew's account of Jesus' birth. In addition, Jeremiah is read on five weekdays during Lent, addressing two ethical themes in Jeremiah: the importance of faithfulness to God and justice toward other people.

On Wednesday of the Second Week Jer 18:18-20 and Matt 20:17-28 describe the suffering that inevitably comes with discipleship. On Thursday of the Second Week we hear 17:5-10 with Luke 16:19-31, stories of trust in God. On Thursday of the Third Week Jer 7:23-28 and Luke 11:14-23 contrast the faithful and the unfaithful. On Saturday of the Fourth Week Jer 11:18-20 and John 7:40-53 report of plots against those who remain faithful. On Friday of the Fifth Week Jer 20:10-13 and John 10:31-42, like the readings for Saturday of the Fourth Week, tell of plots against the faithful.

In Year 2 for fourteen days a semi-continuous reading of Jeremiah extends from Wednesday of the Sixteenth Week in Ordinary Time through Thursday in Week Eighteen. These readings include 1:4-10; 2:1-3, 7-8, 12-13; 3:14-17; 7:1-11; 13:1-11; 14:17-22; 15:10, 16-21; 18:1-6; 26:1-9; 26:11-16, 24; 28:1-17; 30:1-2, 12-15, 18-22; 31:1-7; 31:31-34, which include Jeremiah's call, condemnations of the people's unfaithfulness and pleas for them to turn to God, portions of the Temple Sermons, the symbolic action involving the loincloth, a portion of Jeremiah's second Confession, the story of the potter, the contrast between Jeremiah and the prophet Hananiah with his unrealistically optimistic promises, and words of comfort from chapters 30–31. These semi-continuous readings offer a cross section of the major genres and themes in the book, similar to the cross section offered in the options for Sundays in *RCL*.

In the Jewish readings Jeremiah appears in seven weekly Sabbath portions and also on the second day of Rosh Hashanah and the morning of the Ninth of Av. The weekly portions are as follows: 46:13-28 is paired with Exod 10:1–13:16; Jer 34:8-22; 33:25, 26 is paired with Exod 21:1–24:18; Jer 7:21–8:3; 9:22-23 is paired with Lev 6:1–8:36; Jer 32:6-27 is paired with Lev 25:1–26:2; Jer 16:19–17:14 is paired with Lev 26:3–27:34; Jer 1:1–2:3 is paired with Num 30:2–32:42; Jer 2:4-28; 3:4 (in the Sephardi ritual 2:4-28; 4:1, 2) is paired with Num 33:1–36:13. On the second day of Rosh Hashanah Jer 31:2-20 is paired with Gen 22:1-24 and Num 29:1-6. On the morning of the Ninth of Av, Jer 8:13–9:23 is paired with Deut 4:25-40.

Jeremiah's significance for our daily life

The book of Jeremiah spans such a long and critical period of time, and includes such a variety of themes, that its meanings offer an array of applications to life today. Its condemnations of leaders who do not live up to the trust placed in them are as relevant today as they were in the seventh century. Critiques of social injustice and of neglect of the vulnerable are likewise as timely today as they were in Jeremiah's time.

The words of comfort and assurance that Jeremiah offers speak to many who are alienated in today's world, whether because of painful relationships, economic hardships, political differences, or religious tensions. The Lord's promises of new ways of divine inbreaking offer particularly encouraging words to people who are caught in the many dysfunctional aspects of life today, whether institutional, familial, or personal.

Words from Jeremiah have often been set to music, providing opportunities for communities to use the words of the prophet for prayer.

- What hymns do you know with words based on passages from Jeremiah?

- How might we apply Jeremiah's oracles against the nations (chs. 46–51) in today's global society?

Passages for study

3:1–4:4

20:7-18

30:18-22

For Further Reading

Bauer, Angela. *Gender in the Book of Jeremiah.* New York: Peter Lang, 1999.

Berrigan, Daniel. *Jeremiah: The World, the Wound of God.* Minneapolis: Fortress, 1999.

Bright, John. *Jeremiah.* AB 21. Garden City, NY: Doubleday, 1984.

Brueggemann, Walter. *A Commentary on Jeremiah: Exile and Homecoming.* Grand Rapids: Eerdmans, 1998.

Carroll, Robert. *Jeremiah.* OTL. Philadelphia: Westminster, 1986.

Collins, John J. "The Zeal of Phinehas: The Bible and the Legitimation of Violence," *JBL* 122/1 (2003) 3–21.

Diamond, A. R. *The Confessions of Jeremiah in Context.* Sheffield: JSOT Press, 1987.

Holladay, William L. *Jeremiah.* 2 vols. Hermeneia. Philadelphia and Minneapolis: Fortress, 1986, 1989.

———. *Jeremiah: Spokesman Out of Time.* Philadelphia: United Church Press, 1974.

King, Philip J. *Jeremiah: An Archaeological Companion.* Louisville: Westminster John Knox, 1993.

Lewis, C. S. *Reflections on the Psalms.* New York: Harcourt, Inc., 1986.

Lundbom, Jack R. *Jeremiah: A Study in Ancient Hebrew Rhetoric.* Winona Lake: Eisenbrauns, 1997.

McKane, William. *A Critical and Exetetical Commentary on Jeremiah.* Vol. 1. ICC. Edinburgh: T & T Clark, 1986.

Perdue, Leo G. *The Collapse of History: Reconstructing Old Testament Theology.* Minneapolis: Fortress, 1994.

Smith-Christopher, Daniel L. *A Biblical Theology of Exile.* Minneapolis: Fortress, 2002.

LAMENTATIONS

"I called on your name, O Lord, from the depths of the pit;
you heard my plea, 'Do not close your ear to my cry for help,
but give me relief!'" (Lam 3:55-56)

The Book of Lamentations appears directly after Jeremiah in Christian Bibles. It consists of five poems that express grief over the destruction of Jerusalem. The poems are ascribed to Jeremiah because of their style and content: the relationship between the city and its inhabitants, expressions of mourning, and condemnation of unfaithfulness. The first four poems are acrostics; that is, alphabetical poems in which the lines begin with successive letters of the alphabet. That arrangement highlights the divine pattern and orderliness in life when the people were struggling to find meaning in the destructive events that had occurred at the hands of the Babylonians.

Lamentations is read once in the Weekday Lectionary on Saturday of the Twelfth Week in Ordinary Time in Year II, when 2:2, 10-14, 18-19 express the people's mourning over the loss of Jerusalem to the Babylonians.

The book is frequently used during services on Good Friday, to express the sorrow and repentance of the sinners Christ redeemed on the cross. It can give voice to our individual sorrow for sin at times when we reflect on God's love for us and our own failures to love in return.

For Further Reading

Brueggemann, Walter. *Praying the Psalms*. Winona, MN: St. Mary's Press, 1982.

Kraus, Hans-Joachim. *Theology of the Psalms*. Trans. Keith Crim. Minneapolis: Augsburg, 1986.

Lewis, C. S. *Reflections on the Psalms*. New York: Harcourt, 1986.

O'Connor, Kathleen M. *Lamentations and the Tears of the World*. Maryknoll, NY: Orbis Books, 2002.

BARUCH

"Happy are we, O Israel, for we know what is pleasing to God." (Bar 4:4)

Baruch's name appears in the book of Jeremiah twenty-three times in connection with three separate incidents. The first is the purchase of land described in chapter 32. The second incident, in chapter 36, is Jeremiah's dictation of his words to Baruch, who wrote them on a scroll and then read them aloud in the Temple in the hope of convincing the people to turn away from evil. This event is reported as taking place in 605 or 604. When the king's officials received word of the reading they sent for Baruch and requested that he come and read the scroll to them. They were alarmed at the words and questioned Baruch as to the origin of what he had read. They warned Baruch to take Jeremiah and hide, and then they reported the incident to the king. The king sent men to find the scroll and bring it to him, which they did. Then the king asked that

Western Wall of the Terrace that Supported the Temple in Jerusalem

it be read aloud. As the words were read from the scroll, the king cut the scroll, a few columns at a time, and threw them into the fire. Then he sent some of his men to arrest Baruch, who is identified as "secretary," and Jeremiah. But the Lord hid the two men from those sent to arrest them.

Jeremiah then dictated the words to Baruch a second time. In addition, he dictated, "You have dared to burn this scroll. . . . Therefore thus says the LORD concerning King Jehoiakim of Judah: He shall have no one to sit upon the throne of David, and his dead body shall be cast out to the heat by day and the frost by night" (36:30).

The book of Baruch appears in Catholic editions of the Bible immediately after Lamentations, and among the Apocryphal books in other editions. Tradition ascribes it to Jeremiah's scribe, and in fact much of the book is similar to parts of Jeremiah. The superscription sets the book in Babylon at the time of the destruction of Jerusalem.

Baruch appears in the Lectionary on the Second Sunday of Advent in Year C in *LM* and as an option in *RCL*, when 5:1-9 is paired with Luke 3:1-6. The passage offers hope of return to the exiles in Babylon. In the Lectionary its appearance during Advent adds a christological interpretation to the words. We have discussed this type of interpretation above; we note here that, while it is easy to see the Christian interest in the words as descriptions of the coming of Christ, the passage is also rich in encouragement to anyone who experiences alienation of any sort.

During the Easter Vigil in Years ABC, Bar 3:9-15, 32–4:4 is included among the readings in both *LM* and *RCL*. It is a praise of wisdom that has more in common with the Wisdom books than with the prophetic material. In addition, *LM* includes readings from Baruch twice in the Weekday Lectionary, both in Year I during the Twenty-sixth Week in Ordinary Time, after the readings from Haggai and Zechariah. The passages are Bar 1:15-22, whose message is similar to Jer 11:3-5, and Bar 4:5-12, 27-29, which offers encouragement that the Lord will remember the people in spite of their sins.

For Further Reading

Dempsey, Carol J. *Hope Amid the Ruins: The Ethics of Israel's Prophets.* St. Louis: Chalice Press, 2000.

Murphy, Frederick James. *The Structure and Meaning of Second Baruch.* SBLDS 78. Atlanta: Scholars Press, 1985.

Chapter Seven

Ezekiel and Obadiah

General Background Information

Historical and Geographical Setting

When many Jerusalemites were taken into exile in Babylon, some of those left in the land of Judah fled, hoping to settle safely in an area not controlled by the Babylonians. However, some of those who fled were attacked by the Edomites. In the years that followed, Edomites moved westward and settled in the area of Hebron (Mal 1:2-5). During the Persian period Nabateans migrated into Edom, where they were securely established in Petra by the end of the fourth century. In Greco-Roman times this area became known as Idumea.

EZEKIEL

"They shall live in safety in it, and shall build houses and plant vineyards.
They shall live in safety, when I execute judgment upon all their
neighbors who have treated them with contempt.
And they shall know that I am the LORD their God." (Ezek 28:26)

The messages of Jeremiah and Ezekiel offer insights into the theological issues that helped Israel's faith to survive the tragedy of exile. We have seen that Jeremiah preached to the exiles from Jerusalem. Ezekiel was himself an exile; he spoke as one of them in Babylon.

Background Information

Historical and Geographical Setting

The book of Ezekiel gives background information that helps to situate it historically and also provides biographical information about Ezekiel himself. Date formulas appear sixteen times in the book. These formulas place it historically between 593 and 571, from a few years after the first deportation to Babylon until about fifteen years after the fall of Jerusalem.

Ezekiel himself was a priest who began to preach in 593 and continued for at least twenty years, until about fifteen years after Jerusalem's fall. He was married; his wife died during the siege of Jerusalem. He preached in Babylon, where he was most likely taken in 597 with the first group of deportees that included Jehoiachin the king (1:1-3; 24:15-18). His location in exile in Babylon differentiates him from Jeremiah, whose words to the exiles came from Jerusalem. It is quite possible that while Ezekiel was still in Jerusalem he heard Jeremiah preach.

The high literary quality and esoteric imagery of the book suggest that the final version was probably the work of a school loyal to Ezekiel and associated with the Temple cult. Its editors reworked the prophet's words, making them relevant for their own communities.

Organization of the book

The MT and LXX versions of Ezekiel differ in several ways; our study of Ezekiel follows the MT. Our reason for using the MT version is that the oracles in the book relate to one another according to word associations and allusions that can be made only in the Hebrew language; they would be lost in translation, with the result that the probable organizing principles of the book would disappear.

Outline

1–24	Oracles of judgment against Judah	
	1:1–3:27	Call and commission
	4:1–7:27	Fate of Jerusalem and Day of the Lord
	8:1–11:25	Vision of the Lord's glory departing after judgment
	12:1–24:14	Judgment against leaders and people
	24:15-27	Transition: prediction of Jerusalem's fall
25–32	Oracles against foreign nations	
	25:1-17	Against Ammon, Moab, Edom, Philistia
	26:1–28:19	Against Tyre

28:20-26   Against Sidon

29:1–32:32   Against Egypt

33–48   Oracles of salvation for Israel

33:1-33   Transition: news of fall and commissioning anew

34–37   Restoration, new shepherds, covenant, unity, fall of Edom

38–39   Final eschatological battle against Gog

40–48   Vision of restored Temple and land

Genres

DATE FORMULAS. The following dates are identified, arranged canonically in order of appearance in the book:

Reference in Ezekiel	Date in Scripture	Date according to modern calendar
1:1 initial vision	30th year, 4th month, 5th day	593
1:2 initial vision	5th year, 4th month, 5th day	July 593
3:16 appointment as watchman	after seven days	July 593
8:1 temple vision	6th year, 6th month, 5th day	September 592
20:1 Israel's sinful history	7th year, 5th month, 10th day	August 591
24:1 beginning of siege of Jerusalem	9th year, 10th month, 10th day	January 588
26:1 against Tyre	11th year, – month, 1st day	March–April 587–586
29:1 against Egypt	10th year, 10th month, 12th day	January 587
29:17 against Egypt	27th year, 1st month, 1st day	April 571
30:20 against Egypt	11th year, 1st month, 7th day	April 587
31:1 against Egypt	11th year, 3rd month, 1st day	June 587

Reference in Ezekiel	Date in Scripture	Date according to modern calendar
32:1 against Egypt	12th year, 12th month, 1st day	March 585
32:17 against Egypt	12th year, 1st month, 15th day	(March) 585
33:21 fall of Jerusalem announced	12th year, 10th month, 5th day	January 585
40:1 vision of Temple restoration	25th year, 1st month, 10th day	April–October 573

We see that the dates are arranged chronologically for the most part. Only the formula in 29:17, with its 571 date, is out of chronological order. That formula appears thematically in the series of Egypt oracles rather than after the vision of restoration that begins in 40:1, dated in 573.

Almost all the formulas name a year, month, and day, denoting the time from the reference point of Jehoiachin's exile in 597. That date was significant because it marked the end of the monarchy in Jerusalem. Three of the formulas are unique: the first date, given in 1:1, most likely represents Ezekiel's age at the time of his call rather than the date in relation to the exile of Jehoiachin. The second exception is the formula in 3:16, which gives only the number of days since the previous incident. It specifies only "at the end of seven days" and introduces the Lord's commission to Ezekiel to be a watchman for the house of Israel. The second formula in 40:1 is "in the fourteenth year after the city was struck down," reckoning the date from the fall of Jerusalem. All the formulas follow the ancient practice of marking time in relation to significant events rather than according to a fixed calendar.

These formulas remind us that the words in Ezekiel were spoken on particular, significant occasions. They associate the book's words with their historical settings and indicate the passing of twenty-two years from 593 to 571, during which the events associated with Ezekiel's words took place. Chapters 1–24 refer to events prior to the fall of Jerusalem, chapters 25–32 to the period between the beginning of the siege of the city and its fall, chapter 33 to the fall itself, and chapters 34–48 to the time after the fall of the city. This time period overlaps by a few years with the dates assigned to the book of Jeremiah, 627–587.

CALL NARRATIVE. Ezekiel's call comes at the beginning of the book, in 1:1–3:15. This call narrative is significantly longer than most. It begins with a detailed description of the vision that announced the Lord's presence in 1:1-28. The first part of the call itself is in 2:1-8. This is followed by a symbolic act in 2:9–3:3, after which the call continues in 3:4-11. Then in 3:12-15 another incident intervenes, an experience that harkens back to the initial vision. There is no conversation between Ezekiel and the Lord in this report, thus no response or question from Ezekiel. Rather, the Lord addresses Ezekiel repeatedly throughout the incident, in 2:1, 3, 6, 8; 3:1, 3, 4. The repetition of the term "mortal" or "son of man" highlights the divine origin of the words by contrasting the listener with the speaker.

The initial vision comes to Ezekiel in Babylon. It takes place "by the river Chebar," near Nippur. This description recalls the opening words of Psalm 137, "By the rivers of Babylon—there we sat down and there we wept when we remembered Zion," implying that Ezekiel was in a group of exiles gathered for worship near a river when this vision came to him. It involves wind, a cloud, fire, and four living creatures with unusual configurations of human and animal body parts including faces, wings, legs, feet, and hands. Among the creatures a wheel appears and becomes four wheels full of eyes. These move with the wind, in tandem with the movement of the four living creatures. Then a dome appears over the heads of the four living creatures. The number of wings on the creatures changes from four to two, and the sound of their flight is compared to water, an earthquake, and an army. Then above the wings a voice is heard and a jeweled throne appears with a human-like figure with light emanating from it: gleaming amber, fire, and splendor, and a rainbow. This figure is identified as the glory of the Lord.

This complex and highly imaginative description freely combines realistic and fantastic elements into a bewildering, highly figurative account of a very unusual experience. It is an apt description of the uprooting and displacement the Jerusalemites experienced when they were driven from their homeland and exiled to Babylon with its foreign gods, customs, and languages. We get the impression of life turned upside down and rearranged into unfamiliar and disconcerting shapes and movements, which was the experience of the exiles who arrived in Babylon from Jerusalem. In the midst of it all Ezekiel recognizes "the likeness of the glory of the Lord" (1:28).

The voice addresses Ezekiel here and throughout the book as "son of man," translated in the *NRSV* as "mortal." It commands Ezekiel to stand up; then the wind lifts him to his feet. Another translation we need to note is the word "spirit," which literally means "wind," the same word we find in Gen 1:2 to describe the creative power of God. The voice sends Ezekiel to the people of Israel, described as impudent and stubborn (Hebrew: hard-hearted) rebels and transgressors. The voice instructs him, "You shall speak my words to them, whether they hear or refuse to hear; for they are a rebellious house" (2:7). The voice instructs Ezekiel not to fear the people or be rebellious like them, comparing them to briars, thorns, and scorpions. It then directs him to open his mouth and eat what is given him. This call further develops the disconcerting tone of the initial vision by indicating that a force beyond the human overtakes Ezekiel and directs him to go into a hostile environment. He is to go as the Lord's messenger and speak, whether or not his listeners heed his word.

The next section, 2:9–3:3, describes the symbolic act. The Lord unfurls a scroll with words written on both sides of it. Ezekiel recognizes words of lamentation, mourning, and woe. The Lord feeds Ezekiel the scroll, which he takes and eats, noting the sweetness of its taste or the consolation of receiving the word of the Lord. The account includes five commands to Ezekiel: eat, eat, speak, eat, fill your stomach, highlighting the symbolism of the action: Ezekiel fills himself with the word the Lord commands him to speak, filling himself at the same time with the Lord's promised presence and support. The words are reminiscent of Jer 15:16, "Your words were found, and I ate them, and your words became to me a joy and the delight of my heart; for I am called by your name, O LORD, God of hosts."

The symbol of the scroll to connote the divine word recalls events recorded in two previous books. Isaiah instructed his listeners to "bind up the testimony" (Isa 8:16), and Jeremiah dictated the Lord's words to Baruch to record at the Lord's request (Jer 36:2-4). The scroll eventually came into the possession of the king, who, when he heard what was written on it, cut up the scroll and burned it. These two previous references to a written word suggest that by Ezekiel's day the concept of the Lord's word written on a scroll was already familiar.

The second part of the commission follows in 3:4-11, when the Lord instructs Ezekiel to speak to the house of Israel. First, in vv. 4-6 the Lord makes clear that Ezekiel is being sent to a people whose speech he understands because they are the house of Israel. Second, vv. 7-9 emphasize the unwillingness of the people to listen. Ezekiel will be able to deal with them because the Lord will give him a hard forehead, that is, a strong determination, like the hard foreheads of the people to whom he will speak. Then in vv. 10-11 the Lord repeats the commission from 2:7 to speak the Lord's word to the exiles, whether or not they accept it. The Lord's message to Ezekiel highlights the tenacity and resolve the prophet will need in order to deliver the word of the Lord to this stubborn people.

The final section of Ezekiel's call, in vv. 12-15, returns to the living creatures described in 1:4-28. Ezekiel hears the rumble of the creatures and wheels moving as the wind picks him up and takes him away. Ezekiel finds himself among the exiles at Tel Abib near the river Chebar, where he was when the vision began. The text tells us of his stunned and bitter reaction to the experience.

Throughout this call narrative it is clear that the Lord acts within the events of history. The Lord goes to Ezekiel in Babylon, where the people are in exile, and commissions him to preach to them. The Lord who acts within the events of history is not bound by the local confines of the Holy of Holies, or even the land of Judah, but goes with the people, even into a foreign land. This divine visit to Babylon was revolutionary insofar as it introduced a new, unconfined understanding of divine presence among the people. It harkened back to the years of wandering in the wilderness, when the people recognized the divine presence among them in the Ark. Ezekiel's fresh approach opened up the possibility of divine presence in a foreign land, even in the absence of Ark, Temple, or king. It opened the way for the people to worship the Lord in exile, knowing the divine presence was among them.

• Compare and contrast the calls of Jeremiah (chapter 1) and Ezekiel.

VISION REPORTS. Three times the book gives detailed descriptions of visions: the first in connection with Ezekiel's call, discussed in the previous section; then chapters 8–11, which describe the vision of the Lord's glory departing from the Temple after judgment; and finally chapters 40–48, the vision of restored Temple and land.

In chapters 8–11 the vision picks up elements found in chapters 1–3: four flying creatures, wheels with eyes, unwavering direction in flight. It adds other elements that highlight the presence of light that accompanies the glory of the Lord departing from the temple. As in the previous vision, Ezekiel is picked up and moved, this time to the east gate of the Temple, where the Lord instructs him to speak words of judgment to the people for their unfaithfulness. Words of assurance follow in which the Lord promises to give the people new hearts to replace their stony hearts. These new hearts of flesh will allow the people to be faithful. We can relate this idea of new, fleshy hearts to two other points. First, Jeremiah promised the people that the law would be written not on stone but in their hearts (Jer 31:31-34). Now Ezekiel relates to the people God's promise to remove the people's hardheartedness. He had decried it in the first vision (Ezek 3:4-11); centuries earlier hardheartedness had prevented Pharaoh from making wise decisions on behalf of the people. Just as the Lord was able to control Pharaoh's hardheartedness, likewise the Lord intervenes in the lives of the hardhearted people of Jerusalem and offers a new opportunity for faithfulness. After the promise, the vision ends as the glory of the God of Israel leaves, Ezekiel is transported to Babylonia, and he reports to the exiles what he has seen.

Just as we learned from the earlier vision, again we see the Lord finding new ways of appealing to the people to be faithful. Their sins are condemned and punished; then a new beginning for the covenant can take place and the Lord can promise, "Then they shall be my people, and I will be their God" (11:20).

- Note the specific similarities in the visions in 1:1–3:15 and chapters 8–11.

The third vision, in chapters 40–48, shares characteristics of the first and second. It opens with Ezekiel being transported back to the Temple in Jerusalem. In chapters 40–42 he is shown the restored Temple, described in minute detail. All the dimensions of the different precincts are given, as well as a few details about the furnishings for the offering of sacrifices. Then in chapter 43 he witnesses the return of the glory of the God of Israel by the same way that it had left. Ezekiel is instructed to describe the Temple to the exiles after they have repented of their unfaithfulness. The description of the restored Temple continues, alternating with stipulations for proper conduct in each of its areas. These include instructions for carrying out the sacrifice of rededication, a listing of the duties of the levitical priests, the terms of land distribution, values of weights and measures, prescribed offerings for festivals and sabbaths. Then in 47:1-12 Ezekiel sees water flowing in the Temple area, a sign of new life originating in the Temple and spreading throughout the land. The vision concludes with prescriptions for distribution of the land into tribal allotments analogous to, but not exactly the same as the allotments when the people first entered the land after their wandering in the wilderness. All, including resident aliens, are to receive a portion in the land distribution (47:22-23).

A special allotment of land will be given to the prince, the descendant of David, with a section for the Levites as part of the prince's allotment (48:21-22). This stipulation acknowledges the promise to David that he would always have descendants, but implies at the same time that there will not be a king. In fact, when the exiles did return to their land during the newly triumphant Persian empire, they were ruled by a Persian appointee, not by a king from among them.

The details of this final vision highlight the connection between Israel's past and future. References and allusions to the terms of the covenant form the nucleus of the vision, which describes a new life in Israel after the exile. That new life will have many similarities with the life of those who first lived in the promised land, but it will also reflect the changed circumstances of the post-exilic community.

• Compare and contrast the land allotments in Ezek 47:13–48:35; Num 34:1-15; and Josh 13:8–19:51.

REPORT OF SYMBOLIC ACTION. Ezekiel reports at different points that he is told to perform symbolic actions. In 4:1–5:4 he is directed to perform four such acts:

4:1-3	sketch a city on a clay brick
4:4-8	lie on his side
4:9-17	bake unclean bread
5:1-4	cut his hair.

In the first of these actions Ezekiel is to depict a city under siege by tracing it on a mud brick. The mention of mud bricks alludes to the people's oppressive situation in Egypt when they were forced to make bricks. Other than that, there is no interpretation given in the text except: "This is a sign for the house of Israel" (4:3).

The second action contrasts sharply with the first: Ezekiel is to lie on his side, first the left and then the right, for a prescribed number of days. He is not to do anything here except endure what is imposed on him. Again no interpretation is given, but the explanation of the symbolism of the number of years of exile offers a clue that this action symbolizes the exile itself, when the people of Jerusalem must endure years of alienation from their former lives and their independent status. The explanation of the number forty suggests that the passage reached its final form sometime after the exile ended, when the writer knew from hindsight how long the time in Babylon would last.

The third symbolic action is to prepare patties made from six ingredients—wheat, barley, beans, lentils, millet, and spelt—and to eat a specified amount each day. The combination resulted in an unclean food, a violation of the command in Lev 19:19: "You shall not sow your field with two kinds of seed." The command to eat unclean food is not interpreted; it may highlight the uncleanness of unfaithfulness that characterized the lives of the people or the uncleanness of the environment of exile to which Jerusalemites were banished.

The fourth symbolic act is to cut his hair with a sword, then divide the cut hair into three equal parts, with specific instructions as to what to do with each of the three parts. The first is to be burned inside the city when the siege is completed, or when the enemy takes over the city. The second is to be beaten and the third scattered. These acts symbolize what will happen to the inhabitants of the city when the Babylonians take over: some will be burned, others beaten, and still others scattered. But a remnant will be saved, symbolized by the few hairs to be bound in Ezekiel's robe.

Each of these symbolic actions involves everyday materials that are used in an unusual way. The strangeness of the symbolic actions mirrors the strangeness of the people's experience. They were uprooted from all that was familiar to them and inserted into an alien environment with foreign languages, customs, and religious practices. Ezekiel's bizarre expression can throw the reader off balance, just as did the experience of life in Babylon for many of the exiles.

 • In 12:1-16 and 37:15-28 what are the symbolic actions, and what are the interpretations?

WORDS OF JUDGMENT AGAINST ISRAEL. These appear throughout chapters 12–24, in which the prophet condemns the people's many forms of unfaithfulness throughout their entire history. (Israel here refers to the people of God rather than to the geographical identity of the former Northern Kingdom.) The forms alternate between prose descriptions and poetic images of the people's unfaithfulness, interspersed with words of salvation. For example, chapter 14 addresses their worship of idols and their attention to false prophets, warning that these actions will be punished by destruction. But the judgment is followed immediately by assurance that sons and daughters will survive the destruction of Jerusalem and will console the people. Then chapter 15 depicts a metaphor of a piece of wood that is useless because both ends have been burned (vv. 1-5). An explanation follows in vv. 6-8, comparing the wood to the inhabitants of Jerusalem who have made themselves useless by their unfaithfulness.

Chapter 16 looks back over the people's long history of unfaithfulness, beginning with their creation. The chapter ends in vv. 59-63 with the promise of a new covenant and divine forgiveness. Then 17:1-10 recounts the allegory of two eagles and two trees (the trees represent Babylon and Egypt). Its meaning follows in vv. 12-15: the Babylonians carried king Zedekiah off to Babylon. But Zedekiah requested help from Egypt against Babylon. As a result, Jerusalem will not withstand the Babylonian on-slaught. Then vv. 22-24 pick up the imagery of vv. 1-10, offering assurance that God would send a new leader for the people.

Throughout the book, and especially in these chapters, the refrain "you shall know that I am the LORD" recurs frequently. The formula highlights the divine activity and purpose throughout all the events and sufferings associated with the Babylonian exile: these things are taking place in order to assure the people of the Lord's power to care for them.

Chapter 18 is a disputation that begins with a proverb: "The parents have eaten sour grapes, and the children's teeth are set on edge." Then the chapter goes on to interpret the proverb. Here Ezekiel warns against the hopelessness of assuming that one cannot repent on account of the sins of one's forebears, or that even one person who is righteous cannot expect divine care when the community as a whole is guilty. On the contrary, God promises life to everyone who turns away from sin (vv. 28-32).

• In chapter 22, what accusations are made against the city?

ORACLES AGAINST THE NATIONS. The second major section of the book, chapters 25–32, consists of oracles against seven foreign nations: Ammon, Moab, Edom, Philistia, Tyre, Sidon, and Egypt. The words against most of the nations are relatively short, but against Tyre there are three lengthy oracles and against Egypt five long ones. Many of the oracles begin with a metaphor, then develop it, sometimes to the extent that it becomes allegory. For example, chapter 26 begins the series of four oracles against Tyre. The first one opens with the metaphor of a broken gateway to de-scribe Tyre's opinion of Jerusalem. Tyre delights in the prospect of taking advantage of the broken gateway to enhance its own ends. But the Lord will bring upon Tyre the same end it wished for Jerusalem: its own walls will fall at the hands of destroying nations who plunder the city.

The oracle ends with the formula Ezekiel often repeats: "They shall know that I am the LORD" (26:6). In other words, the whole event is actually a demonstration of the Lord's power over all, including the foreign nations.

- In chapter 27, trace the metaphor of a shipwreck to describe the city of Tyre.

The fourth oracle against Egypt, in 30:20-26, uses the metaphor of a broken arm to highlight the Lord's power. In 31:1-18 the metaphor of a tree provides the background for Ezekiel to insist that all power ultimately belongs to God. He explains, "Because it towered high and set its top among the clouds, and its heart was proud of its height, I gave it into the hand of the prince of the nations; he has dealt with it as its wickedness deserves. I have cast it out" (31:10-11).

In all the oracles against foreign nations, the condemnation of their sins offers reassurance to the people of Jerusalem in several ways. First, it shows that the power of the nations is not absolute; they will eventually fall to a power greater than they are. Second, it reminds the people of Jerusalem that God's continuing care for them will outlive the destruction of their enemies.

- In 32:1-16, how does the metaphor of the dragon enhance the meaning of the words against Egypt?

WORDS OF SALVATION. The third section of the book, chapters 33–48, actually follows chapter 24. In the final arrangement of the book, however, the oracles against the nations are inserted between the words of judgment against Israel (the people rather than the geographical entity) and the words of salvation. These words are given in a variety of forms, often combinations of several forms. These forms are, for the most part, subordinate to their message, which consists of original words with interpretations developed over a period of time and inserted into the text. The result is a complex composite of words from different times that highlight the ongoing importance of the message. For that reason we will emphasize the message rather than the forms of these words of salvation.

That message is given within a variety of topics and images: chapter 33 is a transition from judgment to salvation; chapter 34 uses the metaphor of sheep and shepherds to offer assurance to Israel. Chapters 35–36 condemn Edom and encourage Israel; chapter 37 describes the vision of dry bones; chapters 38–39 describe the battle against Gog and Magog; and chapters 40–48 offer a vision of a new temple. We will look at several

Shepherd and Sheep (see Ezekiel 34)

of these words of salvation to see how Ezekiel uses the different forms and images to express the message of hope to the exilic community.

Chapter 33 begins with a messenger formula identifying Ezekiel as the Lord's sentinel. Ezekiel receives instructions to assure the people that their sins will be punished, but the purpose of the punishment is to lead the people back to God. That message is interrupted by a terse announcement from a fugitive who reports the fall of the city (vv. 21-22). Ezekiel then regains the ability to speak, which he had been promised in 24:27 (see also 16:63).

Chapter 34 compares the leaders of Israel to shepherds and the people to their flocks. In vv. 1-10 the Lord condemns the shepherds who use their flocks for their own ends rather than caring for them. The Lord promises to remove those shepherds from their flocks. Then vv. 11-22 assure the people that the Lord will be their shepherd who will gather back the scattered ones and protect the weaker sheep from the stronger ones. In v. 23 the metaphor shifts, and the shepherd becomes David. The Lord promises a Davidic successor who will care for the sheep as their divinely appointed ruler. Ezekiel repeats the familiar refrain, "they shall know that I, the LORD their God, am with them, and that they, the house of Israel, are my people, says the Lord GOD" (34:30), then reiterates the terms of the covenant within the sheep and shepherd metaphor: "You are my sheep, the sheep of my pasture, and I am your God, says the Lord GOD" (34:31).

Chapter 37 contains the vision of dry bones restored to life, the best-known passage in the book of Ezekiel. Verses 1-10 begin similarly to Ezekiel's call in 1:1–3:15. They describe the vision of bones scattered over the ground, then a wind that breathed life into the bones so that they reassembled themselves into living people. Verses 11-14 interpret the vision with a divine promise to restore the exiles to their own land, enlivened by the spirit of the Lord. The purpose of this divine action is the familiar refrain throughout Ezekiel: "You shall know that I, the LORD, have spoken and will act" (v. 14). That is, the vision highlights the ongoing power of God to care for the people, healing their unfaithfulness and offering them another opportunity to live as a faithful covenant people.

We looked at chapters 40–48 above in our consideration of vision reports. Here we call attention to the salvation dimension of the vision. The divine promise of a new temple is an assertion of a hopeful future. The temple, the religious center of the people, will again serve as the place of worship and sacrifice for the people who will return to Jerusalem from exile.

Within the vision report, a digression in 44:4-31 explains the shift in duties of the Levites, who had admitted foreigners into the Temple (perhaps a reference to 2 Kings 23:9). In the new Temple they will assume caretaking responsibilities but will not perform priestly duties: those will be reserved to the Zadokites, who remained faithful.

Chapter 47 describes a river flowing from under the Temple, bringing life and fertility to the entire area. This detail underscores the promise of restoration, highlighting the centrality of the restored Temple as source of new life for the people. It recalls the mention of the stream that would water the ground in Gen 2:6: the divine gift of water that makes life possible is another assurance of God's power in the midst of exile.

- Compare and contrast the depiction of the Temple in Ezekiel 40–48 with the descriptions of the Temple in 1 Kings 6–7 and 2 Chronicles 3–4.

Rhetorical Features

Repetition. Repeated words and phrases throughout the book call attention to significant points in Ezekiel's message. For example, in 3:5-6 the phrase "obscure speech and difficult language" appears twice, emphasizing to Ezekiel that he is being sent to deliver the Lord's message to his own people, not to foreigners. In 13:2-4 forms of the words "prophet" and "prophesy" recur five times: "Mortal, prophesy against the prophets of Israel who are prophesying; say to those who prophesy out of their own imagination: 'Hear the word of the Lord!' Thus says the Lord God, Alas for the senseless prophets who follow their own spirit, and have seen nothing! Your prophets have been like jackals among ruins, O Israel." The repetition highlights the purpose of the instructions to Ezekiel, to condemn the false prophets who lead the people astray by preaching their own word rather than the Lord's message.

In 20:5-6 "I swore to them" appears three times. The repetition underscores the Lord's gift of the covenant to the people, with its inherent promise to care for them throughout their history. In 14:3-7 the word "idols" recurs six times and the words "stumbling block" three times, calling attention to the divine eagerness for the people to turn back to the Lord.

- In 20:7-26, what examples of repetition do you find? What does the repetition add to the message of the prophet?

IMAGERY. Images appear frequently in Ezekiel. The imagery takes familiar objects and give them new meaning in order to teach, condemn, or encourage the people. We have looked at several uses of imagery in our discussion of genres in Ezekiel, especially in the visions and symbolic acts: for example, wheels, eyes, and a scroll in the call of Ezekiel and a brick, bread, and a haircut in the accounts of symbolic acts. Ezekiel gives each of these everyday objects and actions a deeper meaning when he uses imagery to illustrate a point, as we saw above.

Images often appear within metaphors in Ezekiel. We have seen instances of this usage in our discussion of the piece of wood in chapter 15, the sheep and shepherds in chapter 34, and the dry bones in chapter 37. These metaphors are sometimes extended into allegories, such as the eagles and trees in chapter 17. All these examples share the common characteristic of using something familiar to the listener and looking at it from a new perspective to illustrate the point Ezekiel makes.

This combination of the familiar and the strange was an apt way to talk about the situations in which the people found themselves during the period leading up to the exile and then during the exile itself. The very foundations on which their life had been built—land, king, and Temple—were shaken in discombobulating ways. The people were bewildered and confused by the uprooting of the familiar and by their presence in a foreign land with strange customs, languages, and religious practices. By using familiar images Ezekiel offered reassurance that in the midst of all their uncertainties the Lord's faithfulness to them did not waver.

EXTREME LANGUAGE. Related to Ezekiel's use of imagery is his extreme language. This rhetorical feature overlaps with imagery and metaphor but is unique in its intensity of speech. For example, chapter 16 relies on imagery we have already met in Hosea and Jeremiah: the people are an unfaithful spouse. Their unfaithfulness begins with Jerusalem's ancestry among foreigners and continues through the city's birth without proper care or nurturing and during the divine courtship when the Lord bestowed on the city gifts of fine clothing and jewelry. But the city took its finery and made it into idols, turning to prostitution among the nations. In consequence the unfaithful people will be delivered into the hand of the foreigners. Finally, toward the end of the chapter, the Lord promises restoration after punishment.

- Look at the specific images in chapter 16 and note how they express the theme of faithfulness and unfaithfulness.

- Look also at chapter 23 and note its extreme language. Compare and contrast it with chapter 16.

- How do you personally respond to the extreme language in these chapters?

KEY WORDS. The key words *mišpat* (lawful) and *ṣedeq, ṣadiq* (righteous) or *ṣedaqah* (right, righteousness, righteous deed) appear frequently in Ezekiel, sometimes in word pairs. For example, 18:5: "If a man is righteous and does what is lawful and right. . . ." Then throughout vv. 19-27 the words appear in different combinations to highlight the importance of "lawful and right" living. The Lord is always ready to forgive sins; in words reminiscent of Jeremiah the prophet announces: "I have no pleasure in the death of anyone, says the Lord GOD. Turn, then, and live" (18:32).

The word *mišpat* is repeated in several passages. For example, in 5:6-8 *mišpat* appears five times, translated "ordinances" and "judgments." In chapter 20 *mišpat*, translated "ordinances," occurs eight times in vv. 11-25, paired with "statutes" or *ḥuqot* and "sabbaths" or *šabbtot*. These word pairs call to mind the giving of laws at Mount Sinai, when the Lord swore to the people, "I am the LORD your God" (20:5) and made explicit the terms of the covenant. Here the Lord reminds the people of those terms, accuses them of breaking the terms, and urges them to turn back to the Lord by following those terms.

- In 33:14-19 compare and contrast the use of "lawful," "right," "statutes," and "righteousness" to their use in chapter 20.

Ezekiel's Message

Themes

"THEY SHALL KNOW THAT I AM THE LORD." More than thirty times the Lord declares, "They shall know that I am the LORD." This assertion makes clear that divine actions serve the purpose of making known the creative power of the one Lord, whether in punishment of Israel's sin or in forgiveness or in condemnation of foreign nations. This is the Lord who initiated the covenant with the people and who remains faithful to them throughout all the ups and downs of life. The Lord was with the people as they wandered in the wilderness, as they settled in the land, as they built their monarchy and Temple, as they worshiped and carried out the ordinary affairs of their lives, whether faithfully or unfaithfully.

The Lord is with them not only in their own land, but also in the land of exile. All the judgments and promises the Lord gives to the people throughout their lives in these different places serve to make known to the people that it is the Lord who cares for them. Ezekiel calls attention to the Lord's ongoing revelation in new ways under different circumstances. This understanding offers reassurance to the exiles that they can still count on the Lord in the absence of their land, king, and Temple. They gradually come to know the Lord's inbreaking in unexpected ways, such as receiving new hearts to replace their hearts of stone.

"THE GLORY OF THE LORD." This phrase appears frequently throughout the book. It denotes the appearance of the Lord in light such as Moses saw on Mount Sinai (see Exod 34:29-35). The word connotes honor, dignity, and otherness as in the Priestly materials in the Pentateuch. In Ezekiel the expression appears throughout the accounts of Ezekiel's call, the departure of the Lord from the Temple, and the divine return to it. Ezekiel's vision of the Lord by the River Chebar included bright light described as fire, gleaming amber, lightning, and a rainbow. Ezekiel found the light overwhelming; we are told that he fell on his face at the sight of it.

The presence of the glory of the Lord in Babylon shattered the belief that God was present only in Jerusalem and opened up the possibility of worship in a place other than the Jerusalem Temple. Together the two expressions "they shall know that I am the LORD" and "the glory of the LORD" connote the awesome presence of the Lord among the people rather than in a particular location. The Lord was with them in exile, caring for them as always according to the covenant promise, while at the same time offering them new ways of knowing and worshiping the Lord in their changed circumstances. Just as in the days of the ancestors, the Lord continues to find new ways of being present among the people wherever they are.

TEMPLE. Ezekiel includes several priestly concerns among its prominent themes, among which is the focus on the Temple. The departure of the glory of the Lord from the Temple toward the beginning of the book and the return to the restored Temple at the end highlight the Temple's centrality in the lives of the people: it was the site of their pilgrimage, worship, and sacrifice. The people felt its absence keenly when it had been destroyed and they were hundreds of miles away from its former location. But Ezekiel offered the people a new understanding of place by announcing the presence of the Lord among the people in exile, even in the absence of a designated house of the Lord.

This development is one of several ways in which the exilic prophets announced a process of internalization that located the religious center not in a particular geographical location, but rather within the people themselves. We will look further at this internalization process in the next theme, the people's new heart.

A NEW HEART. Ezekiel condemns the stubbornness of the people by using language reminiscent of the encounters among God, Moses, and Pharaoh leading up to the Exodus. God told Moses "I will harden his [Pharaoh's] heart" (Exod 4:21), assuring Moses of the divine ability to prevent Pharaoh from making wise decisions. This assertion, repeated throughout the account of the plagues, is reinforced by declarations of Pharaoh's own stubbornness: for example, "Pharaoh's heart was hardened" in Exod 7:13 and 8:19. Ezekiel, speaking as the divine messenger, asserts, "But the house of Israel will not listen to you, for they are not willing to listen to me; because all the house of Israel have a hard forehead and a stubborn heart" (Ezek 3:7).

But for Ezekiel the people's hard-heartedness is an opportunity for the Lord to offer something new: a new heart of flesh to replace their stony hearts. He assures them: "A new heart I will give you, and a new spirit I will put within you; and I will remove from your body the heart of stone and give you a heart of flesh" (Ezek 36:26). This gift is even more revolutionary than the promise we find in Jeremiah, that the law will be written on the people's hearts (Jer 31:33). Here the hearts themselves will be new. (See also Ezek 11:17-21; 18:31-32.)

PRIESTLY CONCERNS. In addition to its focus on the centrality of the Temple, Ezekiel highlights other topics associated with priestly concerns, such as we find in the P strand of the Pentateuch. We can see this emphasis by comparing passages of Ezekiel with the Holiness Code in Leviticus 17–26.

Leviticus	Ezekiel
18:4-5	20:11
19:3	20:12
19:33-34	22:7-8
20:2-6	14:1-4
26:3-13	34:25-31
26:27-33	7:24-25; 24:21

In the first example, Lev 18:4-5 reads: "My ordinances you shall observe and my statutes you shall keep, following them: I am the LORD your God. You shall keep my statutes and my ordinances; by doing so one shall live: I am the LORD." Ezekiel 20:11 asserts: "I gave them my statutes and showed them my ordinances, by whose observance everyone shall live." Both passages focus on the necessity of keeping the statutes and ordinances of the Lord in order to have life. We note that these words are among the key words that appear frequently throughout the prophetic books. They denote the specific responsibilities given to the people by the Lord, by which the people are to live in grateful response for all the Lord has done for them.

The articulation of these duties in the Holiness Code identified them as the special responsibilities of the people who were chosen as God's holy people, that is, a people set aside for God.

- Note the similarities in the other passages from Leviticus and Ezekiel.

Ezekiel and Jeremiah

Several passages in Ezekiel share commonalities with the book of Jeremiah.

Jeremiah	Ezekiel
3:19-20	20:6-8
6:1	7:14-15
15:1	14:12-16
23:9-15	13:2-19
24:5-7; 31:31-34	11:16-21; 18:31; 36:24-28

These pairs illustrate the gratitude for God's faithfulness and the concern that the people be faithful to God that are common to both Jeremiah and Ezekiel. For example, Jer 23:9-15 and Ezek 13:2-19 both condemn false prophets who lead the people astray by their evil actions and their empty promises.

- What similarities do you find in the other pairs of passages?

Ezekiel in the New Testament

Images that appear in Ezekiel recur in several New Testament books. For example, the image of the shepherd in Ezek 34:11-31 is found in three of the gospels: Matt 18:12-14; Luke 15:3-7; and John 10:2-18. The vine imagery in Ezek 15:1-8 reappears in John 15:1-11.

Several of Ezekiel's images can be found in Revelation as well. For example, the four living creatures, precious metals and stones, and fire, all named in the call of Ezekiel in chapter 1, are also found in Rev 4:3-10. The city of Jerusalem, to which Ezekiel refers in 40:1–41:26 and 48:30-35, appears in Rev 21:1-27. Finally, Rev 20:7-10 refers to the nations of Gog and Magog, who face defeat at the hand of God. Ezekiel refers to Gog as a person and Magog as a place in chapters 38–39.

Ezekiel's Meaning for Us Today

Ezekiel in the Lectionary

Ezekiel is one of the readings for the Vigil of Easter in all three years in both *LM* and *RCL*. In *LM* the reading is 36:16-28 and in *RCL* 36:24-28 and 37:1-14, the promise of a new heart. On the Vigil of Pentecost in all three years *LM* assigns 37:1-14 as one of several options. The reading is Ezekiel's vision of dry bones coming to life.

In Year A Ezekiel appears four more times. On the Fifth Sunday of Lent *LM* pairs Ezek 37:12-14 with John 11, selections from vv. 1-45, and *RCL* pairs 37:1-14 with John 11:1-45, passages that promise new life. These readings teach practical concern for one another. On the Twenty-third Sunday in Ordinary Time *LM* pairs Ezek 33:7-9 with Matt 18:15-20 and *RCL* offers 33:7-11 as one option with the same gospel as *LM*. On the Twenty-sixth Sunday of Ordinary Time *LM* pairs Ezek 18:25-28 with Matt 21:28-32 and *RCL* gives the option of Ezek 18:1-4, 25-32 with Matt 21:23-32, admonishing us to turn to God. On the Feast of Christ the King *LM* pairs 34:11-12, 15-17 with Matt 25:31-46 and *RCL* pairs Ezek 34:11-16, 20-24 with the same gospel reading on the duties of a shepherd.

In Year B, *RCL* offers the option of 37:1-14 on Pentecost (*LM* suggests it on the Vigil of Pentecost) with John 15:26-27; 16:4b-15. In Ordinary Time, on the Eleventh Sunday *LM* pairs Ezek 17:22-24 with Mark 4:26-34, in which trees are images of faith. *RCL* gives the same Ezekiel reading as an option, assigning the same gospel reading. On the Fourteenth Sunday *LM* pairs Ezek 2:2-5 with Mark 6:1-6 while *RCL* assigns Ezek 2:1-5 and Mark 6:1-13 on the implications of being a prophet. Neither lectionary assigns readings from Ezekiel for Year C, other than those common to all three years.

In the Weekday Lectionary Ezekiel is read three times during Lent: on Friday of the First Week Ezek 18:21-28 highlights the importance of reconciliation and is paired with Matt 5:20-26. On Tuesday of the Fourth

Week Ezek 47:1-9, 12 describes Ezekiel's vision of waters flowing from beneath the restored Temple and John 5:1-16 offers instruction on the healing power of water. On Saturday of the Fifth Week Ezek 37:21-28 promises restoration after cleansing the people of their sins, and John 11:45-56 includes God's promise to gather all together in unity.

In addition, Ezekiel is read on the twelve weekdays in the Nineteenth and Twentieth Weeks of Year II. These readings are 1:2-5, 24-28 and 2:8–3:4, both from the call of Ezekiel; 9:1-7; 10:18-22, the departure of the glory of the Lord from Jerusalem; 12:1-12, instructions to carry his bags into exile; 16:1-15, 60, 63 or vv. 59-63, describing Israel's faithlessness and the Lord's faithfulness to the covenant; 18:1-10, 13, 30-32, highlighting the importance of turning back to God; 24:15-23, a prediction of Jerusalem's fall; 28:1-10 against Tyre; 34:1-11 about false shepherds; 36:23-28, a promise of restoration; 37:1-14, the vision of dry bones; and 43:1-7, the vision of the return of the divine glory to the Temple. These weekday readings offer a representative sample of the themes and images found throughout the book.

- Explain how the Ezekiel reading for the Easter Vigil fits its liturgical setting.

- Discuss the relationship between the readings from Ezekiel and Mark on the Eleventh Sunday in Ordinary Time in Year B.

The Jewish community includes five Sabbath readings from Ezekiel, paired with the readings from the Pentateuch. These are:

Genesis 44:18–47:27	Ezekiel 37:15-28
Exodus 6:2–9:35	Ezekiel 28:25–29:21
Exodus 27:20–30:10	Ezekiel 43:10-27
Leviticus 16:1–18:30	Ezekiel 22:1-19 (vv. 1-16 in the Sephardi ritual)
Leviticus 21:1–24:23	Ezekiel 44:15-31

- What interpretation does the reading from Ezekiel offer to the Genesis passage?

- What relationship do you find between the Exod 27:20–30:10 and Ezek 43:10-27 readings? Between the Leviticus 21–24 and Ezekiel 44 readings?

In addition, Ezek 38:18–39:16 is read on the Sabbath during Sukkot, paired with Exod 33:12–34:26. Ezekiel 36:37–37:14 is read on the Sabbath that falls during Passover; and Ezek 1:1-28; 3:12 is read on the first day of Shavuot, the feast of Weeks.

Ezekiel's Significance for Our Daily Life

Ezekiel has much to offer twenty-first-century readers, for whom uncertainty and instability are often the characteristics of everyday life. People who grew up accustomed to clear boundaries and now find themselves on shifting sand with regard to family life, educational opportunities and expectations, social and religious customs, national and international politics can discover in the book of Ezekiel assurance from several perspectives. For example, the prophet emphasizes that faithfulness is always in season: God remains faithful to us and asks for our faithfulness in return. Furthermore, God's presence is within us, not simply in our religious buildings or in any specific location. Divine inbreaking in our lives continues in unexpected ways, helping us to live faithful lives in the midst of uncertainty and alienation. In short, God is always eager to forgive and transform us.

The bizarre imagery Ezekiel uses lends itself to depiction in art, drama, and poetry. An example is Daniel Berrigan's *Ezekiel: Vision in the Dust*, including art by Tom Lewis-Borbely. The bibliographic information is given below.

• How would you depict Ezekiel's message in an artistic medium?

Passages for study

    10:1-22
    16:59-63
    36:22-32
    43:1-12

For Further Reading

Berrigan, Daniel. *Ezekiel: Vision in the Dust,* with art by Tom Lewis-Borbely. Maryknoll, NY: Orbis, 1997.

Duguid, Iain. *Ezekiel and the Leaders of Israel.* Leiden and New York: Brill, 1994.

Eichrodt, Walther. *Ezekiel.* OTL. Philadelphia: Westminster, 1970.

Greenberg, Moshe. *Ezekiel 1–20. Ezekiel 21–48.* AB 22, 22A. Garden City, NY: Doubleday, 1983, 1997.

Halperin, David. *Seeking Ezekiel: Text and Psychology.* University Park, PA: Pennsylvania State University Press, 1993.

Levenson, Jon. *Theology of the Program of Restoration of Ezekiel 40–48.* Cambridge, MA: Published by Scholars Press for the Harvard Semitic Museum, 1976.

Wevers, John W. *Ezekiel.* NCBC. Grand Rapids: Eerdmans, 1969.

Zimmerli, Walther. *Ezekiel.* 2 vols. Hermeneia. Philadelphia: Fortress, 1979, 1983.

———. *I Am Yahweh.* Trans. Douglas W. Stott. Ed. and introduction by Walter Brueggemann. Atlanta: John Knox, 1982.

OBADIAH

"You should not have gloated over your brother
on the day of his misfortune." (Obadiah 12)

Background Information

Obadiah is a short book, with only twenty-one verses and no chapter divisions. The numerals in references indicate the verses; for example, Obad 1-18 refers to vv. 1-18.

Several proper names in the book have significant historical backgrounds. Edom, which means "red," was the name given to Jacob's brother Esau when he begged for some of the stew that Jacob cooked (Gen 25:29-30). Esau and his family eventually settled in Edom (Genesis 36). Obadiah appears in 1 Kings 18 as the administrator of the estates of King Ahab. It was he who hid the prophets in a cave to protect them from Jezebel. It is difficult to situate the book of Obadiah at such an early date, though, in light of the references to the destruction and looting of Jerusalem and Judah in vv. 11-14.

Obadiah most likely originated around 587 or within a few years after that, at the time of the deportation to Babylon. This date is based on vv. 11-14, which suggest some Edomite complicity with the Babylonian conquerors at the time of the destruction of Jerusalem. This arrangement afforded protection for the relatively small Edomite population, who feared the power of the conquering Babylonian army. Furthermore, in vv. 11-14 the angry tone of the condemnation of Edom for not coming to the aid of Judah is quite raw, as would be expected in a description of a fresh and very painful memory. In addition, Edom probably ceased to be an independent state in the mid-sixth century, when it was taken by Nabonidus and incorporated into the Babylonian Empire (Mal 1:2-5); hence the book was most likely written before then. Ezekiel 25:12-14; 35:15; 36:5 also support an early exilic date of composition of the book.

Organization of the Book

The book begins with a historical sketch and ends with eschatological prophecy. Its condemnation of Edom can be interpreted nationalistically or as allusion to the establishment of the Yahwistic community. Likewise, the Day of the Lord can be understood as either a day of reckoning or an abstract eschatological idea. We will concentrate on the historical meaning of the book and will mention the other interpretive possibilities in our discussion of the themes of the book.

Outline

The book of Obadiah is very likely not a composite, unlike many of the prophetic books, but rather a unit that expresses a realistic and compelling condemnation of Edom. The book is easy to outline according to its four messenger formulas in vv. 1-18 and the change from poetry to prose after v. 18. The messenger formulas in vv. 1, 4, 8, and 18 separate the first eighteen verses into three oracles against Edom, followed by Obadiah's comment on the third oracle.

Verses 1-4, 5-7, 8-18	Oracles against Edom
Verses 19-21	Obadiah's prose comment

Genres

MESSENGER FORMULAS. Verse 1 begins: "Thus says the Lord GOD concerning Edom" and v. 4 ends: "says the LORD," marking the beginning and end of the first oracle. The formulas "says the LORD" in v. 8 and "for the LORD has spoken" in v. 18 begin and end the third oracle.

ORACLES AGAINST THE NATIONS. These announcements of judgment are "apostrophes" or speeches to one party when the actual intended listener is another party. Here the announcements address Edom, but the intended listener is the people of Judah. The speaker hopes that they will take heart at the Lord's ongoing care for them, demonstrated in the destruction of the enemy Edom. In this case it is possible that the words were meant to be heard by the people of Edom as well. A variety of motifs announce Edom's impending doom in spite of their defensive advantages: status among the nations in vv. 1-2, inaccessible location in the mountains in vv. 3-4, hiding places and wealth in vv. 5-6, allies in v. 7, wisdom in v. 8, and military might in v. 9.

The first oracle, in vv. 1-4, plays on the image of height to contrast the present status of Edom with its imminent future. The second announcement, in vv. 5-7, focuses on ambush. The third, in vv. 8-18, names specific outrages perpetrated against the inhabitants of Jerusalem, indicating that in the end the perpetrators will be conquered and Jerusalem will triumph.

- In vv. 11-14, in what specific ways did the Edomites augment the destructive acts of the Babylonians against the Jerusalemites?

WORDS OF SALVATION. Verses 17-21 elaborate on the final words of the previous oracle. Verses 17-18 offer assurance that in the end Jerusalem will triumph over Edom, and vv. 19-21 spell out specific ways in which that will take place. The words of salvation conclude with the promise that in the end it will not be the people who triumph, but rather the Lord. Verse 21 sums up this future status with a reference to Mount Zion as the place where the remnant will gather to rule over Mount Esau or the people of Edom. The verse begins with a phrase poorly translated into English in the *NRSV* as "those who have been saved." The Hebrew is "the saviors," and the assertion leads the reader to expect that they will be the new possessors of Mount Esau; but the final proclamation is "the kingdom shall be the LORD's." All are the Lord's people: the children of Jacob and the children of Esau. Israel's future restoration is proclaimed unconditionally. All four passages, even those addressed to Edom, offer hope to Judah that the Lord has not rejected them and will reverse the status quo, leaving Edom destroyed and Zion ruling over it.

- Compare and contrast Obadiah 21 with Amos 1:11-12; Jer 49:7-22; Lam 4:21-22; Mal 1:2-5.

Rhetorical Features

Several rhetorical features intensify the power of the book's message.

IMAGERY. Verse 4 compares Edom to an eagle with its ability to fly and build its nest very high in the sky, "among the stars." The imagery highlights Edom's dramatic fall by contrasting its original height with its lowly end. Verses 5-6 use the images of grape-gatherers and thieves to compare the totality of the destruction with the purposeful activity of harvest and theft. These two groups would take only what was useful to them, while the enemy will totally plunder Edom. Verse 11 uses the image of casting lots for the city of Jerusalem, as if it were a common prize to be awarded to the lucky winner of the draw. Verse 18 uses fire imagery to describe the reversal of power: Edom the destroyer will be consumed by the fire of its victim Israel.

- Note the words that connote "high" and "low" in vv. 1-4.

- How does the fire imagery contribute to the meaning of v. 18?

Another specific image that recurs throughout the book is that of family. The first verse specifies that the oracle is about Edom. But v. 6 refers to Edom as Esau and v. 8 uses the two terms in a parallel construction. In fact, throughout the book the word Edom appears only twice while Esau is used seven times. Four times the place Mount Esau is named; twice the phrase "house of Esau" appears. Both those times are in v. 18, where "house of Jacob" and "house of Joseph" also appear, contrasting the fate of the two peoples. The use of the family name Esau rather than the place name Edom personalizes the tension between the two groups and reminds us of the struggles between Jacob and Esau that began before they were born, and continued throughout their lives. ("House of Joseph" is a symbol for the Northern Kingdom.) The phrase "house of Esau" appears only in Obadiah; it is not found in any other biblical book.

Verse 10 accuses Edom of violence to "your brother Jacob," intensifying the personal, familial reference. The violence is not simply that of one people against another; it is one brother's violent treatment of another. The crime is all the more heinous because when the Israelites were wandering in the wilderness on their way from Egypt to Canaan they had been forbidden to attack Edom because Jacob and Esau were brothers.

Verse 12 again calls Judah "your brother," identifying him with Judah in the following phrase. The familial imagery continues in v. 18 when the destruction of Edom is described as the result of the fire of the house of Jacob and the house of Joseph, which will destroy the house of Esau. Finally, the two references to Mount Esau in vv. 19 and 21 both use the place name to indicate the people who live there. Verse 21 contrasts it with Mount Zion, the home of Jacob's descendants. We are reminded here of the opening words of Psalm 133: "How very good and pleasant it is when kindred live together in unity!" The tragic tension between Jacob and Esau, which continued into the sixth century, reminds us not only of how pleasant it is when brothers and sisters get along, but also how difficult it often is for those closest to one another to be at peace together.

• How does the family imagery intensify the conflict in the book?

PARALLELISM. The pairing of phrases, often including the imagery described above, increases the visual and emotional impact of Obadiah's words. For example, in v. 15b the two clauses "as you have done, it shall be done to you; your deeds shall return on your own head" both make clear that Edom's punishment is no more than what it has imposed on its victims. Obadiah often uses very elaborate parallelism, sometimes in conjunction with chiasms. For example, in v. 11 the middle of the verse describes the destruction of Jerusalem in three parallel ways: "strangers carried off his wealth, and foreigners entered his gates and cast lots for Jerusalem." The same verse begins and ends with reminders that Edom stood idly by while the destruction was taking place. "On the day that you stood aside . . . you too were like one of them." In fact, not only did Edom stand idly by, in doing so it incurred the same guilt as the active destroyers.

REPETITION. In vv. 12-14 the phrase "you should not have . . ." appears eight times. In Hebrew the words are even stronger: "Do not . . . !" Each of these phrases is followed by a clause that names Edom's complicity with increasing intensity, from acts of observation to actual participation in the destruction of Jerusalem in its time of trouble. The repetition hammers home Edom's guilt for not coming to the aid of their brother Judah.

• Find similar examples of repetition in Ezekiel 15 and Psalm 137:7.

TERSE LANGUAGE. There are no extra words in the oracles. The message is expressed in pithy imagery and parallelism. The result is a sharp, concise condemnation of Edom's evil and a succinct announcement that in the end the situation will be reversed and the Lord will reign.

IRONY. Verse 7 mentions the allies of the Edomites, who eventually turned against them. Edom trusted its allies, who enjoyed Edom's hospitality, then turned against Edom in ambush. The treachery of the deceit amazes even the writer, who observes: "there is no understanding of it."

Obadiah's Message

Themes

DAY OF THE LORD. Like many of the prophets, Obadiah makes reference to the Day of the Lord. Obadiah explicitly refers to it in v. 8 as the epitome of destruction of Edom: they will receive the kind of treatment they have inflicted on their own victims. It is thus a day of judgment, of balancing the scales of justice against oppressors and in favor of those who have suffered at their hands.

HOPE FOR THE FUTURE. Obadiah looks forward to a future time when the evils of the present will be transformed and God's reign will prevail. Edom the destroyer will be taken by the previously destroyed Judahites. Mount Zion will be the new center of power from which the Lord will rule over everyone.

SACREDNESS OF FAMILY TIES. Obadiah illustrates the tragic consequences of tensions among family members, who have both the privilege and the responsibility to care for one another. Neglect of family members is even more tragic than neglect of people who are not related to us.

Eschatological Interpretation

The word Edom took on a symbolic meaning in the time of Roman oppression of the Jews, when it became a "code" word for Rome. Members of the community could use the words of Obadiah in reference to the Roman oppressors without risking accusations of sedition against the government. Gradually "Edom" became a code word for any place or people the community hoped would be destroyed.

Obadiah and Jeremiah

Obadiah reiterates and elaborates on the oracle against Edom in Jer 49:7-22. The more detailed description in Obadiah suggests that it is a later text than the Jeremiah oracle.

Obadiah's Meaning for Us Today

Obadiah in the Lectionary

Obadiah is the only prophetic book that does not appear in the *LM*, *RCL*, or Ashkenazi Jewish readings. In the Sephardic community, Obad 1-21 accompanies Gen 32:4–36:43. This pair of readings highlights the Edomite roots of Sephardic Jews as well as the family relationship between Jacob and Esau.

Obadiah's Significance for Our Daily Life

Even though Obadiah is not used in the liturgy, its focus on the sacredness of family relationships is a valuable pastoral resource. It offers an opportunity to review the family beginnings of ancient Israel as they are told in Genesis. It also provides an opportunity to reflect on the importance of caring for one another in the world family to which all people in our global society belong.

• How might Obadiah call us to respect everyone in the global community?

Passages for study

> Obadiah 1-4
>
> Obadiah 5-7

For Further Reading

Raabe, Paul R. *Obadiah: A New Translation with Introduction and Commentary.* AB 24D. New York: Doubleday, 1996.

Sweeney, Marvin A. *The Twelve Prophets,* vol. 1. Berit Olam. Collegeville: Liturgical Press, 2000.

Wolff, Hans Walter. *Obadiah and Jonah: A Commentary.* Trans. Margaret Kohl. Minneapolis: Augsburg, 1986.

Chapter Eight

The Final Years of the Exile: Second Isaiah

After Ezekiel's time about twenty years elapsed before another prophetic voice was heard and preserved. Those twenty years proved to be
decisive ones for the people in exile in Babylon and for the beginnings
of Judaism. We will look first at the background information, and will
then discuss Second Isaiah in the light of the late Babylonian exile.

Background Information

Historical and Geographical Setting

Nebuchadnezzar's army destroyed virtually all the fortified towns in
Judah. The population declined from 250,000 in the eighth century to
about half that many after the first deportation in 597. It continued to
decline until the first return in 538, after which it grew to about 20,000.
Nebuchadnezzar ruled the Babylonian empire until his death in 562. At
his death Jehoiachin was liberated from prison by Nebuchadnezzar's
successor, Evil-Merodach (2 Kings 25:27-30). This began a period of
increasing instability for the mighty Babylonian empire. In thirteen years,
four emperors ruled: Evil-Merodach reigned from 562 to 560, followed
by Nergal-Sharusur from 560 to 556. Then Labashi-Marduk ruled for
part of the year 556.

In 556 Nabonidus took the throne and reigned until 539. He alienated
the local priests of Marduk and eventually fled from Babylon, continuing
to conquer territories for the empire, but even as he did, the empire grew
more and more unstable under the crown prince, Belshazzar. Then a new
conqueror arose from another quarter: Cyrus, who reigned in Medea
from 556 to 530, began to take over the areas that were under Babylonian
control. As it became clear that Cyrus' seizure of Babylon was only a

matter of time, the voice of Second Isaiah began to be heard. Nabonidus tried to forestall Cyrus' forward march by bringing into Babylon the gods of outlying areas. But Cyrus' army took Babylon without resistance when he entered the city and was welcomed as its liberator. Thus the mighty Babylonian empire came to an anticlimactic end and the Persian empire began.

Socioeconomic Situation

We have little concrete information about the situation of the exiles in Babylon. Lamentations and Psalm 137 express bitter grief over the loss of the land and the ramifications for worship. Jeremiah 50–51 hints at suffering, but this is more likely the agony of abandonment by God than physical oppression. Both Jeremiah and Ezekiel allude to reasonable freedom, settlement in communities, marrying, managing their own affairs, working for the Babylonians or in agriculture with a view to exile of long duration. Evidence does not seem to indicate any type of physical persecution of the Judahites or any other exiles at the hands of the Babylonians. On the contrary, many exiles thrived in their new surroundings, contributing to the grandeur of the city of Babylon, learning trades, and adopting ideas from their captors and their fellow exiles from other places.

Religious Issues

The burning question for the exiles was the meaning of the events of the exile and the circumstances in which the people found themselves. The book of Ezekiel and Psalm 137 address the people's questions about the possibility of divine presence among them in Babylon. The response to this question determined the characteristics of life in exile, especially issues related to the relationship between God and the people. They had, since the time of Joshua, lived on land they believed had been given to them by God. Furthermore, since Solomon's day they had understood the Temple as the house of God, the central place for worship, pilgrimage, and sacrifice. In addition, they had seen the monarchy as a divinely-established institution through which God governed the people. All three institutions—land, Temple, and monarchy—had been either destroyed or rendered nonfunctional.

The people were left with fundamental questions about the meaning of their lives. Where was God in all this? Which God would they honor, the one God whose promises seemed to be broken, or the Babylonian gods who had defeated them? How would they worship apart from their sacred space? How would they live as people of the covenant among other exiles who worshiped other deities? Who would help them maintain their identity in the absence of a king who had the power to rule them?

In their state of separation from their sacred place, sacred time assumed new importance. Sabbath observance came into prominence during the exile, as did the practice of male circumcision. Perhaps synagogues, or gathering places, began during this time as well.

As the years passed in Babylon, various efforts to grapple with this basic question of meaning created new ways of understanding the people's own identity and their relationship with God. Among these are the Deuteronomistic History, which reflected on the people's life from the time they came into the land and determined that they, and particularly their leaders, had repeatedly violated the terms of the covenant and consequently had brought the exile on themselves by their own unfaithfulness.

The Priestly History took shape during the exile in an effort to preserve the memory of the public practice of religion. That document recorded topics related to the Temple, priesthood, and sacrifice as well as questions regarding how to live as a people chosen by God.

The earlier prophetic materials were interpreted in fresh ways that reflected on their messages in light of the new circumstances in which the people found themselves. Jeremiah and Ezekiel made highly creative contributions to the effort of resignifying the beliefs and practices of the people. In a word, Jeremiah's promise that the covenant would be written not on stone, but in the hearts of the people, showed that God was still actively intervening in the life of the people, finding new ways to maintain the covenant relationship. Ezekiel's report of a vision of the Lord in Babylon offered assurance that the divine presence was not limited to land or Temple, but continued in the people wherever they happened to be. These insights made it possible for the Judahites to remain faithful to the basic core of their beliefs while adapting their practices to the new situation in which they found themselves.

Second Isaiah came on the scene late in the exilic period and took this resignification process a step farther by transcending the idea of return and suggesting the possibility of a whole new way of life for the people of God.

SECOND ISAIAH

"Comfort, O comfort my people, says your God.
Speak tenderly to Jerusalem, and cry to her that she has served her term,
that her penalty is paid, that she has received from the
LORD's hand double for all her sins." (Isa 40:1-2)

Background Information

Earlier we looked at Isaiah 1–39, or First Isaiah. Now we study chapters 40–55 or Second Isaiah. This part of the book of Isaiah most likely comes from the period toward the end of the Exile, between 550 and 540, most likely closer to 540. The reasons for this determination are thematic, as we will see in our discussion of the prominent themes in these chapters.

Organization of the Book

Even though Second Isaiah is understood to be about two hundred years later than First Isaiah, the chapters are together in one scroll, along with chapters 55–66 or Third Isaiah, in the earliest available manuscripts. Several Isaiah scrolls were found in the caves at Qumran, and these manuscripts include all sixty-six chapters of Isaiah as a unity. We can assume that, just as later prophetic materials were inserted throughout other prophetic books, the same is true of Isaiah with the exception that these later insertions were organized differently. They were placed together after the earlier chapters rather than being inserted immediately after the words they resignify. This organization simplifies our task of understanding, because we can easily see the relevance of these chapters to the people in exile in Babylon with their concerns about alienation, marginalization, loss of power, even loss of identity. (A few passages that appear to be set in the time of the exile are included in chs. 1–39, for example chs. 34–35. We will concentrate on chs. 40–55, knowing that the understanding we reach about this material can help us read the exilic portions of chs. 1–39.)

There are no clues that might help us identify the prophet known as Second Isaiah. This anonymity might be related to political realities of the time such as the possibility of retribution for polemics against Babylonian religious practices (see, for instance, 46:1-2 and 47:1-15).

Reasons for setting Second Isaiah in Babylon toward the end of the exile are the indications within these chapters that the fall of Jerusalem happened in the past (40:1-2), polemics against Babylonian religious practices mentioned above, and references to Cyrus of Persia as a contemporary in 44:28–45:3.

Outline

Chapters 40–55 form a tightly unified whole in which a few genres interweave around themes of promise for the exiles. There is a shift, though, in the focus of the message after chapter 48 that suggests the following two-part structure:

| 40–48 | Messages of hope to the exiled community |
| 49–55 | Zion poems |

Genres

MESSENGER FORMULA. The expression "says the LORD" appears thirty-five times, sometimes including a second title in the formula, especially in chapters 40–48; for example, "Thus says the LORD, the King of Israel, and his Redeemer, the LORD of hosts" in 44:6 and "Thus says the LORD, your Redeemer, the Holy One of Israel" in 48:17. Two messenger formulas appear in 41:21: "Set forth your case, says the LORD; bring your proofs, says the King of Jacob." Isaiah's references to Israel are not to the geographical location but rather to the people and traditions of Jerusalem.

Several messenger formulas include a clause that names a divine action; for example, "Thus says God, the LORD, who created the heavens and stretched them out, who spread out the earth and what comes from it, who gives breath to the people upon it and spirit to those who walk in it" in 42:5; "Thus says the LORD, who makes a way in the sea, a path in the mighty waters" in 43:16; and "Thus says your Sovereign, the LORD, your God who pleads the cause of his people" in 51:22. These formulas recall the divine deeds of creation, release from Egypt, and ongoing care for the people by naming royal honorifics such as "King of Israel," "King of Jacob," "your Sovereign;" using military titles such as "Lord of hosts;" and highlighting divine holiness with the phrase typical of First Isaiah, "Holy One of Israel." The formulas emphasize God's ongoing concern for the people and ability to care for them even in exile in Babylon and in spite of what appeared to be a crushing military defeat.

ASSURANCE OF SALVATION. This form, which we find in the Old Testament primarily in Second Isaiah, includes five elements: a statement of

God's past dealings with Israel, the formula "Fear not," assurance of divine presence or a promise of divine intervention, a description of the results of God's acts, and an explanation of why God chooses to act. The verbs that name divine actions are in the perfect tense in Hebrew, connoting completed action. A description of 41:8-13 is included above in the introduction to basic forms of prophetic speech.

Another example is 43:1-7. It recalls the Lord's past dealings of creation and redemption, assures the people of divine intervention with an allusion to crossing the Red Sea and the Jordan River, promises to gather together all God's people from the ends of the earth, pledges that as a result they will not be harmed by water or fire but will come together as God's people, and explains the reason for this promise: "because you are precious in my sight, and honored, and I love you." The words express the power and love of God by recalling creation and divine saving deeds throughout history and promising new saving actions on Israel's behalf. The assurance that it is God the creator who brings about the new ingathering puts the people in touch with their belief in the one God and demonstrates that God remains uniquely able to care for the people by bringing about a new beginning for those in exile.

- In 44:1-5 identify the elements and the message of assurance of salvation.

ANNOUNCEMENT OF SALVATION. We recall from the introduction to the basic forms of prophetic speech that announcements of salvation are very similar to assurances of salvation except that in Hebrew they are in different tenses. In many prophetic books the difference between them is not recognizable in English, so we refer to both forms as "words of salvation." But in Second Isaiah the words of salvation are so important a part of the book that we point out the distinction in the two forms. We looked above at a few assurances of salvation; here we consider announcements of salvation.

These frequently begin with a messenger formula and refer to a particular difficulty. Then they announce salvation, connecting the saving act with divine purpose. The announcement is expressed in the imperfect tense, which carries a future, or unfinished, meaning. Isaiah 41:17-20 is an example of an announcement of salvation. The first part of v. 17 refers to the thirst the people experience. Then vv. 17b-18 are the Lord's promise to provide the thirsty people with water: rivers, fountains, a pool, and springs. What is more, the presence of water will enable trees to grow in the wilderness: cedar, acacia, myrtle, olive, cypress, plane, and pine.

The variety of trees attests to the plenitude of water the Lord will send. The announcement ends with a statement of the divine purpose, "so that all may see and know, all may consider and understand, that the hand of the LORD has done this, the Holy One of Israel has created it" (41:20). Just as we have seen in the other genres we have discussed, here, too, the concern is to convince the people that the LORD has the power to provide for the people and is eager to do so.

In 42:14-17 it is not the people's prior difficulty that begins the announcement, but rather the acknowledgment of the Lord's silence. Now, however, the opposite occurs: the Lord declares, "I will cry out like a woman in labor, I will gasp and pant." The cry will be spontaneous and genuine, as will be the acts of reversal. Nature will be thrown into reverse, and the Lord will reverse the people's situation as well. The blind will know the way, darkness will become light, rough places will become level. (We are reminded here of one of the opening verses of Second Isaiah (40:4): "Every valley shall be lifted up, and every mountain and hill be made low; the uneven ground shall become level, and the rough places a plain.") Then the Lord's purpose becomes clear: to shame the people who worship false gods. The Lord will demonstrate the ability to turn creation upside down, not as an end in itself but in order to demonstrate power over nature and life, something the gods carved by the people are not able to do.

In 43:16-21 the announcement begins with a messenger formula that includes several divine acts: "Thus says the LORD, who makes a way in the sea, a path in the mighty waters, who brings out chariot and horse, army and warrior." These allusions to the crossing of the sea in Exodus recall the divine power that was manifest on that day and announce a new demonstration of God's ability to act on behalf of the people. The promise is given with the kind of references to nature and animals we find throughout Second Isaiah. The new thing about to take place will be so amazing that it will overshadow everything the Lord has done in the past. The reason for this divine action is to refresh the people the Lord has made, in order that they might praise the Lord.

• In 49:7-12 what announcement of salvation does the Lord give the people?

POLEMIC. Isaiah frequently rails against the nations and their gods, and against his own people as well. These speeches are similar to the oracles against the nations we find in other books insofar as they offer assurance of salvation to the exiles. The polemics are often included in prophetic lawsuits and disputations, two forms we will examine below. The appearance of polemics within legal forms illustrates a shift within prophetic discourse. The examples of divine power are no longer military; after all, the Babylonians would say that they have clearly demonstrated the military superiority of their army and therefore of their deities. Now another kind of example emerges, and that is the legal testimony we find in lawsuits and disputations. Several examples follow.

PROPHETIC LAWSUIT. We looked at this form in the introduction to basic forms of prophetic speech, noting that it includes the summons to trial, speeches by one or both parties, and a sentence. Second Isaiah uses this form to condemn idolatry. For example, the trial in 41:21-24 opens with a summons to the gods to show their evidence that might take the form of disclosing events, either in the past or in the future, to confirm their divine powers. Alternatively they are requested to perform some action, either good or evil, that would frighten the people and convince them of the power of the gods. Then we can imagine a pause in the trial while all wait for evidence to be brought forward. The outcome implies that no evidence was produced: it proclaims the nothingness of the gods and condemns anyone who believes in them.

In 45:20-25 we find another trial against idolatry. The survivors are summoned for trial. Immediately, even before they are invited to present their case, the worshipers of wooden gods are ridiculed. Then they are called upon to present their case by giving information about the past. The judge then offers opposing evidence that the one God, the righteous savior, alone knows the past. The divine judge then (45:22) calls on the assembled audience: "Turn to me and be saved, all the ends of the earth! For I am God, and there is no other." The unique value of trusting in the one God is proclaimed, and the final verdict is: "In the LORD all the offspring of Israel shall triumph and glory" (45:25).

In 48:14-16 all are assembled and the trial begins with a puzzling question: "Who among them has declared these things?" It is not clear what individual or group is meant in the question. But the speech continues with assurance of the Lord's love and guidance of this person, who will act successfully against the Babylonians. Then the speaker acknowledges having been present from the beginning, in words echoed in Prov 8:22-23.

- In 43:26-28, identify the elements of the trial speech and explain the theme.

DISPUTATION. This form is related to the lawsuit insofar as it can be thought of as one element in a trial. It presents an argument against a particular viewpoint, thereby supporting the legal case. Its line of reasoning often resembles that of wisdom writings like the example we saw above in 48:16 that is similar to Prov 8:22-23. A disputation often quotes the opinion to be disputed, followed by the refutation itself.

Isaiah 40:27-31 quotes Israel's assertion that the Lord does not see them. The refutation that follows highlights several divine characteristics: existence from the beginning, understanding, and gift of power to the weak, with the result that "those who wait for the LORD shall renew their strength, they shall mount up with wings like eagles, they shall run and not be weary, they shall walk and not faint" (40:31). In other words, they will exemplify the strength they receive from the Lord, proving that the Lord has not abandoned them.

In 49:14-25 Zion voices the same concern that the Lord has forgotten them. The refutation comes in the tender expression of family relationships. Even if a mother were to forget her nursing infant, the Lord will not forget the people. They are written on the Lord's hands; the barren women will bear many children whom the Lord will carry back to the once-desolate land. Those who oppressed them will become their prisoners. Twice, in vv. 23 and 26, the disputation emphasizes that these things will happen so that the Lord may be revealed.

- Whom does 42:18-25 address? What is the theme of the disputation?

- In 45:9-13, what opinions are refuted? What is the line of argument in the refutation?

SERVANT SONG. Four passages in Second Isaiah are called Servant Songs because they celebrate someone called a servant, who remains anonymous. The passages are 42:1-4; 49:1-6; 50:4-9; 52:13–53:12. In many respects they are unique: they do not follow a typical Old Testament genre or language. Their closest resemblance is to Jeremiah's Confessions. In fact, the four songs themselves are not examples of a common form. They do share a common theme: God has assigned the servant the task of proclaiming God to everyone, including the Gentiles. This task will involve suffering; in fact, the servant is often called the Suffering Servant in view of the burdens that person or group will be asked to bear.

In 42:1-4 the servant is introduced with affirmations of being chosen by the Lord: "whom I uphold," "in whom my soul delights," and "I have put my spirit upon him." The servant's task is to bring forth justice, a commission repeated three times in the Song. This will be done gently: "He will not cry or lift up his voice, or make it heard in the street." The servant will show concern for the vulnerable: "a bruised reed he will not break, and a dimly burning wick he will not quench." Finally, the Song proclaims the eagerness of the nations to receive his message. The Song has a royal tone in the attributes it gives to the servant. It also calls to mind the ancestors Abraham and Jacob as well as Moses, who were called "servant."

In 49:1-6 the servant calls on the Gentiles to listen and identifies himself as a prophet with a "mouth like a sharp sword." The servant is like Jeremiah in several respects: he was called from the womb to be the Lord's servant, and he expresses his trust in the Lord while lamenting the hardships his life has brought him. His task is to restore Israel and to be a beacon to all so that the Lord's salvation might extend to the whole earth.

In the third Song, 50:4-9, the servant is identified as a teacher who will both teach and be taught the Lord's word. In this song as in the previous one the servant describes the suffering that goes with fulfilling his commission: he is struck, spat upon, and insulted; the hairs on his face are pulled out. He is not disgraced by this abuse; rather, he remains determined and confident in the Lord's help as he fulfills his commission. His persecutors will suffer the final defeat: "All of them will wear out like a garment; the moth will eat them up."

The fourth Song, in 52:13–53:12, highlights the suffering the servant endures: he is despised, rejected, infirm, wounded, bruised, oppressed, and finally killed. The Song repeats throughout that he suffers these hardships at the Lord's hands on account of the people's sins, in order for the Lord's will to thrive. The servant's reward will be victory and a long life, a paradoxical ending for one who suffers so much physical battering in carrying out his commission.

The composite impression of the four Songs is of one called by God as king, prophet, teacher, and mediator to proclaim God's word to the nations. Two themes are new here: the focus on the Gentiles and the idea of expiatory suffering. The songs make it clear that God is eager for the salvation not only of the Judahites in exile but of all people. Furthermore, that salvation will be accomplished even in the absence of sacrificial offerings in the Temple. Instead, a person will accomplish this when his life, suffering, and death become a sacrificial offering of expiation for the sins of all.

Rhetorical Features

IMPERATIVES. Second Isaiah uses an abundance of verbs that give commands. The first two verses of the book, 40:1-2, include four imperatives: comfort, comfort, speak, cry. All four verbs are plural (in Hebrew there are different forms for singular and plural commands), commissioning unknown parties to console Jerusalem by announcing that the punishment for unfaithfulness has ended. Verse 9 includes five verbs: get up, lift up your voice, lift it up, do not fear, say to the people. . . .

Lawsuits begin with imperatives that summon the parties to trial; for example, 41:21 begins, "Set forth your case, says the LORD; bring your proofs, says the King of Jacob." This particular lawsuit continues with imperatives that request some show of divinity from the foreign gods: three times the request is made: "tell us," followed by "do good, or do harm." The absence of reply leads to the conclusion in v. 24: "You, indeed, are nothing."

- In 45:20-23, what imperative verbs do you find? To whom are they addressed?

Hymns and words of salvation also begin with imperatives. Isaiah 42:10 begins: "Sing to the LORD a new song"; 43:1 counsels: "Do not fear, for I have redeemed you"; 43:5-6 advises: "Do not fear, for I am with you . . . Give them up . . . do not withhold; bring my sons from far away and my daughters from the end of the earth." This verb form engages the listener and the reader in the action by its sense of immediacy. One does not read Second Isaiah passively; one is drawn into its message by the imperative forms that speak directly, not only to an unknown ancient listener but also to today's reader. Furthermore, commands are forms that leaders use when addressing those they lead. The imperatives in Second Isaiah call attention to the Lord's power to lead, even in exile.

- Note the imperative verb in 43:18. What message does it have for you?

- In 44:1-2, what imperatives do you see? What invitation do they extend to the reader?

- What imperative forms do you find elsewhere in Second Isaiah? How do you respond to them?

RIDICULE. Particularly in the polemical sections the book uses sarcasm or ridicule in its denunciations of foreign gods and their worshipers. In the lawsuits the judge asks the gods to speak or act, then ridicules their silence and inaction; for example, 41:24 concludes: "You, indeed, are nothing and your work is nothing at all; whoever chooses you is an abomination." In 44:1-20 the polemic describes at length the labor involved in "creating" a god. It says with regard to the carpenter, "The rest of it he makes into a god, his idol, bows down to it and worships it; he prays to it and says, 'Save me, for you are my god!'" Later it wonders: "Half of it I burned in the fire; I also baked bread on its coals, I roasted meat and have eaten. Now shall I make the rest of it an abomination? Shall I fall down before a block of wood?" While the claim that the people actually worship the statues they have made is an exaggeration, it nevertheless calls attention to the silliness of placing one's trust in what one has made rather than in the God who made us. Ridiculing the gods highlights the power of the one God.

Second Isaiah's Message

Themes

The overarching intent of Second Isaiah is to reveal the one God who is able and eager to care for the people. Each of the book's themes contributes to that one larger idea.

GOD IS CREATOR. In our discussion of the polemics against idols and their makers we have observed the contrast Second Isaiah makes between the gods made by human hands and the Lord who singlehandedly creates human beings and all of creation. Calling on creation themes links Second Isaiah with the earliest beginnings of the universe. We see this focus on creation in the assertion, "For thus says the LORD, who created the heavens (he is God!), who formed the earth and made it (he established it; he did not create it a chaos, he formed it to be inhabited!): I am the LORD, and there is no other" (45:18). Here the prophet identifies the one and only Lord as the one who created all in an orderly manner hospitable to its creatures, a testimonial to God's power to care for the people and also God's love for them.

But creation does not stop with bringing the universe into being. God continues to create the people by caring for them and providing what they need throughout their lives. For example, we find in 44:21-22: "Remember these things, O Jacob, and Israel, for you are my servant; I formed you, you are my servant; O Israel, you will not be forgotten by me. I have swept away your transgressions like a cloud, and your sins

like mist; return to me, for I have redeemed you." Here the Lord reminds
the people that they have been created by God, and that God will continue to "create" them by forgiving their sins through divine power and
love.

- Note the references to creation in 40:12-17; 42:5-9; 43:1-7, 14-21; 44:2-
  5, 21-22, 24-28; 45:9-12; 51:1-3. What indications of ongoing creation
  do you find in these passages?

FEMININE CHARACTERISTICS OF GOD. Second Isaiah turns to images of
motherhood to describe divine nurturing power and presence. For
example, 44:2 declares that the Lord formed Israel in the womb, while
46:3-4 comforts the people with assurance that the Lord has carried them
since birth. These tender depictions portray yet another facet of divine
creative power: its tenacious maternal strength that endures and overcomes any threat to the wellbeing of the child.

- What maternal image of God do you find in 42:14?

DIVINE LOVE FOR THE PEOPLE. The Lord freely declares divine love for
the people in 43:4; 48:14; 54:8, 10; 55:3. That love is the reason for divine
action on behalf of the people, just as we find in the declarations of love
in the book of Deuteronomy.

- Compare and contrast Isa 43:4; 48:14; 54:8, 10; 55:3 with Deut 7:7-8;
  10:15-18; 23:5.

THE EXODUS. We notice frequent references and allusions to the Exodus
in Second Isaiah. This was the founding event in the creation of Israel
as the people of God, and thus the example *par excellence* of God's power
to care for the people and eagerness to do so. For example, Isaiah ex-
claims in 43:2, "When you pass through the waters, I will be with you;
and through the rivers, they shall not overwhelm you." The words recall
the parting of the waters of the Reed Sea and the Jordan River when the
people left Egypt and entered the new land at the beginning and end of
the time in the wilderness. At the same time the indefinite phrasing
expands the context of divine care beyond the specific events of the forty
years in the wilderness, to include instances of God's providence in the
past and in the future. This expression of ongoing protection brings
together the two themes of creation and redemption; God's continuing
creation of the people takes various forms, especially forgiveness and
transformation.

• Note the references and allusions to the Exodus in Isa 43:16-19; 48:21; 51:10. What broader meanings do you find in the passages?

THE TRADITIONS OF ISRAEL. In addition to the creation and Exodus themes, Second Isaiah refers and alludes to other traditions of Israel to demonstrate God's ongoing power and concern. We find references and allusions to Noah, Israel's ancestors, the chosen people, David, and Zion, often interwoven with assurances of continuing care in the present and future. These references to the past do not include recitals of divine deeds throughout specific periods in Israel's history like those in Amos 2:9-11; 5:25, or in Isa 7:1-9. Here the mention of them strengthens the historical ties between God and the people, giving additional credibility to the divine promises of new things to come.

• In the following passages, what references and allusions to Israel's traditions do you find: 41:8-16; 44:26; 45:17; 48:12; 49:7, 14-21; 51:2; 52:1-2; 55:3? How do these references to the past strengthen the promises about the future?

ONE GOD. In Second Isaiah we find unequivocal announcements of monotheism. The refrain "I am God, and there is no other" recurs throughout the book in the only unequivocal statements of monotheism in the Old Testament aside from Deut 4:35, 39. These statements form the climax of Second Isaiah's teaching about God's power and concern for the people. The God of Israel is not only able and willing to care for the people, even in the humiliation and alienation of exile; the Lord is the only God. The Babylonian gods are not more powerful than the Lord; they do not even exist. These statements speak to immensely creative ideological developments among the exiles: the people who questioned whether their God was able to care for them effectively, and was still interested in their wellbeing, reached a profound level of belief and understanding about the very nature of God.

• Note the declarations of monotheism in 44:8; 45:5-7, 14, 18, 21-22; 46:8-9. Whom does Isaiah call to witness these declarations in each case?

A NEW BEGINNING. The declarations of monotheism exemplify a new level of understanding and belief that emerged among the people in exile. Several explicit references to something new occur; the allusions to making a way in the wilderness and desert suggest a new Exodus for the people in exile. For example, 43:18-19 advises, "Do not remember the former things, or consider the things of old. I am about to do a new thing; now it springs forth, do you not perceive it? I will make a way in the wilderness and rivers in the desert." These words announce that a major qualitative change is imminent.

- How do Isaiah 40:24-27; 42:9; 52:12; Hos 2:14-20 announce a new beginning?

- What other new beginning in Israel's past does Isa 54:9 recall?

That beginning will actually empower the exiles to announce the Lord to all people. Therein lies the drama: the same people who struggled to come to terms with the apparent loss of their God are now commissioned to announce God's presence to all. We find in 40:9: "Get you up to a high mountain, O Zion, herald of good tidings; lift up your voice with strength, O Jerusalem, herald of good tidings, lift it up, do not fear; say to the cities of Judah, 'Here is your God!'" This charge announces a new day of courage when the exiles, strengthened by God's power and concern, become the spokespeople who will convince others to believe in God. This new beginning is even more significant than the question of return to Jerusalem. The people will not go back to life as before; they are changed by their experience of God in Babylon.

- What do 42:9-10 and 48:1-8 proclaim about something new?

- Compare and contrast Second Isaiah's promise of a new beginning with Jeremiah's letter to the exiles in Jer 29:1-23 and his words in 31:2-6, and with Ezekiel's words to the people in Ezek 11:14-25; 18:30-31; 20:33-38; 33:21-22.

CYRUS THE ANOINTED ONE. The Lord will bring about the promised new beginning through one who does not even know the Lord: Cyrus the Mede. We know that Cyrus conquered the Babylonian empire and decreed that exiles should return to their own lands to rebuild their former lives. Second Isaiah mentions him without naming him in 41:2-4, then refers to him as the Lord's shepherd in 44:28 and the Lord's anointed in 45:1. The divine messenger says of him, "I have aroused Cyrus in righteousness, and I will make all his paths straight; he shall build my city and set my exiles free, not for price or reward, says the LORD of hosts" (45:13). With these words Second Isaiah asserts that Cyrus is a messiah, an anointed one who will guide the people according to the terms of the divine-human relationship even though he does not know the Lord who leads him. In this respect his position is similar to that of the Assyrian conqueror Shalmaneser V (see 7:20).

• What promises does the Lord make to Cyrus in 45:1-7?

Similarities and differences between First and Second Isaiah.

Now that we have looked at the significant aspects of both First and Second Isaiah we can compare and contrast them. We note first of all the major similarity in the two Isaiahs: the emphasis on the transcendent God, including the frequent use of the title "Holy One of Israel" in both First and Second Isaiah. In Second Isaiah this title contrasts God with the idols of the nations.

But there are significant differences as well, and these indicate the passage of time from First to Second Isaiah. In Second Isaiah there is no mention of Assyrian political events from the period of Hezekiah as there is in First Isaiah. Instead, the destruction of Jerusalem is past (40:1-2; 47:6) and Cyrus of Persia is a contemporary figure (44:28; 45:1) connected to the imminent fall of Babylon and repatriation of the exiles who are addressed in chapters 40–55.

We will look again at these similarities and differences when we study Third Isaiah, chapters 55–66.

Second Isaiah in the New Testament.

We are all familiar with the similarity between Isa 40:3 and Matt 3:3; Mark 1:3; Luke 3:4-6; John 1:23. All urge their listeners and readers to prepare the way of the Lord. In Second Isaiah the words are spoken by an unknown voice urging the people to make ready for the coming of the God of Israel, drawing on language and imagery from the Babylonian New Year's festival of enthronement. The gospels attribute the words to John the Baptist, suggesting that he is living in the wilderness and adding a christological dimension to the command.

Matthew 12:18-20 quotes Isa 42:1-3 almost verbatim, applying the words to Jesus and adding a christological identity to Isaiah's anonymous servant. Acts 8:32-33 quotes Isa 53:7-8, part of the Fourth Servant Song, applying them to Jesus when Philip responds to the question "About whom, may I ask, does the prophet say this, about himself or about someone else?" (Acts 8:34). As we will see below, the Lectionary assignment of Servant Songs during Holy Week further highlights the Christian tendency to interpret the Songs in light of Christ's redemptive suffering. It is helpful to keep in mind that the first meaning of the Songs makes clear that all are called to participate in redemptive suffering.

In other instances New Testament passages allude to words from Second Isaiah and apply them to the disciples' teaching. For example, the Fourth Gospel alludes to Second Isaiah in John 7:37-38, where John applies the image of water to the Holy Spirit. The words recall Isa 55:1, which names water as an essential source of human life. Likewise James 2:23 refers to Abraham as God's friend, as does Isa 41:8.

- Compare and contrast Isa 40:3 and John 1:23; Isa 42:1-3 and Matt 12:18-20.

Second Isaiah's Meaning for Us Today

Second Isaiah in the Lectionary

The Sunday Lectionary draws frequently on readings from Second Isaiah. Several readings are used in Years ABC: in the Christmas Mass during the Day Isaiah 52:7-10 and John 1:1-18 both proclaim the presence of the word among us. The Sunday after Epiphany (the Baptism of our Lord) includes Isa 42:1-4, 6-7, the First Servant Song, in *LM* for all three years. The *RCL* gives 42:1-9 for Year A, *LM* offers 55:1-11 as a second option for Year B, and in Year C the option of 40:1-5, 9-11. The *RCL* gives 43:1-7. Each year the gospel account of Jesus' baptism is read. On Palm Sunday Isa 50:4-7 in *LM*, 50:4-9 in *RCL*, part of the Third Servant Song, is read with the gospel account of the Passion for that year. On Good Friday Isa 52:13–53:12, the Fourth Servant Song, and John's account of the Passion are read. In *LM* the Easter Vigil includes Isa 54:5-14 and 55:1-11, both of which offer assurances of divine care and protection for the people. The *RCL* includes only 55:1-11.

In addition, during Year A, Second Isaiah appears six times on the Sundays of Ordinary Time. On the Second Sunday, Isa 49:3, 5-6 in *LM* and 49:1-7 in *RCL*, part of the Second Servant Song, is read with John 1:29-34 in *LM* and 1:29-42 in *RCL*, the words of those who serve the Lord. On the Eighth Sunday, *LM* Isa 49:14-15 and *RCL* 49:8-16 and Matt 6:24-34 offer assurance that the Lord remembers the people. On three Sundays the readings are parts of chapter 55. On the Fifteenth Sunday, in Isa 55:10-11 in *LM* and 55:10-13 in *RCL* and Matt 13:1-23 images of growing crops teach about the word of God; on the Eighteenth, Isa 55:1-3 in *LM* and 55:1-5 as an option in *RCL* and Matt 14:13-21 remind us that God nourishes us; and on the Twenty-fifth in *LM*, Isa 55:6-9 and Matt 20:1-16a recall for us that God is beyond our understanding. On the Twenty-ninth Sunday of the Year Isa 45:1, 4-6 and Matt 22:15-21 in *LM* and Isa 45:1-7 (an option) and Matt 22:15-22 point out the relationship between God and civil authorities.

In Year B Second Isaiah appears four times. On the Second Sunday of Advent Isa 40:1-5, 9-11 in *LM* (40:1-11 in *RCL*) and Mark 1:1-8 announce the coming of God, Isaiah at the end of the exile in Babylon and Mark with regard to the ministry of John the Baptist. On the Seventh Sunday of Ordinary Time Isa 43:18-19, 21-22, 24-25 in *LM*, 43:18-25 in *RCL*, and Mark 2:1-12 announce new things God will do among the people in spite of their unfaithfulness. On the Twenty-fourth Sunday of Ordinary Time Isa 50:5-9 (50:4c-9 in *NAB*), part of the Third Servant Song, and Mark 8:27-35 in *LM*, 8:27-38 in *RCL* both pertain to suffering on behalf of others. On the Twenty-ninth Sunday Isa 53:10-11 in *LM*, 53:4-12 (an option) in *RCL*, part of the Fourth Servant Song, and Mark 10:35-45, like the readings for the Twenty-fourth Sunday, teach about suffering on behalf of others.

In Year C, Second Isaiah is read on the Fifth Sunday of Lent: Isa 43:16-21 announces a new thing among God's people, and *LM* John 8:1-11 illustrates something new when Jesus refuses to condemn the woman caught in adultery. The *RCL* pairs the Isaiah reading with John 12:1-8, Mary's anointing of Jesus.

In the Weekday Lectionary, Second Isaiah is read during Advent and Lent, when the readings for Years I and II are the same. During Advent the readings are semi-continuous, following the readings from First Isaiah. On the Second Tuesday Isa 40:1-11 and Matt 18:12-14 remind us that God lets no one be lost. On the Second Wednesday Isa 40:25-31 and Matt 11:28-30 urge us to rely on God for comfort. On the Second Thursday Isa 41:13-20 and Matt 11:11-15 teach us about God's presence among us in other people. On the Second Friday Isa 48:17-19 and Matt 11:16-19 teach the importance of obedience. In the following week, on the Third Wednesday, Isa 45:6-8, 18, 21-25 and Luke 7:18-23 portray divine acts of power: creation in Isaiah and healing in Luke. On the Third Thursday Isa 54:1-10 and Luke 7:24-30 remind us that God cares for us. On the Third Friday, Isa 56:1-3, 6-8 and John 5:33-36 point out several witnesses to the Lord.

In Lent the reading for Monday of the First Week is Isa 55:6-9; for Tuesday of the First Week, Isa 55:10-11 highlights the power of the divine word and Matt 6:7-15 teaches us the Lord's Prayer. On Thursday of the Fourth Week, in Isa 49:8-15 and John 5:17-30 the Lord comforts the people. Then on Monday, Tuesday, and Wednesday of Holy Week parts of three Servant Songs are read. On Monday Isa 42:1-7 and John 12:1-11 teach us to serve the Lord by serving other people. On Tuesday Isa 49:1-6 and John 13:21-33, 36-38 describe faithful and unfaithful servants of God. On Wednesday Isa 50:4-9 and Matt 26:14-25 focus for the third time in Holy Week on servants of the Lord.

Readings from Isaiah 40–55 appear frequently in the Jewish community, including ten times in the weekly Sabbath readings. At the beginning of the yearly cycle of readings, Isa 42:5–43:11 in the Ashkenazi calendar and 42:5-21 in the Sephardi calendar are read with Gen 1:1–6:8. Then Isa 54:1–55:5 in the Ashkenazi calendar and 54:1-10 in the Sephardi calendar are read with Gen 6:9–11:32. Isaiah 40:27–41:16 is paired with Gen 12:1–17:27. Isaiah 43:21–44:23 is read with Lev 1:1–5:26. Several passages from Second Isaiah are read with Deuteronomy as well. Isaiah 40:1-26 is paired with Deut 3:23–7:11. Isaiah 49:14–51:3 is paired with Deut 7:12–11:25. Isaiah 54:11–55:5 is read with Deut 11:26–16:17. Isaiah 51:12–52:12 appears with Deut 16:18–21:9. Isaiah 54:1-10 is read with Deut 21:10–25:19. Isaiah 55:6–56:8 is paired with Deut 31:1-30.

In the afternoon of the Ninth of Av, Isa 55:6–56:8 is read with Exod 32:11-14; 34:1-10. This same pair of readings is used on other days of fast, in both morning and afternoon.

We note that the Fourth Servant Song is not included in the Jewish Lectionary. This passage has become so closely associated with the Passion of Christ in the Christian community that the Jewish community does not use it for liturgical purposes.

Second Isaiah's significance for our daily life

The disillusionment and confusion of the experience of exile in Babylon expressed itself in the people's questions and uncertainties. It eventually led to a new conviction about themselves, their God, and their relationship to other peoples. They emerged from their sufferings strengthened and renewed by the new insights born of their struggle to find meaning in the upheavals of their lives.

People today can take comfort in the exiles' experience of transformation. Just as God was with them in their efforts to come to terms with their situation of alienation and disarray, God is with us in our own confusion and upheaval. This kind of experience permeates today's world of economic and political turbulence, social and familial instability, military confrontation, strong individualism, isolation, and loneliness.

• Name a particular situation of alienation or upheaval of which you are aware. Select three passages from Second Isaiah you would recommend for reflection on God's presence in that situation.

Passages for study

>   40:1-11
>
>   41:1-5
>
>   43:1-4
>
>   50:1-3

For Further Reading

Brueggemann, Walter. *Hopeful Imagination: Prophetic Voices in Exile.* Philadelphia: Fortress Press, 1986.

————. *Texts That Linger, Words That Explode.* Minneapolis: Fortress Press, 2000.

Clifford, Richard J. *Fair Spoken and Persuading: An Interpretation of Second Isaiah.* New York: Paulist, 1984.

McKenzie, John L. *Second Isaiah.* AB 20. Garden City, NY: Doubleday, 1967.

Smith-Carpenter, Daniel L. *A Biblical Theology of Exile.* Minneapolis: Fortress Press, 2002.

Westermann, Claus. *Isaiah 40–66: A Commentary.* Trans. David M. G. Stalker. OTL. Philadelphia: Westminster, 1969.

Whybray, Roger N. *Isaiah 40–66.* NCBC. Grand Rapids: Eerdmans, 1975.

Willey, Patricia T. *Remember the Former Things: The Recollection of Previous Things in Second Isaiah.* Atlanta: Scholars, 1997.

Chapter Nine

The Persian Period and the Second Temple:
Third Isaiah, Haggai, Zechariah 1–8

Background Information

Historical and Geographical Setting

Cyrus's rule was characterized by respect for the conquered peoples of his empire. One of his first official acts, in 538, was to issue an edict that sent the exiles back home to their own territories to rebuild their lives and cities. The edict was recorded on the Cyrus Cylinder; it is informative to compare and contrast it with the versions in Ezra 1:1-4 and 6:2-5. As a result of the edict a few Judahites returned to Jerusalem, reinstituted the sacrificial rituals, and began work on rebuilding the Temple (Ezra 1–4).

In 525 Cyrus's successor Cambyses (530–522) conquered Egypt, strengthening the Persian hold on the entire region. He was the only Persian ruler who did not honor the practice of installing and supporting local rulers. He commissioned Sheshbazzar as Persian governor of the region, an unsuccessful appointment, as it turned out. Little was accomplished during Cambyses' lifetime. When Cambyses died without heir in 522 the kingship fell to Darius I (522–486).

Darius's early reign was marked by much unrest, which he quelled successfully except in Egypt. He was an able administrator who restored order by establishing careful organization and expecting regular accountability. During his reign Syria-Palestine became important to the Persians because of its location as a bridge between Persia and Egypt. Early in his reign, in 520, Tattenai (governor of Syria-Palestine under Darius I) negotiated with Haggai and Zechariah to continue the rebuilding effort (Ezra 5:1–6:12), giving new energy to the project. (Hag 1:3-11 and 2:15-17 suggest that a major wave of return of exiles had already taken place quite a few years before 520.) That year saw the beginning of serious work on rebuilding the Temple in Jerusalem, where sacrifice had already been reinstituted a few months earlier. The new Temple was dedicated in 515, in the sixth year of Darius's reign. It provided a rallying place for the remnant of returnees, but they had no political autonomy. The Temple was referred to as the Second Temple (Ezra 6:13-22).

At Sheshbazzar's death Zerubbabel, Jehoiachin's grandson and Sheshbazzar's nephew, was appointed Persian governor of the region. His tenure was a successful one, supported by the stability Darius brought to the Persian throne. Nevertheless, this was a time of significant disappointment and hardship for the returnees in Israel. The realities of life did not at all match the magnificent vision Second Isaiah had articulated. The returnees suffered from bad weather (Hag 1:6-11; 2:15-17), political insecurity, claims to the land by those who had remained and by Samaritans. The result was disenchantment (Zech 8:10). Zerubbabel disappears from the literary record after 518, probably because of the growing importance of the high priests in both the civil and religious spheres and the increasing significance of the soon-to-be-rededicated Temple.

The Bible is virtually silent about the seventy years after the completion of the Second Temple except for what we can infer from Obadiah and Malachi around the year 450. The Temple assured the continuity of the Jewish community as a religious body, but the political and civil future of the people was uncertain. Darius continued to expand the boundaries of the Persian empire; he established a system of government that balanced central and local administration. At his death his son Xerxes (486–465) succeeded him. Xerxes conquered Babylon, then reinstated Persian control over Egypt. However, the heyday of the Persian empire had passed. Xerxes was succeeded by Artaxerxes I (464–424), during whose reign Nehemiah and Ezra brought about reform in Jerusalem. In 464 the second Egyptian revolt gave Artaxerxes his first opportunity to confront the newly emerging Greek presence. The relationship between Persians and Greeks was complex from the start. At first the Persians welcomed the Greeks into their homeland, while the Persian army passed through Judah en route to and from battle with the Greeks.

Second Zechariah tells us that Persian policy included militarization, commercialization, ruralization, and ethnic collectivization that led to intermarriage between returnees and foreigners. These policies can be understood in several different ways, either as enhancing the viability

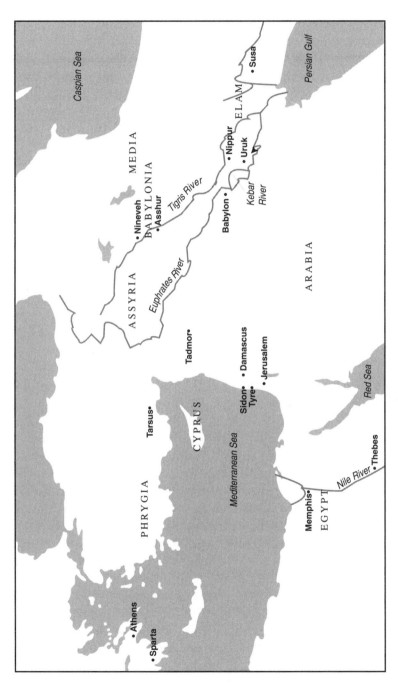

The Extent of the Persian Empire

of the newly settled territories or as threats to the integrity of the Lord's people. In actuality, both of these things occurred.

Artaxerxes was succeeded by Darius II (423–404), Artaxerxes II (404–360), Artaxerxes III (360–338), Arses (338–335), and Darius III (335–332). Then in 332 a new conqueror brought fear and conquest to the area: Alexander the Great.

Socioeconomic Situation

The early returnees found that Judah offered them only limited agricultural opportunities. The land was now owned by people who had served the previous owners. These new landholders and their families required larger plots of land than they had tilled as tenant farmers. In addition, major economic trading centers, including Jerusalem, had been destroyed. The returnees began to develop larger collectivities called "father's houses," whose origins could be traced to pre-exilic times. This system made possible some integration of returnees with the people who had been working the land while its former owners were in Babylon.

Meanwhile, Jewish communities continued to flourish in Babylon and elsewhere throughout the Persian empire, including Egypt, as we know from the papyri found at Elephantine. These communities followed their own local customs, adopting various syncretistic practices with which they had become familiar in their dealings with other local communities. And Jews continued to trickle back to the towns they had been forced to abandon under the Assyrians and Babylonians. Their high priests probably provided the only official leadership; Persian civil appointees were not concerned about the best interests of their Jewish subjects. Eventually, probably around 445, the Jewish people began to fortify the city of Jerusalem in order to protect themselves (Ezra 4:23; Neh 1:3). The Persian rulers in Samaria, not wanting to see the Jewish community regain any power or influence, put a stop to this work.

Religious Issues

The religious life of the people continued and, except for the absence of a king, probably resembled the pre-exilic cult. The people very likely saw themselves as the remnant of Israel (Hag 1:12, 14; Zech 8:6, 12). However, their disillusionment expressed itself in a lack of zeal for religious life, as faithfulness did not seem to be worthwhile (Mal 2:17; 3:13-15). Malachi gives us details about this state of affairs: the offering of imperfect sacrifices to God (1:6-14), partiality in the application of the Law (2:1-9), intermarriage with Gentiles (2:11-12), the prevalence of divorce, accompanied by threats to the integrity of the community (Mal 2:13-16; Neh 13:23-27), cheating and taking advantage of the vulnerable (Mal 3:5; Neh 5:1-5), and non-payment of tithes, making it impossible for Levites to earn a living (Mal 3:7-10; Neh 13:10-14). Nehemiah condemns violations of the Sabbath (Neh 13:15-22). All in all, the community was in danger of disintegration unless the people could find a way to pull together.

From around 450, Nehemiah and Ezra provided the leadership necessary to reorganize the Jewish community, Nehemiah in political affairs and Ezra in spiritual concerns. Nehemiah arrived in Jerusalem in 445 and was there until around 433, as we know from the Elephantine texts and from administrative records that set his term at twelve years. It is not at all clear when Ezra came there; three possible dates have been suggested: 458, 428, and 398. The date that fits most readily with our reconstruction of the history of that time is 428.

Nehemiah was a Jew in the court of Artaxerxes. The difficulties the Jews were experiencing in Jerusalem were brought to his attention, and he arranged with Artaxerxes to provide resources for rebuilding the walls of the city (Neh 5:14; 10:1). By 440 he was in Jerusalem, rallying the people and organizing the rebuilding project. The city wall was rebuilt in spite of opposition from several parties including the Samaritan governor, who found Nehemiah's efforts a threat to his own authority. Once the walls were built, Nehemiah encouraged the people to return to the city. When his twelve-year term expired he returned to the Persian court.

After a very short time Nehemiah was reappointed. When he returned to Jerusalem he found serious laxity in religious affairs. He imposed a series of administrative measures in an effort to curb these irregularities, but it was Ezra the priest who brought about reform among the people. He arrived in Jerusalem around the year 428 with a copy of the Law and a commission from the king to regularize the religious life of the people who identified themselves as Jews in Jerusalem and the surrounding area. Ezra began his work by assembling the people, reading the Law, and having it translated into Aramaic for them. Very shortly afterward the people celebrated the feast of Booths. In spite of their first fervor, though, they did not easily abandon their violations of the Law. Ezra continued his efforts, publicly confessing the people's sins to the Lord. This moved the hearts of the men, who agreed to divorce their foreign

Jaffa Gate in the Old City of Jerusalem

wives. They assembled in Jerusalem to solemnize this promise, and Ezra appointed a commission to study each case and dissolve the applicable marriages.

Shortly afterward the people assembled again, this time publicly to accept life under the Law. The specific terms that were important at the time were agreement to keep the Sabbath, not to intermarry with foreigners, to give the land a rest every seventh year, and to support the Temple cult with annual taxes, first fruits, wood, and tithes. Ezra accomplished his mission of reform in about a year's time, after which he disappears from the record. He is often called the founder of Judaism because of the significance of his work of reform and organization of the community into a group of observant Jews whose commitment to the covenant insured their continuity as a religious body.

There is some question as to which law Ezra actually brought with him to Jerusalem: the Priestly laws? the Pentateuch? It is not certain. What is clear, however, is that the commitment of the people to live by the Law gave them recognized status within the Persian empire, not as an independent nation but as a community authorized to regulate its own internal affairs according to the Law of Moses. This status as a community gave them the structure and credibility to thrive as a people, and has formed the backbone of their life ever since.

THIRD ISAIAH

"The spirit of the Lord GOD is upon me,
because the LORD has anointed me;
he has sent me to bring good news to the oppressed,
to bind up the brokenhearted,
to proclaim liberty to the captives,
and release to the prisoners." (Isa 61:1)

Background Information

Third Isaiah speaks to three points of tension the returning exiles faced as they attempted to put their lives back together. The first was the strained relationships between themselves and those who had occupied the land during the years of exile. The second, related to the first, was the vast discrepancy between the promises Second Isaiah had made and the reality the people discovered on their return: the discouraging reality was a land of devastated buildings and depleted soil. The third was dissension and lack of incentive to rebuild the Temple.

Organization of the Book

Chapters 60–62, and perhaps also 57:14-20; 65:16b-25; 66:6-16 are considered the nucleus of the book. These chapters seem to coincide with the years 537–521 (see especially 60:13). They form a literary unit, with a message of salvation that hearkens back to Second Isaiah. The date of the rest of the work is impossible to determine, but it was probably completed by the year 455.

Outline

Third Isaiah is difficult to outline because, except for chapters 60–62, which form the nucleus of the book, it is a collection of loosely related sayings. The following outline offers a general way of looking at the book's contents.

56–59	Independent sayings that contrast the righteous and the unrighteous
60–62	Nucleus: Third Isaiah's proclamation of salvation
63–66	Independent sayings that contrast the righteous and the unrighteous

Genres

ANNOUNCEMENT OF SALVATION. Third Isaiah does not include assurances of salvation, the distinguishing genre of Second Isaiah, in which promises are given in the perfect, or completed, tense. Here the promises are announcements of salvation, given in the imperfect or unfinished tense, and strongly in the spirit of Second Isaiah. The nucleus, chapters 60–62, contains a series of four announcements of salvation: 60:1-22; 61:1-3; 61:4-11; and 62:1-12.

The first of these, 60:1-22, has two parts: vv. 1-9 and 10-22. Imperatives in vv. 1 and 4 set the tone for the first part: "Arise, shine" and "Lift up your eyes and look around." The first imperative announces the coming of the Lord, using the contrasting images of light and darkness. The second imperative introduces the ingathering of the nations, supported by the question, "Who are these that fly like a cloud, and like doves to their windows?" Verses 10-22, the second part of this announcement, describe the state of salvation brought about by the ingathering.

The description has three sections: vv. 10-14 describe the rebuilding of Jerusalem, vv. 15-18 the effect on Zion, and vv. 19-22 the implications for the entire cosmos. We can see the shared features with Second Isaiah here: imperatives in vv. 1 and 4 and language in 60:4 that is very similar to 49:18. In the second announcement, 61:1-3, the Anointed One describes the mediating actions he will perform.

- What similarities do you find between 61:1-3 and the Servant Songs in 42:1-4 and 49:1-6?

The third announcement of salvation, 61:4-11, which elaborates on 61:1-3, forms the centerpiece of Third Isaiah. Its promises in vv. 4-7 presuppose a prior lament about the damage that had been done to Jerusalem. Then vv. 8-9 announce the divine promise of blessing. Verses 10-11 respond to the Lord's promise with words of praise. Metaphors that rely on weddings and on garden growth express the people's praise of God, who brings righteousness to all people.

Chapter 62 reiterates the announcements from chapters 60–61 that Jerusalem will be vindicated in the eyes of all people. It picks up the marriage metaphor from the previous announcement in vv. 4-5, and the section ends with new names promised to the people in 56:5 and 62:2: "Holy People, The Redeemed of the Lord," "Sought Out, A City Not Forsaken," culminating in 62:4: "My Delight Is in Her" and "Married," in contrast to "Forsaken" and "Desolate."

- Compare and contrast 62:10-11 and 40:10.

Autobiographical report. A limited amount of autobiographical information about the prophet appears in 61:1-2 and 62:1. These few verses depict Third Isaiah as a prophet in the spirit of Second Isaiah, reworking the exilic message for the new situation in which the returnees find themselves. The promised salvation, according to Third Isaiah, depends on perseverance in rebuilding their former lives.

- What echoes of Second Isaiah do you find in 61:1-7?

Response to a Lament. Isaiah 59:1-21 is a response to a lament. It begins with an assertion that the Lord is not helpless, responding to an unspoken accusation that God has not helped the people. Then vv. 2-8 indict the people for their sins of violence, injustice, and deceitfulness. In vv. 9-11 the people bemoan the difficult situation they face, but in vv. 12-15a they acknowledge that their suffering is the result of their own sins. The Lord responds in vv. 15b-21, decrying the lack of justice and announcing divine deliverance to the people.

In 63:7–64:12, vv. 7-14 describe the Lord's past acts on behalf of the people. Then the people describe the difficulties they face, seeing themselves deserted by their ancestors and oppressed by God. Throughout their complaint they interject words of confidence and cries for help. The first is in 63:15, where the people appeal to divine power and compassion. In 64:1 they plead that God's name be revealed through divine assistance to the people, and in 64:8 they appeal to the familial relationship between God and themselves. In the final verse they accuse God of remaining silent in the midst of their struggles.

- In 63:7–64:2, what sins do the people acknowledge that they have committed?

ADMONITION. In 58:1-12 we find an admonition on the subject of fasting. It is addressed to all and declares that giving up food has no religious value unless it leads to actions on behalf of the vulnerable—that is, the oppressed, the hungry, the homeless, and the naked.

- In 66:1-4, what religious institution is given secondary importance in relation to care for the vulnerable?

ORACLE AGAINST THE NATIONS. The oracle in 63:1-6 opens with questions to establish the identity of someone approaching from Edom. The response, however, does not offer precise identifying details but rather establishes the divine nature of the visitor: "It is I, announcing vindication, mighty to save." As this stranger comes closer, the sentry asks a second question, this time about the visitor's red-stained clothing. The divine visitor's response acknowledges that a battle has been fought, continuing the metaphor of treading grapes that the sentry used in framing the question. The response focuses on the singlehanded victory of the visitor against the enemy, alluding to the great cosmic battle between the Lord and Pharaoh leading to the Exodus. Just as the Lord defeated Pharaoh in the plagues and finally at the Reed Sea, so the Lord was victorious over the present enemy. The precise identity of the enemy, and the reason for battle, are not explained in the oracle. It focuses only on the divine victory, accomplished without assistance from allies. The victory over enemies is assurance to God's people that they can count on divine protection from their foes.

- What characteristics of an oracle against the nations do you find in 66:6?

Rhetorical Features

SIMILES. Third Isaiah frequently uses similes to illustrate the coming salvation. Some of these depict the change that will come over the people: for example, "Then your light shall break forth like the dawn" (58:8) and "Who are these that fly like a cloud, and like doves to their windows?" (60:8). Some illustrate ritual uncleanness: for example, "We have all become like one who is unclean, and all our righteous deeds are like a filthy cloth. We all fade like a leaf, and our iniquities, like the wind, take us away" (64:6) and "a people who provoke me to my face continually, sacrificing in gardens and offering incense on bricks" (65:3). Others describe the Lord: for example, "So those in the west shall fear the name of the LORD, and those in the east his glory; for he will come like a pent-up stream that the wind of the LORD drives on" (59:19) and "For the LORD will come in fire, and his chariots like the whirlwind" (66:15). The comparisons are based largely on imagery of animals and natural phenomena familiar to the audience.

• How do the similes in the following verses enhance Third Isaiah's message: 57:20; 58:1; 59:10-11; 62:1?

KEY WORDS. All the key words that appear throughout the prophetic books are found in Third Isaiah. The words *mišpat* and *ṣedeq* or *ṣedaqah*, frequent among all three Isaiahs, appear together several times in Third Isaiah. For example, in 56:1 we find "Thus says the LORD: Maintain justice *(mišpat)*, and do what is right *(ṣedaqah)*, for soon my salvation will come, and my deliverance *(ṣedaqah)* be revealed." In 58:2 we read "Yet day after day they seek me and delight to know my ways, as if they were a nation that practiced righteousness *(ṣedaqah)* and did not forsake the ordinance *(mišpat)* of their God; they ask of me righteous judgments *(mišpete-ṣedeq)*, they delight to draw near to God."

• Compare and contrast the use of "justice" *(mišpat)* and "righteousness" *(ṣedaqah)* in 59:9, 14 with 56:1 and 58:2.

Other key words also appear. The word *ʾemunah* in 59:4 is translated "honestly." The word *ḥesed* appears twice in 63:7, along with *raḥamim*: "I will recount the gracious deeds *(ḥesed)* of the LORD, the praiseworthy acts of the LORD, because of all that the LORD has done for us, and the great favor to the house of Israel that he has shown them according to his mercy *(raḥamim)*, according to the abundance of his steadfast love *(ḥesed)*." These key words link Third Isaiah's message with First and

Second Isaiah and all the other prophets expressing essential character-istics of the covenant relationship between God and the people, and among the people themselves.

Third Isaiah's Message

Themes

SALVATION. For Third Isaiah salvation is understood in terms of this world, and within history for the most part. The promised salvation includes peace and security, joy and honor brought about by the presence of the Lord among the people. These qualities will overcome the eco-nomic hardship and political insecurities (60:1-18), ruins, devastation, and shame (61:4-7; 62:4-9) faced by the returning exiles. On the other hand, empty observance of religious rituals will delay the advent of salvation among the people. In a few instances salvation is described in apocalyptic terms, outside the realm of history (60:19-20; 65:25), but these are rare in Third Isaiah.

- How does 65:18-23 depict salvation in Jerusalem?

- Compare and contrast 11:6-9 and 65:25.

SERVANT ROLE OF THE PEOPLE. The servant people of Israel have a part in the great transformation that divine salvation will bring about. This transformation does not depend on destruction of Israel's enemies; instead, nations and kings will come to the light (56:3-7; 60:3; 66:18-23) and bring back the dispersed (60:4; 66:12); they will bring their treasure to Jeru-salem (60:9) and acknowledge the mighty acts of God (60:6; 61:9; 62:2).

WORSHIP AND SACRIFICE. Third Isaiah assumes that the community will worship and sacrifice in the Temple (60:6-7, 13; 62:9). In addition, the people are enjoined to keep the Sabbath (56:1-2; 58:13-14), avoid idol worship (57:3-13), and uphold their covenant obligations in their deal-ings with one another (58:1-12; 66:1-7); all of these actions are essential accompaniments of right worship.

- To what covenant obligations do 58:1-12 and 66:1-7 call the people?

Third Isaiah's Meaning for Us Today

Third Isaiah in the Lectionary

In Year B, readings from Third Isaiah appear twice during Advent. On the First Sunday in Advent *LM* pairs Isa 63:16b-17; 64:1, 3b-[7]8 with

Mark 13:33-37 and *RCL* pairs 64:1-9 with Mark 13:24-37, readings that express expectation of the Lord. Then on the Third Sunday in Advent *LM* assigns 61:1-2, 10-11 with John 1:6-8, 19-28 while *RCL* pairs 61:1-4, 8-11 with the same reading from John, about those who announce the Lord.

In *LM* in all three years the First Reading for the Christmas Vigil is Isa 62:1-5, which tells of the Lord's delight in the people, paired with Matt 1:(1-17) 18-25, the genealogy of Christ. For the Second Mass on Christmas (at Dawn) *LM* assigns Isa 62:11-12 and Luke 2:15-20, and *RCL* has Isa 62:6-12 and Luke 2:(1-7) 8-20, all of which describe the presence of a savior.

On the Feast of the Holy Family, the First Sunday after Christmas, for Year A, *RCL* pairs Isa 63:7-9 with Matt 2:13-23 in readings about family relationships and activities. For Year B *RCL* assigns Isa 61:10–62:3 with Luke 2:22-40. The Gospel gives an account of the presentation of Jesus in the Temple, borrowing words from Isaiah that appear in the First Reading. In all three years on Epiphany both *LM* and *RCL* assign Isa 60:1-6 about the ingathering of all who are scattered, and Matt 2:1-12, the account of Jesus' birth.

In Year C, *RCL* offers Isa 65:17-25, God's promise of a new creation, as an option for Easter, paired with John 20:1-18 or Luke 24:1-12, both of which are Resurrection accounts.

In Year A on the Fifth Sunday in Ordinary Time *LM* pairs Isa 58:7-10 with Matt 5:13-16 and *RCL* assigns Isa 58:1-9a (9b-12) with Matt 5:13-20. All these readings represent God's presence as light. On the Twentieth Sunday in Ordinary Time *LM* pairs Isa 56:1, 6-7 with Matt 15:21-28, and *RCL* gives Isa 56:1, 6-8 as an option with Matt 15:(10-20) 21-28. The readings emphasize the importance of concern for the marginalized.

In Year C on the Second Sunday in Ordinary Time *LM* pairs Isa 62:1-5 with John 2:1-12 and *RCL* assigns the same reading from Isaiah with John 2:1-11. In these readings, weddings announce God's concern for people. On the Fourteenth Sunday in Ordinary Time *LM* pairs Isa 66:10-14c with Luke 10:1-9 (10-12, 17-20) and *RCL* gives the Isaiah reading as an option, paired with Luke 10:1-11, 16-20, assuring us that God's presence brings peace and prosperity. On the Twenty-first Sunday in Ordinary Time *LM* assigns Isa 66:18-21 with Luke 13:22-30 and *RCL* gives Isa 58:9b-14 as an option with Luke 13:10-17, reminding us that God's reign encompasses everyone. On the Thirty-third Sunday in Ordinary Time *RCL* gives Isa 65:17-25 as an option with Luke 21:5-19. These readings highlight endings and beginnings.

In the *LM* Weekday Lectionary, in Years I and II, Isa 56:1-3, 6-8 is read on the Third Friday in Advent with John 5:33-36, focusing on the importance of faithfulness to God. The *RCL* offers the option of Isa 58:1-12 on Ash Wednesday. On the Friday after Ash Wednesday, Isa 58:1-9 is read with Matt 9:14-15, about the spirit of fasting. Isaiah 58:9-14 and Luke 5:27-32 are read on the Saturday after Ash Wednesday, calling for a spirit of concern for the vulnerable. On Monday of the Fourth Week of Lent, Isa 65:17-21 and John 4:43-54 rejoice in the healing action of God.

In the Jewish community Third Isaiah appears in three Sabbath readings: 60:1-22 is read with Deut 26:1–29:8; 61:10–63:9 is read with Deut 29:9–30:20; and 55:6–56:8 is read with Deut 31:1-30. The same Isaiah passage is read with Exod 32:11-14; 34:1-10 on the afternoon of the Ninth of Av, the day that commemorates the destruction of the Temple by the Babylonians. (Second and Third Isaiah are not understood as separate documents in this lectionary.) In addition, Isa 57:14–58:14 is read on the morning of Yom Kippur with Lev 16:1-34 and Num 29:7-11. Isaiah 66:1-24 is read on Rosh Ḥodesh and Shabbat Hanukkah.

Third Isaiah's significance for our daily life

Third Isaiah speaks to us in times of regrouping, reorganizing, and refocusing after events of major stress. It calls us to hang onto basic beliefs and practices and to the confidence that God is with us in our daily efforts to remain faithful when there is no public recognition of our struggles or our efforts at fidelity.

• Select three passages in 3 Isaiah that might offer encouragement to people trying to be faithful in the midst of difficulties today.

Passages for study

> 61:1-7
> 65:1-7
> 66:14-16

For Further Reading

Berquist, Jon L. *Judaism in Persia's Shadow: A Social and Historical Approach.* Minneapolis: Fortress, 1995.

Habel, Norman C., ed. *The Earth Story in the Psalms and the Prophets.* Earth Bible 4. Cleveland: The Pilgrim Press, 2001.

McKenzie, John L. *Second Isaiah.* AB 20. Garden City, NY: Doubleday, 1967.

Westermann, Claus. *Isaiah 40–66: A Commentary.* Trans. David M. G. Stalker. OTL. Philadelphia: Westminster, 1969.
Whybray, Roger N. *Isaiah 40–66.* NCBC. Grand Rapids: Eerdmans, 1975.

HAGGAI

"On that day, says the Lord of hosts,
I will take you, O Zerubbabel my servant, son of Shealtiel,
says the Lord, and make you like a signet ring;
for I have chosen you, says the Lord of hosts." (Hag 2:23)

Haggai and Zechariah are often discussed together because the date formulas in the two books overlap, as we will see in the chart below. We will actually look at the two books in three parts: first Haggai, then Zechariah 1–8, and finally Zechariah 9–14. The reason for separating Zechariah into two parts is chronological: as we will see, the final six chapters seem to be set at a time considerably later than chapters 1–8.

Haggai is a traditionalistic and pragmatic book with a hands-on message of encouragement to rebuild the Temple. This pragmatism fits the needs of the time, when rebuilding the Temple was understood as the first step in reconstituting the cultic practices of the community and providing a home for God's blessing. It is traditionalistic insofar as it affirms much that appears in earlier prophetic books.

Background Information

Haggai's message corresponds to events related in Ezra 2:68–3:13, which include building an altar, beginning to offer sacrifices on it, and laying the foundation for the new Temple. The upheaval within the Persian empire at that time gave Haggai and Zechariah an opportunity to encourage the community in the rebuilding effort. There was no king to initiate and fund the project, motivate the people to participate, or reconstitute the cult in the tradition of its monarchic beginnings. Furthermore, the governor appointed by the Persian emperor was occupied with external affairs rather than the needs of the Jewish people. This lack of effective civil leadership left a void the religious leaders could fill, providing security and encouragement to the people.

Haggai's message is easy to set historically because of the date formulas throughout the book. We noted these above; they cover a period of about four months from August 29 to December 18, 520. Two dates mark significant milestones in the rebuilding project: 1:15 sets the date of September 21, 520 as the starting date for the concerted effort to rebuild, and 2:15 refers to an event similar to ancient Near Eastern rededication ceremonies; this took place on December 18, 520.

Organization of the Book

Haggai and Zechariah are often discussed together because the dates listed in the formulas in the two books overlap, as we can see below.

Reference	Date in Scripture	Date according to today's calendar
Hag 1:1	2nd year, 6th month, 1st day	August 29, 520 B.C.E.
Hag 1:15	2nd year, 6th month, 24th day	September 21, 520
Hag 2:1	2nd year, 7th month, 21st day	October 17, 520
Zech 1:1	2nd year, 8th month	October–November 520
Hag 2:10	2nd year, 9th month, 24th day	December 18, 520
Hag 2:20	" "	" "
Zech 1:7	2nd year, 11th month, 24th day	February 15, 519
Zech 7:1	4th year, 9th month, 4th day	December 7, 518

As we can see, the first date in Zechariah precedes Haggai's final oracle, and the second date in Zechariah comes two months after Haggai's final oracle.

Outline

Date formulas throughout the book define its historical setting as the four-month period from August 29 to December 18, 520. The five date formulas help to delineate three principal parts of the contents of the book.

1:1-15a   Positive response to Haggai's encouragement to rebuild the Temple during a 24-day period

1:15b–2:9   Haggai's encouragement to continue the project, 28 days
after the first encouragement

2:10-23   Haggai's instructions to the priests and to Zerubbabel
for a new time, two months after the second
encouragement.

Genres

MESSENGER FORMULAS throughout the book stress that Haggai's words
came not from himself but from the Lord. The Temple rebuilding venture
was ultimately God's project, and God promised to be with the people
throughout the rebuilding effort. The rebuilt Temple would be a visible
sign of the Lord's presence among the people, just as the pillars of cloud
and fire were signs of God's presence during the wandering in the
wilderness.

PROPHETIC HISTORY. The genre of the book is prophetic history: that
is, history that is understood as revelatory. It was written by people who
had both scribal training and access to records of prophetic activity. The
text is the result of reflection on the developing role of the prophets during the period of restoration: they were seen as a source of information
and guidance for both civil and religious leaders (that is, the governor
and the high priest). In addition, the text shows the prophetic interest in
the Temple as an institution that impacted not only the community's
religious practice but also its social and economic life.

BIOGRAPHICAL INFORMATION. The superscription gives genealogical
information for the two recipients of Haggai's words: Zerubbabel son
of Shealtiel, governor of Judah, and Joshua son of Jehozadak, the high
priest. The information concerning these two men supports our understanding that the civil leadership at the time was Persian and the religious leader was the local high priest. Details about both Haggai and
Zechariah and their work are given in Ezra 5–6 but not in the books
named for them. For Haggai the lack of genealogical information moves
the focus away from him as a person, toward an emphasis on his call
from the Lord as the source of his prophetic authority.

Rhetorical Features

REPETITION. Several words and phrases recur throughout the book.
We have already noted the date and messenger formulas. In addition,
the word "consider" appears five times, in 1:5, 7; 2:15, and twice in 2:18,

urging the people to reflect on their circumstances. Twice, in 1:5 and 7, Haggai proposes that the people think about their own reduced circumstances during the time when they concentrated on rebuilding their own homes rather than the Lord's house. Then in 2:15-19 he challenges them twice to think about the reversal of fortune their repentance will cause: he assures them as the divine messenger "I will bless you," repeating the formula that recurs frequently throughout Genesis.

The words "I am with you" appear twice, in 1:13 and 2:4. Then in 2:5 Haggai adds "do not fear." These phrases link Haggai's words with Second Isaiah's in 41:10 and 43:5: "Do not fear, for I am with you." These assurances offer the people a further pledge of the value of their rebuilding efforts: God is with them in this work.

- What other examples of repetition do you find in Haggai? What meaning do they add to the book?

KEY WORDS. The key words often found in the prophetic books are not present in Haggai. Two other expressions do occur, and both are significant for Haggai's message.

Remnant of the people. Haggai includes the remnant of the people among those who took his words to heart, mentioning them in 1:12 and 1:14. The remnant joined Zerubbabel and Joshua in obeying the Lord and making a serious effort to rebuild the Temple. Haggai speaks to the remnant with Zerubbabel and Joshua in 2:4 as well, assuring them of the Lord's presence among them in their rebuilding effort. "Remnant," by now familiar in the prophetic books, specifies those in Jerusalem after the return from Babylon who participated in the rebuilding effort, thus giving witness to their commitment to the Lord.

Spirit (ruaḥ). This word first appears in Gen 1:2, where it is translated "wind": "a wind from God swept over the waters." It connotes power and is often used to describe the power of God. Elsewhere in the Old Testament the word is translated "spirit," another way of describing divine energy. Translations such as "rushing energy," "abiding power," or "sweeping power" capture the ancient understanding of the word. While the Christian understanding of the Holy Spirit is related to this ancient idea of divine energy, that connotation does not inhere in the word itself as it is used in the Old Testament. Here the word connotes energetic commitment to the rebuilding project, the result of divine power among the people. In 1:14 it describes the energy of Zerubbabel, Jehozadak, and the remnant of the people. In 2:5 it refers to divine power and appears with "do not fear" and "I am with you," offering assurance that God stirs up the people to undertake the rebuilding project.

Haggai's Message

Themes

HAGGAI'S ROLE IN THE REBUILDING PROJECT. The text tells us that Haggai encouraged the people to rebuild the Temple by relating their situation to the Deuteronomistic theme of retribution. Their concentration on rebuilding their own homes rather than the Temple was seen as an act of unfaithfulness, which resulted in a lack of resources for the rebuilding effort. When the people redirected their efforts toward rebuilding the Temple they were rewarded with the resources necessary for the project, as Haggai 1:2-14 explains.

Haggai encourages the reconstitution of religious practices by supporting the authority of the priests. He urges the priests to interpret the laws about ritual purity in 2:10-13. He then relates that request to the rebuilding effort, inviting the people to reflect on its meaning in 2:14-19 by promising God's blessing. His words highlight the importance of the rebuilt Temple and the reconstituted cult in the lives of the people.

ZERUBBABEL'S ROLE. Haggai refers to Zerubbabel as governor, servant, and chosen one. The language that focuses on him in 2:20-23 is reminiscent of Second Isaiah's references to the people as chosen servant (Isa 42:1 and 43:10), of Second Isaiah's commission to Cyrus (45:1-4), and of Jeremiah's condemnation of Jehoiachin (Jer 22:24). Some see Zech 3:8 and 6:12-13 as additional references to Zerubbabel because of the repetition of the title "Branch." Zerubbabel would serve as an instrument of the Lord even if he actually believed in a different deity.

- Compare and contrast Hag 2:20-23; Isa 41:8-9; 42:1; 43:10; 44:1-2; Ps 78:70-72.

TRUST IN GOD. Haggai commissions and encourages the people to rebuild the Temple, reassuring them with two important reminders. The first is that God is present among them: "I am with you, says the LORD" (1:13; 2:4). He recalls God's presence among the people at the time of the Exodus in Hag 2:5, and promises that the Lord is eager to live among them in the rebuilt Temple (1:8). The second reassurance is that the people can depend on the Lord's strength, as we saw above in the discussion of the word *ruaḥ*. God's energy will underwrite the rebuilding effort; the people are enjoined to catch that spirit and use it to rebuild their Temple and their cultic life under the leadership of Joshua and Zerubbabel.

These two promises connect the immediate program of Temple rebuilding with the eschatological hope of blessing based on God's presence. Haggai's words assert that these two realities go hand in hand to assure the people that God is with them, and to motivate them to proceed with the work of rebuilding. Haggai also encourages the people in their disappointment when they see that the rebuilt Second Temple does not measure up to the magnificence of the first. Again he assures them that the Lord's presence among them does not depend on the splendor of the Temple.

Haggai's Meaning for Us Today

Haggai in the Lectionary

Haggai does not appear in the Sunday *LM*. It does appear once in *RCL*, as an option on the Thirty-second Sunday in Ordinary Time in Year C, when Hag 1:15b–2:9 is paired with Luke 20:27-38. Both readings address questions about the future.

In the Weekday Lectionary in Year 1, Haggai is read on Thursday and Friday of the Twenty-fifth week in Ordinary Time. On these two days 1:1-8 encourages the people to rebuild the Temple while Hag 2:1-9 promises that the Temple will be filled with God's glory. Haggai does not appear in the Jewish readings.

Haggai's significance for our daily life

Haggai's words of encouragement are like a pep rally, energizing the people for the task of rebuilding that confronts them. That message can stimulate us today to undertake tasks that might prove tedious but are necessary nonetheless. We, like Haggai's audience, can take heart in his reminder, "do not fear," knowing that God is with us in our efforts.

• What temples in our own lives need rebuilding today?

Passages for study

  2:10-19

  2:20-23

RSV, NRSV	*NAB*, MT, LXX
1:18-21	2:1-4
2:1-13	2:5-17

As we noted above, Zechariah 1–8 includes date formulas showing that Haggai and Zechariah 1–8 overlap in their historical settings. We copy the chart here, to focus on the dates in Zechariah 1–8.

Reference	Date in Scripture	Date according to today's calendar
Hag 1:1	2nd year, 6th month, 1st day	August 29, 520 B.C.E.
Hag 1:15	2nd year, 6th month, 24th day	September 21, 520
Hag 2:1	2nd year, 7th month, 21st day	October 17, 520
Zech 1:1	2nd year, 8th month	October–November, 520
Hag 2:10	2nd year, 9th month, 24th day	December 18, 520
Hag 2:20	" "	" "
Zech 1:7	2nd year, 11th month, 24th day	February 15, 519
Zech 7:1	4th year, 9th month, 4th day	December 7, 518

Genres

Even though First Zechariah overlaps with Haggai in its historical setting, its style is quite different. Haggai is pragmatic and straightforward, and Zechariah 1–8 is symbolic and abstract. This difference is evident in the genres of the books. First Zechariah as a whole is a theological reflection, as we explain below. Within that overarching designation we find a variety of genres in particular passages; dominant are messenger formulas, date formulas, revelation reports, vision reports, and reports of symbolic action. We have discussed the messenger and date formulas in previous chapters. Here we will focus on the other genres.

THEOLOGICAL REFLECTION. The entire book is a prophetic theological reflection on history as a source of encouragement for the present. It illustrates the post-exilic understanding of the role of the earlier prophets as interpreters of the meaning of events, in such a way as to challenge the people to reflect on how the Lord might be involved with their own generation and how the messages of the earlier prophets might shed light on the present time. The book is a report about, rather than by, Zechariah.

BIOGRAPHICAL INFORMATION. The superscription gives the names of both Zechariah's father Berechiah and his grandfather Iddo. We find a mention of Zechariah son of Iddo in Neh 12:16, causing puzzlement as to the exact relationships among Zechariah, Berechiah, and Iddo. The word "Zechariah" means "The Lord has remembered," connoting continuity with Israel's past and its reliance on the divine memory as well as hope for its future in God's presence and care.

REVELATION REPORT. This type of report describes a message privately received by a prophet from YHWH. It may be given in autobiographical or biographical form, and it includes two elements: a formulaic statement that the word of the Lord came to the prophet, and a quotation of the actual message to the prophet. Zechariah 1:1-6 and 7:1–8:23 are prophetic revelation reports that record the Lord's instructions to Zechariah.

• What messages does Zechariah receive in 1:1-6 and 7:1–8:23?

VISION REPORT. Chapters 1–6 report on eight visions, all on the same date: February 15, 519. They are found in 1:7-17; 1:18-21; 2:1-5; 3:1-10; 4:1-14; 5:1-4; 5:5-11; 6:1-8. Historically we do not know if all the visions actually took place in one night, but an answer to that question is not necessary for interpreting the visions. Vision reports consist of two elements: an introductory statement that the prophet has seen a vision, and a description of the vision itself. In First Zechariah each vision refers in some way to a problematic issue in the early Persian period, in the years of rebuilding after the return from exile. The highly symbolic language illustrates the prophet's efforts to describe ideas and insights for which there were no straightforward explanations. The visions address issues similar to those in Haggai and in Ezekiel 40–48, but express them quite differently, in symbolic rather than concrete language.

• Identify the visions and their meanings in 1:7-17; 1:18-21; 2:1-5; 3:1-10; 4:1-14; 5:1-4; 5:5-11; 6:1-8.

Rhetorical Features

REPETITION. The word "return" appears four times in 1:3-6. ("Repent" in v. 6 is a form of the same Hebrew word, *šub*.) This repetition sets the tone and highlights the message of the introduction. The Lord pleads with the people to change their hearts, in a way reminiscent of the repeated use of the verb "return" in Jeremiah 3–4.

SPECIFIC DETAILS. Zechariah's visions are described in precise detail including numbers (especially the number four), colors, and body parts. These descriptions create vivid word pictures that enable the reader to see the vision along with Zechariah. In addition they have symbolic value that was probably historical at first and eventually became typological. The details are often similar to those found elsewhere; for example, Daniel 7 uses the number four and names different body parts with unusual configurations.

• Compare and contrast the details in Zech 2:1-5; Jer 5:1; and Amos 7:7-9.

SYMBOLIC LANGUAGE. We noticed the specific details Zechariah uses to describe the visions. Many have symbolic value, as the text explains. For example, Zechariah 4 begins with a vision of a lampstand and olive trees. The meaning of these symbols is explained in 4:14: "These are the two anointed ones who stand by the LORD of the whole earth."

Several images and symbols from First Zechariah appear in the book of Revelation. For example, the colors of the four horses that appear when the seals are opened in Rev 6:1-8 are similar to those in the vision of the four horses in Zech 6:1-8. Many other allusions and similarities between these two books can be found, as both use symbolic language to talk about something new that is about to come.

COMMANDS. Chapter 8 includes several commands in which the Lord makes clear that the covenant responsibilities remain essential for the people. In 8:16-17 we find commands to speak the truth, make true judgments, avoid plotting evil against another, and avoid making false oaths. In addition, the command "do not be afraid" is given twice in the chapter, reminding the people of the Lord's presence among them in the midst of their struggles.

KEY WORDS. Three key words frequently found in the prophetic books, *ḥesed, mišpat,* and *raḥamim,* all occur in 7:9, in the oracle that encompasses 7:8-14: "Render true judgments *(mišpat),* show kindness *(ḥesed)* and mercy (*raḥamim*) to one another." This admonition about how to live is followed by a description of the punishment that befell the people for hardening their hearts and abandoning their covenant responsibility to care for the widows, orphans, resident aliens, and the poor.

• Compare and contrast Zech 7:8-14 and Exod 22:21-25.

"Sons of oil" in 4:11-14 highlights both Zerubbabel and Joshua as divine intermediaries. They are called "sons of oil," a term with several implications. First, "son" is a title often given to a divine representative, especially the king; for example, Ps 2:7 proclaims: "I will tell of the decree of the LORD: He said to me, 'You are my son; today I have begotten you.'" Next, the Hebrew word for oil used here in Zechariah refers to olive oil, but it is not used for describing the act of anointing. Thus the meaning of the oracle is vague in several respects, but it is not the same as "messiah" ("anointed one") given in some translations. The words do, however, indicate that the civil leader Zerubbabel and the high priest Joshua are equal partners before the Lord.

• Compare and contrast the descriptions of the relationship between civil and religious leaders in 3:8-9 and 6:11-13.

First Zechariah's Message

Themes

CHARACTERISTICS OF RESTORED TEMPLE AND COMMUNITY. Zechariah offers insight into how the restored community will live in relation to the Temple, their leaders, and the Law. He specifies that the Lord will be present not only in the rebuilt Temple, but as "a wall of fire" (2:5) "in your midst" (2:10-11). And before the Temple is completed Joshua the high priest will be purified by the heavenly council, making possible the reinstatement of the cult (3:1-10). The governor and the high priest will jointly lead the people according to the Mosaic Law.

HOPE FOR THE FUTURE. Zechariah sees the future in terms of Israel's traditions and thus delivers his message of hope using the language of the past. We noticed this tendency in our discussion of the specific details and symbols in the text as well as the key words in 7:9. Another example is Zechariah's use of Deuteronomistic language. For example, in 3:6-7 the angel explains the responsibilities of the high priest, using language similar to 1 Kings 3:14; 9:1-9; 11:38.

In another example Zechariah looks forward to the ingathering of all people in Jerusalem in 8:20-23, using language similar to Isa 2:2-4 and 66:18-23. In this way the prophet highlights the continuity of the present and future with the past. Something new is about to happen with the rebuilding of the Temple; it will be in continuity with the past and at the same time it will be new, far beyond the imaginings of the people. This sense of continuity with the past and inbreaking of something new is fundamental to Zechariah's message. The Lord remained faithful to the people throughout the past and will continue to do so in new ways in the future. And the Lord will continue to ask for faithfulness on the part of the people, just as had been the case throughout their history.

Zechariah 1–8 continues Haggai's hope that the life of faithfulness to the covenant symbolized by the rebuilt Temple will mark the beginning of what had been promised with the second Exodus, the return from Babylon. This move marked a significant shift from the earlier understanding of eschatology—that is, the new age to begin with the return from Babylon—to the coming of the end-time at some time in the future. We will see the further development of this theme in our discussion of Zechariah 9–14, with its focus on the divine activity that will transform the world.

DIVINE SPIRIT. Zechariah refers to the divine spirit in 4:6; 6:8; and 7:12. These three occurrences of the word equate the divine spirit with divine effective presence among the people. The third, in 7:12, focuses on the power inherent in that presence, which is mediated by the prophets (see p. 256).

First Zechariah's Meaning for Us Today

Zechariah 1–8 in the Lectionary

Zechariah 1–8 does not appear in the Sunday *LM* or *RCL*. In the Weekday *LM*, Year I, it appears three times in semi-continuous reading, immediately after Haggai from Saturday of the Twenty-fifth week to Tuesday of the Twenty-sixth week in Ordinary Time, describing visions of the new Jerusalem. On Saturday, Zech 2:1-5, 10-11 (*NAB* 2:5-9, 14-15) gives a promise of divine presence among the people; on Monday, 8:1-8 teaches that God's presence brings new life; and on Tuesday, 8:20-23 describes the gathering of all who seek the Lord.

The Jewish community assigns 2:14–4:7 with Num 8:1–12:16, and also for the first Sabbath during Hanukkah with the regular weekly portion.

First Zechariah's significance for our daily life

This highly symbolic book serves as a reminder that we can recognize God's presence among us in metaphorical ways. Our experiences of natural and meteorological phenomena, daily events, and other people can increase our awareness of God's attributes and actions in our own lives.

The book also invites us to hopefulness. Just as it beckoned the returned exiles to remember their past experiences of God, and from them to take courage in looking toward the future, likewise it can challenge us to look hopefully toward the future, despite all its uncertainties, with the confidence that remembers God's presence among us in our own past.

• Name a metaphor for God's presence among us today.

Passages for study

> 2:6-13
>
> 7:1-7

For Further Reading

Meyers, Carol L., and Eric M. Meyers. *Haggai, Zechariah 1–8: A New Translation with Introduction and Commentary.* AB 25B. Garden City, NY: Doubleday, 1987.

Petersen, David L. *Haggai and Zechariah 1–8: A Commentary.* OTL. Philadelphia: Westminster, 1984.

Sweeney, Marvin A. *The Twelve Prophets,* vol. 2. Berit Olam. Collegeville: Liturgical Press, 2000.

Chapter Ten

Fifth- and Fourth-Century Prophets: Malachi, Joel, Zechariah 9–14

Background Information

The historical, geographical, socioeconomic, and religious background of the Persian Period was described at the beginning of Chapter Nine. These concerns continued to influence life in Jerusalem and Judah until Alexander the Great began his conquests in the latter fourth century. Malachi, Joel, and Zechariah 9–14 are best understood in the context of the late Persian Period.

MALACHI

"They shall be mine, says the LORD of hosts,
my special possession on the day when I act,
and I will spare them as parents spare their children who serve them."
(Mal 3:17)

Background information

The information in the book does not enable us to assign Malachi to a particular historical setting. The period between 500 and 450 or even a bit later is consistent with the message, though, because by then the Temple was operational, with a functioning priesthood offering regular animal sacrifices. Both of these institutions, Temple and priesthood, are understood in this book to be in practice, especially in 1:6–2:3.

It is likely that the book relates to the reign of Xerxes (486–464) or the early reign of Artaxerxes (464–425). Perhaps the defeat of the Persians by the Greeks at Marathon prompted its oracles. It is quite possible that the Jewish restoration community had an unsympathetic overlord at the time in which the book is set. Malachi is particularly sympathetic to the cause of the Levites and to "those who revered the LORD" (3:16), who were becoming marginalized by the community.

The socioeconomic context of Malachi's teaching is probably best understood from a pragmatic perspective. A natural disaster as well as political corruption in the local government, including heavy taxation (Neh 5:15), contributed to a depressed local economy. This in turn could have been responsible for the cultic and social ills Malachi condemns: offering imperfect animals in sacrifice (Mal 1:6-10), divorce (2:16), neglect of the vulnerable (3:5), neglect of tithe duties (3:8-10). In addition, religious apathy was probably at least partially caused by the smaller size of the new Temple compared to the first. Its stature was also diminished: the First Temple had been a sign of national identity and autonomy but the new one was dependent at least in part on the leadership and financial resources of the Persian government.

Malachi's emphasis on the levitical priests as religious educators (2:7-8; see also Ezek 7:26) might well indicate that he recognized the importance of the Temple as a stabilizing institution for the community during this time.

Organization of the Book

Malachi is the last of the prophetic books. In the Christian Scriptures it is the last book of the Old Testament. This placement reflects the early Christian interpretation of chapters 3 and 4 as references to the coming of Christ. As we will see in our study of the book, its message applied originally to the returnees, especially the religious leaders, who were rebuilding their Temple and their worship.

The versification of Malachi differs among the versions of the Bible. The MT and LXX, and also the *NAB*, organize the book in three chapters, but the *RSV* and *NRSV* have four. This difference occurs when the MT and LXX 3:19 becomes 4:1 in *RSV* and *NRSV*, with the result that the final six verses in *RSV* and *NRSV* are numbered 4:1-6.

RSV, NRSV	MT, LXX, *NAB*
4:1-6	3:19-24

Outline (according to NRSV versification)

1:1	Superscription
1:2–3:24 [4:6]	Main body
1:2-5	Introduction
1:6–3:24	Exhortation

         1:6–2:16   Prophetic questioning about impure cultic practices
             1:6–2:9   Speech to the priests
             2:10-16   Speech to the people

         2:17–3:24   Prophetic concern over the people's cynicism
             2:17–3:12   Call to the people to support the Temple cult
             3:13–4:6   Report to the people of how a group accomplished this.

Genre

ORACLE. The superscription identifies the book as an oracle *(maśśa).* The genre has three characteristics: it is an oracular speech of the Lord that reports past or present events and gives commands or prohibitions to the audience, either in a prophetic report of the Lord's speech or in the prophet's own words. It explains how some previously communicated expression of the divine will is now being realized, or is about to be realized, in the realm of human affairs. Thus it is a revelation that interprets the present applicability of a previous revelation, guiding the audience toward an appropriate response.

All the units of the book include oracular speech of the Lord, although there is great variety in the way it is combined and alternated with the prophet's own words. The units serve the basic function typical of this genre: to identify the contemporary events in which the Lord is at work and to guide the people's involvement in them. For example, the last unit (3:16–4:3) is a report based on events narrated in 3:13-15. The events include conversation about the futility of serving God because the evildoers, rather than righteous people, seem to be the ones who prosper. The report describes the result of this conversation: the faithful ones prepared a list of those who "revered the LORD," and the Lord responded: "They shall be mine, says the LORD of hosts, my special possession on the day when I act, and I will spare them as parents spare their children who serve them. Then once more you shall see the difference between the righteous and the wicked, between one who serves God and one who does not serve him" (3:17-18). The report then describes the punishment to be meted out to evildoers and the reward for the faithful.

• Identify the elements of the oracles in 1:6–2:9 and 10-16.

Rhetorical Features

QUESTIONS. This device introduces each of the topics to be discussed. In fact, 1:6-9 includes eight questions that highlight the topic under discussion and set up the dialogue between the Lord and the other party in the conversation. They also engage the reader in the discussion, calling attention to the ongoing relevance of the topic.

• What are the questions in 1:6-9? How do they organize the conversation between the Lord and the priests?

ALLUSION AND QUOTATION FROM THE LAW AND THE PROPHETS. The book appeals to other parts of the Law and the Prophets, highlighting the continuity between the traditions of Israel and the situation in Malachi's day. Malachi includes references to the ancestral period, e.g., Jacob and Esau; to the time of Moses, e.g., Horeb and Levi; and to the monarchic period, e.g., Elijah. The Law and the Prophets are understood to proclaim the same message. The prophet condemns the current priestly cultic practices because they violate the norms of the Law, which forms the ground of Israel's existence. The references to Moses and Elijah at the end of the book offer further support to the ongoing relevance of the Law and the Prophets. The reference to Moses in 4:4 calls on all to respect and follow the Law given at Horeb (Sinai). The promise to send the prophet Elijah at a future time highlights three themes: the ongoing continuity between the Law and the Prophets, the past, present, and future of the covenant community, and God's ongoing care for the people.

CONTRAST. This device serves to highlight the characteristics of one element of the message by setting that element off against another. Examples are the contrast between Jacob and Esau and between building and tearing down in 1:2-5, between faithfulness and faithlessness to the covenant in 2:13-16, and between understandings of good and evil in 2:17.

DEUTERONOMIC STYLE. The book includes frequent references and allusions to Deuteronomy and Deuteronomic style. For example, the chart shows vocabulary and motifs found in the two books.

Motif	Deuteronomy	Malachi
God's love for Israel	7:7-8	1:2
Father-son relationship	32:5-6	1:6; 2:10; 3:17
Name of the Lord	14:23-24	1:6, 11, 14; 2:2, 5; 3:16; 4:2
The Lord the one God	6:4	2:15
Laws regarding sacrificial offerings	15:21; 17:1	1:8, 13-14
Abomination of Israel's transgressiveness	14:3; 17:1, 4	2:11
Levitical priesthood	17:8-13; 21:5; 24:8; 27:9-10; 33:8-10	2:4-8; 3:3
Divorce	24:1-4	2:14-16

- Compare and contrast the paired readings above. What examples of Deuteronomic style do you find in them?

Malachi's Message

Themes

ACTUALIZATION. The book is largely a prophetic actualization of rules from the Law of Moses, designed to show that the priestly interpretation of such rules can have prophetic status. The intent of actualization is to interpret Torah to guide the community through difficult times. Its starting point was the historical reality that a vestige of Israel had survived both the trauma of exile and at least the beginnings of restoration. This fact stands as a sign of the Lord's constant love for the people. Malachi focuses on the nexus of cultic and family life as key to the community's survival and prosperity.

The previous revelation actualized by Malachi's *maśśa* is thus some form of the Pentateuch. This revelation is described as the book of the law that the Lord commanded Moses at Horeb (4:4), which clearly associates it with Deuteronomy. Malachi's concept of tradition also includes patriarchal legends from other Pentateuchal sources (e.g., 1:2-3; 2:4-5, 12), as well as laws from the Priestly Code. Thus it seems that for Malachi "the law of Moses" includes much of what eventually became incorporated into the Pentateuch, but not necessarily all of the Pentateuch in its final form. We can observe three specific reactualized themes.

1. Torah regarding acceptable sacrifices is reinterpreted to call the priests to account for not properly fulfilling their responsibilities and for allowing the people to be irresponsible in their cultic obligations. Similarly, Torah regarding intermarriage and divorce is reinterpreted to call the people to account for both contracting and dissolving marriages in ways that threaten the community's survival as a religious minority.

2. Torah regarding tithes is reinterpreted to urge people to abandon their cynicism and mediocrity and contribute wholeheartedly to the maintenance of the cult. This effort was motivated by the ripple effects of the reform of the priesthood. This reform portends a wider moral renewal of society at large in accord with Torah's norms for a just social order, as well as eventual economic viability of both cult and society. A vital pattern of communal existence began to emerge based on prophetic reinterpretation of the Mosaic Torah tradition in written form; that is, reading it in light of what can be learned from such prophets as Elijah with regard to what the Lord holds in store.

3. For modern readers, who are confronted in an analogous way with the mysterious historical fact that God's people have retained their identity to this day even in the face of disdain and abuse, while other peoples have lost their identity, Malachi suggests the possibility of actualizing Torah traditions today in a way analogous to their actualization in the text so as to guide the modern covenant community through its difficult times and turn its tendency to cynicism back toward hope.

COVENANT. This theme permeates Malachi, for example in the role of the levitical priests in 2:4-9, the requirement to care for the vulnerable in 3:5, the words "my special possession" in 3:17, and the references to Moses and Elijah in 4:4-6. It is closely related to Malachi's references and allusions to the Law and the Prophets.

GOD AS FATHER. Malachi refers to God as Father in 1:6 and 2:10. While the New Testament frequently uses this title for God, the Old Testament uses it only rarely, for example in Isa 9:6.

- Compare and contrast Mal 3:5 and Exod 20:14, 16; Lev 19:13; Deut 5:18, 20; 18:10; 24:17.

- Compare Numbers 16 with Mal 2:17–4:3. What similarities do you find in vocabulary, motifs, and themes?

- Compare and contrast Mal 1:6–2:9 and Num 6:24-26 (the Priestly Blessing).

- Compare and contrast Mal 3:8-10, Lev 27:30, and Num 18:21-24.

DAY OF THE LORD. Like many of the prophets, Malachi refers to the Day of the Lord as one of terror. He uses images of fire to describe the destruction that will take place (4:1), and the sun's healing warmth to describe the protection the Lord will extend to the righteous on that day. Furthermore, Elijah will come to bring about reconciliation between the generations in order to avoid destruction.

ESCHATOLOGY. Malachi looks forward to a future time of new life when the people will "go out leaping like calves from the stall" (4:2). Like all Old Testament references to the future, this is understood as an era within time as we know it, not beyond our conception of it. The two appendices in Malachi balance the memory of the past with expectation of the future. The book of Ecclesiastes ends similarly, with a look backward and a look forward. In the Christian canon the two appendices at the end of Malachi form the end of the Old Testament. They link Malachi's message with that of the entire Old Testament, from the beginning of the covenant to that time in the future when the most sacred and complex relationships, those within the family, will be reconciled.

Malachi in the Christian Scriptures

We mentioned earlier that Malachi is the last book in the Christian Old Testament. Its canonical position immediately preceding the New Testament expresses the link made by the early church between Malachi and several New Testament books. For example, Mal 1:10-11 was understood as a statement in support of permitting Gentiles to become Christians. "Sun of righteousness" (4:2) became an epithet for Jesus Christ.

Explicit references to passages from Malachi appear: for example, Mark 1:2 and Luke 1:17 refer to both Isa 40:3 and Mal 4:5-6, the final verses of the book, using the words to describe John the Baptist. In addition, Rom 9:13 quotes Mal 1:2-3.

Malachi's Meaning for Us Today

Malachi in the Lectionary

The *RCL* assigns Mal 3:1-4 as an option for the Second Sunday of Advent in Year C, pairing it with Luke 3:1-6. Both readings announce the coming of one who prepares the way of the Lord. In Year A, in *LM* but not *RCL,* on the Thirty-first Sunday in Ordinary Time, Mal 1:14–2:2, 8-10 condemns the priests for not living up to their responsibility as leaders of the people. It is paired with Matt 23:1-12, which condemns the scribes and Pharisees for not living up to their responsibilities. In Year C, in both *LM* and *RCL,* on the Thirty-third Sunday in Ordinary Time, Mal 4:1-2a (3:19-20a in *NAB*) announces the coming Day of the Lord and teaches perseverance, paired with Luke 21:5-19, which announces impending persecution.

In the Weekday *LM* on December 23, Mal 3:1-4; 4:5-6 (3:1-4, 23-24 in *NAB*) announces the coming of the divine messenger, identified in 4:5 (3:23 in *NAB*) as Elijah. The early Christian community retrospectively identified the messenger as Christ, hence the assignment of this reading a few days before Christmas. The Gospel for that day is Luke 1:57-66, the birth of John the Baptist. In addition, 3:13-20 [3:13–4:2], which promises protection for the faithful ones on the Day of the Lord, appears on Thursday of the Twenty-seventh Week in Ordinary Time in Year I, following three days of readings from Jonah.

The Jewish Lectionary pairs Mal 1:1–2:7 with Gen 25:19–28:9. In addition it assigns Mal 3:4-24 on Shabbat Hagadol, the Sabbath before Passover.

Malachi's significance for our daily life

Malachi invites us to actualize the message of Scripture for our own lives, just as he did for the postexilic community. Modern prophetic reinterpreters of Scripture can focus on the connections between cultic and community life that are crucial for God's people to survive, prosper, and serve the common good. Prophetic re-interpretation of the Scriptures supports the ongoing vitality of communal existence; that is, we can learn from past prophets to recognize and trust God's intervention in life today.

• Name a specific passage from which we can learn a lesson for today.

Passages for study

>   2:4-9
>
>   3:1-7

For Further Reading

Hill, Andrew E. *Malachi*. AB 25D. New York: Doubleday, 1998.

Petersen, David L. *Zechariah 9–14 and Malachi*. OTL. Louisville: Westminster John Knox, 1995.

Sweeney, Marvin A. *The Twelve Prophets,* vol. 2. Berit Olam. Collegeville: Liturgical Press, 2000.

JOEL

"Rend your hearts and not your clothing.
Return to the LORD, your God, for he is gracious and merciful,
slow to anger, and abounding in steadfast love,
and relents from punishing." (Joel 2:13)

Background Information

The historical setting of Joel eludes us because we have only the words of the book itself to guide us, and the information they offer is ambiguous. For instance, the superscription gives only the prophet's name, Joel ben Pethuel, a name that does not appear anywhere else in the Bible. But the text does offer some information that lets us know there was a temple in Jerusalem at the time. Joel 1:9, 1:13, and 2:17 refer to the house of the Lord. In addition, 1:9 and 1:13 refer to different offerings and 2:17 names areas in the temple compound: vestibule and altar.

• What indicators of the geographical setting do you find in 1:2, 14; 2:1, 15-16; 2:32; 3:1, 16-20?

The text does not mention a king or other royal figure, but it does refer to priests and elders in 1:2, 13-14; 2:15-17. The time in Israel's history when there was a temple but no king was the Second Temple period, when the monarchy no longer existed and the priests and elders led the people as a religious body. We can narrow down the date a bit more because we know that Sidon was destroyed by Artaxerxes in 343 and Tyre by Alexander the Great in 332. The two cities are named in 3:4; therefore the historical setting is most likely before their destruction. This information leads us to conclude that the setting of the book is sometime between 515 and 332.

Another ambiguous aspect of the book is its liturgical references in 1:9, 13-14; 2:12-17. Some have suggested that these references indicate that the book had a liturgical setting; perhaps its words were originally part of an actual liturgical service or communal lament. Again, we cannot know this for sure, but the suggestion is a plausible one.

An additional puzzling dimension of the book is the double metaphor that runs through it. There is a detailed description of a plague of locusts that devastates the land, and also a lengthy description of an attack by an enemy army. It seems that one is a metaphor for the other, but which is which? The clever artistry of the book could lead to either conclusion. For instance, 1:4-12 concentrates primarily on the locust plague but v. 6 refers to a powerful invading nation. Then 2:1-11 concentrates on the military attack but includes such phrases as "like blackness spread upon the mountains a great and powerful army comes" and "before them the land is like the garden of Eden, but after them a desolate wilderness, and nothing escapes them" (2:2-3). These aptly describe an infestation of locusts. Perhaps both the plague of locusts and the enemy invasion are real, perhaps both are metaphors, or perhaps one is real and the other a metaphor. These possibilities remain ambiguous. Then the promised future is described in both agricultural and military terms in 2:18-27, continuing the ambiguity.

Finally, the assertion "You shall know that . . . I, the LORD, am your God and there is no other" in 2:27 appears only in late exilic or postexilic texts (Deuteronomy and Second Isaiah).

Organization of the Book

Different versions use slightly different versification in the second half of the book. The English, as well as Latin and Greek versions, have three chapters. The Hebrew has four: it ends chapter 2 with v. 27 and numbers 2:28-32 as 3:1-5. Then the English, Latin, and Greek chapter 3 is the Hebrew chapter 4. We will follow the English versification here.

RSV, NRSV	MT, LXX, *NAB*
2:28-32	3:1-5
3:1-21	4:1-21

Outline

> 1:1–2:17   Devastation
>> 1:1-20   Locust invasion in the country
>> 2:1-17   Military invasion of the city
>
> 2:18–3:21 Restoration after the devastation
>> 2:18-27   Divine response to laments
>> 2:1-17   Restoration in the cosmos
>> 3:1-21   Restoration in Judah

Genres

MESSENGER FORMULA. The book has only two messenger formulas, "The word of the LORD" in 1:1 and "says the LORD" in 2:12.

WORDS OF JUDGMENT. The first part of the book describes two kinds of destruction: the first is a locust invasion that devastates the country-side and the second a military invasion that destroys the city. The first, 1:2-20, begins with an introductory summons to the elders and all the inhabitants of the land. It continues in vv. 5-14 with a combination of calls to wake up and mourn the all-pervasive destruction by locusts. The calls address wine-drinkers, farmers, vinedressers, priests, and ministers. A prayer of lament in vv. 15-20 describes the famine that results from the destruction by locusts, and cries out to the Lord for help in vv. 19-20. The second description, in 2:1-11, portrays the devastation, vv. 12-17a call the people to repentance, and v. 17bc is the lament.

> • Whom do vv. 12-17a specifically address? What specific acts of re-pentance do these verses name? What liturgical connection do you find in these verses?

WORDS OF SALVATION. After 2:17 the message shifts to one of salvation. Joel 2:18–3:21 concerns the restoration the Lord promises after the de-struction. The words assure the people of divine intervention in the form of the land's return to prosperity. They allude to an army in v. 20. (The *NRSV* includes the word "army" in the text. This word is not explicit in

Hebrew, but it is realistic to understand the word "northern" as a reference to an army because the sentence mentions its front, rear, and foul
smell.) The land and its animals are enjoined, "Do not fear" in vv. 21 and
22. Then the results of God's intervention are spelled out in the rest of
the oracle. Verses 23-26 describe the effect on the land and on the everyday lives of the people. Verse 27 reveals the purpose of God's action in
an assertion of monotheism. Verses 28-32 describe the cosmic effects of
the divine action. Then chapter 3 outlines the effect of the Lord's action
on the nations.

- In 2:19–3:21, what specific effect will the Lord's action have on the
  land and the life of the people? On the cosmos? On the nations?

- Many words of salvation in Joel are expressions of judgment against
  the nations. In chapter 3, what nations does the text name? What
  words of condemnation are addressed to them?

Rhetorical Features

METAPHOR. We looked briefly in the introductory comments at metaphors, the predominant literary feature in the book. In 1:4 the text describes total destruction by a plague of locusts. Four adjectives—cutting,
swarming, hopping, destroying—highlight the waves of activity that
consume all the vegetation. The next verse specifies that grape vines
have been hit by the plague, and the crop destroyed. But then the metaphor changes to a military invasion that lays waste all vegetation, point-
ing out its effects on people, animals, and the ground itself. The items
in the list alternate with calls for repentance addressed to drunkards and
wine-drinkers, farmers, vinedressers, priests, and ministers of the altar.
The climactic cry commissions the religious leaders: "Sanctify a fast, call
a solemn assembly. Gather the elders and all the inhabitants of the land
to the house of the LORD your God, and cry out to the LORD" (v. 14). Then
comes the cry for help: "To you, O LORD, I cry. For fire has devoured the
pastures of the wilderness, and flames have burned all the trees of the
field. Even the wild animals cry to you because the watercourses are
dried up, and fire has devoured the pastures of the wilderness" (vv.
19-20).

Both the locust plague and the military invasion destroy life, but the
calls to repentance make clear that both forms of invasion result from
the destructive power of sin. The people themselves have caused the
waves of devastation, whether by locusts or by an invading army. Sin

destroys life; prayer and fasting acknowledge the sin and express the people's repentance, in the hope that God will heal the people. The metaphorical power of the descriptions of destruction rests in their different levels of meaning: destruction by locusts and invading armies is a real phenomenon and at the same time is a metaphor for the annihilation of life that results from sin.

- What insights do the locust and army metaphors offer into the devastating effects of sin?

COMMANDS. As we have seen in our study of other prophets, imperative verbs stress the urgency of the prophetic message. The commands to hear, wake up, sanctify, call, gather, return, etc. call the listeners to attention and enjoin them to repent. At the same time the commands draw the readers or hearers into the prophetic message, directing us to follow suit and repent of our own sins.

- What commands do you find in 2:1-17? To whom are they addressed? To what acts of repentance might they call today's reader?

REPETITION emphasizes important parts of the prophet's message. For example, "Tell your children of it, and let your children tell their children, and their children another generation" (1:3) highlights the importance of passing on the message to later generations. The triple command, "Blow the trumpet in Zion; sanctify a fast; call a solemn assembly" in 2:15 repeats what the text enjoins in 1:14 and 2:1 and underscores the urgency of the situation.

- What repetition do you find in 2:12-13? In 2:23? How do these enhance the prophet's message?

- What phrase is repeated in 2:28-29? What divine promise does it highlight?

LISTS. These add vividness to the message. For example, four kinds of locusts are named: cutting locusts, swarming locusts, hopping locusts, and destroying locusts in 1:4 and 2:25. Likewise, five different fruits are named in 1:12: grape (vine), fig, pomegranate, date (palm), and apple in 1:12; a shorter list appears in 2:22. The lists underscore the totality of the destruction and eventual rebirth of life.

- What other lists do you find in the book? How do they enhance the prophet's message?

Person Blowing a Ram's Horn (see Joel 2:1, 15)

RHETORICAL QUESTIONS. Questions in 1:2, 16; 2:14, 17; 3:4 engage the reader by calling attention to the situation and challenging both Joel's audience and today's reader to think about the message and decide how to respond to it.

REVERSAL OF PREVIOUS PROPHETIC MESSAGE. Joel 3:10 reverses the words of Isa 2:24 and Mic 4:14. The severity of the battle will necessitate turning farm implements into weapons. Afterward they can be turned back into farm implements, as Isaiah and Micah counsel. This reversal of messages highlights the importance of reading the prophets' messages in their historical context, to the extent that it is possible to do so. Here we find instruction to deal with the circumstances in which one lives, whether in time of peace or of war.

APOCALYPTIC ELEMENTS. Joel contains a few apocalyptic elements such as the depiction of the day of the Lord in 2:1-11. It includes a cosmic battle with meteorological elements of earthquake, darkness, and fire.

• Which of these elements do you find in 2:30-31?

In 2:28-29 we find reference to outpouring of the spirit, or power, of God to make seemingly impossible things happen. This is part of Joel's vision of the future, when evil will be defeated and goodness will prevail.

QUOTATION OF OTHER OLD TESTAMENT BOOKS. Joel frequently uses the words of other books. For example, 3:16 quotes Amos 1:2, "The LORD roars from Zion, and utters his voice from Jerusalem." Joel uses several expressions found also in Psalms; for example, Ps 79:10 cries: "Why should the nations say, 'Where is their God?'" in language that resembles Joel 2:17.

• Compare and contrast the language in the following examples:

Joel 2:13 and Exod 34:6; Jonah 4:2

Joel 2:14 and Jonah 3:9

Joel 2:21 and Ps 126:3

Joel 2:28 and Ezek 36:26-29

Joel 2:32 and Obad 17

Joel 3:2 and Isa 66:18; Zech 14:2

Joel 3:17 and Ezek 36:11

KEY WORDS. Joel uses two key words: *ḥesed*, "steadfast love," in 2:13, and *ṣedaqah*, "vindication," in 2:23, to express the divine approach to the people. Both words indicate the Lord's eagerness to transform the people.

Joel's Message

Themes

DAY OF THE LORD. We have seen this theme in several prophetic books. Joel 1:15 hints at the connection between destruction and divine activity. Then 2:1 explicitly combines the two calamities of locust plague and military invasion into a third: the Day of the Lord. The description of the Day begins in 2:1 with the sounding of the trumpet *(šofar)*, the eerie sound of which evokes fear and awe in the listener. It is associated with Yom Kippur (see 2:12-17). Chapter 2:1-12 gives a vivid description of the day, evoking the imagery of both the locust plague and the military invasion. Then 2:31 links the cosmic upheaval with the Day of the Lord, naming its human causes, divine actions, and divine commands for the Day, which will ultimately result in salvation for God's people.

Three times, in 2:10; 2:31; and 3:15 we find images of the darkened sun. These relate to the Ḥamsin, the wind that blows during the transition from dry summer to wet winter. Here the images are a demonstration of divine power to punish or to deliver the land and people.

A result of the Day of the Lord will be the internalization of the divine spirit among all people, as 2:28-29 promises. This assurance recalls Jeremiah's promise of a covenant written on the hearts of the people, and Ezekiel's promise of new hearts of flesh that will strengthen the people's ability to be faithful.

- What specific promises does 2:28-29 include?

- Compare and contrast the depictions of the Day of the Lord in Joel 1:15; 2:1, 11; Isa 13:6; Ezek 13:5; Amos 5:18; Obad 15; Zeph 1:7, 14-16.

LITURGICAL WORSHIP. Joel affirms that worship is essential to the relationship between God and Israel. The book encourages the community to turn to God in fasting and lamentation, in the hope that God will turn to the community in transformative redemption. There is a keen sense of urgency in the calls to worship in 1:14 and 2:15-17.

- Compare Amos 5:24 with Joel 1–2, especially 1:14 and 2:16.

ONE GOD. In 2:27 the assertion, "I, the LORD, am your God and there is no other" reiterates the unequivocal statements of monotheism found elsewhere only in Deut 4:35 and 39 and Second Isaiah (Isa 44:8; 45:5, 6, 14, 18, 21, 22; 46:9).

Joel in the New Testament

In addition, the New Testament makes references to Joel.

- Note the similarities in the following pairs of references:

    Joel 1:4, 6; 2:4 and Rev 9:7-8

    Joel 2:11 and Rev 6:17

    Joel 2:28-32 and Acts 2:17-21

    Joel 2:31 and Rev 6:12

    Joel 2:32 and Rom 10:10-13

    Joel 3:13 and Mark 4:29; Rev 14:15

    Joel 3:18 and Rev 22:1

Joel's Meaning for Us Today

Joel in the Lectionary

In Years ABC, in *LM* Joel 3:1-5 is an option for the Vigil of Pentecost, announcing divine judgment on all the nations. It is paired with John 7:37-39, promising the water of life. In Year C, on the Thirtieth Sunday in Ordinary Time, *RCL* lists Joel 2:23-32 as an option with Luke 18:9-14.

In the Weekday Lectionary in Years I and II, on Ash Wednesday Joel 2:12-18 and Matt 6:1-6, 16-18 in *LM*, and Joel 2:1-2, 12-17 and Matt 6:1-6, 16-21 in *RCL* call the people to repent. The book of Joel also appears on two weekdays in Year I, Friday and Saturday of the Twenty-seventh Week in Ordinary Time, after the semi-continuous readings from Jonah and Malachi: The readings from Joel are 1:13-15; 2:1-2, a call for repentance, and 3:12-21 (4:12-21 in *NAB*), an announcement of the coming Day of the Lord.

Joel appears once in the Jewish readings, when 2:15-17 is read with Hos 14:2-10 and the weekly portion from the Pentateuch on Shabbat Shuvah.

Joel's significance for our daily life

The book's liturgical focus highlights for us the importance of communal practice of religion, especially prayer and fasting. Joel called the postexilic community to acts of worship and repentance that strengthened their ties as a community united in petition to God. In addition, as we see with particular clarity in the reading for Ash Wednesday, the book's message calls us to remember that religious practice is rooted in our hearts. It is not the actions in themselves that are important, but rather their ability to express the desires of our hearts makes them effective means of communicating with our God.

In addition, Joel's descriptions of the effects of battle on the land and its ability to produce food illustrate the interconnectedness of all creation. Our actions affect the earth for better or for worse, as the book's depictions of destruction and its far-reaching consequences show. We can work to raise consciousness of how our actions today affect the ground, the water, and the air not only for our own generation but for generations to come, and we can take steps to reverse destructive trends and promote respect for the earth.

- What passages in Joel can speak to today's need to care for the environment?

Passages for study

>   2:1-14

>   3:17-21

For Further Reading

Crenshaw, James L. *Joel: A New Translation with Introduction and Commentary.* AB
  24C. New York: Doubleday, 1995. Detailed discussion of the book's historical setting on pp. 21–29.

Sweeney, Marvin A. *The Twelve Prophets,* vol. 2. Berit Olam. Collegeville: Liturgical Press, 2000.

Wolff, Hans Walter. *Joel and Amos: A Commentary on the Books of the Prophets Joel
  and Amos.* Trans. Waldemar Janzen, S. Dean McBride, Jr., and Charles A.
  Muenchow; ed. S. Dean McBride, Jr. Hermeneia. Philadelphia: Fortress,
  1977.

ZECHARIAH 9–14 OR SECOND ZECHARIAH

"They will call on my name, and I will answer them.
I will say, 'They are my people'; and they will say,
'The Lᴏʀᴅ is our God.'" (Zech 13:9)

As we saw in our discussion of First Zechariah, there is a strong thematic relationship between First and Second Zechariah. Both relate the
historical introduction in 1:1-6 to their own day; chapters 1–8 to the early
Persian period and chapters 9–14 to the early Hellenistic period. Thus
they provide us with early examples of actualization of the biblical message for one's own time. In fact, all the later prophetic books, especially
Malachi and Second Zechariah, illustrate the evolution in the role of the
prophet toward a twofold task: interpreting the traditions of Israel found
in the earlier books, and showing the relevance of those traditions for
later communities. In this way the later prophetic books offer us an example of how to understand the biblical message in our contemporary
communities. By the end of the second century B.C.E. these interpretations were no longer incorporated into the books themselves but were
written in separate commentaries such as the Targums (Aramaic translations and interpretations), many of which have been found among the
scrolls hidden in the Judean desert.

Background Information

Second Zechariah does not contain any date formulas like those in Haggai and First Zechariah. In fact, it gives very little idea of the historical setting of the oracles it contains. On the one hand, the material fits the Hellenistic period, after the long history of conflict between Persians and Greeks that started with Darius's campaigns against Thrace and Macedonia in 516 and throughout Alexander's campaigns. These began in 334 and included the subjugation of Tyre and Gaza, which are mentioned in Zechariah 9. At first the Jewish communities were grateful that Alexander was defeating their traditional enemies; their joy was tempered, though, by apprehension over what would become of Jerusalem.

On the other hand, the same material could easily fit other historical settings: the earlier periods of Assyrian and Babylonian ascendancy were equally difficult for Jerusalem. This lack of historical specificity allows modern readers to situate the book in a number of time periods and to read it typologically—that is, as a book about God's ongoing care for the people in many different eras. We will read it within the historical setting of the Persian empire because, as we have seen throughout our study of the prophets, their messages relate first to their current historical settings and then to other times and places.

There are various opinions regarding the process of collection and redaction of the material in Second Zechariah and its eventual inclusion in the book of Zechariah. Some think that two anonymous collections of material were eventually added to Zechariah 1–8, becoming chapters 9–11 and 12–14. Others propose a long process of collection of disparate materials that eventually became Zechariah 1–14. It is not known with certainty which, if either, of these possibilities explains how the book reached its final form. What is clear, though, is that, whatever the redaction process, a thematic similarity unifies the entire book, chapters 1–14. We will look at chapters 9–14 in two sections, chapters 9–11 and 12–14, in keeping with the heading at the beginning of both of these sections.

9:1–14:21	Zechariah's insights applied to later events	
	9:1–11:17	Zechariah's perspective on the new Hellenistic regime
	9:1-8	Yhwh will maintain people and Temple
	9:9–11:3	Directives to the people for this time
	11:4-17	Yhwh will accomplish this end through a bad leader

Head of Alexander the Great from a museum in Anatolia (Turkey)

12:1–14:21   Creation of a new world
    12:1–13:6   New leadership good for defense, not for
               prophecy
    13:7-9   The people will become a leaderless remnant
    14:1-21   Jerusalem the center of Yhwh's new world

Genres

ORACLE. Chapters 9–11 and 12–14 are each identified as an oracle or *maśśa*. (See the discussion of this genre in Malachi.) The two parts of Second Zechariah differ insofar as chapters 9–11 include mostly commands while chapters 12–14 are largely narration.

MODIFIED MESSENGER FORMULAS. Both 9:1 and 12:1 begin with the modified messenger formula "An oracle: the word of the LORD," followed by the object of the divine word. These two formulas divide Second Zechariah into its two major parts, chapters 9–11 and 12–14.

ANNOUNCEMENT OF JUDGMENT. Judgment against the cities of Phoenicia and Philistia occurs in 9:1-8 with mention of the four cities of Damascus, Hamath, Tyre, and Sidon in 9:1-2, a description of the specific sin of greed and self-sufficiency of Tyre in 9:3, and an announcement of the consequences the Lord will bring upon these and other cities in 9:4-8. These include destruction followed by salvation for the remnant under the Lord's protection.

• Compare and contrast 9:1-8 and 11:1-4.

CALL TO REJOICE. This form is based on women's leading of victory songs and dances as in Exod 15:20-21. In Zechariah the calls address "Daughter Zion" or "Daughter Jerusalem," invite the party to rejoice, then announce the act of the Lord that calls for rejoicing. In Zech 9:9-10 the invitation to lead the community in singing anticipates a victory that will put an end to war.

REPORT OF SYMBOLIC ACTION in 11:4-14, 15-17. This genre includes three elements: a divine command to perform a task, the report of its performance, and the interpretation of the act. Here the report has two parts, the first in vv. 4-14 and the second in vv. 15-17. Both use the symbol of the shepherd who is commissioned to shepherd a flock doomed to slaughter. The symbols describe the Lord giving up direct control to others, raising up a shepherd who will not provide adequate leadership.

These actions highlight the distress and destruction that will come to the people on account of their sins and the futility of actions that do not rely on God.

The report reflects the dismay of the people of Judah at their lack of power in the Persian empire, and at the dispiriting lack of leadership from their Persian governors. Elsewhere Cyrus is called "shepherd" in Isa 44:28, and the Lord's people are called "sheep" in Mic 2:12-13. The positive connotations of those two references intensify the contrasting negative depiction here in Zechariah. However, in keeping with symbolic discourse the report in Zechariah is not univocal, but rather picturesque and impressionistic. It takes a cosmic perspective, allowing for interpretations that apply to different periods throughout history in addition to the Hellenistic era.

The report raises the question of payment of wages to the shepherd in 11:12. The merchants weigh out thirty shekels of silver and give it to him, then the Lord instructs him to throw it into the treasury. Much effort has been made to determine the value of that amount: was it a little? a lot? In Exod 21:32 the same amount is prescribed as recompense for a slaveowner whose slave has been gored by an ox. It is not the value of the sum that is important here; rather, Zechariah focuses on living according to the ancient traditions. In the New Testament, Matthew specifies that the chief priests paid that amount to Judas for handing Jesus over to them. He then threw it in the Temple, and the priests used it to purchase a burial place for strangers. Matthew mistakenly identifies this action as fulfillment of words of Jeremiah in Matt 26:15; 27:3-10.

WORDS OF SALVATION. In 9:9-17 and 10:6-12 Zechariah's words offer assurance to the people of Jerusalem that the Lord will protect them in the midst of their enemies. In 9:9-17 the Lord promises to defeat the invading armies, set the prisoners free, and save the people, whom he describes as the sheep of the Lord's flock.

• What promises does the Lord make in 10:6-12?

Rhetorical Features

REPETITION. The phrase "on that day" appears seventeen times in chapters 12–14 in reference to the Day of the Lord. This repetition heightens the sense of expectation of the Lord's intervention on that day. The phrase appears within apocalyptic statements.

APOCALYPTIC LANGUAGE. Zechariah 14:1-21 begins with a reference to a "day," a motif that is repeated in vv. 6, 8, 9, 20, and 21 as well as in chapters 13–14. We have met that expression in several other books; here, however, the "day" is described in apocalyptic terms.

Apocalypticism is a mindset rooted in Persian religious thought, particularly Zoroastrianism. It sees the world in dualistic terms. It defines two powerful, opposing cosmic forces, good and evil. Regarding time, it sees two ages: the present and the future. In Judaism and Christianity apocalyptic belief holds that human power is insufficient to withstand the forces of evil. God is in control of the cosmos and will assure that goodness prevails to usher in the age to come.

The assertion, "[the Lord's] feet shall stand on the Mount of Olives . . . and the Mount of Olives shall be split in two from east to west" (14:4) describes an earthquake in terms that place it outside the normal course of human events, which are seen as powerless to resolve the problems the people face. Only a force beyond the human and everyday is thought to be powerful enough to combat the otherwise insurmountable difficulties the people face, described in geological and meteorological images. The future is beyond the imaginings of those who dream about it; Jerusalem will exist peacefully with "the nations," but this state of things can be described only in metaphorical language.

- What apocalyptic elements do you find in 14:6-8? What other apocalyptic elements do you find in the chapter? How do these elements support the people's belief that the situation is beyond their ability to rectify it?

- Compare and contrast this passage with Ezekiel 9 and Amos 8:9.

COMMANDS. Throughout chapters 9–11, twelve commands appear in the *NRSV* translation. These vary from "rejoice" and "shout" in 9:9 to "ask rain" in 10:1 and "open your doors" in 11:1 and are addressed to different audiences: daughter Zion and daughter Jerusalem, Lebanon, and unspecified hearers. They add a sense of immediacy to the oracle. That immediacy is enhanced by the next feature, divine assertions.

DIVINE ASSERTIONS. Chapters 9–10 contain twelve first-person future verbs in which the Lord promises to do something; for example, "I will take away . . . encompass . . . restore . . . bring home . . . gather . . . make strong." The immediacy of the verb form offers assurance that God is near, is aware of the needs of the people, and is ready to intervene on their behalf.

• On whose behalf are the divine assertions in chs. 9–10 made?

ALLEGORY. Zechariah 11:4-17 recounts the divine request to shepherd flocks destined for slaughter. From the outset the futility of the shepherd's task suggests that it is meant to be read on a level other than literal. The allegorical quality of the story is evident in the symbolic names of the two staves, Favor and Unity, the breaking of the staves, the final words of condemnation of the worthless shepherd in 11:17, and the literary similarity to the allegory of the two sticks in Ezek 37:15-28. Specifically, in real life it would be unusual for a shepherd to carry two staves and it would be unheard of to give the staves names or labels. These details let us know that this is more than a straightforward report of activity. When each staff is destroyed, the interpretation of the action sheds light on the allegory. Verse 10, "I took my staff Favor and broke it, annulling the covenant that I had made with all the peoples," and v. 14, "Then I broke my second staff Unity, annulling the family ties between Judah and Israel," clarify that it is agreements that are being broken: first the covenant between God and all people (see Genesis 9) and then the unity between the northern and southern parts of the kingdom. Some suggest that v. 14 refers to the breaking of the covenant with David.

Second Zechariah's Message

Themes

DESCRIPTIONS OF GOD in Second Zechariah include the divine warrior coming in victory for Judah and Jerusalem in chapters 9 and 14, and God as the good shepherd in 9:16-17; 11:1-17; 13:7-9. These two opposite characteristics highlight the many facets of divine power and presence among the people.

• How do the details in these descriptions enhance the depictions of God as warrior and shepherd?

FALSE PROPHETS. For both First and Second Zechariah the question of reliable transmission of the word of God was a serious one. We saw in 7:12 the understanding that the spirit is mediated through the prophets. Second Zechariah expresses disdain: "For the teraphim utter nonsense, and the diviners see lies; the dreamers tell false dreams, and give empty consolation. Therefore the people wander like sheep; they suffer for lack of a shepherd" (10:2). In 13:2-6 both idols and false prophets are condemned in the same breath.

- Compare and contrast 13:2-6 and Deut 13:1-5; 18:20; Amos 7:14-15.

ESCHATOLOGY. Chapters 12–14 convey an eschatological message throughout. This incorporates several post-exilic motifs: attack on Jerusalem by the nations in Ezek 38–39; the end of true prophecy in Neh 6:10-14; eschatological transformation of Jerusalem in Isa 65:17-25; conversion of the nations in Isa 56:6-8. Zechariah uses apocalyptic language to convey this message about a transformed future, as we have seen above in our discussion of apocalyptic language.

The eschatological message conveys the importance of faithfulness, which is even more essential than survival. Sometimes this involves letting go of a past mode of existence and trusting the Creator's capacity to bring new realities into being, as we see, for example, in 13:9.

Similarities and Differences Between First and Second Zechariah

Now that we have studied both chapters 1–8 and 9–14 we can look at the two parts of the book from a canonical perspective; that is, as parts of one book. Quite possibly the two circulated independently at first and were eventually combined around their common theme of Jerusalem as the cultic center in the age to come. This theme is particularly evident in 8:20-22 and 14:16. Both parts of the book rely on and develop the same religious traditions. For instance, they use covenant language in promising a hopeful future in 8:8 and 13:9. Both promise punishment for those who swear falsely in the name of God, for example, in 5:4 and 13:3. Both foresee a messianic figure who comes in humility, for example in 4:14 and 9:9.

- What commonalities do you note between 8:7 and 10:9 and between 4:6 and 12:10?

We can also notice several differences between chapters 1–8 and 9–14. For instance, both parts present highly symbolic messages, but in contrasting ways. Chapters 1–8 are specific in giving dates for the different visions while chapters 9–14 offer no specific historical clues at all and do not identify any of the material as visions, but as oracles. First Zechariah refers to the Temple, especially in chapter 6, but Second Zechariah does not mention it at all, even though it does promise that Jerusalem will be the center of cultic activity. First Zechariah refers several times to Zerubbabel and Second refers several times to the house of David.

- Compare and contrast 2:5; 9:8; 14:11.

- Compare and contrast 5:3 and 14:11.

The two parts of the book need to be understood in light of each other. Chapters 1–8 use Exodus language to refer not to a second exodus but rather to the coming of the end-time. The second part of the book expands, develops, and sharpens the theological pattern of the end-time that begins to emerge in the first part. The language in chapters 9–14 is not related to the Exodus; here the end is portrayed in apocalyptic terms.

How, then, are we to understand the present time in relation to the end-time? The addition of chapters 9–14 offers a prophetic word by which to understand the period before the end. In them we find detailed development of the contours of a new eschatological pattern that addresses not only eschatological hope but the community's present history as well. The issues include severe judgment against the nations in 9:1-8 and 11:1-3, and divine anger against God's own people who disobey under false leaders like a flock scattered without a shepherd (10:3-12; 11:15-17; 13:7-9). The shepherd allegory speaks of a period of indignation in which the covenant is broken and Israel is abandoned under the abusive hand of a false shepherd. The land is filled with pollution and false prophecy.

Then a change occurs. Divine compassion purges the land and the repentant Jerusalem hears a new assurance of divine presence and protection to which it responds in faith. Chapter 14 focuses completely on the end-time, when God again miraculously redeems the remnant of suffering Jerusalem.

- In chapter 14, what images highlight the description of the end-time?

Zechariah 9–14 in the New Testament

The New Testament writers incorporated phrases from Zechariah 9–14 into their work, particularly in the Passion narratives in the Gospels. Zechariah 9:9, "Rejoice greatly, O daughter Zion! Shout aloud, O daughter Jerusalem! Lo, your king comes to you; triumphant and victorious is he, humble and riding on a donkey, on a colt, the foal of a donkey" appears in Matthew 21:5 to describe Jesus' entry into Jerusalem a few days before his death.

- Compare and contrast Zech 9:9 and Mark 11:1-7; Luke 19:30; John 12:15.

Another example is Zech 11:12-13, "I then said to them, 'If it seems right to you, give me my wages; but if not, keep them.' So they weighed out as my wages thirty shekels of silver. Then the LORD said to me, 'Throw it into the treasury'—this lordly price at which I was valued by them. So I took the thirty shekels of silver and threw them into the treasury in the house of the LORD." Matthew 27:9 applies these words to Judas's betrayal of Jesus, attributing them to Jeremiah: "Then was fulfilled what had been spoken through the prophet Jeremiah, 'And they took the thirty pieces of silver, the price of the one on whom a price had been set, on whom some of the people of Israel had set a price, and they gave them for the potter's field, as the LORD commanded me.'"

- Compare and contrast this verse from Matthew with Exod 21:32.

- Compare and contrast Zech 11:17 and John 10:12-13; Zech 12:10 and Rev 1:7; Zech 14:8, Ezek 47:1-12, and Rev 22:1.

Second Zechariah's Meaning for Us Today

Zechariah 9–14 in the Lectionary

In the Sunday Lectionary Zechariah 9–14 appears twice. In Year A, *LM* assigns 9:9-10 on the Fourteenth Sunday of the Year with Matt 11:25-30. *RCL* offers Zech 9:9-12 as an option with Matt 11:16-19, 25-30. Here Zechariah promises the king's protection and Matthew promises divine comfort. In Year C, on the Twelfth Sunday in Ordinary Time, *LM* pairs 12:10-11; [13:1], which refers to looking at "the one whom they have pierced," with Luke 9:18-24, on the inevitability of suffering when we follow Christ. The Zechariah reading was retrospectively understood by the early Christian community as referring to Christ. Zechariah 9–14 does not appear in the Weekday Lectionary.

In the Jewish community, Zech 14:1-21 is the reading for the first day of Sukkot, paired with Lev 22:26–23:44; Num 29:12-16.

Second Zechariah's significance for our daily life

Zechariah provides a prophetic picture of God's plan for the people by which to instruct every future generation of Israel who awaits the coming of God's reign. The book emphasizes faithfulness to God and to our covenant commitments, but it does not advocate adherence to the status quo as an end in itself. Rather, the book encourages us to trust that God continues to create a new reality; it invites us to join in bringing about that new thing.

The canonical shape of the book points to a bizarre, intense, overwhelming dimension of reality, as does Ezekiel. This challenges the reader to wrestle with the content in other forms of actualization: art, poetry, drama.

- How might you depict Zechariah's message of hope for the future in an artistic form?

Passages for study

> 10:6-12
>
> 12:1-9
>
> 14:16-21

For Further Reading

Floyd, Michael H. *Minor Prophets, Part 2*. FOTL 22. Grand Rapids: Eerdmans, 2000.

Meyers, Carol L., and Eric M. Meyers. *Zechariah 9–14* AB 25C. Garden City, NY: Doubleday, 1993.

Petersen, David. *Zechariah 9–14 and Malachi: A Commentary*. OTL. Louisville: Westminster John Knox, 1995. Very good history section.

Sweeney, Marvin A. *The Twelve Prophets*, vol. 2. Berit Olam. Collegeville: Liturgical Press, 2000.

Chapter Eleven

Jonah, the Unique Prophet

We save Jonah for last in our study of the prophets for several reasons. First, as we will see below, the book offers only indirect hints as to its historical setting; the few clues it does give suggest a late date of composition. Second, the prophet Jonah is unique among the prophets for his reluctance and the minimal fulfillment of his prophetic commission. Closely related is the third reason: Jonah proclaims only one sentence to the audience to whom God sends him. The book consists largely of the story of his efforts to remain unengaged from the task assigned to him. The remarkable aspect of the book's message is that the Lord accomplishes the divine task in spite of Jonah's resistance. The book thus has its own unique fascination, as we will see.

JONAH
"The word of the Lord came to Jonah a second time,
saying, 'Get up, go to Nineveh, that great city,
and proclaim to it the message that I tell you.'" (Jonah 3:1–2)

Background Information

Nothing is known with certainty about the historical setting of Jonah. The Bible does offer several clues as to language and geography. The first is in 2 Kings 14:25, which mentions a Jonah, son of Amittai, who lived during the reign of Jeroboam II of Israel (786–746) and predicted success for Jeroboam's campaign to restore Israel's borders. Even though the names are the same, the reference cannot unequivocally be associated with the prophet of the book, and thus cannot be used to assign a clear date to the book. Second, Sir 49:10 refers to twelve prophets, after naming Isaiah, Jeremiah, and Ezekiel in 48:22 and 49:6-8. This information tells us that by the time Sirach was written at the beginning of the second century B.C.E. three major and twelve minor prophets were known and referred to as a body. We can assume that the twelve were the same as those we include today; this information sets the early second century as the *terminus ad quem* (the last possible time) for Jonah as a written document.

Extra-biblical information offers additional insight into the question. First, the language of the book includes postexilic words, phrases, and syntax. This information suggests that the written form of the book as we know it is postexilic. Geography also offers information about two of the cities named in the text. Joppa was probably not an Israelite city in the eighth century, but it was an important city in postexilic times. Nineveh was the capital of Assyria in its days as an empire, but in postexilic times it was a major city-state. (See Zeph 2:13 and Tob 14:4, 8 regarding its destruction.) This information suggests that the composer of the story did not base the settings on eighth-century realities, but rather transposed their postexilic importance to a pre-exilic time.

It is realistic to locate the story in Jerusalem, not far from Joppa, with Nineveh to its east and Tarshish to its west (if, in fact, Tarshish was in the area that is modern Spain). These two locations to the west and east of Jerusalem would allow the story to move Jonah away from God toward Tarshish, in the opposite direction from Nineveh, where God sent him.

The story fits the postexilic community, offering a corrective to that group's nationalistic tendencies by illustrating God's concern for non-Israelite people. This information places Jonah, in the written form we know today, in the postexilic period, perhaps the fourth century.

Organization of the Book

Outline

The story follows a simple outline:

    1, Jonah flees from God geographically

    2, Jonah prays to God in thanksgiving

    3–4, Jonah flees from God spiritually

Genre

NOVELLA. The imprecision of the historical references suggests that the book is not historical but fictional. The book as a whole is a novella, a short fictional piece with a plot that moves toward a climax and includes characterization, similar to the Joseph story in Genesis 37–50.

The division of the plot into two main parts is evident when we compare chapters 1 and 3. Both begin with divine instructions to Jonah, followed by his response. In chapter 1 Jonah goes in the opposite direction from the divine commission. In chapter 3 he travels to the place where God sends him. In both parts of the story his travels involve him in adventures that illustrate God's concern for him and for those with whom he comes in contact.

Jonah in the story is a reluctant follower of God. In chapter 1 he actually goes directly away from where God sends him. Then in chapter 3 he goes to the place where he is sent, but accepts only minimally the commission to preach to the Ninevites. His reluctance continues throughout the story.

PRAYER OF THANKSGIVING. Chapter 2 is a prayer of thanksgiving similar to those found in the book of Psalms. It consists of a statement of the petitioner's need and how God relieved it, and vows a sacrifice of thanksgiving to God. The prayer in Jonah follows this format, using phrases typical of psalm language. The irony of Jonah's thanksgiving is its context: Jonah thanks God for placing him in the belly of the fish, a situation most of us would not see as reason for thanksgiving. But the fish had rescued Jonah from drowning in the sea, hence Jonah's prayer of thanks.

Rhetorical Features

REPETITION. Chapters 1 and 3 begin with the same formula. In 1:1–2 we read: "Now the word of the LORD came to Jonah son of Amittai, saying, 'Go at once to Nineveh, that great city . . .'" and in 3:1 we find "The word of the LORD came to Jonah a second time, saying, 'Get up, go to Nineveh, that great city. . . .'" This repetition emphasizes the second opportunity God creates for Jonah to accept the divine commission. This time, though, since God saw that the commission frightened Jonah away the first time, the instructions state only where to go, with the promise that, once Jonah reaches Nineveh, God will tell him what to say to the people.

• Contrast Jonah's position with that of Abraham in Gen 18:16-33.

The Lord's actions in the story use the same Hebrew verb in 1:17; 4:6, 7, 8, often translated "appoint." While the *NRSV* does not use the same verb in English, it is informative to note that all the divine actions that directly affect Jonah are expressed in the same verb, "to appoint."

NUMBERS. Several numbers appear throughout the book, serving as mnemonic devices in the story.

- How many appearances of the number "three" do you find in the book? The number "four"? Compare and contrast this repetition with Amos 1–2.

CONTRAST. In addition to repetition, the book also uses contrasts or opposites to deliver its message. One example is the two places where Jonah went: Tarshish to the west and Nineveh to the east. Another example is the actions of the mariners in contrast to those of Jonah: when the storm came up, the mariners prayed to their gods but Jonah went to the lowest part of the ship and fell asleep. This contrast is all the more significant in light of Jonah's claim to worship the Lord in 1:9. Eventually the mariners prayed to Jonah's God, whom he professed to worship, but in fact did not.

- In chapter 3, what contrast do you find in the ways Jonah and the king of Nineveh speak to the people of Nineveh? What impression do Jonah's words give you about how he carried out his prophetic commission?

HYPERBOLE. Several details in the story are clearly exaggerated, highlighting specific dimensions of the narrative. For example, the story leaves Jonah in the belly of the fish three days and three nights, an exceptionally long time that is possible only in fiction. Another example is the repentance of the animals of Nineveh by fasting, prayer, and the wearing of sackcloth. These exaggerations serve the story by their improbability. While they are not humanly plausible, their occurrence in the story underscores God's presence and power in the events described.

- What instances of hyperbole do you find in chapter 4? How do they enhance the message of the book?

IRONY OF SITUATION, PLOT, AND CHARACTER. The above examples of rhetorical features illustrate several ironies in the book in which the situations themselves, the twists of the plot, and the actions that characterize the different people are not as we would expect. For example, characters act in contrast to what we would normally anticipate: the mariners pray when Jonah sleeps, even though Jonah identifies himself as one who worships the Lord. In the same vein, the mariners first each pray to their own gods, then they pray, offer sacrifices, and make vows to Jonah's god, the Lord (1:5, 14, 16). Jonah does not pray until he is in the belly of the fish, from which he thanks God for rescuing him. We would expect him to pray that God would deliver him rather than thank God for saving him (ch. 2).

Another ironic twist is the contrast between the actions of Jonah and the king in Nineveh. While Jonah's message to the city is a warning that consists of only five words in Hebrew, the king issues a decree calling for the people, and even the animals, to repent in the hope that God also will repent of the destruction Jonah has predicted. Jonah contrasts sharply with all the other biblical prophets, proclaiming only five words, while all the other biblical prophets spoke on numerous occasions, giving lengthy speeches to the people. And in this story we would expect that Jonah would advocate prayer and sacrifice, but instead it is the Ninevites themselves who decide to repent; their king issues the decree that one would have expected to come from Jonah.

KEY WORDS. Jonah, the name of the prophet, means "dove." This word carries two different connotations: on the one hand it suggests the capricious lack of direction that characterizes Jonah in the book, while on the other hand the dove is a symbol for peace, the divine goal in the book.

- See the use of the word "dove" in Hos 7:11–12.

The word "sleep" in Jonah 1 connotes a particular kind of sleep. It is the same as the word in Gen 2:21, where God puts Adam to sleep in order to take a rib from which to create Eve. The word also appears in Gen 15:12: from a deep sleep Abram hears the voice of God telling him that his descendants will "be aliens in a land that is not theirs." We find it again in Isa 29:10: "For the LORD has poured out upon you a spirit of deep sleep; he has closed your eyes, you prophets, and covered your heads, you seers." These three examples illustrate sleep induced by God for some divine purpose.

- What divine purposes do you see in the three examples above? Compare and contrast them with Jonah 1:5-6.

Ḥesed. In 2:8 the word is translated "true loyalty" and in 4:2 "steadfast love." In both instances Jonah uses the word in talking to God, naming a divine attribute. We can note the irony in Jonah's use of this word to describe God in light of Jonah's actions.

Raḥum. This word is related to another word found often in the prophetic books, *raḥamim.* In Jonah 4:2 it is translated "merciful." Like the phrase "abounding in steadfast love" in the same verse, "merciful" is ironic in light of Jonah's refusal to cooperate in the divine project to save the Ninevites.

Jonah's Message

Themes

DIVINE FORGIVENESS. When the Ninevites repent and God's mind changes about punishing them, Jonah wants to die because, he says, he has known all along that God would relent. While this interchange highlights Jonah's unreasonable line of thinking, it also underscores God's eagerness to forgive. Divine forgiveness is immediate and non-discriminatory. As soon as the Ninevites repent, God relents. The mariners and the Ninevites, all Gentiles, worship God while the Israelite prophet Jonah balks, sleeps, and whines. God, seeing their devotion, saves the mariners and forgives the Ninevites in spite of the fact that they are enemies of Israel.

GOD'S LIMITLESS PRESENCE AND ACTION. The saving of the mariners highlights the unlimited sphere of divine presence and action. God is present among the people, not only in Israel but also on the sea and in Nineveh. The mariners sacrifice to God and God accepts their offering even though they are not in the designated place for sacrifice (see Deut 12:5–12). Likewise, the Ninevites fast and wear sackcloth and God accepts their repentance.

DIVINE FREEDOM. Divine action in the story highlights God's freedom and offers an alternative to the strict belief in divine retribution (for example, Judg 2:11–23). God relents, showing mercy to people in their inadequacy (Jonah 4:11) in spite of Jonah's protest. God is free to show mercy both to Israelites and to non-Israelites. The flip side of this divine characteristic is the importance of trust in God. The mariners and the Ninevites trust God and are saved. Jonah claims to trust God, but his words and actions contradict that claim (Jonah 1:6, 9; 3:5, 9; 4:2-5, 8–11). Only when he is inside the fish does Jonah express trust in God (2:9).

The irony we have observed regarding Jonah in the fish suggests that Jonah trusts God only under unreal circumstances. When he is face to face with real life, he complains about God's mercy.

Jonah and Other Parts of the Bible

The book of Jonah engages in dialogue with earlier biblical traditions regarding the character of the Lord and the divine relationship with Israel, with non-Israelites, with the righteous and the unrighteous, with the repentant and the unrepentant. In the late fifth and early fourth centuries this kind of hopeful message offered support to the returned exiles in their efforts to rebuild their life in Jerusalem and Judah.

- Compare and contrast the Lord's relationships with different peoples in Exod 20:5-6; 34:6-7; Num 14:18; Deut 5:9–10; 7:7–11; Judg 2:11–23. See also Jer 18:7–10; Ezek 18:21–24; Joel 2:13–14.

Jonah includes several similarities with other biblical books as well. For example, Jonah and Elijah share several traits: both consider themselves zealous for God, both require two commissionings from God, both involve people who worship gods other than the Lord, and both ask God to take their lives, as they would rather die than continue to live in their present circumstances.

- Compare and contrast Jonah with 1 Kings 17–19 in this regard.

- Compare and contrast Jonah and Ruth in this regard.

- Tobit 14:4-9 refers to Nahum's predictions of the fall of Nineveh. Compare and contrast Nahum's view of the Ninevites with their depiction in Jonah.

Matthew refers to the story of Jonah to illustrate a point about signs. In response to the scribes' and Pharisees' request for a sign, Jesus tells them:

> An evil and adulterous generation asks for a sign, but no sign will be given to it except the sign of the prophet Jonah. For just as Jonah was three days and three nights in the belly of the sea monster, so for three days and three nights the Son of Man will be in the heart of the earth. The people of Nineveh will rise up at the judgment with this generation and condemn it, because they repented at the proclamation of Jonah, and see, something greater than Jonah is here! (Matt 12:39-41; see also Luke 11:29-32).

Here Matthew uses Jonah's stay inside the fish as the requested sign, which for Matthew is an oblique reference to Jesus' coming death and resurrection. Again in Matt 16:1-4 the people ask for a sign, and again Jesus refers to the sign of Jonah. These references are examples of Matthew's tendency to use Old Testament references to illustrate his lessons. They are not to be understood as proofs of the historicity of Jonah, but rather as literary and rhetorical devices and teaching tools for Matthew.

Jonah's Meaning for Us Today

Jonah in the Lectionary

In both *LM* and *RCL*, on the Third Sunday in Ordinary Time in Year B Jonah 3:1-5, 10 is paired with Matt 1:14–20. Both of these readings are calls to repentance. In addition, 3:1–10 is read on Wednesday of the First Week in Lent, with Luke 11:29-32. The Jonah passage recounts God's second commission to Jonah to go to Nineveh, and the positive response of the Ninevites; the Gospel reading makes reference to Jonah.

In the Weekday Lectionary, on Monday, Tuesday, and Wednesday of the Twenty-seventh Week of Year I, Jonah 1:1–2:2, 11 in *NAB* tells of Jonah's first call and his refusal to answer it; 3:1–10 is as above; and 4:1–11 describes Jonah's unwillingness to rejoice in the works of God on behalf of the Ninevites.

In Jewish liturgy the book of Jonah is read on the afternoon of Yom Kippur, the Day of Atonement, the holiest day in the Jewish year, with Lev 18:1-30 and Mic 7:18–20.

Jonah's significance for our daily life

Jonah invites us to reflect on our own willingness to follow God's word in the events of our own lives. Are we eager like Isaiah? Willing in spite of the inevitable difficulties like Jeremiah? Reluctant like Jonah?

Jonah also invites us to inclusiveness in our dealings with people in today's global society. Just as God eagerly transformed the repentant Ninevites, the book challenges us to recognize that God's love encompasses all people.

• How would you respond to God's final question to Jonah?

• What specific situations today call us to inclusiveness?

Jonah is a popular literary and artistic subject as well. Some examples of modern interpretations are Herman Melville's *Moby Dick,* especially Father Mapple's sermon in Chapter Nine; Robert Frost's *A Masque of Mercy;* James Limburg, "Jonah and the Whale Through the Eyes of Artists," *Bible Review* 6/4 (August 1990) 18–25; Wolf Mankowitz, "It Should Happen to a Dog: A Play in One Act" (in his *Five One Act Plays* [London: Evans Brothers, 1956]); Hart Crane, "After Jonah,"; Thomas Merton, "All the Way Down (Jonas Ch. 2)"; and Paul Murray, o.p., *A Journey with Jonah: The Spirituality of Bewilderment* (Dublin: Columba Press, 2002).

- Read and comment on one of the interpretations listed above.

- Create your own contemporary depiction of the Jonah story.

Passages for study

> 2:1-9
> 4:1-5
> 4:9–11

For Further Reading

Limburg, James. *Jonah: A Commentary.* OTL. Louisville: Westminster John Knox, 1993.

Sasson, Jack M. *Jonah: A New Translation with Introduction, Commentary, and Interpretation.* AB 24B. New York: Doubleday, 1990.

Sherwood, Yvonne. *A Biblical Text and Its Afterlives: The Survival of Jonah in Western Culture.* Cambridge: Cambridge University Press, 2000.

Sweeney, Marvin A. *The Twelve Prophets,* vol. 1. Berit Olam. Collegeville: Liturgical Press, 2000.

Trible, Phyllis. *Rhetorical Criticism: Context, Method, and the Book of Jonah.* Minneapolis: Fortress, 1994.

Conclusion

Now that we have looked at the different prophets, the situations in which they lived and spoke, and their particular messages, we find certain particularities that can serve us in interpreting the prophetic message for today. Each prophetic voice rose in a specific historical and geographical context. Sometimes this information is included in the book, as is the case with First Isaiah, who names the different rulers during the Syro-Ephraimite Crisis in the late eighth century. At other times the book's superscription provides the only explicit identification of a historical and geographical context. Sometimes it is difficult to know the context that gave rise to the message, and we rely on the message itself and on how it might relate to a particular time and place. Within the historical and geographical context, each prophetic message related the divine stirring presence in the midst of the socioeconomic, political, and religious concerns of the people. Prophets spoke God's word about the widening socioeconomic gap between different groups of people in the eighth century, the threat of invasion by the Assyrians in the eighth century and the Babylonians in the late-seventh and early-sixth centuries, exacerbated by the religious complacency of the Jerusalemites. They addressed the crisis of faith precipitated by the Exile in Babylon, the ongoing struggle for faithfulness to the one God and to the covenant relationship between God and the people during the Persian and Hellenistic Periods when the Judahites were subject to the rule of foreign governors.

In addition, we have observed that each prophet spoke in a particular style. That style corresponded to the conventions of the ancient Near East, and also included the personal ways of expression of each prophet. It included the use of the genres and rhetorical features of the day, lending a highly persuasive dimension to each message, in keeping with the prophets' eagerness that the divine words be heard and followed. The words condemned injustice, encouraged faithfulness to God and covenant, announced new modalities of divine presence among the people, and invited the people into a hopeful future.

These features were only part of the prophets' messages, though. Underneath the words was the pervasive conviction that the one God loved and cared for the people in the midst of all the difficulties and challenges they faced. In return, God asked for faithfulness, to be expressed in prayerful worship and in righteous living. The latter included, in particular, special concern for the vulnerable members of the community.

A further characteristic we have noted is the tendency of the later prophets to base their teaching on the words of the earlier prophets, and to interpret them for their own audiences in the light of current needs. These later prophets have given us models for announcing God's presence in our own world: they began with the essence of God's message, and delivered it in new ways to call their audiences to faithful living in their own day.

These elements of the prophetic message: historical and geographical context, socioeconomic, political, and religious concerns that make up what we referred to in Chapter One as the world behind the text; the actual prophetic words, based on the prophets' experience of God's stirring presence and delivered in the genres and rhetorical framework of their day, or the world of the text; inform our own awareness of the world in which we live, and of God's creative presence in our midst, or the world in front of the text.

The biblical prophets teach us the importance of being rooted in our ancient monotheistic heritage as well as the necessity to address our world within today's context. They show us the need to speak from a solid knowledge of the issues that surround us. In addition they exemplify the importance of using contemporary media to deliver the message of divine stirring among us. The current status of electronic development puts worldwide audiences within instant reach, creating a new kind of space for God's message to unfold in our day. How will we rise to the challenge?

- Focus on a specific concern in your community today. Compose a prophetic message within a contemporary genre and rhetorical style, that you can announce by using a contemporary medium.

Index of Authors and Subjects

Acrostic, 136, 138, 185
Admonition (genre), 19, 57, 60, 164, 248, 264
Advent, 16, 97, 117–118, 120–121, 134, 182–183, 188, 236, 250–251, 274
Ahaz, 46–48, 50, 87, 105–108, 112, 113, 115, 116, 118
Alexander the Great, 242, 267, 276, 285
Allegory, 199, 290, 292
Anderson, Francis I., 68, 99
Announcement of judgment
  to Israel, 17–18, 54–56, 64, 66, 67, 71–72, 88–89, 104, 129–130, 132, 146, 198–199, 277
  to the nations, 18, 54–56, 67, 104–105, 129–130, 132, 137–138, 146, 169, 199–200, 248, 287
Announcement of salvation, 20, 58–59, 90, 224–225, 246–247
Apocalyptic, 4, 250, 280, 288–289, 291–292
Assurance of salvation, 16, 19, 26–27, 59, 225–226, 227, 246
(Auto)biographical report, 22, 52, 70, 148, 160, 161, 247

Barstad, Hans M., 121
Barton, John, 121
Bauer, Angela, 185
Berlin, Adele, 135
Berquist, Jon L., 252
Berrigan, Daniel, 122, 185, 211
Blank, Sheldon, 122

Blenkinsopp, Joseph, 31, 44
Bright, John, 31, 44, 185
Brueggemann, Walter, 185, 186, 238

Call narrative, 22, 36, 41, 101–102, 136, 147, 159, 171, 192, 195
Carroll, Robert, 185
Christ, 4, 96, 116–119, 168, 182–183, 186, 188, 209, 235, 237, 251, 268, 273, 274, 293
Christmas, 16, 98, 181, 235, 251, 274
Clements, Ronald E., 122
Clifford, Richard J., 238
Collins, John J., 185
Confessions of Jeremiah, 4, 163–164, 181–183, 227
Conrad, Edgar, 122
Creation, 9, 58, 62, 77, 112, 132, 146, 150–151, 168, 179, 199, 223–225, 230–232, 236, 251, 260, 283, 287
Crenshaw, James L., 284

David, 37–39, 56, 58–59, 96–98, 103, 116, 119, 124, 156, 157, 161, 177, 183, 186, 197, 202, 232, 290, 292
Davies, Eryl, 122
Death, meaning of, 11, 30, 161, 205, 228
Dempsey, Carol J., 85, 99, 188
Diamond, H. R., 185
Disputation, 21, 91, 162–163, 199, 226–227
Doorly, William J., 68
Duguid, Iain, 211

Easter, 16, 134, 181, 188, 209–210, 235, 251

Edom/Edomites, 58, 65, 123, 169, 189, 199, 200, 212–217, 248

Egypt, 9, 12, 46, 49, 53, 55, 60, 62, 65, 71, 77, 84, 96, 97, 106, 123–124, 125, 156, 162, 165, 169,170, 176, 180, 191–192, 197, 199–200, 215, 224, 231, 239–240, 242

Eichrodt, Walther, 211

ʾemunah, 78, 111, 249

Equality/inequality, 17, 49–50, 264

Evans, Craig, 122

Exile, 2, 18, 23, 31, 49–50, 54, 56–63, 88–90, 92, 94, 96, 98, 100–101, 116, 125, 139, 155–156, 158–159, 165–169, 171–173, 175–176, 180–181, 183, 189–190, 192–193, 195–199, 202–204, 206, 210, 219–225, 227–229, 231–237, 239–240, 245, 250, 260, 262, 266, 271, 301, 305

Exodus, Book, 20, 30, 41, 137, 225
    Event, 35, 41, 62, 78, 97, 166–168, 174, 180, 207, 231–232, 248, 257, 265, 292

Ezra, 240, 243, 245

Faithfulness, divine, 1, 10, 68, 77–85, 104, 130, 168, 204–205, 208, 210–211, 265

Faithfulness/unfaithfulness, human (see also ʾemunah), 3, 11, 23, 41, 51, 61–65, 68, 70–74, 77–85, 91, 93–94, 96–97, 104, 109, 114, 116, 120, 130–131, 132–134, 135, 140, 141, 148, 151–152, 156, 161–163, 165, 167–169, 171–174, 176–177, 179–180, 183, 185, 195–196, 198–199, 202–205, 208, 211, 221, 229, 236–237, 242, 252, 257, 265, 269–270, 274, 282, 291, 294, 305–306

Floyd, Michael H., 294

Forgiveness, 53, 65, 94, 136, 167–168, 179–180, 199, 205, 211, 231, 300

Freedman, David Noel, 68

Gray, John, 44

Greenberg, Moshe, 212

Habel, Norman C., 85, 252

Halperin, David, 212

Heschel, Abraham, 31

ḥesed, 78, 93, 97, 249, 263, 281, 300

Hezekiah, 48–51, 68, 87, 115, 116, 121, 124–129, 176, 234

Hill, Andrew E., 275

Hillers, Delbert, 99

Holladay, William L., 185

Hymn, 21, 29, 57–58, 62, 66, 108, 136, 144–145, 185, 229

Hypocrisy, 29, 36, 64, 93, 120

Imagery, 18, 54, 75, 77, 83, 104, 106, 138, 190, 199, 204, 209, 211, 214–216, 234, 249, 281

Instruction, prophetic, 21, 90, 98, 108, 147

Interpretation, Christocentric, 16, 96, 98, 116–120, 182–183
    Theocentric, 16, 116–120, 182, 183, 291
    Typological, 16, 263, 285

Irony, 93, 165, 216, 297–301

Jehoiachin, 49, 116, 124, 158, 176, 190, 192, 257

Jehoiakim, 19, 22, 49, 124–125, 144, 155, 160, 176, 188

Jeremias, Jörg, 68

Jewish Community, 4, 6, 15, 67, 116, 156, 240, 242–243

Jewish Sabbath Readings, 67, 83–84, 98, 121, 134, 142, 152, 184, 210–211, 218, 237, 252, 258, 265, 274, 283, 293, 302

Jones, G. H., 44

Josiah, 49, 51, 124–128, 129, 155, 159, 176–177

Justice/injustice (see also mišpat), 1, 6, 17–18, 21, 29–30, 42, 51, 52, 55, 57, 60–68, 72–73, 78, 87, 88–89, 93–99,

109–111, 114–118, 125, 128, 137, 143–144, 146, 148, 151–152, 170, 175, 177, 183–184, 217, 228, 247–249, 305

King, Philip J., 185
Koch, Klaus, 31
Kraus, Hans-Joachim, 186

Lament, 4, 21, 40, 59, 80, 91, 92, 99, 102, 145–149, 152, 153, 163, 179–180, 194, 228, 247, 276, 277, 282
Lawsuit, prophetic, 13, 21, 73–74, 90, 226–227, 229–230
Lectionary for Mass, 15–16, 66–67, 83–84, 97–98, 117–121, 134, 142, 152, 181–183, 186, 188, 209–210, 218, 235–237, 250–252, 258, 265, 274, 283, 293, 302
    Jewish, 67, 83–84, 98, 121, 134, 142, 152, 184, 210–211, 218, 237, 252, 258, 265, 274, 283, 293, 302
    Revised Common, 15–16, 66–67, 83–84, 97–98, 117–121, 134, 142, 152, 181–183, 188, 209–210, 218, 235–237, 250–252, 258, 265, 274, 283, 293, 302
Legend, 6, 23, 41, 45, 101, 272
Lent, 16, 84, 98, 120, 182–183, 209, 236, 252, 300, 302
Letter, 24, 27–28, 165–166, 171, 184, 187, 233
Levenson, Jon, 212
Lewis, C. S., 185, 186
Limburg, James, 303
Love (see also *ḥesed*)
    Divine, 9, 12, 65, 68, 73, 77, 84–85, 134, 174, 177, 179, 186, 224, 226, 230–231, 271, 275, 306
    Human, 19, 57, 60, 63, 72–73, 77, 80, 82, 87, 99, 186
Lundbom, Jack R., 185

Mays, James Luther, 68, 85, 99
McKane, William, 185

McKenzie, John L., 238, 252
Messenger formula/speech, 17, 18, 20, 24, 52, 54, 69, 106, 169–170, 202, 213, 223–225, 255, 261, 277, 287
Messianic Figure, 96, 116, 233, 264, 291
    Passage, 98, 117, 119, 182, 183
    Reference to Christ, 10, 118
Metaphor, 53–54, 60, 70, 73–77, 79, 83, 84, 89, 102, 104, 148, 162, 171–173, 179–180, 182, 198–202, 204, 247, 248, 266, 276, 278–279, 289
Meyers, Carol L. and Eric M., 259, 266, 294
mišpat, 78, 93, 110, 205, 249, 263
Moses, 1, 6, 8, 11, 37, 41–44, 53, 102, 105, 125–126, 206, 228, 270
Mowinckel, Sigmund, 31
Murphy, Frederick James, 188

Nebuchadnezzar, 28, 49, 124, 164, 176–177, 219
Nineveh/Ninevites, 6, 27, 31, 49, 123–124, 135–140, 296–302
Nissinen, Martti, 31

O'Brien, Julia Myers, 143
O'Connor, Kathleen M., 186
Ordinary Time, 10, 16, 66, 83–84, 98, 118–120, 134, 142, 152, 181–183, 186, 188, 209–210, 235–236, 251, 258, 265, 274, 283, 293, 302
Orphans, 6, 10, 63, 109, 128, 165, 264

Paul, Shalom, 68
Pentecost, 209, 283
Perdue, Leo G., 185
Personification, 74, 77, 110, 132, 139–140
Petersen, David L., 32, 259, 266, 275, 294
Polemic, 222–223, 225–226, 229–230
Pontifical Biblical Commission, 32, 116
Portrayal of salvation , 19–20, 106, 112
Pritchard, James B., 32
Pun, 61, 110, 171, 172

Raabe, Paul, 218
Rad, Gerhard von, 32
raḥamim, 78, 249, 263–264, 300
Resident aliens, 6, 10–11, 63, 196, 264
Rhetorical question, 23, 24, 58, 66, 91, 109, 137, 140, 280
Ridicule, 104, 148, 226, 229–230
Righteousness/unrighteousness (see also *ṣedaqah, ṣedeq*), 6, 17, 29, 51, 55, 62–66, 68, 72–73, 78, 91, 93–96, 104, 110–111, 115, 130, 132, 145, 149, 151, 177–179, 199, 205, 226, 233, 2 46–247, 249, 269–270, 273, 301, 306
Roberts, J.J.M., 135, 143, 153
Robertson, O. Palmer, 135, 143, 153
Rosh Hashanah, 84, 98, 184

Samaria, 34, 40, 46–51, 59, 68–69, 79, 94, 242
Sasson, Jack M., 303
Sawyer, John F., 122
Schmitt, John, 122
ṣedaqah, 78, 93, 110, 205, 249, 281
ṣedeq, 78, 110, 205, 249
Sermon, 164–165, 170, 175, 184, 303
Shavuot, 211
Sherwood, Yvonne, 303
Simile, 60, 72, 74–77, 80, 92, 96, 139, 249
Smith-Christopher, Daniel L., 185, 238
Soliloquy, 145, 147, 149
Stacey, W. D., 32
Suffering, 11, 34–36, 46, 51, 56, 58, 77, 81, 89, 98–99, 102, 106, 137, 140–143, 149, 151, 158, 160–165, 170–174, 182–183, 199, 217, 220, 227–228, 235, 237, 240, 247, 290, 292, 293
    Redemptive, 228, 235–236
    Suffering Servant, 227
Sweeney, Marvin A., 32, 68, 85, 99, 135, 143, 153, 218, 259, 266, 275, 284, 294, 303
Symbolic act, 13, 22, 70–72, 108, 184, 193–194, 197–198, 204, 261, 287

Thanksgiving hymn, 21, 108, 296–297
Thompson, Michael E. W., 122
Treaty, 10, 24, 36
Trible, Phyllis, 303
Trust in God, 22, 91, 105–109, 120, 130–131, 133, 134, 141, 151, 163–166, 182–184, 226, 228, 257, 274, 291, 294, 300–301

Vision report, 22, 52–53, 172, 195, 202–203, 261–262
Vulnerable members of community, 6, 10–11, 21, 30, 55–56, 63–64, 67, 77, 93, 96, 104, 111, 115, 116, 165, 175, 177, 182, 184, 228, 243, 248, 252, 268, 272, 306

Weems, R., 32
Weinfeld, Moshe, 32
West, Fritz, 32
Westermann, Claus, 32, 238, 252
Wevers, John W., 212
Whybray, Roger N., 238, 252
Widows, 6, 10, 23, 40, 63, 109, 128, 165, 264
Wildberger, Hans, 122
Willey, Patricia A., 238
Woe oracle, 18–19, 56, 105, 130, 136, 144–145, 147–148, 149
Wolff, Hans Walter, 68, 85, 99, 218, 259, 284
Words of judgment, 17–19, 63, 69, 72, 83, 88, 92–94, 104, 129–130, 132, 138, 195, 198– 200, 248, 277
Words of salvation, 19, 25, 72, 88, 89, 92, 94, 105–106, 130, 166–167, 198, 200–203, 214, 224, 229, 277–278, 288

Yom Kippur, 84, 98, 252, 281, 302

Zedekiah, 34–35, 49, 124–125, 155, 169, 175–176
Zerubbabel, 116, 240, 255–258, 264, 292
Zimmerli, Walther, 212
Zucker, David J., 32

Index of Biblical References

Genesis
1	9, 12
1:1	150, 179, 256
1:1–6:8	237
1:2	194
2	9
2:6	203
2:7	150
2:21	299
6:7	132
6:9–11:32	237
11:1-9	131
12:1–17:27	237
15:12	299
18:16-33	297
18:22-33	180
22:1-24	184
22:17	150
25:29-30	212
28:10–32:3	84
32:4–36:43	84, 218
32:12	150
36	212
37:1–40:23	67
40:9, 16	25
41:17, 22	25
41:49	150
44:18–47:27	210

Exodus
1:1–6:1	121
3	41
3:10	24
3:12, 20	105
3:14	8
4:2-5, 6-8, 9	105
4:21	102, 207
6:2–9:35	210
6:7	71
7:13	207

7:13, 14, 22	102
8:15, 19, 32	102
8:19	207
9:7, 12, 34, 35	102
10:1, 20, 27	102
10:1–13:16	184
11:10	102
13:2	165
14:4, 8	102
14:13	26
15:20-21	287
16:1–17:7	172
18:1–20:23	121
20	44, 81
20:5	141
20:5-6	301
20:14	273
20:18-20	44
20:18-21	30
21:1–24:18	184
21:32	288, 293
22:21-22	10, 63
22:21-25	264
22:26-27	55
23:9	63
27:20–30:10	210
32	78
32:11-14	237, 252
33:12–34:26	211
34:1-10	237, 252
34:5-7, 14	141
34:9	53
40:10-15	116
34:6-7	301
34:6	281

Leviticus
1:1–5:26	237
6:1–8:36	184
8:10-12	116

16:1-34	252
16:1–18:30	210
18:1-30	98, 302
18:4-5	207, 208
18:15	55
19:1–20:27	67
19:3, 33-34	207
19:13	273
19:19	198
20:2-6	207
20:12	55
21:1–24:23	210
22:26–23:44	293
25:1–26:2	184
25:39-46	55
26:3-13, 27-33	207
26:3–27:34	184
26:12	71
26:16, 18, 22, 30, 37	82
26:19	172
26:21-22	180
27:30	273

Numbers
1:1–4:20	84
6:24-26	273
8:1–12:16	265
10:35	26
11	78
11:1-15	172
14:18	141, 301
14:19-20	53
16	273
18:21-24	273
22–24	27
22:2–25:9	98
24:2	25
28:19-25	121
29:1-6	184
29:7-11	252

311

29:12-16   293
30:2–32:42   184
33:1–36:13   184
34:1-15   197

Deuteronomy
1:1–3:22   121
3:23–7:11   237
4:9   82
4:9-31   72
4:25-40   184
4:35, 39   9, 133, 232, 282
5:9-10   301
5:18, 20   273
6:4   271
6:5   165
6:6-13   82
6:12   72
7:6-8   12
7:7-8   231, 271
7:7-11   301
7:12–11:25   237
7:17-24   26
8:11-19   72
8:11-20   82
9:15-21   82
10:15-18   231
10:16   173
10:18   10
11   180
11:26–16:17   237
12–26   125
12:5-12   300
12:13-18   126
13:1-5   30, 291
13:17   70
14:3, 23-24   271
14:28-29   128
15:1-3, 7-11, 12-18   128
15:18   44
15:19–16:17   121
15:21   271
16:11-14   10
16:16-20   128
16:18–21:9   237
17   29
17:1, 4, 8-13   271
17:14-20   128
17:14-15   82
18   30
18:1-8   128
18:10   273
18:15   129

18:15, 18   42, 126
18:15-22   30, 42
18:20   291
18:22   31
19:1-3, 14   128
20:1-4   26
20:5-9   128
21:5   271
21:10–25:19   237
22:6-7   128
23:8-10   271
23:15-16, 19-20   128
24:1-4   180
24:1-4, 8   271
24:5, 6, 7, 10-13, 17-22   128
24:12-13   55
24:17   273
24:17-21   10
26:1–29:8   252
26:12-15   128
27:9-10   271
27:15-26   126
28:1-68   82
28:15-68   126
29:9–30:20   252
30:3   70
30:6   173
31:1-8   26
31:1-30   237, 252
31:9-11   82
32:21, 43   141
33   146
33:10   82

Joshua
2:4   256
13:8–19:51   197

Judges
2:11-23   300, 301
2:16   36
3:9, 15   36
3:10   25
6:14   36
11:29   25
14:6, 19   25
15:14   25

1 Samuel
1:12-17   36
1:20   35
2:12-17, 22, 26   36
3:11-17, 19   36

3:19   12, 38
4:11, 15   36
8:1   36
8:5, 6-9   37
9:1–10:27   37
10:6, 10   25
11:6   25
15:1   116
16:1-13   37
16:3   25
17   37
23:4   26
24:6-10   116
26:8   26
26:9-16   116
28:6   19

2 Samuel
1:1–25:14   157
1:14-16   116
2:4   116
5:14   38
5:22-24   19
7:1-17   38
7:12-16   156
7:16   98
7:24   71
9:7-8   28
12:24-25   39
24:11   27
25:15   157

1 Kings
1:5-53   39
3:14   264
5:1   116
6–7   203
6:23-28   101
9:1-9   264
11:29-39   41
11:38   264
12   29
12:21-24   41
13:1-32   41
14:1-18   41
15:11-15   128
16:1-4   41
16:32   40
17–19   40, 301
17–2 Kings 1   33
17:2-6, 8-16   40
18   40, 212
19   40

18:7-46 30
18:20-40 40
19:4-8 40
20:1-43 34
21 40
21:1-16 70
22:1-38 33
22:1-53 30, 34
22:19-23 102
22:43-46 128

2 Kings
1:1–2:12 40
2:1–9:13 41
4:1-7 23, 55
9:14-37 70
14:25 295
15:19-20 46
15:35 50
16:1-18 50
16:5-10 48
17:1-6 46
17:24-41 50
18:4 50
18:4, 22 128
18:13-16 48
19:35-37 48
19:37 49, 123
20:12-19, 20 48
20:21–21:18 124
21:3-16 125
21:18-25 124
21:19-26 51
21:26–23:30 126
22:1–23:30 51
22:3–23:25 125
22:13-20 124
23:9 126, 203
23:30-34 124
23:35–24:7 124
24:6-17 124
24:17–25:21 124
24:18–25:30 159, 181
25:1-12 161, 162, 181
25:6-7 125
25:22-25 161
25:22-26 125, 181
25:27-30 124, 158, 161, 219

2 Chronicles
3–4 203
20:14 25

24:20 25
32:30 48
32:33–33:20 124
33:20-25 124
33:25–36:23 126
34:1–35:19 125
36:1-4, 4-8, 8-10 124
36:11-21 125

Ezra
1–4 239
2:68–3:13 253
4:23 242
5–6 255
5:1–6:12 239
6:13-22 240

Nehemiah
1:3 242
5:1-5, 14 243
5:15 268
6:10-14 291
10:1 243
13:10-14, 15-22, 23-27 243

Tobit
14:4, 8 296
14:4-9 135, 301

Job
21 11
38–42 149

Psalms
2:7 28, 264
4:6 26
7:1 151
10 131
14 180
17 141
25 131
34 131
37 131, 141
53 180
58 141
68:2 26
77:17-20 146
78:70-72 257
79:10 281
89:11 26
126:3 281
133 215
137 220

137:7 216
143:1-2 162
144:6 26
147 131

Proverbs
8:22-23 226, 227
15:33 131
18:12 131
22:4 131

Sirach
46:1 42
49:10 296

Isaiah
1–39 45, 110, 222
1:1-27 121
1:2 114
1:5 109
1:8 115
1:10-17 21, 120
1:11-12 109
1:11-17 29
1:16-17 109
1:17 9
1:18–20 113
1:21-23 29
1:21-25 104
1:23 9
1:27 110
2:1-5 117
2:2-4 111, 265
2:3, 5-6 114
2:24 280
3:9, 11-13 131
3:14 111
3:16-26 104
4:2-6 106
4:3-5 115
5:1-7 105, 114, 119, 173
5:7 110, 111
5:8-10, 11-13, 18-24 105
5:16 111
5:19 109
6 35
6:1-8 120
6:1-13 101, 121
6:1–7:6 121
6:3 100
6:5-7 28
6:6-7 105
6:9 24

6:13	104	17:1-6	48	41:8-13	19, 224
6:13-15	30	17:7-8	113	41:8-16	232
6:18-25	105	18:7	115, 131	41:10	256
7:1-3	105	21:8-9, 12	109	41:13-20	236
7:1-9	120, 232	22:1-14, 19-23	119	41:17-20	224
7:1–8:15	48	23:4	110	41:20	225
7:1-20	3	23:9-17	30	41:21	223, 229
7:4	27	24:23	114	41:21-24	21, 226
7:4-9	105, 106	25:1-10	119	41:24	229, 230
7:8	49	26–28	30	42:1	257
7:8-20	88	26:2	111	42:1-3	234, 235
7:10-17	116, 118	26:7-9	111, 121	42:1-4	227, 235, 247
7:10-25	105	26:12, 16-19	121	42:1-7	237
7:14	108	27:6–28:13	121	42:1-9	235
7:17	112	28:1-4	46	42:5	223
8:1-4	108	28:1-17	30	42:5-9	231
8:5-8	104	28:16	115	42:5–43:11	237
8:7	112	29:10	27, 299	42:6-7	235
8:8-10	151	29:22-23	121	42:8	9
8:11-15	113	29:22-24	114	42:9-10	233
8:16	194	30:8-11	113	42:10	229
8:17, 18	114	30:8-14	104	42:14	231
8:19–9:6	108	30:12-14	113	42:14-17	225
8:23–9:3	118	30:12-16	27	42:18-25	227
9:1-7	108, 116, 118	30:15-17	113	43:1	229
9:5	121	32:1-4	115	43:1-7	224, 231, 235
9:6	273	32:1–33:5	111	43:2, 4	231
9:7	110	33:5-6	111	43:5	256
9:8-21	46	33:17-22	116	43:5-6	229
9:8-12, 13-21	104	33:19	131	43:10	257
9:10	109	34–35	222	43:16	223
10:1-2	111, 121	35:1-10	118, 120	43:16-19	232
10:1-4, 5-11	105	35:4-7	119	43:16-21	20, 225, 236
10:3-4, 8-9, 15	109	37:5-7	21–25, 115	43:18	229, 233
10:5-7	120	38:1-8, 21-22	121	43:18-25	236
10:12	115	40–48	223	43:21–44:23	237
10:12-19	104	40–55	222, 223	43:26-28	226
10:13-16	120	40:1-2	222, 228, 233, 234	44–55	234
10:20-27	106	40:1-11	236	44:1-2	229, 257
10:32–12:6	121	40:1-26	237	44:1-5	224
11:1-5	106, 116	40:3	234, 235	44:1-20	230
11:1-10	117	40:4	225	44:2	27, 231
11:4-5	111	40:9	27, 233	44:2-5	231
11:6-9	106, 108, 112, 250	40:9-11	236	44:6	223
11:10-16	112	40:10	247	44:8	232, 282
12:1-6	108	40:12-17	231	44:9-20	148
12:6	115	40:24-27	233	44:21-22	230, 231
13:6	282	40:25-31	236	44:24	9
14:8, 13-14	110	40:27-31	227	44:24-28	231
14:13-16	30	40:27–41:16	237	44:26	232
14:32	115	41:2-4	233	44:28	233, 234, 288
16:1	115	41:8	235	44:28–45:3	223
16:15	111	41:8-9	257	45	133

45:1	233, 234, 236	51:22	223	61:1-3	246–247
45:1-4	257	52:1-2	232	61:1-4	251
45:1-7	233, 236	52:7-10	235	61:1-7	247
45:4-6	9, 236	52:12	233	61:4-7	250
45:5	282	52:13–53:12	227–228, 235	61:4-11	246–247
45:5-7	232	53:4-12	236	61:8-11	251
45:6	282	53:7-8	234	61:10–62:3	251
45:6-8	236	53:10-11	236	61:10–63:9	252
45:9-12	231	54:1-10	236, 237	62:1	247, 249
45:9-13	227	54:5-14	235	62:1-5	251
45:13	233	54:8, 10	231	62:1-12	247
45:14	232, 282	54:9	233	62:2	247, 250
45:17	232	54:11–55:5	237	62:4-9	250
45:18	230, 232, 236, 282	55–66	222, 234	62:6-12	251
45:20-23	229	55:1-11	235	62:9	250
45:20-25	226	55:3	231, 232	62:10-11	247
45:21	282	55:6-9	235, 236	62:11-12	251
45:21-22	232	55:6–56:8	237, 252	63:1-6	248
45:21-25	236	55:10-11	12, 235, 236	63:7	249
45:22	226, 282	55:10-13	235	63:7-9	251
45:25	226	56:1	249	63:7–64:12	248
46:1-2	222	56:1-7	250	63:16-17	250
46:3-4	231	56:1-3, 6-8	251	64:1	250
46:8-9	232	56:6-8	251	64:1-9	251
46:9	282	57:3-13	250	64:3-8	250
47:1-15	222	56:5	247	64:6	249
47:6	234	56:7	26	65:3	249
48:1-8	233	57:14-20	246	65:16-25	246
48:12	232	57:14–58:14	252	65:17-21	252
48:14	231	57:20	249	65:17-25	251, 291
48:14-16	226	58:1	249	65:18-23, 25	250
48:17	223	58:1-9	251	66:1-4	248
48:17-19	236	58:1-12	248, 250, 251, 252	66:1-7	250
48:21	232	58:2	249	66:1-24	252
49–55	223	58:7-10	251	66:6	248
49:1-6	227, 228, 237	58:8	249	66:6-16	246
49:1-7	235	58:9-14	251, 252	66:10-14	251
49:7	232	58:13-14	250	66:12	250
49:7-12	225	59:1-10	249	66:15	249
49:8-15	236	59:1-21	247	66:18	281
49:8-16	235	59:4, 9-11, 14	249	66:18-21	251
49:14-21	232	60–62	246	66:18-23	250, 265
49:14-25	227	60:1-6	251	66:20	26
49:14–51:3	237	60:1-18	249		
49:18	227, 247	60:1-22	246, 252	*Jeremiah*	
49:26	227	60:3	250	1:2–2:3	184
50:4-9	227, 228, 235, 236, 237	60:4	247, 250	1:1–25:14	158
		60:6-7	250	1:4-5, 17-19	182
50:5-9	236	60:8	249	1:4-10	22, 159, 182
50:10	232	60:13	246, 250	1:10	158, 166, 171, 176
51:1-3	231	60:19-20	250	1:11-12	24, 171
51:2	232	61:1	245	1:11-16	172
51:12–52:12	237	61:1-2	247, 251	1:14-19	160

1:17-19	172	13:1-11	183	25:15–52:34	158
2:1-3, 7-8, 12-13	183	14:7-10, 19-22	183	26:1-9	183
2:2	171	14:13-16	177	26:7-19	177
2:4-13	162, 182	14:17-22	183	26:11-16, 24	183
2:4-28	184	14:18	177	26:20-24	28
2:14-37	163	14:19-22	174	27:1–28:17	172
2:21	173	15:1	208	27:5-8	177
2:35–4:8	171	15:1-4	125	28:1-10	181
3–4	263	15:10-21	163, 183	28	31
3:1	172, 180	15:15-21	182	28:1-17	28, 30, 31,
3:2-5	172	15:16	194		178, 183
3:4	184	16:19–17:14	184	28:5-9	181
3:14-17	183	17:5-10	183	28:8-9	157
3:15-16	174	17:24-26	176	28:16	89
3:19-20	208	16:1-3	161	29:1, 4-7	183
4:1, 2	184	17:14-18	163	29:1-23	165, 233
4:1-10	183	17:26	26	29:5	171
4:4	173	18:1-6	183	29:13-14	166
4:11-12, 22-28	183	18:1-11	182	29:15-23	178
4:19-28	179	18:7-10	171, 301	30:1-2, 12-15, 18-22	183
5:1	263	18:18-20	12	30:2-3	8
5:1-6	179	18:19-23	163	30:4-11	167
5:6	171	19:14-15	175	30:10	27
5:12-15	31	20:7-9	181	30:18-22	168
5:13	177	20:7-13	163, 181	31:1-6	168, 181
5:20-31	126	20:10-13	181	31:1-7	183
5:31	177	20:14-18	163	31:5	173
6:1	208	22:1-5	180	31:2-6	233
6:13	177	22:1-9	174	31:2-20	184
6:13-15	31	22:13-17	29	31:7-9	168,182
6:16-21	126	22:13-19	19, 125	31:7-14	181
6:20	29	22:15-16	177	31:14	178
7:1-11	183	22:24	257	31:15-22	180
7:1-15	170	22:26-30	124	31:27-34	183
7:1–8:3	164	23	35	31:28	171
7:4	23, 171	23:1-4	173	31:31-34	167, 169, 178,
7:12-14	175	23:1-6	182, 183		182, 183, 196, 208
7:21–8:3	184	23:3-4	180	31:33	155, 207
7:22	29	23:5	177	32:1-15	23, 169, 183
7:23	71	23:5-8	183	32:6-15	161
7:23-28	183	23:7-8	180	32:6-27	184
8:1-3	165	23:9-15	208	32:15	173
8:13–9:23	184	23:9-40	178	32:36-41	174
8:18–9:1	183	23:11	177	33–52	158
8:22–9:6	179	23:13-14	178	33:1-26	169
9:4	27	23:23-29	182	33:14-16	182
9:22-23	184	24:1-10	172	33:14-26	157, 175
9:25	173	24:5-7	208	33:18	178
11:3-5	188	24:6	171	33:25, 26	184
11:18-20	182, 183	24:9	176	34:8-22	184
11:18–12:6	163	25:1-14	178	35:12-17	178
11:20	141	25:12	144, 177	35:35-37	168
12:1-4	11	25:13	157	36	22
12:10-11	173	25:14–31:44	157, 159	36–45	160

36:2-4	194	1:1–3:27	190	16:1-15	210
36:20-26	124	1:2	191	16:37-43	143
37:7-10	28	1:2-5, 24-28	210	16:59-63	199, 210
38:4-6, 8-10	182	1:4-28	194	16:63	202
39:1-10	161–162, 181	1:28	193	17:1-10, 12-25	199
40:5–41:18	161, 181	2:1-5	209	17:22-24	209
42:10	171	2:1-8	193	18:1-4, 25-32	209
44:15-19	50	2:2	25	18:1-10, 13, 30-32	210
45:4	171	2:2-5	209	18:5, 19-27	205
46:1-26	169	2:7	194	18:21-24	301
46–51	157	2:8–3:4	210	18:21-28	209
46:13-28	184	2:9–3:3	193, 194	18:28-32	199
47:1-7	169	3:1, 3, 4	193	18:30-31	233
47:2	172	3:4-11	193, 194, 196	18:31	208
48:1-47	169	3:5-6	131, 203	18:31-32	207
49:1-39	169	3:7	207	18:32	205
49:7-22	214, 217	3:12	211	20:1	191
49:11	27	3:12-15	193	20:5	205
50–51	220	3:16	191, 192	20:5-6	203
50:1, 4	170	3:24	25	20:6-8	208
50:28	176	4:1-17	197	20:7-26	203
50:33	170	4:1–5:4	197	20:11	207, 208
50:1–51:58	169	4:1–7:27	190	20:11-25	205
51:1	170	5:1-4	197	20:12	207
51:11	176	5:6-8	205	20:33-38	233
52	181	6:2-5	239	22:1-19	210
52:4-16	161, 181	7:14-15	208	22:7-8	207
52:9-11	124	7:24-25	207	24:1	191
52:28-30	181	7:26	268	24:15-18	190
52:31-34	162	8–11	195	24:15-23	210
		8:1	191	24:15-27	190
Lamentations		8:1–11:25	190	24:21	207
1:7-10	143	8:6	172	24:27	202
2:2, 10-14, 18-19	186	9	289	25:1-17	190
3:55-56	185	9:1-7	210	25:12-14	213
4:21-22	214	10:18-22	210	26:1	191
		11:14-25	233	26:1–28:19	190
Baruch		11:16-21	208	26:6	199
1:15-22	188	11:17-21	207	28:1-10	210
3:9-15, 32–4:4	188	11:20	196	28:25–29:21	210
4:4	186	12:1-12	210	28:26	189, 191
4:5-12, 27-29	188	12:1-16	198	29:1	191
5:1-9	188	12:1–24:14	190	29:1–32:32	191
32	186	13:1-23	30	29:17	191, 192
36	186	13:2-4	203	30:20	191
36:30	188	13:2-19	208	30:20-26	200
		13:5	282	31:1	191
Ezekiel		14:1-4	207	31:1-18	200
1–3	195	14:1-11	30	32:1	192
1:1	191, 192	14:3-7	203	32:1-16	200
1:1-3	190	14:12-16	208	32:17	192
1:1-4	239	15	216	33:1-33	191
1:1-28	193, 211	15:1-5, 6-8	198	33:7-9	209
1:1–3:15	192, 196, 202	15:1-8	209	33:7-11	209

33:14-19	205	1:4-5	69	7:7	46
33:21	192	1:10	74	7:6-7, 8, 11	75
33:21-22	202, 233	1:10-11	72, 83	7:9	80
34–37	191	2	77	7:11-12	299
34:1-10, 11-22	202	2:1-22	84	7:13	81
34:1-11	210	2:2-3	83	8:3, 4, 5-7, 12	82
34:1-17, 20-24	209	2:2-9	73	8:4	46
34:11-31	208	2:2-15	84	8:4-6	79
34:25-31	207	2:3	75	8:4-7, 11-13	84
34:29-35	206	2:5-7	143	8:9, 14	75
34:30, 31	202	2:7	82	8:14	77
35:15	213	2:8	80, 82	9	78
36:5	213	2:8-9	83	9:7-8	79
36:11	281	2:9-13	81	9:10, 13	75
36:16-28	209	2:13	69, 82, 83	9:10–13:16	69
36:23-28	210	2:14-15	172	9:11	75
36:24-28	208, 209	2:14-20	83, 233	9:16	75
36:26	207	2:14-23	81	9:16-17	83
36:26-29	281	2:16	69, 82	10:1	75
36:37–37:14	211	2:16, 17, 21-22	83, 84	10:1-2	83
37:1-10	202	2:16-23	71, 72–73	10:1-3, 7-8, 12	84
37:1-14	209, 210	2:17	82	10:3-8	79
37:11-14	202	2:19-20	68, 78	10:4	75, 78, 81
37:15-28	198, 210, 290	2:20	80	10:8	83
37:21-28	210	2:21	69	10:9-15	69
38–39	191	2:23	8, 83	10:10	82
38:18–39:16	211	3	70	10:11-12	83
40–48	191, 195, 203	3:1-5	70–71	10:11-13	75, 83
40:1	192	3:2	68	10:12, 13	78
40:1–41:26	209	4:1	78, 80	11	78
40:38-43	26	4:1-3	73–74, 82	11:1, 3, 4	77
43:1-7, 10-27	210	4:1–9:9	69	11:1, 3-4, 8-9	84
43:18-27	26	4:2, 5, 10	82	11:1-3	82
44:4-31	203	4:3	77	11:1-4	78
44:15-31	210	4:4-5	79	11:1-11	84, 85
47:1-9, 12	210	4:4-10	73–74	11:2	82
47:1-12	196, 293	4:12	81	11:5-7	79
47:13–48:35	197	5	78	11:5-11	81
47:22-23	196	5:1, 11	78	11:7–12:12	84
48:22	296	5:1-2	71–72, 79	11:8	78
48:30-35	209	5:3, 4	80	11:8-11	80
49:6-8	296	5:7	77	11:9, 12	112
		5:8-15	69	11:10	75
		5:8–9:9	48	11:11	69
Daniel		5:10	79	12:2-6, 12-14	78
7	263	5:14	75, 82	12:13	42
		5:14-15	180	12:13–14:10	84
Hosea		5:15–6:6	83	13:1	82
1	70	6:1-6	84	13:1-3	79
1–3	69, 83	6:3, 5	75	13:3	75
1:2	69, 70–71, 77	6:3-6	83	13:4-8	71
1:2-3	70	6:4-6	78, 80	13:7-8	75
1:2-9	83	6:11–7:7	46	13:9-11	46
1:2-10	84	7	79	13:13	77

13:15	75	2:31	281, 232, 282	5:4-5	57, 63
14	69, 77	2:32	281, 282	5:6	60
14:1-7	80	2:32–3:1, 16-20	275	5:6-7	57
14:2-10	84, 283	3:1-5	276, 283	5:6-7, 10-15	66
14:4-8	72–73, 83	3:1-21	277	5:7	63
14:7, 8	75	3–4	276	5:8-9	57–58, 62
		3:2	281	5:11	64
Joel		3:4, 10	280	5:14-15	57, 60, 66
1:1-20	277	3:12-21	283	5:18	282
1:1–2:17	277	3:13, 15	282	5:18-20	56
1:2	275, 280	3:16	280, 281	5:19, 20	60
1:2, 9, 13-14	275	3:17	281	5:21-24	57, 63, 66
1:3, 14	279	3:18	282	5:24	17, 51, 60, 282
1:4	278, 279, 282	4:12-21	283	5:25	232
1:4-12	276			6:1-3	56
1:6	282	*Amos*		6:1-7	67
1:9, 13-14	276	1:1	51, 64	6:4-6	64
1:12	279	1:1-2	52	6:4-7	56, 66
1:13-15	283	1–2	14, 298	6:8, 11	64
1:14	278, 282	1:2	59, 281	6:13	60–61
1:15	281, 282	1:2-5	18	6:14	64, 65
1:16	280	1:3-5	54	7:1-3	53, 65
1:19-20	278	1:3–2:5	56, 65	7:1–9:10	52
2:1	279–281, 282	1:3–2:16	52, 61	7–9	46
2:1-2	283	1:6-8, 9-10, 13-15	54, 56	7:4-6	53–54, 65
2:1, 15-16	275	1:11-12	54, 56, 214	7:7-9	22, 53, 263
2:1-11	276, 280	1:13-14	59	7:7-17	66
2:1-12	281	2:1-3, 4-5	54, 56	7:10-15	52
2:1-17	277, 279	2:6-7	10	7:10-17	66, 161
2:2-3	276	2:6–3:8	67	7:12	27
2:4	282	2:6-8	64	7:12-15	66
2:10, 11	282	2:6-16	18, 54–56, 66	7:13	51
2:12	277	2:9-11	65, 232	7:14-15	44, 51, 53, 291
2:12-13	279	2:10	62	7:17	64
2:12-17	276, 281, 283	2:13-16	64	8:1-2	61
2:12-18	283	3:1-2	62	8:1-3	53
2:13	275, 281	3:1-8	58, 66	8:1-12	66
2:13-14	301	3:1–6:14	52	8:2	64
2:14	280, 281	3:2	8, 64–65	8:4-7, 9-12	66
2:15-17	275, 282, 283	3:3-5	21	8:9	289
2:16	282	3:3-8	23	8:10	60
2:17	275, 277, 280, 281	3:11	64–65	9:1	64
2:18-27	276, 277	3:12	59	9:1-4	53
2:18–3:21	277–278	3:15	64	9:1-6	67
2:21	281	4:1	10, 60, 64	9:5	60
2:22	279	4:4	51	9:5-6	57–58
2:23	279, 281	4:4-5	63–64	9:7	62
2:23-32	283	4:6-12	58	9:7-15	67
2:25	279	4:11-12	66	9:8	65
2:27	282	4:13	57–58, 62	9:10	60
2:28	281	5	19, 57	9:11-12	58
2:28-29	279, 280, 282	5:2	21, 58, 60	9:11-15	52, 65, 66
2:28-32	276, 277, 282	5:3	64	9:13-15	59
2:30-31	280	5:4	65	9:14	63

Obadiah
(all references are to verses)
1 — 213
1-2 — 214
1-4 — 213–215
1-18 — 213
1-21 — 218
3-4 — 214
4 — 213, 214
5-6 — 214, 215
5-7 — 214
6 — 215
7 — 214, 216
8 — 214, 215, 217
8-18 — 214
9 — 214
10 — 215
11 — 215
11-14 — 212, 214
12-14 — 215
15 — 215, 282
17 — 281
17-21 — 214
18 — 215
19-21 — 213, 214, 215

Jonah
1:1-2 — 297
1:5-6, 14, 16 — 299
1:6 — 300
1:9 — 298, 300
1:1–2:2, 11 — 302
2:8, 9 — 300
2:29 — 21
3:1-2 — 295
3:1-5, 10 — 302
3:5 — 300
3:9 — 281, 300
4:1-11 — 302
4:2 — 281, 300
4:2-5, 8-11 — 300
4:5 — 147
4:11 — 300

Micah
1:1 — 88
1–3 — 94
1:2 — 88
1:2-6 — 96
1:2-7 — 89
1:2–2:11 — 88
1:4 — 92, 99

1:8 — 92
1:8-16 — 91
1:10-15 — 93
2:1-5 — 98
2:1-9 — 96
2:2 — 128
2:6-11 — 21, 91
2:12 — 92
2:12-13 — 88, 90, 94, 288
3:1 — 88, 89
3:1-4 — 88
3:1-7 — 96
3:5-8 — 88–89, 91, 93
3:5-12 — 98
3:8, 9 — 89
3:9-12 — 18, 88–89, 96, 133
3:11-12 — 93
3:30 — 92
4:1-2 — 92
4:1-3 — 111
4:1–5:15 — 88
4–5 — 94
4:6-8 — 97
4:8-10, 13 — 92
4:14 — 280
5:1-5 — 97
5:2-4 — 96
5:5-9 — 94
5:6–6:8 — 98
5:7 — 97
5:7-8 — 92
6:1 — 88
6:1-4, 6-8 — 98
6:1-5 — 90, 96
6:1-8 — 98
6:1–7:7 — 88, 94
6:3-5 — 97
6:5, 6-7 — 93
6:6-8 — 29, 90
6:8 — 87, 93, 99
6:9 — 133
6:9-16 — 89
7:1-7 — 29, 91, 99
7:5 — 27
7:7-9 — 98
7:8-10 — 97
7:8-20 — 88
7:9 — 93–94
7:10 — 93
7:12 — 96
7:14-15, 18-20 — 98
7:17 — 92
7:18 — 93

7:18-20 — 96, 98, 302
7:20 — 93

Nahum
1:2-14 — 136
1:6-8 — 140
1:12-15 — 140
1:12–2:4 — 152
1:12, 14 — 136
1:15 — 135, 138, 139, 140, 142
2:1 — 138
2:2 — 138, 142
2:2-5 — 152
2:3-6 — 138
2:4 — 139, 140
2:7, 9, 10 — 139
3:1-3, 6-7 — 142
3:1-17 — 136-137
3:3-4, 13 — 142
3:4, 5 — 140, 142
3:5-7 — 143
3:7 — 137, 140, 142
3:10, 15-17 — 139
3:18 — 29
3:18-19 — 137, 140, 142
3:19 — 137

Habakkuk
1:1 — 143
1:1-4 — 152
1:2 — 150
1:2-3 — 152
1:2-4 — 145, 149
1:4 — 148
1:5-11 — 146–147, 149
1:6 — 148, 150, 151
1:8 — 151
1:9, 10 — 150
1:12-17 — 147
1:12–2:1 — 145
1:16, 17 — 148
2:1 — 147, 149, 151
2:1-4 — 152
2:2 — 149, 151
2:2-3 — 149
2:2-4 — 152
2:2-5 — 147, 148
2:2-6 — 149
2:3 — 143
2:4 — 151, 152
2:6 — 147, 149
2:6-8 — 148

2:8	150	1:1-8	258	4:14	263, 291
2:9-11	148	1:1-15	254	5:1-4	262
2:9, 12, 15, 19	147	1:2-14	257	5:3	292
2:12-14	148	1:3-11	239	5:4	291
2:15-17	150	1:5, 7	255, 256	5:5-11	262
2:18-20	148	1:6-11	240	6:1-8	262, 263
3:1	144	1:8	257	6:8	265
3:1-19	22	1:12, 14	242, 256	6:11-13	264
3:2-15	145–146, 148	1:13	257	6:12-13	257
3:3, 6, 9, 12	150	1:14	256	7:1	254, 261
3:8, 9	151	1:15	254, 261	7:1–8:23	260, 262
3:16-19	152	1:15–2:9	255, 258	7:2-3	260
3:17	148, 151	2:1	254, 261	7:4–8:23	260
3:18	149	2:4, 5	256, 257	7:8-14	263, 264
3:19	144	2:5	27	7:12	265, 290
		2:10	254, 261	8:1-8	265
Zephanizh		2:10-13	257	8:6, 12	242
1:2, 3	132	2:10-23	255	8:7, 8	291
1:4	133	2:14-19	257	8:10	240
1:4-6, 8-9, 12	130	2:15	254, 255	8:13	27
1:4-9	125	2:15-17	239, 240	8:16-17	263
1:7-13	130	2:15-19	256	8:20-21	259
1:7, 12-18	134	2:18	255	8:20-22	291
1:7, 14-16	282	2:20	254, 261	8:20-23	264, 265
1:14-18	129, 131	2:20-23	257	9:1-2	287
2:1-15	130	2:23	253	9:1-8	260, 285, 287, 292
2:3	131, 132, 133, 134			9:1–11:17	260, 285
2:5, 6	132	*Zechariah*		9:1–14:21	260, 285
2:7, 11	133	1:1-6	260, 284	9:3, 4-8	287
2:9	132, 133	1:1, 7	254, 261	9:8	292
2:13	296	1:3	17	9:9	289, 291, 292
2:13-14	132	1:7-17	262	9:9-10	287, 293
3:1	133	1:7–14:21	260	9:9-12	293
3:1-2, 9-13	134	1:3-6	263	9:9-17	288
3:1-5	130	1:8–3:10	260	9:9–11:3	260, 285
3:1-7	125	1:17, 21	260	9:16-17	290
3:3-5	133	1:18-21	261, 262	10:1	289
3:5, 9	131	2:1-4	261	10:2	291
3:8-20	132, 133	2:1-5	262, 263	10:3-12	292
3:9-10	133	2:1-5, 10-11	265	10:6-12	288
3:9-13	130	2:1-13	261	10:9	291
3:10	26	2:5	264, 292	11:1	289
3:11	130	2:5-17	261	11:1-3	292
3:11-13	134	2:10-11	264	11:1-4	287
3:12	128	2:14–4:7	265	11:1-17	290
3:12-13	133	3:1-10	262, 264	11:4-17	260, 285, 287, 290
3:13	131	3:6-7	264	11:12-13	293
3:14	132	3:8	257	11:15-17	292
3:14-20	134	3:8-9	264	11:17	290, 293
3:16	27	4:1-14	262	12:1	287
		4:1–6:15	260	12:1–13:6	260
Haggai		4:6	265, 291	12:1–14:21	260
1:1	254, 261	4:11-14	264	12:10	291, 293

12:10-11	293
12:16	262
12:1–14:21	287
13:2-6	291
13:7-9	260, 287, 290, 292
13:9	284, 291
14:1-21	260, 287, 289, 293
14:2	281
14:11	292
14:16	291

Malachi •

1:1	269
1:2	271
1:2-3	272, 274
1:2-5	189, 213, 214, 269, 270
1:2–3:24	269
1:6	271, 273
1:6-9	270
1:6-10	268
1:6-14	243
1:6–2:3	267
1:6–2:9	269, 273
1:6–2:16	269
1:8, 13-14	271
1:10-11	273
1:11, 14	271
1:14–2:2, 8-10	274
2:1-9	243
2:2, 5	271
2:4-8, 12	272
2:4-8; 3:3	271
2:7-8	268
2:10	273
2:10-16	269
2:11	271
2:11-12	243
2:13-16	243, 270
2:14-16	271
2:16	268
2:17	242, 270
2:17–3:24	269
2:17–4:3	273
3:1-4	274
3:1-4; 4:5-6	274
3:3-4	26
3:5	243, 268, 272, 273
3:7-10	243
3:8-10	268, 273
3:13-15	242, 269
3:13–4:6	269
3:16	268, 271

3:16–4:3	269
3:17	28, 267, 272
3:17-18	270
3:19-24	268
4:1	268, 273
4:1-2	274
4:1-6	268
4:2	271, 273
4:4	270–271
4:4-6	272

Matthew

1:1-7, 18-25	251
1:14-20	302
1:18-25	118, 183
2:1-12	251
2:13-23	251
3:1-5	276
3:3	234
4:1-21	276
4:12-23	118
5:1-12	98, 134
5:13-16	251
5:13-20	251
5:20-26	209
6:1-6, 16-21	283
6:7-15	236
6:24-34	235
7:21-27	120
8:5-11	120
9:9-13	83
9:9-13, 18-26	83
9:14-15	252
9:27-31	120
9:35–10:8	120
10:24-39, 40-42	181
11:2-11	118
11:11-19	236
11:16-19, 25-30	293
12:18-20	234, 235
12:39-41	301
13:1-23	235
14:13-21	235
15:10-28	251
15:29-37	120
16:1-4	302
16:13-20	119
16:21-28	182
17:14-20	152
18:12-14	209, 236
18:15-20	209
18:28-30	236
20:1-16	235

20:17-28	183
21:5	293
21:23-32	209
21:28-32	134, 209
21:33-46	119
22:1-10	119
22:15-22	236
23:1-12	98, 120, 274
24:37-44	117
25:14-20	134
25:31-46	209
26:14-25	237
26:15	288
27:3-10	288
27:9	293

Mark

1:1-8	236
1:2	274
1:3	234
2:1-12	236
2:13-22	83
3:1-12	117
4:26-34	209
4:29	282
6:1-6	209
6:1-13	209
6:7-13	66–67
6:14-29	66
6:30-34, 53-56	182
7:24-37	119
8:27-38	236
9:30-37	182
10:33-37	251
10:35-45	236
10:46-52	182
11:1-7	293
13:24-37	251

Luke

1:17	274
1:39-45	98, 134
1:57-66	274
2:1-14	118
2:1-20, 22-40	251
3:1-6	188, 274
3:4-6	234
3:10-18	134
3:13-42	274
4:21-30	182
5:1-11, 17-26	120
5:27-32	252
6:17-26	182

7:18-30	236	7:14-15, 18-20	98	*Hebrews*	
9:18-24	293	7:37-38	235	1:17	298
10:1-12, 16-20	251	7:37-39	283	2:1, 2	140
10:21-24	120	7:40-53	183	2:14–3:17	140
10:25-42	66	8:1-11	236	4:6-8	298
11:1-13	84	9:1-41	98	8:8-13	169
11:14-23	183	10:2-18	209	9:15-22	169
11:29-32	301, 302	10:12-13	293	10:16-17	169
12:13-21	84	10:31-42	183		
12:49-56	182	11:1-45	209	*James*	
13:10-17, 22-30	251	11:45-56	210	2:23	235
15:3-7	209	12:1-8	236		
16:1-13	66	12:1-11	237		
16:19-31	66, 183	12:15	293	*Revelation*	
17:5-10	152, 182	12:20-33	182	1:7	293
18:9-14	283	13:21-33, 36-38	237	4:3-10	209
19:30	293	15:1-11, 26-27	209	6:1-8	263
20:27-38	258	16:4-15	209	6:12, 17	282
21:5-19	251			9:7-8	282
21:25-36	182	*Acts of the Apostles*		14:15	282
24:1-12	251	2:17-21	282	20:7-10	209
		8:32-34	234	21:1-27	209
John				22:1	282, 293
1:1-18	181, 235	*Romans*			
1:6-8, 19-28	251	10:10-13	282		
1:23	234, 235			*Other Ancient Texts*	
1:29-42	235	*Philippians*		Babylonian text	29
2:1-12	251	4:11-13	149	Egyptian texts	28–29
4:43-54	252			Lachish texts	28
5:1-16	210	*Thessalonians*		Mari texts	24–26
5:17-30	236	2:1	140	Nineveh texts	26–27
5:33-36	236, 237	2:13–3:17	140	Sumerian hymn	29

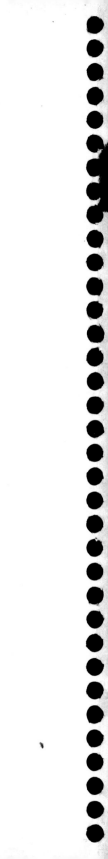